Only connect: readings on children's literature

Only connect

readings on children's literature

second edition

Edited by
Sheila Egoff, G. T. Stubbs, and
L. F. Ashley

TORONTO/NEW YORK/OXFORD UNIVERSITY PRESS/1980

CANADIAN CATALOGUING IN PUBLICATION DATA
Main entry under title:

Only connect : readings on children's literature

Bibliography: p.
Includes index.
ISBN 0-19-540309-6 pa.

1. Children's literature — History and criticism —
Addresses, essays, lectures. I. Egoff, Sheila.
II. Stubbs, Gordon T., 1918-   III. Ashley, L.F.

PN1009.A1E28 1980   028.5   C80-094252-3

© Oxford University Press (Canada) 1980
ISBN 0-19-540309-6
1 2 3 4 5 6 - 5 4 3 2 1 0
Printed in Canada by John Deyell Company

Contents

3 Some Writers and Their Books

Illustrations

Acknowledgements

EDWARD ARDIZZONE: *Creation of a Picture Book*. Reprinted from *Top of the News* (December 1959) by permission of the American Library Association.

JORDAN BROTMAN: *A Late Wanderer in Oz*. Reprinted from the *Chicago Review* (vol. 18, no. 2), 1965. © 1965 Chicago Review.

ROGER DUVOISIN: *Children's Book Illustration: The Pleasures and Problems*. Reprinted from *Top of the News* (November 1965) by permission of the American Library Association.

SHEILA EGOFF: *The Problem Novel* will appear in a book by Sheila Egoff to be published by the American Library Association and appears here by permission of the American Library Association; copyright © by the American Library Association.

T. S. ELIOT: *Huckleberry Finn: A Critical Essay*. Reprinted by permission of Faber and Faber Ltd from the Introduction to Cresset Library Edition of *Huckleberry Finn*.

SYLVIA ENGDAHL: *Perspective on the Future: The Quest of Space Age Young People*. © 1972 by Sylvia Engdahl. Reprinted from *School Media Quarterly* (Fall 1972) by permission of the American Library Association.

JASON EPSTEIN: *'Good Bunnies Always Obey'*. Reprinted from *Commentary* (February 1963) by permission; all rights reserved.

CLIFTON FADIMAN: *Professionals and Confessionals: Dr Seuss and Kenneth Grahame*. Reprinted from *Enter, Conversing* by Clifton Fadiman by permission of the author.

MARTIN GARDNER: *A Child's Garden of Bewilderment*. © Saturday Review, 1965. All rights reserved. Reprinted from *Saturday Review* (17 July 1965) by permission of the author.

JOHN GOLDTHWAITE: *Notes on the Children's Book Trade: All Is Not Well in Tinsel Town*. Copyright © 1976 by Harper's Magazine. All rights reserved. Reprinted from the January 1977 issue by special permission.

ROGER LANCELYN GREEN: *Andrew Lang in Fairyland.* Reprinted from *The Junior Bookshelf* (October 1962) by permission.

ROGER LANCELYN GREEN: *The Golden Age of Children's Books.* Included here by permission of the author, Roger Lancelyn Green, from *Essays and Studies 1962*, published for the English Association by Messrs John Murray Ltd and reprinted by Messrs Wm Dawson and Sons Ltd.

GRAHAM GREENE: *Beatrix Potter.* From *Collected Essays* by Graham Greene. Copyright © 1969 by Graham Greene. Reprinted by permission of the author, Viking Penguin Inc., The Bodley Head Limited, and Laurence Pollinger Limited, London.

MICHAEL HORNYANSKY: *The Truth of Fables.* Reprinted from *The Tamarack Review* (Autumn 1965) by permission of the author.

ELIZABETH JANEWAY: *Meg, Jo, Beth, Amy, and Louisa.* Reprinted from *The New York Times Book Review* (29 September 1968). Copyright © 1968 by Elizabeth Janeway. Reprinted by permission of Paul R. Reynolds, Inc. © 1968 by The New York Times Company. Reprinted by permission.

FREDERICK LAWS: *Randolph Caldecott.* Reprinted from *The Saturday Book*, No. 16, by permission of The Cupid Press.

EDMUND LEACH: *Babar's Civilization Analysed.* Reprinted from *New Society* (20 December 1962). Copyright *New Society*, London.

C. S. LEWIS: *On Three Ways of Writing for Children.* Reprinted from the *Proceedings* of the Bournemouth Conference, 1952, by permission of The Library Association, London.

MARION LOCHHEAD: *Clio Junior: Historical Novels for Children.* Reprinted from *Quarterly Review* (January 1961) by permission of the author.

WALTER LORRAINE: *An Interview with Maurice Sendak.* Copyright © 1977 by The H. W. Wilson Company. Reprinted from the October 1977 issue of the *Wilson Library Bulletin* by permission of the author.

HELEN LOURIE: *Where is Fancy Bred?* Reprinted from *New Society* (6 December 1962). Copyright *New Society*, London.

DONNARAE MAC CANN: *Wells of Fancy, 1865-1965.* Reprinted by permission from the December 1965 issue of the *Wilson Library Bulletin.* Copyright © 1965 by The H. W. Wilson Company.

WILLIAM H. MAGEE: *The Animal Story: A Challenge in Technique.* Reprinted from *The Dalhousie Review* (Summer 1964) by permission of the author.

PATRICK MERLA: *'What Is Real?' Asked the Rabbit One Day.* Reprinted from *Saturday Review* (4 November 1972). © Saturday Review, 1972. All rights reserved.

PENELOPE MORTIMER: *Thoughts Concerning Children's Books.* Reprinted from the *New Statesman* (11 November 1966) by permission.

WILLIAM NOBLETT: *John Newbery: Publisher Extraordinary.* Reprinted from *History Today* (April 1972) by permission of the author.

JOHN PUDNEY: *The Publication of Alice's Adventures in Wonderland.* Reprinted from *Lewis Carroll and His World* by John Pudney. Copyright © 1976 John Pudney. Used by permission of the author, Thames and Hudson Ltd, and Charles Scribner's Sons.

EDWARD W. ROSENHEIM, JR: *Children's Reading and Adults' Values.* Reprinted from *The Library Quarterly* (January 1967) by permission of The University of Chicago Press and the author.

LILLIAN H. SMITH: *News from Narnia.* Reprinted from the *CLA Bulletin* (July 1958) by permission of the *Canadian Library Journal* and the author.

PETER A. SODERBERGH: *The Stratemeyer Strain: Educators and the Juvenile Series Book, 1900-1980.* Reprinted from the *Journal of Popular Culture* (Spring 1974) by permission.

ANTHONY STORR: *The Child and the Book.* Reprinted from the *New Statesman* (12 November 1960) by permission.

ROSEMARY SUTCLIFF: *Combined Ops.* Reprinted from *The Junior Bookshelf* (July 1960) by permission.

J. R. R. TOLKIEN: *Children and Fairy Stories.* From *Tree and Leaf* by J. R. R. Tolkien. Copyright © 1964 by George Allen & Unwin Ltd. Reprinted by permission of Houghton Mifflin Company.

JOHN ROWE TOWNSEND: *Didacticism in Modern Dress.* Reprinted from *The Horn Book Magazine* (April 1967) by permission of The Horn Book, Inc. and the author.

JOHN ROWE TOWNSEND: *Are Children's Books Racist and Sexist?* Reprinted from *New Community* (Summer 1976) by permission of the author.

P. L. TRAVERS: *Only Connect.* Reprinted from the *Quarterly Journal of Acquisitions of the Library of Congress* (October 1967) by permission of the author's agents, David Higham Associates, Ltd, London.

ALAN MORAY WILLIAMS: *Hans Christian Andersen.* Reprinted from *Time and Tide* (7-13 February 1963) by permission.

ILLUSTRATIONS

The title-page opening of *The Royal Primer*, published by John Newbery, is reprinted courtesy of The Osborne Collection of Early Children's Books, Toronto Public Library.

The illustration by JEAN DE BRUNHOFF from *Babar the King* is reprinted by permission of Random House, Inc., New York, and Librairie Hachette, Paris. Photograph courtesy Toronto Public Library.

The illustration by BEATRIX POTTER from *The Tale of Tom Kitten* (1907) in The Osborne Collection of Early Children's Books, Toronto Public Library, is reprinted by permission of Frederick Warne & Co., Ltd, London.

The drawing by EDWARD ARDIZZONE from *Tim All Alone* is reprinted by permission of the Oxford University Press, London.

The illustration by ROGER DUVOISIN from *Petunia* (copyright 1950 by Alfred A. Knopf) is reprinted by permission of Alfred A. Knopf, Inc., New York. Photograph courtesy Toronto Public Library.

The illustration by RANDOLPH CALDECOTT is from *Sing a Song for Sixpence* (George Routledge and Sons, 1880) in The Osborne Collection of Early Children's Books, Toronto Public Library.

The illustration from *The Juniper Tree and Other Tales from Grimm* by Lore Segal and Maurice Sendak. Picture copyright © 1973 by Maurice Sendak. Reprinted by permission of Farrar, Straus & Giroux, Inc.

Preface
to the second edition

In compiling a Second Edition of *Only Connect*, which was first published in 1969, the editors have been guided by the same considerations that prompted the original volume. The criteria stated in the original Preface are the ones that were followed in reaching decisions about what was to be included in the Second Edition.

When a revision was contemplated, and the articles were re-read against the background of developments of the 1970s, it became evident that about a quarter of the material would need to be replaced or up-dated. In fact, eleven articles have been deleted, and nine added. We have attempted to pay due attention to the changes in attitude towards children and their literature that have characterized the ten years from 1970 to 1980. Of the new pieces, one by Sheila Egoff, 'The Problem Novel', is published for the first time in this collection. Professor Egoff's historical summary, 'Precepts and Pleasures', has been retained in the Second Edition, but revised somewhat and extended in the light of recent trends.

The last section of the book, 'The Modern Scene', consists almost entirely of new material. Elsewhere there have been a few substitutions; as, for example, the exchange of Peter A. Soderbergh's 'Stratemeyer Strain' for the 1934 *Fortune* article on Stratemeyer; and instead of Nat Hentoff's profile of Maurice Sendak, we present the artist's own mature reflection on picture-books in 'An Interview with Maurice Sendak'.

The First Edition of *Only Connect* met with an encouragingly warm reception in many parts of the English-speaking world—

and in Japan, since the publication in 1976 of a Japanese translation. We hope this Second Edition will continue to promote an interest in children's books, old and new, and to give the reader stimulating ideas and fresh insights.

February 1980   G.T.S.

L.F.A.

Preface
to the first edition

Every author or editor likes to think he is offering the public something unique. The editors of this volume are aware that a number of collections of articles and essays on children's literature have already been published. Without making any unreasonable claims, we feel justified in stating that in no previous collection has the material come from so many diverse quarters; nor has there been so broad a representation of writers from both North America and Great Britain.

Our primary aim has been to find selections that deal with children's literature as an essential part of the whole realm of literary activity, to be discussed in the same terms and judged by the same standards that would apply to any other branch of writing. We do not subscribe to the view that the criticism of children's books calls for the adoption of a special scale of values. We looked for insight and informed contemporary thinking, and rejected any material that was too concerned with recapturing childhood or with presenting coy and sentimental attitudes. With these criteria in mind we also sought writers who had a distinctive message to offer: one that is fresh, original, and illuminating and not necessarily unorthodox or provocative (though a few can be so described).

In the quest for material, byways of periodical literature were explored as well as more familiar ground, and before the process of compilation was finished, several hundred articles in journals and newspapers from all parts of the English-speaking world were examined. Essays and critical reviews were also considered, though in the final selection periodical articles are in the majority. The original plan was to include only publications of the 1960s. Maintaining an arbitrary restriction to a single decade, however, seemed to impose an artificial limitation; therefore it was relaxed in some cases to admit important earlier contributions to the criticism of children's literature, such as the essays by T. S. Eliot and C. S. Lewis and the profile of Edward Stratemeyer, 'For It Was Indeed He'*. This collection, then, is devoted mainly to topics of current interest, but a few pieces were written earlier than 1960.

Within the limits already defined, we have attempted to cover as many aspects of children's literature as possible. However, no article has been included simply because it discusses a certain subject or a certain writer: questions of balance or comprehensiveness have not taken precedence over literary considerations. For example, a careful search was made for a critical treatment of children's poetry, but nothing we read seemed to be significant enough to merit a place in the collection. That is the reason —the only reason—why no space has been allotted to the subject of poetry. However, two subjects that had not been adequately dealt with in the periodical literature we examined, of special interest to one of the editors, were written about specially for this book. One of these new essays is on science fiction* and the other presents a capsule history of writing for children, 'Precepts and Pleasures'; both are by Sheila Egoff. Where there was a choice of articles on particular authors or illustrators, our decisions for inclusion were based mainly on the interest of the content and the quality of the writing rather than on the popularity or fame of the subject.

For the title *Only Connect* we are indebted both to E. M. Forster who made the phrase memorable in *Howards End* and to Pamela Travers who borrowed it to form the title and motif of her address at the Library of Congress, reproduced here in the second section. Our interpretation of the Forster epigraph, like Miss Travers's, implies a need to gain understanding through the linking of one world with another. In *Howards End* it was the

---

*The essays referred to here have been replaced in the Second Edition.

life of warm personal relationships and that of unfeeling commercialism. In this collection the two worlds that are brought into focus are Youth and Age, traditionally beset by problems of rapport, today perhaps more than ever before separated by mutual distrust. Some of our contributors, for example Jason Epstein and Nat Hentoff*, feel that only here and there in contemporary writing for children is there evidence of a true understanding of young people's needs and interests. The connection between author and audience is often tenuous.

In 1965 a *Times Literary Supplement* article on a new study of children's literature began, 'Alas! This must be a review of a book yet to be written: *the* book about children's books.' The article was entitled 'Themes in Search of an Author' and the reviewer was pessimistic about the emergence of any single author who might succeed in producing a truly definitive work. He commented, however, on the existence of many 'interesting fragments' by notable writers 'mostly appearing—and therefore disappearing—in periodicals'.

We still do not have '*the* book about children's books'. Perhaps what is needed is a symposium. In the meantime the present volume gathers together some 'interesting fragments', of which a few are already well known while many have been rescued from obscure corners of specialized periodicals. We have wanted to make them permanently accessible because individually they are of more than merely passing interest and collectively they comprise a body of writing that we hope will be of lasting value. The book is designed to appeal particularly to librarians, parents, teachers, and students; but for anyone at all concerned with children and their literature there is material here that will repay scrutiny. We have reason to believe that the comment and discussion in the following pages will contribute to a better understanding of an important and influential field of writing.

G.T.S.

L.F.A.

1 *Books and children*

The golden age of children's books

ROGER LANCELYN GREEN

Histories of Literature seldom mention books written primarily for children, except when in cases like *Tales from Shakespeare* and *The Rose and the Ring* they represent amiable eccentricities on the part of writers famous for other and adult works.

Of recent years one or two favoured volumes have been promoted; but even for such works as *Alice in Wonderland* and *The Wind in the Willows* it has seemed that an excuse must be found, and painstaking (and painful) efforts have been made to prove that they are really allegories, or deeply psychological parables, intended to convey disguised truths to initiated adults.

The consideration of children's literature as such found its most noteworthy exponent in F. J. Harvey Darton, whose *Children's Books in England* was published in 1932. Even so, however, he felt constrained to add the sub-title 'Five Centuries of Social Life', and he does not in fact touch on anything which could be described as Literature until his last two chapters. Percy Muir's *English Children's Books 1600-1900* (1954) is written largely from the book-collector's point of view, and the delight in rare editions tends to divert both author and reader from consideration of content to that of format.

The most compendious and painstaking work on the subject

was published in America in the previous year (1953), *A Critical History of Children's Literature*, a 'survey' in four parts under the editorship of Cornelia Meigs.

Now while these excellent works describe the growth and development of writing for children over several centuries, they reveal curious differences in approach from any similar works on the whole or any section of adult literature. Not only are they apt to consider children's books as a separate species rather than a branch of literature, but they tend more and more to accumulate a vast sea of books in which the reader becomes lost as he struggles desperately between the few definite islands which are just allowed to emerge above the flood.

Under these circumstances there seems to be some point in attempting to write at least the first draft of what might be developed by some expert into a chapter in a future history of English Literature: an attempt to chart some of the more or less definite islands off a portion of the mainland of our more generally recognized literary heritage.

There were few books written before the middle of the nineteenth century which can be said to have more than an antiquarian interest today. Several adult books like *Robinson Crusoe*, *Gulliver's Travels*, and *Baron Munchausen* which have become nursery property (usually now in abridged or simplified versions) are beside the point, as are ballads, popular rhymes, and folktales. Beyond a few translations of foreign fairy tales (Perrault and Grimm) and of *The Arabian Nights*, Lamb's *Tales from Shakespeare* (1807) is the only book from before the middle of the century which is still read, or which deserves any place among children's classics. Apart from this, and from a few representative poems in anthologies, Marryat's *The Children of the New Forest* (1847) and Ruskin's *The King of the Golden River* (1851—but written some years earlier) are the only islands still visible in those early waters.

The only book which hovers on the border between actual and academic interest is Catherine Sinclair's *Holiday House*

(1839). From the historical point of view it is one of the most important books in the history of children's literature, for it was written with the intention of changing the quality and kind of reading supplied for young people, and it was so successful that not only did it achieve its purpose but it remained in print and was read by children for precisely a hundred years.

At a time when 'informative' books (they are now called, significantly, 'non-fiction') are once again swamping the junior-book counters, it is worth looking at what Catherine Sinclair wrote (for parents) in her preface:

Books written for young persons are generally a mere dry record of facts, unenlivened by any appeal to the heart, or any excitement to the fancy . . . but nothing on the habits and ways of thinking natural and suitable to the taste of children. Therefore, while such works are delightful to the parents and teachers who select them, the younger community are fed with strong meat instead of milk, and the reading which might be a relaxation from study becomes a study in itself . . .

In these pages, the author has endeavoured to paint that species of noisy, frolicsome, mischievous children which is now almost extinct, wishing to preserve a sort of fabulous remembrance of days long past, when young people were like wild horses on the prairies, rather than like well-broken hacks on the road; and when, amid many faults and many eccentricities there was still some individuality of character and feeling allowed to remain.

Her battle was not won without a long struggle, and her children seem fairly tame now in the light of subsequent developments. The only part of the book which stands out as a notable achievement that is still fresh and entertaining is the 'Wonderful Story' about Giant Snap-'em-up (who was so tall that he 'was obliged to climb up a ladder to comb his own hair'), which is the earliest example of Nonsense literature and a direct precursor of Lewis Carroll and E. Nesbit.

It was some time before either the nonsense fairy tale or the story of true-to-life childhood achieved any worthy representations; but meanwhile a new development was started by Marryat and developed by Charlotte Yonge—the simple historical romance, usually with a child hero. In an age when the Waverley Novels were read avidly even by young children (Mrs Molesworth, born 1839, was reading them at the age of six when *Peveril of the Peak* proved too difficult, though she had found *Ivanhoe* and *The Talisman* 'so much nicer and easier'), and when Scott's followers such as Bulwer Lytton and Harrison Ainsworth were not forbidden like the majority of adult novels, it was natural that, sooner or later, such books would be written with the young reader specially in view. An obvious development came also by way of the 'desert island' story, since *Robinson Crusoe* and *The Swiss Family Robinson* had been followed by the intensely pious *Masterman Ready*: R. M. Ballantyne avoided the didactic brilliantly in *The Coral Island* (1858), and followed it with excellent adventure stories in other fields which, like the meticulously historical thrillers of G. A. Henty, grew together towards the close of the century into the semi-adult movement of the 'storytellers' headed by Stevenson, Haggard, and Conan Doyle.

The really distinctive children's book grew more slowly and in less expected forms. Traditional fairy tales and stories from myth and legend found a period of great popularity about the time of the first translation of Hans Andersen (1846) and of Kingsley's *The Heroes* (1856), the Kearys' *Heroes of Asgard* (1857) and Dasent's *Tales from the Norse* (1859). But the original tale of fantasy developed slowly. Probably the earliest of any was F. E. Paget's *The Hope of the Katzekopfs* (1844), which showed real imagination and invention, but gave way to an undue weight of direct moral teaching which cripples its last two chapters hopelessly. It has not been reprinted since a shortened version renamed *The Self-willed Prince* came out about 1908.

Ruskin's *The King of the Golden River* (1851), a brilliant imitation of Grimm, made the grade, though an interesting experiment in the Border Ballad tradition of fairy tale, by Mrs Craik, *Alice Learmont* (1852), failed to hold its audience. But at Christmas 1854 (though dated 1855), Thackeray produced the first classic of fairy-tale nonsense and set the stage for all future stories of the 'Fairy Court' with *The Rose and the Ring*.

Although there is a basic moral in Thackeray's fantasy, the story, the characters, and the spirit of fun are all more important. With the paradox of all true originality, Thackeray owed several debts for the materials with which he built: the general fairy-tale background of writers like Madame d'Aulnoy and the pantomime tradition which was growing in the able works of Planché and H. J. Byron; perhaps *The Hope of the Katzekopfs*, certainly Fielding's heroic burlesque *Tom Thumb the Great* whose language is echoed in the royal blank verse and in the brilliant use of bathos ('He raised his hand to an anointed King, Hedzoff, and floored me with a warming pan!' 'Rebellion's dead—and now we'll go to breakfast').

The Rose and the Ring had very few direct followers, or few that survive. Tom Hood 'the Younger' wrote probably the best imitation, *Petsetilla's Posy* (1870), though it is too like its original to escape destructive criticism, and there were others of even less importance. It was not, in fact, until thirty-five years later that a major work in the same tradition appeared, Andrew Lang's *Prince Prigio* (1889)– which owes only the same kind of debt to *The Rose and the Ring* and the traditional fairy tales as Thackeray owed to his sources. In each case a writer of real genius was using, as it were, the same company and setting to put on a play of his own devising, and such as only he could have written.

Thackeray's indirect influence may, however, be traced in another original if somewhat controversial genius, George MacDonald, whose first children's story, *The Golden Key* (1861), was pure allegory in a setting only superficially that of any known fairyland, but who showed a strong dash of the comic Fairy Court tradition by the time he reached his third, *The*

Light Princess, in 1864 (written two years earlier). After this he attempted longer stories, beginning with the full-length *At the Back of the North Wind* (1870, dated 1871) which combines dream, allegory, and fairy tale in a not completely successful whole, but reached his real heights with the *The Princess and the Goblin* (1871) and its even better sequel *The Princess and Curdie* (1882, but serialized 1877).

Critical judgement of MacDonald's work is rendered difficult, as in the case of several writers with superlative powers of imagination which far out-run their skill as literary craftsmen. The classic example of this uncomfortable dualism is Rider Haggard, whose amazing imagination and narrative powers would place him among the truly great did not his woefully inept use of language and creation of character press him back amongst the very minor novelists.

MacDonald's deficiencies are most notable in his adult novels and least apparent in his *Unspoken Sermons* and the best of his children's books and imaginative works.

The quality of the *Princess* books to a child is that of a haunted house—but a house haunted by entirely good and desirable ghosts. They leave behind a feeling of awe and wonder, the excitement of the invisible world (we may call it Fairyland at the time, but it is always something more) coming within touchable distance: the door into the fourth dimension is situated in the places that we know best—we may chance upon it at any moment, and with the thrill of delight and excitement quite divorced from any fear of the unfamiliar. Though the stories are not memorable, the experience and its enriching quality remain vivid, and MacDonald's greatness is shown by the fact that to reread him in later life is equally rewarding and brings no sense of disappointment.

Two excursions into utterly different realms of the imagination which appeared at much the same time as MacDonald's finest children's books have also this quality of an appeal that continues through life: *Alice's Adventures in Wonderland* (1865) and *Through the Looking-Glass* (1871).

Coming when they did, these two books revolutionized writing for the young. They captured the irresponsible fantasy in the minds of most children, and with it the unrealized urge towards rebellion against the imposed order and decorum of the world of the Olympians; but the capture was made by a writer of exceptional powers, a scholar in love with the richness of language and the devastating precision of mathematics. This seemingly inharmonious concatenation of elements produced two masterpieces, of which the second, being a little farther away from the spontaneous inspiration of oral storytelling, is the more perfectly integrated whole.

It is unsafe to attempt to get nearer to Dodgson's sources of inspiration. There seems to be no doubt that he made up the stories on the spur of the moment, telling them to children who were supplying much of the inspiration while he told by the interruptions, suggestions, and criticism which are inseparable from composition in this kind. It is also true that on account of his stammer, from which he was only free when talking to children, Dodgson was seeking an escape into childhood and thereby recapturing or preserving his own to some extent past the normally allotted limits. The result is what matters, and in this case it was two of the best-known, best-loved, and most often quoted books in the language.

Although 'Lewis Carroll' set free the imagination, he had no original followers, though his imitators were legion—'People are always imitating *Alice*,' complained Lang in 1895. In fact the only writers to draw anywhere near him in his peculiar realm of fantasy, nonsense, and felicitously haunting turns of phrase are Rudyard Kipling with the *Just So Stories* (1902) and A. A. Milne with his two *Pooh* books in 1926 and 1928. One has only to turn to Tom Hood again (*From Nowhere to the North Pole*, 1875) to see how completely impossible it is to write a memorable imitation of *Alice*.

Perhaps because of this impossibility, the last quarter of the nineteenth century tended to produce fewer and fewer examples of the child's quest for the 'perilous seas' of fairyland and concentrate with more and more skill on the presentation of childhood in the world of every day.

This was the main theme of Catherine Sinclair's protest, but its application was slow and tortuous. Superficially it was not new, since Maria Edgeworth and Mrs Sherwood professed to be writing about real children in their daily lives. A distinct step forward was taken by Charlotte Yonge with her novels for teenage girls, such as *The Daisy Chain* (1856), and in the following year by Thomas Hughes in his outstanding story of public school boys, *Tom Brown's Schooldays*.

Smaller children, however, were still being subjected to the lachrymose-pious, as in *Jessica's First Prayer* (1867) and *Misunderstood* (1869), though a new writer first made her mark in the second of these years, Juliana Horatia Ewing (1841-85), with *Mrs. Overtheway's Remembrances*. She progressed to *A Flat Iron for a Farthing* in 1872 (which year also saw Elizabeth Anna Hart's one outstanding child-novel, *The Runaway*), and reached her greatest heights with *Six to Sixteen* (1875) and *Jan of the Windmill* (1876).

The impact of these first outstanding child-novels is shown by Kipling's reference to *Six to Sixteen* in his autobiography: 'I owe more in circuitous ways to that tale than I can tell. I knew it (in 1875) as I know it still, almost by heart. Here was a history of real people and real things.'

Although Mrs Ewing may have had a better style, and on a small scale could produce better work, she was far surpassed as a child-novelist by Mrs Molesworth (Mary Louisa, née Stewart, 1839-1921). Although several of her longer books remain popular and stand up to rereading, Mrs Ewing is best remembered by her miniature novels, or long short stories, *Jackanapes* (1884) and *The Story of a Short Life* (1885); but their appeal is now more strong to the adult than the child, since they both turn on child-deaths[1] which needs a conscious return to the days of high infant mortality on the part of the reader for any appreciation, and seem awkward and sentimental to a modern child. Though often derided, stories of this kind should not be condemned out of hand: Mrs Ewing's two remain classics, and they have close runners-up in Mrs Molesworth's *A Christmas Child* (1880) and Frances E. Crompton's *Friday's Child* (1889).

This was, however, almost the only death-bed in Mrs Molesworth's voluminous works for the young (two short stories and an opening chapter complete her list of early deaths; no parents meet their end during the course of any book, though a few endure dangerous illnesses, and only one child becomes a cripple). Her greatness lies in the fact that she was at once the faithful mirror of her own age and yet wrote, at her best, about the universal aspects of childhood.

It is no exaggeration to describe Mrs Molesworth as the Jane Austen of the nursery. Although her works are to Jane's as the miniature is to the great painting, such books as *The Carved Lions* and *Two Little Waifs* and *Nurse Heatherdale's Story* are as nearly perfect in their small kind as the great novelist's are in hers. Like her novel they are 'period' without being dated; they appeal to the heart as well as to the intellect; they remain in the memory and enrich the experience; they not only played an important part in their own branch of our literature but deserve an abiding place on our shelves to be read and reread by young and old.

Not only is one told in Mrs Molesworth's stories what it was like to be a child seventy-five years ago; as one reads one can experience all the hopes and fears, all the miniature loves and hates, passions and despairs, plots and counterplots of that distinct, if rather restricted, little world. She truly understood children and could see life again with their eyes, and give vividness

---

[1] Jackanapes in fact jumps into manhood before dying, but the effect is that of a child-death.

and poignancy to their small troubles in such a way that even to the adult reader the suspense may be as strong and as compelling as if it were a matter of life and death among grown men and women. So many of the basic problems and conflicts of life make themselves felt at all ages that this novel view of them back through the telescope into the eye of childhood seems in her best work to clarify and accentuate their relevance.

Although after such early stories as *Carrots* (1876) and *Hoodie* (1881) Mrs Molesworth avoided any hint of direct preaching, there is always a certain underlying intention in her stories. Well though she and such writers as Mrs Ewing and Mrs Hodgson Burnett understood children, they had not quite escaped from the tradition of the child as a miniature adult, as always in training for grownup life. This tends to make the children seem a little on their best behaviour, and it gives perhaps an undue emphasis to the continual moulding of character, occasionally an exaggerated importance to a small sin or backsliding. The children are just a little better than ourselves; to some extent the same is still true in such recent masterpieces as Arthur Ransome's stories of holiday adventures, but most of the conscious recognition of and combat with temptation has now gone. Acute introspection plays a relatively small part, however, in Mrs Molesworth's stories, though one told in the first person like *The Carved Lions* (1895), which is probably her masterpiece, gains greatly by the insight into the heroine's mind which it allows.

For more pronounced introspection we must turn to Mrs Hodgson Burnett, who wrote many minor works but only three which are on the definitely higher level which still makes them vividly alive. The first, *Little Lord Fauntleroy* (1886), suffers both from its intractable material—the balance without sentiment or patronizing between the democratic child of America and the aristocratic child in England—and from its unenviable reputation derived mainly from its translation into a stage sweetmeat for sentimental adults. Given a sympathetic reader who is ready to accept the limitations imposed by its period, the book is still remarkably readable both by young and old. Less difficult, though less convincing to the adult, is her second major story, *A Little Princess* (1905—but a revised version of an earlier book published in 1887), which exploits the theme of the lonely child fallen from high fortune to poverty and persecution and then rescued at the eleventh hour by means which seem supernatural until satisfactorily explained at the end. The book is brilliant fare for children, but not one which weathers the test of adult rereading with complete success.

Her last book, *The Secret Garden* (1911), is one of great individuality and astonishing staying power. It is the study of the development of a selfish and solitary little girl later in contact with an hysterical and hypochondriac boy of ten: a brilliant piece of work, showing unusual understanding of introspective unlikeable children with a sincerity that captures many young readers and most older ones.

Children with a country upbringing have found a similarly satisfying quality in *The Carved Lions*, with its less introspective and more sympathetic heroine, and Mrs Molesworth's less convincing *Sheila's Mystery* (also 1895), which deals not quite so happily with the salvation of one of her few unpleasant children. The significant difference is that while Sheila's solution is found for her by intelligent adults, Mary in *The Secret Garden* works out her salvation for herself–with the aid of an imposing array of coincidences. Between the writing of these two books another change had come over the child-novel and one of considerable importance; it seems to owe its main impetus to Kenneth Grahame's *The Golden Age*, also published in 1895.

Now *The Golden Age*, undoubtedly one of the most important landmarks in the history of children's literature, is not a children's book at all. Misguided parents have frequently thought that it was: so far as I can remember *The Golden Age* was the only book which, as a child, I really and violently hated. The reason, curiously enough, seems to be that Kenneth Grahame knew too much. Here was an adult writing in an adult style about things which touched the very heart of our mystery; he was profaning the holy places—perhaps (for his manner was elusive) he was laughing in his detestable Olympian fashion at the things which really mattered.

The Golden Age, said Oswald Bastable in *The Wouldbe-goods*, 'is A1, except where it gets mixed with grown-up nonsense.' Even E. Nesbit did not quite realize where the trouble lay, since she had never read it as a child. For to the older reader *The Golden Age* (with its sequel *Dream Days*, 1898) is, as Swinburne said of it, 'well-nigh too praiseworthy for praise': it is not merely one of the greatest books of its period, but a classic in its own right and an outstanding example of English prose.

Its importance in the present survey rests in its approach to childhood and its amazing understanding of the workings of the child's imagination and outlook. Hitherto the child had been pictured to a greater or less extent as an undeveloped adult, and all his books were intended in some degree to help force him into life's full flowering. Sheer instruction may have faded into the background, but an undercurrent of teaching in morality, in manners, in the sense of duty was always present. Even Mrs Molesworth never escaped from this background purpose, close though she came to the real thoughts and sensations of childhood—to the child looking forward to adulthood rather than the adult pushing the child into it. In the greater writers even the conscious push was not necessarily a blot: Mrs Ewing, Mrs Molesworth, and Mrs Hodgson Burnett could make of it a triumph as, in a completely different way, could George MacDonald.

But *The Golden Age* suddenly presented childhood as a thing in itself: a good thing, a joyous thing—a new world to be explored, a new species to be observed and described. Suddenly children were not being written down to any more—they were being written up: you were enjoying the spring for itself, not looking on it anxiously as a prelude to summer.

The immediate result was a loosening of bonds similar to that wrought by the outbreak into mere amusement of *Alice* thirty years earlier. It had a marked effect even on writers already well in their stride; even Mrs Molesworth, nearing the end of her literary career, found it impossible to resist the new elixir altogether, and at least two of her later books, *The House that Grew* (1900) and *Peterkin* (1902), have a gaiety and a youthfulness that sets them among her half-dozen best child-novels. As for minor writers, one has only to compare the sickly sentimentality of S. R. Crockett's *Sweetheart Travellers* (1895) with the adventurous boyishness of *Sir Toady Lion* (1897) to see the difference at its most extreme.

The oddest omission from the majority of earlier child-novels which Kenneth Grahame brought into the front of the picture was the imaginative life of children, and its importance to the children themselves. It had cropped up in several books written with more than half an eye on the adult reader, notably in Dickens's *Holiday Romance* (1868), Jefferies's *Bevis* (published as a three-volume novel in 1882), and in Mark Twain's *Tom Sawyer* and *Huckleberry Finn* (1875, 1884). But when it appears in the child-novel proper, as in the first chapter of Mrs Molesworth's *Two Little Waifs* (1883), it is merely incidental, or a means (as in *Hermy*, 1881) of starting a train of incidents. Not until *The Three Witches* (1900) and *Peterkin* could she make it the centre of her story.

Grahame had many direct imitators, but only one broke away from imitation and produced great and original work, and that was Edith Nesbit. She had been a hack journalist whose ambition was to be a poet for nearly twenty years when, in July 1897, a series of reminiscences of her schooldays in *The Girl's Own* ran away with her when she came to write of her childhood games of 'Pirates and Explorers'. From this grew the idea of producing sketches or short stories of the *Golden Age* variety, but purporting to be written by one of the children concerned. Most of Oswald Bastable's earlier adventures were contributed to the *Windsor* and *Pall Mall* magazines, both intended purely for adults, and only in the autumn of 1899 did she revise and link them, with a little rewritten earlier material from *The Illustrated London News* and several of *Nister's Holiday Annuals*, as *The Story of the Treasure-Seekers*.

A few reviewers took it as an adult book: 'Don't be content to read *The Treasure Seekers*, but give it also to children. They will all bless the name of Mrs Nesbit,' wrote Andrew Lang, who described the Bastables as 'perfect little trumps' and preferred them to the heroes of *Stalky & Co.* which appeared at the same time. He went on to describe it as 'a truly novel and original set of adventures, and of the finest tone in the world'.

Lang himself was of an older generation and could still not quite reconcile the apparent lack of a moral with a children's book about contemporary children. Albeit with a twinkle in his eye, he had looked for and found a moral in his own original fairy stories (just as Dodgson had done with *Alice*, many years after its publication) and could at least make excuses for the moral shortcomings of such traditional tales as *Puss in Boots*.

E. Nesbit, though she could lapse into sentimentality with the best, made the shift from conscious 'elevation' to unconscious improvement, substituting tone for teaching with the untidy impetuosity which characterizes even her best work. In the second Bastable compilation, *The Wouldbegoods* (1901), she even rounded on the moral tale, made a face at *The Daisy Chain*, and (apart from the one monumental lapse over the supposed dead Boer War hero) wrote her best non-magical children's book. Most of the Bastable stories were based on incidents or inspirations from her own childhood, and the thorough assumption of the child's outlook in the person of the narrator, Oswald, allowed her to use the joyous freedom and colloquial verve which carried the child-novel right out into the spring sunshine once and for all.

In the 'real-life' line she could not follow up her initial success: *The New Treasure-Seekers* (1905) already shows strain and self-imitation, and *The Railway Children* (1906) tends to lapse back into the sentimentality from which she was usually able to escape. Moreover, surprisingly few child-novels followed hers that win anywhere near the status of classics (apart from *The Secret Garden*, 1911) until Arthur Ransome produced *Swallows and Amazons* in 1930.

Apart from achieving complete freedom, E. Nesbit's real claim to greatness lies, however, in her series of Wonder Tales. Short stories in the Fairy Court tradition accompanied the earlier Bastable tales into the world (they were collected as *The Book of Dragons*, 1900, and *Nine Unlikely Tales*, 1901) and she continued writing them, producing as many again over the next dozen years. The best of these would have assured her of a place not so very much lower than Thackeray and Lang; but by combining her styles and expanding her scope she produced eight full-length stories in which magic is introduced into family circles and surroundings as convincingly and prosaically real as those of the Bastables.

Magic to most children is only just out of reach: it fills their imaginings and informs their games. With the sure, deft touch and the rather pedestrian matter-of-factness which she knew so well how to use to advantage, E. Nesbit turned the games and the imaginings into actual events. 'Actual' is the key word; here she has never been equalled. She may have learnt how convincing magic can be, if strictly rationed and set in the most ordinary surroundings possible, from 'F. Anstey' (Thomas Anstey Guthrie, 1856–1934) of *Vice Versa* and *The Brass Bottle* fame; she certainly knew and admired Mrs Molesworth's blendings of fact and fantasy such as *The Cuckoo Clock* and *The Tapestry Room*—the Cuckoo and Dudu the Raven are close relations of the Psammead, the Phoenix, and the Mouldiwarp: but the total effect is, at its best, original with the originality of sheer genius.

Her mounting skill is shown in her first series of three, *Five Children and It* (1902), *The Phoenix and the Carpet* (1904), and *The Amulet* (1906), each better than the last. Then came perhaps her supreme achievement, *The Enchanted Castle* (1907), with a delightful new family, unexpected and most credible magic, and a really cohesive plot instead of the string of adventures in her other books. *The House of Arden* (1908) and its overlapping sequel *Harding's Luck* (1909) keep to the same high level, though the construction begins to falter; and then the decline comes, through *The Magic City* (1910) to *Wet Magic* (1913), after which she had written herself out.

The period ends sharply with E. Nesbit. But to follow out her career three notable writers have been shouldered aside, each author of individual works of such recognized importance and popularity as to need no comment: Kipling with *The Jungle Books* (1894-5), *Stalky & Co.* (1899), *Just So Stories* (1902), and *Puck of Pook's Hill* (1906); Kenneth Grahame for that ambivalent masterpiece *The Wind in the Willows* (1908), an adult's book for children written by one of the few adults who could re-enter childhood at will; and Beatrix Potter, the only writer for very small children to produce works of real literature which adults can still enjoy—helped perhaps by her inseparable and equally outstanding illustrations.

Finally, spilt over from another medium, comes *Peter Pan*, the essence and epitome of all that the writers of the Golden Age were striving to capture. 'It has influenced the spirit of children's books,' wrote Harvey Darton, 'more powerfully than any other work except the *Alices* and Andersen's *Fairy Tales*.' From its shores (the play has been revived every year but one since it began in 1904, and the book, *Peter Pan and Wendy*, 1911, is only a little less immortal) we may sail adventuring in I know not how many new directions, but to the Never, Never Land we shall always return–led away for magic moments by the Boy who wouldn't grow up, before turning refreshed and reinvigorated to seek those joys in the world of real men and women from which he was for ever shut out. For such, to all of us of whatever age, is the true message of the great children's books.

[1962]

Clio Junior: historical novels for children

MARION LOCHHEAD

'Such good news! Such good news! The Black Knight has got into the castle!' So two of his twelve children once greeted Dr Moberly, headmaster of Winchester. They spoke of *Ivanhoe*, and their jubilation was typical not only of their own book-loving family but of more than one generation of Victorian children to whom Sir Walter Scott made history a delight, an excitement, almost a passion. Indeed, one of the differences between them and the modern young is that the former regarded the Waverley novels as a treat not a task, and, far from being driven to read them, were allowed, as reward and privilege after lessons were done, to indulge in one of those enchanting volumes. Charlotte Yonge, friend of 'they Mulberries', as an old woman called them, could recall that way of reading them in her own school-room in the 1830s. Towards the end of the century Maurice Baring saw his sisters promoted to reading Scott at a suitable age. The Barings also read the historical novels of Miss Yonge herself, who besides being a devotee of Sir Walter, was by that time his spiritual daughter and heiress, and with him a great historical influence upon the children of the century.

History was her own favourite study, and her excellent education by her mother and father gave her that sure foundation of learning—a habit of solid reading. She was well equipped in mind and knowledge when she began her long career as author. Her first novel, *Abbeychurch*, appeared anonymously in 1844; then in 1850 began the double stream of domestic and historical fiction with, respectively, *Henrietta's Wish* and *Kenneth; or, The Rearguard of the Grand Army*—a tale of the Retreat from Moscow. In 1851 she began editing *The Monthly Packet*, which continued for more than forty years, every number with two serials by herself: a domestic chronicle and an historical. Besides these, she contributed her *Cameos from History:* scenes and episodes from our rough island story and that of the rest of Europe. Girls in the schoolroom, having learned a chapter of Mrs Markham or some other approved historian (the elder among them perhaps reading Miss Strickland's *Queens of England*), then relaxed over one of Miss Yonge's novels, could hardly help developing a sense of history. The list of her historical tales is impressive, and makes no mean contribution to English fiction, indeed no meagre lifework altogether: *The Little Duke, Pigeon Pie, The Lances of Lynwood, The Chaplet of Pearls, The Dove in the Eagle's Nest, The Prince and the Page, The Armourer's Apprentice. The Caged Lion, Two Penniless Princesses, Unknown to History*—these and others take us on a journey through many countries and many centuries. A few are still read by children: *The Little Duke, The Lances of Lynwood*, perhaps *The Chaplet of Pearls*; but from the 1850s till the end of the century their readers were legion; their influence was profound. For girls, they supplemented and enlivened history lessons in the schoolroom; for their brothers they were sometimes the only approach to the past, except that of Greece and Rome.

At school these boys were drilled in the classics. In imbibing Thucydides and Xenophon, Cæsar and Livy, they might absorb some ancient history, but that of their own country and Christian Europe was rarely imparted to them in formal lessons. Thanks to Clio junior, daughter of the Muse of History and of a father who can only be guessed (though we might hint at an entirely chaste liaison with Sir Walter Scott), they were led into the past through the pleasant gate of fiction. Scott undoubtedly began it, and his influence endured. He told a story, he gave pictures; children in the last century may have had a quicker sense of selection, more agility in skipping than they have today. Those long first chapters did not appear to hamper enjoyment. Indeed one Edwardian child was captivated by *The Talisman*—admittedly not one of the great novels—because of the incident in the chapel, where Sir Kenneth keeping vigil sees the procession of veiled ladies, one of whom, his own lady-to-be, drops a rose at his feet. Great as was his influence, it was possibly surpassed by that of some of his successors, whether they wrote directly for youth, as Charlotte did and as he himself did in *Tales of a Grandfather*, or found themselves being adopted by children and given the unexpected accolade of their approval.

Among the latter is Harrison Ainsworth, whose *Tower of London* (1840) began for children the visible renaissance of the city, in her buildings and memorials. It also presented a heroine whose reign in the schoolroom would be so much longer than her pitiful ten-days' queenship of England—Lady Jane Grey: a model for girls in her devoutness, her learning, her virtue and courage. At the same time he could do justice to Mary Tudor, giving some sense of her personal tragedy as well as of the fearful complications of the time. Readers of every age were captivated by a story packed with incident and rich in colour, while girls in particular were pleased by the details of costume and appearance: so useful if one wanted to dress up and act the story. *Old St Paul's* continued this tradition—or renaissance—and the author's native Lancashire was given what is almost a county history in a series of novels, ranging from Tudor to Georgian times. The Civil War was treated in more than one tale; the Fifteen and the Forty-Five were not forgotten.

The Civil War might be regarded as the favourite period of Clio junior. Charlotte Yonge dealt with it in a short serial, *Pigeon Pie*; and before she had begun her *Monthly Packet*, Captain Marryat published, in 1847, his *Children of the New Forest*, which would win many young adherents to the Royal cause and strengthen others in their allegiance to the Martyr King. The adventures of Edward and Humphrey, Alice and Edith in old Jacob's cottage in the Forest made excellent reading. The story was warmly approved by parents and governesses, for it inculcated sound morals and piety, showing how brave and resourceful boys could be, how diligent and adaptable little girls. The example of Alice and Edith may well have made her task of sewing a long seam endurable to many a reluctant small needlewoman. In masculine eyes, it was all the better for being so meagre in love interest. Edward, certainly, complicated matters by falling in love with Patience, a Puritan maid; but her father, always moderate in opinion, saw the light and abjured Cromwell and his cause. A suitable wife was found for Humphrey—after an exciting adventure—two gallant and virtuous cavaliers paired off with Alice and Edith grownup. There was a fine wedding feast after King Charles II came into his own, but there was no silly love-making. It was indeed a capital story, and the spell of it endures. The Edwardian child aforementioned was so confirmed in Royalism by reading it that any novel that presented Cromwell with sympathy—such as Marjorie Bowen's *Governor of England*—seemed improper and heretical.

This leads to the question of how far historical convictions and prejudices are made for us by Clio junior before we begin to listen to the mature Muse. Charlotte Yonge, out of her own deep loyalty, strengthened her readers in allegiance to High Church and Royalist ideals. She was English and Anglican to the marrow, but she scrupulously avoided attacking Roman Catholicism, which was, indeed, a very good religion for foreigners and for people in the Middle Ages and earlier. One of the great lacks in Roman Catholic literature and culture in England is that of the two kinds of novel Charlotte so delightfully wrote: the *roman jeune fille,* showing the life and ethos of contemporary families, and the historical novel for children;

but young papists could read Charlotte's without hurt to their faith or feelings.

Charles Kingsley on the other hand, who came near her in popularity, was as much her opposite in style as in churchmanship: strident and voluble in his patriotism, his Protestantism, his views on education, social reform, and everything that came within his survey. He was at all times the preacher and lecturer, though one with a gift for storytelling. *The Water Babies* has too much magic to be spoiled by the moral remarks; these are pleasantly few in *The Heroes*; and no one who has discovered the enchantment of Greek legend through his rendering can ever lack gratitude to Kingsley. *Hereward the Wake* is introduced by a lecture on history and thereafter weighted by comments. There are hints of Protestant animosity, as in the description of Edward the Confessor, whose sanctity did not appeal to Kingsley. (So unlike the Prince Consort!)

The conduct which earned him the title of Confessor was the direct cause of the Norman Conquest and the ruin of his people.

Instruction's warning voice may be uplifted overmuch; but after all a child can skip, and *Hereward,* being so remote in time, is comparatively free from prejudice. The patriotism is objective, emotion is expressed in action; as everyone who was not a pagan was at that time a papist, there is no need to inveigh against Roman corruption. In *Westward Ho!* instruction's warning voice becomes louder and still louder, to the accompaniment of a trumpet-blast against popery. Any contemplation of our separated brethren of Rome drove Kingsley into a frenzy bordering on hysteria; his attitude was not so much fraternal as fratricidal. Nowhere in his work are the two strains in his mentality—the religious mania and the narrative gusto—more apparent than in this epic of seafaring and patriotism: the former in the prelude of praise for those Devon men who destroyed the Armada, but for which victory 'what had we been by now but a popish appanage of a world-tyranny as cruel as heathen Rome itself and far more devilish?', and in a chapter which resembles too closely our knowledge of Nazi and Communist ways to make good reading. Amyas Leigh, having captured a bishop and a Dominican, reviles them for their sins and refuses them time to make their confession before being hanged: " 'I will have no such mummery where I command," said Amyas sternly. "I will be no accomplice in cheating the devil of his due!' "

But if one skips the introduction to *Westward Ho!* one may begin with a promising description of young Amyas:

One bright summer's morning in the year of grace, 1575, a tall and fair boy came lingering along Bideford Quay in his scholar's gown, with satchel and slate in hand, watching wistfully the shipping and the sailors,

and presently coming upon John Oxenham as he holds forth upon his own exploits and those of Francis Drake. Children probably did skip the outburst, but Protestant parents may have read it with approval and then looked benignly upon juvenile absorption in the tale. Clio junior owed much of her popularity to the pervading desire for improvement. Food for the young mind, as for the growing body, should be both nourishing and delectable, and historical novels fulfilled this ideal. Children read them with pleasure, and in the process were edified. These books were not precisely powder in jam; they were more like porridge with lashings of cream, or a well-made rice pudding with plenty of sugar and raisins 'intil't' and an agreeable hint of lemon or cinnamon.

Scott, honest man, was not without his prejudices, but everything in his writing is mellowed and transfused by a double warmth: that of genius and that of his own generous temper. His influence did not lessen, but it was enhanced and complemented by that of Dumas—especially upon Robert Louis Stevenson. This adherent of Clio junior has left a delightful account, in one of his essays, of his enthralment by Dumas: reading him on a winter's night in Swanston Cottage, rising at intervals to draw back the curtains and look out on the snow, then returning to the warmth and lamplight and the magic of the tale. From that enchantment he emerged to write his own spell-binders: *The Black Arrow* being directly in the Dumas tradition, *Kidnapped* containing the historical mystery of the Appin Murder.

Stevenson was still playing the sedulous ape when, in the 1870s, G. A. Henty began his long series of books for boys—and usually for their sisters as well. 'He took all history for his province'—to quote his biographer in the *Dictionary of National Biography*—from the recent Franco-Prussian War in *The Young Franc Tireurs*, backwards to ancient Egypt, enlivening nearly every century and every war or expedition with his narratives: *With Clive in India; Under Drake's Flag; St George for England; In Freedom's Cause: a Story of Wallace and Bruce* (which might have been called *St Andrew for Scotland*). The Civil War, Ireland, Orange and Green, of 1688, Venice, Holland, Mexico, Russia—he swept through them all in a gusto of action that left little breath for preaching; and was followed by a crowd of enthralled young readers with a goodly group of elders in the rear. Journalism was by this time paying some attention to youth, and he edited three periodicals for boys: *The Union Jack, Boys' Own Magazine*, and *Camps and Quarters*. Dying in 1902 he lived long enough to write of Roberts in Pretoria and Kitchener in the Soudan. Kingston, his predecessor in editing *The Union Jack*, was copious in producing historical tales as well as those of adventure and travel. The popularity of both these authors has long outlived their century.

And Stevenson was still alive, fragile in body, the beloved Tusitala of Vailima, when Conan Doyle began his twofold career —in romance and in detective fiction. In the nineties, too, came that treasury of tales of every kind, *The Strand Magazine*, of beloved and lamented memory. The engaging Brigadier Gerard made his bow and proceeded to relate the adventures of himself and the Emperor, introducing a Napoleonic saga. In the nineties and the early nineteen-hundreds came *Sir Nigel* and

The White Company making vivid and real the late Middle Ages, and *Micah Clark* with his memories of Monmouth's rising. These heroes and others made *The Strand* a vehicle of delight which must have disrupted the peace of many a household as the young defied paternal claims to first possession. These romances continued a tradition; they did not create a form and mould as did the Sherlock Holmes stories, nor have their heroes the sure immortality of the great detective, but their spell lingers, and not only in memory.

France, especially of the late Middle Ages and Renaissance, was the favourite field of Stanley Weyman. His *House of the Wolf* was published in 1890, seven years after it had appeared in serial in *The English Illustrated Magazine*. (The contribution of the Victorian periodical, especially in the latter decades of the reign, to juvenile happiness would demand an essay to itself.) Other admirable chronicles followed: *A Gentleman of France*, *Under the Red Robe*, *The Man in Black*, *The Red Cockade*. By this time there was plenty of fine, rich feeding, possibly confused through very abundance, and the disciple of Clio junior may have had a kaleidoscopic view of history. But it was vivid enough. History was now much more commonly taught at school, but not always inspiringly. The Victorian discipline of the memory was long maintained: children must learn lists of dates, of kings and queens, and great events; and too often they 'did' history up to a particular period and thereafter knew nothing. Nor were they shown any relation between English and European history. There were, no doubt, exceptions: inspired teachers who brought the past to life, and some who used historical novels wisely and well, along with lessons. But for most children history at school was something different from history as presented in those minor masterpieces in fiction.

If Charlotte Yonge remains first among the female devotees of Clio junior, we must not overlook her companions and followers. Emma Marshal, though remembered now only by amateurs of Victoriana, was in her own day popular, and with reason; she wrote, with charm and knowledge, tales of many periods, in tone and principle akin to Charlotte's. Towards the end of the nineteenth and well into the twentieth century came Evelyn Everett Green's accomplished and pleasant stories—also wide in range: *After Worcester; Cloister and Court; The Church and the King; The Children's Crusade* being only a few of them.

The tendency is more and more towards entertainment, towards illustration and re-creation of a period, with less and less instruction and interpolation. History, whether in learned treatise or enticing novel, whether written for scholars or for children, must answer two questions: 'What happened then?' and 'What were they like?'—the kings and queens, the leaders and warriors, the great and the common folk, old and young in this century or that: the people who caused or who witnessed events. Historical fiction should perhaps answer the second question even more fully than the first, and the characters of romance beloved—or hated—by the schoolroom were, for the most part, convincingly alive.

We have been considering almost but not quite exclusively the work of the Victorians, because this was a form that began and flourished in their century; but we cannot end abruptly in 1899 or 1900. One of the most beloved writers for children of yesterday and today and probably tomorrow, E. Nesbit, created the last of the great Victorian families in her Bastables of *The Wouldbegoods*. They inevitably became Edwardian and were succeeded by other families. E. Nesbit had Charlotte Yonge's talent for making each child in a family alive, separate and different from the rest, at once typical and individual, and very like their readers. Presently she infused magic into domesticity in her *Five Children and It* and its sequels, always with the same realism of character and background. Finally she combined the domestic, the magic, and the historical in *House of Arden* and *Harding's Luck*. In these two books the young Ardens, children of an ancient but impoverished house, return one, two, three, and four centuries back in their family history, the spell being worked by the Mouldiewarp or Mole, which is the animal on their badge and crest and coat of arms. The children remain themselves, whether in their own home or in the castle or mansion to which they are transported through the door of time. In their first adventure, incidentally, one of them—Elfrida—throws a sidelight on her own history lessons: 'I wish I could remember what was happening in 1807, but we never get past Edward IV. We always have to go back to the Saxons because of the new girls.'

Kipling took up this idea in his *Puck of Pook's Hill* and *Rewards and Fairies*, where Dan and Una are taken by Puck into that old, enduring England whose reality they had not guessed.

Charlotte Yonge, in all her creative energy and versatility, never dallied with magic. It may be improper to wish she had; certainly it is a whimsy to imagine a book in which her young Underwoods are translated into the past of their own family, preferably to the seventeenth century. It is easy to see Felix and Wilmet as Pillars of the House during the troubles of the Civil War: brave and resourceful, Felix in defending the house, Wilmet in managing its welfare; all of them sheltering fugitives, perhaps the king himself; worshipping in the chapel, their prayer-books and sacred vessels hidden from marauding Cromwellians; coming again to prosperity at the Restoration.

But even her contemporary domestic chronicles are now period pieces, and in another generation or so will rank as historical romances!

Meanwhile, the inspiration has not been lost. Clio junior has still her servants. The present generation has been given many delights: some by novelists of distinction in mature work, some by those who concentrate on 'juveniles'. There is still the romance of adventure, as for example Rosemary Sutcliff's novel of Roman Britain, *The Lantern Bearers*; and the vogue for biography-on-fiction has been followed in juvenile as in adult literature: Jane Oliver has told the life of Saint Columba in *The Eaglet and the Angry Dove* and of Robert the Bruce in

Young Man With a Sword; Elisabeth Kyle that of *The Maid of Orleans* and the *Queen of Scots.* To make any approach to a catalogue would prolong this article beyond measure. It is enough to show that the tradition continues. The teaching of history has changed and developed; writing for children changes under our eyes. There is a new approach, a new technique. But human nature continues to be the most fascinating study for human readers of every age and in every period. The question of what heroes and heroines and the common people of history were like, especially when young, of what they wore and what they ate, how they talked, what games they played—all that must always interest modern children of any intelligence and curiosity.

It is fairly safe to predict that a hundred years or more hence someone will write an article on 'Historical Novels for Children in the Twentieth Century' and possibly another on 'The Period Interest of Children's Books in the Reign of Queen Elizabeth' (Windsor, whom God preserve!).

[1961]

John Newbery: publisher extraordinary

WILLIAM NOBLETT

To most historians and students of English Literature, John Newbery is chiefly to be remembered as the publisher and patron of Oliver Goldsmith. Newbery was the publisher to whom Dr Johnson had taken the MSS of *The Vicar of Wakefield* and it was to Newbery that Goldsmith turned whenever he needed money. Newbery, indeed, was constantly paying the bills owed by Goldsmith to his landlady, Mrs Fleming, and in return he earned the epitaph 'the honestest man in creation'. He was, in fact, none other than the 'philanthropic publisher of St Paul's Churchyard' who, in *The Vicar of Wakefield,* helped Dr Primrose when he was lying sick at a roadside inn.

Newbery's 'philanthropic' nature, however, should not disguise the fact that he was a ruthlessly effective businessman or that his career was a rags-to-riches tale. He was a Dick Whittington among booksellers. Born in 1713, the son of a Berkshire farmer, John Newbery was not destined to work on the land and at the age of sixteen he had been apprenticed to the proprietor of *The Reading Mercury,* William Ayres. In 1737 Ayres died and the paper passed to William Carnan who, having great faith in Newbery's ability, left him half the business when he himself died later that same year. Newbery consolidated his position by marrying, like so many other 'worthy' apprentices, his ex-employer's widow.

Once in control, Newbery established *The Reading Mercury* as one of the leading provincial newspapers. In 1723 the paper had made no mention of salesmen, yet by 1743 it could proudly boast of forty-three in places as far apart as Bicester, Southampton, and Hastings. 'Overwhelmed as he is with Business,' as Dr Johnson later wrote in *The Idler,* 'his chief desire is to have still more.' In Reading this 'desire to have still more' took the form of a great diversification of his business. Newbery, indeed, patented, manufactured and sold the famous Dr James's Fever Powder, while an advertisement in the issue of the paper for September 29th, 1740, announced that he could supply, 'shopkeepers with all sorts of haberdashery goods (such as threads, tapes, bindings, ribbons, pins, needles etc.) as cheap as in London'. Likewise, in December 1742, it was revealed that a local lending library had been established. Perpetually on the lookout for new ways of making money, Newbery even hit on an ingenious method of getting round the 1725 Stamp Act, by which Walpole had imposed a tax on all newspapers in an attempt to silence his virulent journalistic critics. Newbery proposed that he and his partners at Reading should produce what would be, officially speaking, two distinct newspapers—*The Reading Mercury and Advertiser* once a fortnight and *The Reading Mercury and Weekly Post* once a fortnight. Fortnightly production was, in the strict interpretation of the Act, not a newspaper, and by 'that means (he would) save duty on advertisements'.

For such a restlessly ambitious and creative young man, however, the provinces did not have a lot to offer, and in 1743 he moved to London. Within a year of his arrival in the capital, Newbery started on what is perhaps the most interesting aspect of his career—the production of children's books; that is, books intended for the pleasure and instruction of children and totally separate from adult books. In no sense was Newbery the first person to produce children's books and before he broke into the market in 1744—with *A Little Pretty Pocket Book*—both Thomas Boreman and a Mrs Cooper had issued books aimed at 'little

THE
Royal Primer;

Or, an eafy and pleafant

Guide to the Art of Reading.

Authoriz'd by

His MAJESTY King *GEORGE* II.

To be ufed throughout

His MAJESTY's DOMINIONS.

Adorn'd with CUTS.

London: Printed for *J. Newbery*, at the *Bible and Sun*, in St. *Paul's* Church-yard, and *B. Collins* at *Salifbury*. (Price bound 3d.)

A good Boy and Girl at their Books.

HE who ne'er learns his *A, B, C,*
For ever will a Blockhead be;
But he who to his Book's inclin'd,
Will foon a golden Treafure find.

Children, like tender Oziers, take the Bow,
And as they firft are fashion'd always grow:
For what we learn in Youth, to that alone,
In Age we are by fecond Nature prone.

TITLE-PAGE OPENING, ACTUAL SIZE, OF *The Royal Primer*

masters and misses'. But he was, without doubt, the first really successful entrepreneur of what today is taken for granted as a distinct branch of writing—children's literature.

Newbery's books certainly sold in vast quantities. *The Royal Primer* was one of his successful productions. First issued in the 1750s in conjunction with Collins of Salisbury, by 1772 (a few years after Newbery's death) Collins could record a sale of 20,000 copies. Likewise, *A Museum for Young Gentlemen and Ladies* sold 2,200 and 2,000 copies in its seventh and eighth editions respectively, while *Little Goody Two Shoes* ran through twenty-nine editions in the thirty-five years from 1765 to 1800. In his autobiography after his father's death, Newbery's son, Francis, could, indeed, observe that the pressure his father's books were submitted to was 'immense; an edition of many thousands being sometimes exhausted during the Christmas holidays'.

Part of the explanation of Newbery's success lies in his uncanny knack of knowing his market. He was totally up to date as regards the new theories of education and had read Locke's treatise, *Some Thoughts concerning Education*. Echoing Locke—who had argued that 'children may be cozened into a knowledge of their letters . . . and play themselves into what others are whipped for'—he urged parents to teach their children by way of games. His 'A Little Song Book'—which was bound in with *A Little Pretty Pocket Book*—for example, was 'an attempt to teach children the use of the English alphabet by way of diversion'. The essence of many of his books was, in fact, both the instruction and amusement of children.

Although he saw what was fashionable, however, and exploited it, Newbery was aiming at the mass market. He realized that the conservative element was equally important and therefore did not neglect the more traditional mothers and fathers who frowned upon Locke's theories and regarded them as dangerously subversive. His books are full of sound, Christian advice. Every rhyme in *A Little Pretty Pocket Book* is accompanied by a wood-cutting and, more significantly, a moral of 'Rule of Life'.

Typical, is:

> 'RIDING'.
> *In Quest of his game,*
> *The Sportsman rides on;*
> *But falls off his Horse*
> *Before he has done.*
> *The 'MORAL' of which is:*
> *Thus Youth without thought,*
> *Their Amours pursue;*
> *Tho' an Age of Pain*
> *Does often accrue.*

The result of this fusion of the old and the new was a stream of books that are peculiarly of the eighteenth century. Certainly, Newbery's books do not have the timeless hallmark of great literature. None of his small volumes has survived in the same way as, say, Swift's *Gulliver's Travels* or Defoe's *Robinson Crusoe,* which, although not written for children, have been adopted by them. Newbery's books were produced for the eighteenth century and consequently had eighteenth-century themes. In 1761, for instance, he issued a small volume aimed at 'young Gentlemen and Ladies' with the theme, 'the Newtonian System of Philosophy' as told by 'Tom Telescope'. Likewise, the final section of *A Little Pretty Pocket Book,* is full of fables whereby 'little Tommy and Miss Polly' are urged to learn their lessons in order to get just reward. 'All good boys and Girls', runs one of the fables from Jack-the-Giant-Killer, 'take care to learn their lessons and read in a pretty manner; which makes everybody admire them.'

It is *Goody Two Shoes,* however, which really reveals Newbery's market sense. This work—perhaps the most successful of Newbery's successful productions—bears too many marks of its period to have survived as a children's classic, but it is this that surely explains its great success. The book tells the story of Little Margery Meanwell ('Goody Two Shoes' herself) who, as a child, was turned out of the parish of Mouldwell by Sir Timothy Gripe.

After a few years wandering, Margery returns to the parish where she learns her lessons so well, and proves to be such a good scholar, that she becomes, in turn, a 'trotting Tutoress', the Principal of the A B C College and finally, by marrying Sir Charles Jones, a 'lady'. In her new-found position as a lady, she gets Sir Timothy Gripe struck off the list of J.P.s, not for any ulterior motive of revenge—that would be un-Christian—but for his fraudulent practices. The book was, quite simply, for the benefit of those:

> *who from a state of rags and care*
> *And having shoes but half a pair,*
> *Their fortune and their Fame would fix*
> *And gallop in a coach and six.*

Although he had this very desirable skill of knowing just what the market required, Newbery could not have sold his wares extensively and in great quantity—as Josiah Wedgwood was later to discover with his pottery—without a very sophisticated and skilful sales policy. It is this feature that distinguishes Newbery from the Boremans and the Mrs Coopers and explains why— whereas they only achieved a fleeting success—he captured the market and succeeded in selling his books in large quantities for the rest of the century. Newbery's salesmanship and marketing techniques were, if not totally revolutionary, very sophisticated and bore many modern features.

He advertised both extensively and intensively. Of 150 advertisements appearing in the *Universal Chronicle* (whose chief claim to fame is the fact that it first published Dr Johnson's *Idler*) Newbery is to be associated with ninety-seven. Of course, not all these advertisements were for books—both Dr James's Powder and Greenbagh's Tincture, Newbery having a stake in both, were mentioned several times—but the vast majority were for literary works. He also advertised his wares widely in his own productions. He frequently alluded to his goods in the texts of his own stories. In *Goody Two Shoes*, little Margery's father 'was seized with a violent fever in a place where Dr James's Fever Powder was not to be had, and where he died miserably'. On other occasions in the same book little Margery 'then sang the "Cuzz's Chorus" (which may be found in the "Little Pretty Plaything" published by Mr Newbery)', while later she was made principal of the college of 'Mrs Williams of whom I have given a particular Account in my "New Years Gift"'. Likewise, in *The Valentine's Gift*, Mr Worthy relates how, as a little boy who hated school, he was taken into a closet where 'all Mr Newbery's books lay in the window' and he became interested in various Newbery characters. From that day onwards, he learnt his lessons and never looked back. Naturally enough, Newbery also included his own publisher's lists in his own books. At the back of the third edition of *Goody Two Shoes* a list of forty-two items appeared entitled 'the books usually read by the scholars of Mrs Two Shoes are these, and are usually sold at MR NEWBERY'S, at the BIBLE and SUN in St Paul's Churchyard'.

In all these advertisements, whether in the *Universal Chronicle*, his own works or elsewhere, Newbery used the invaluable technique of 'puffing'. 'He was almost as great in the art of puffing his wares,' as his nineteenth-century biographer, Charles Welsh, put it, 'as the immortal Puff himself.' An advertisement placed in the *Penny Morning Post* for March 17th, 1759, which began, 'To the Parents, guardians and Governesses of Great Britain and Ireland', can be taken as typical.

At a time when all complain of the depravity of human nature, and the corrupt principles of mankind, any design that is calculated to remove the evils, and enforce a contrary contract, will undoubtedly deserve the attention and encouragement of the publick. It has been said, and said wisely, that the only way to remedy these evils is to begin with the rising generation . . . How far Mr Newbery's little books may tend to forward this good work may be, in some measure, seen by what are already published.

Newbery did, however, vary the art of puffing. Not all of his advertisements are immediately obvious. Advertising the publication of 'Nurse Truelove's New Years Gift, or the Book of

Books for Children', Newbery stated that it was 'designed as a present for every little boy who would become a great man and ride upon a fine horse, and to every little girl who would become a great woman and ride in a Lord Mayor's gilt coach. Printed for the author, who has ordered these books to be given gratis to all little boys and girls at the Bible and Sun in St Paul's Churchyard, they paying for the binding which is only 2d. each book'. Like many later philanthropists, Newbery, while appearing benevolent, kept a very sharp eye on the profit margin.

Occasionally the advertisements were accompanied by sales-tricks. One of Newbery's many commercial ventures was the manufacture of games and he had invented a set of fifty-six squares 'with cuts and directions for playing with them' which taught children—whether alone or with assistance—how to spell, write, read, add-up and make figures. Sometimes, these games were tied to particular children's books as an extra selling device. *The Little Lottery Book for Children,* for instance, contained a 'new Method of playing them into a Knowledge of the Letters, Figures, etc.', while *A Little Pretty Pocket Book* was sold for sixpence, but for an extra two-pence parents could buy a ball for 'little Master Tommy' and a pincushion for 'Pretty Miss Polly'. Both items were 'infallibly' guaranteed to 'make Tommy a good Boy and Polly a good Girl'.

A bookselling device used more often was Newbery's publication of multi-volume works. He was the first book-seller/publisher to produce a magazine devoted entirely to children—*The Lilliputian Magazine*—and in this respect may be regarded as an innovator and forerunner of the nineteenth-century producers of children's comics. This periodical was announced as a monthly issue, whose aim was 'by way of History and Fable, to sow in their Minds, the seeds of Polite Literature and to teach them the great Grammer [sic] of the Universe: I mean the knowledge of Men and Things'. As a periodical it failed, although as a bound volume it succeeded. *The Circle of the Sciences: Or The Compendious Library* was a variation on the same theme, being a type of early encyclopaedia. It was issued in ten volumes between 1745 and 1748, and included such titles as 'A Spelling

Dictionary on a Plan entirely new' or 'Geography made familiar and easy to young Gentlemen and Ladies'. Likewise, Tommy Two Shoes, Goody's brother, at the end of the book promises to acquaint the reader with the 'History of His Life and Adventures', in 'a volume soon to be published'. Newbery had, indeed, learnt one of the fundamental truths of the publishing business: that invasion of the market has to be constant and continuous, so that the reader has little time to forget an imprint. In the twenty-three years from *A Little Pretty Pocket Book* to his death in 1767, Newbery produced over fifty new books—an average of nearly two a year—each of which ran through many, re-advertised editions.

With so many books coming from his presses, Newbery found it expedient to offer reduced rates for those who purchased in bulk. On the title page of *A New French Primer* it was boldly stated that 'an allowance will be made to those that buy them by the dozen to sell again', while in the *Pennsylvania Gazette* for November 15th, 1750—already by this time Newbery had begun to export a little—it was announced that 'Mr Newbery' had for sale to 'schoolmasters and shopkeepers who buy in quantities to sell again', varied titles including *The Museum*, and *A New French Primer*. Likewise, *Corderius* (a Latin Primer) was published in 1744 and advertised as costing 1s. 6d. a copy or 15s. 'a dozen to schoolmasters, or those who take quantities as Reading'.

Most of these advertising techniques were tied to royal or aristocratic patronage. The 1752 edition of *The Lilliputian Magazine* had a list of young subscribers at the back. Newbery had learnt the priceless secret of a bookseller's success, a list of 'good' addresses. Likewise, *The Royal Primer* was, according to the title page, 'authorised by His Majesty King George III to be used throughout His Majesty's Dominions'. In this respect, Newbery was not a pioneer and was, indeed, conforming to established practice. Josiah Wedgwood, for instance, later used this fashionable patronage extensively. Sales to the aristocracy and royalty were, in themselves, not vitally important, but their patronage gave a *cachet* to the goods—whether children's books or pottery—

and thus made them far more desirable to the emerging middle classes who felt their own standards to be insecure.

Herein lies the fundamental explanation of Newbery's success as an entrepreneur of children's literature. He was exploiting the emerging middle classes who were hungry for status, learning and culture, and who insisted on the very best for their children. Newbery, without doubt, aimed his goods at this class. His products, like Wedgwood's, were not cheap—cheapness would have made them less desirable to this new class. His little volumes rarely, if ever, sold for less than 6d. and this put them beyond the pocket of the ordinary working man. Again, the books themselves reveal the demand that Newbery was exploiting and their title pages usually contain the words 'young gentlemen and ladies'. Typical was the 1763 edition of *A Compendious History of the World from the Creation to the Dissolution of the Roman Republic* which was subtitled, 'compiled for the use of young gentlemen and ladies by their old friend Mr Newbery'. Likewise, the narrators of the stories were often Nannies and Nurses and on one occasion 'A History of England' was told in a 'series of letters from a Nobleman to his Son'. And finally, the 'young masters and misses' are often urged to be charitable to the poor. 'All good boys and Girls', starts the message on page 76 of *A Little Pretty Pocket Book,* and continues, 'when they see a Poor Man, or Woman or Child in Want, will give them either money or Such Meat and Drink as they have to spare: which makes the whole world love them'.

As his books were relatively expensive, Newbery was able to employ high quality artists to write and illustrate them. Although he naturally did not employ 'Titian', 'Raphael', and 'Michael Angelo' as his title pages proclaimed—they were his apprentices who, on his recommendation, had changed their names—he was the first person to employ engravers specifically to illustrate his books. Consequently, the little etchings that accompany the tales are relevant to the story, a feature that no bookseller before Newbery could claim. Similarly, he did not use hack authors to write the stories. Although he did not have the nerve to claim that they were written by a 'Shakespeare' or a 'Milton', Goldsmith himself repaid some of the money that Newbery had advanced to him by writing stories for the Newbery creations. Although it is not clear whether in fact he wrote *Goody Two Shoes,* it is certain that he wrote both the preface and introductions to the six volumes of *A New and Accurate System of Natural History* (for which he received 30 guineas) and *Tommy Trip's History of Birds and Beasts.* Again Newbery used the best quality paper and ink, and the latest techniques of printing. The result was a series of brightly covered books with impressive illustrations, flowered and gilt decorations and a simple elegance which is typically Georgian.

Newbery's success naturally enough aroused competition and imitation, on both sides of the Atlantic. By 1762 Hugh Gaine of New York had begun to produce a series of books that sounded suspiciously like Newbery's, including such titles as 'A Pretty Book for Children . . . with two letters from Jack the Giant Killer'. In England itself the imitators were even more numerous and some eighty-three years after the Copyright Act, in 1818, H. Roberts issued, in London, a small work entitled 'Little Gaffer Two Shoes, otherwise called "Tommy Two Shoes"'. Even during Newbery's lifetime the copiers were active and the inevitable result was that, like Hogarth, Newbery became a vigorous champion and defender of the Copyright Act. At times he even took his campaign into the pages of the London Press. In October 1765, in *Lloyd's Evening Post,* he denounced the pirated editions of his latest dictionary and urged 'all parents and guardians as well as the young gentlemen and ladies for whose emolument' his books were produced, to do him 'a favour and the justice to ask for his books, and observe that his name is prefixed to those that they buy, that he, who has entered so heartily into their service, and been ever studious of their improvement, may, at least, reap some of the fruits of his labour'.

[1972]

Children's reading and adults' values

EDWARD W. ROSENHEIM, JR

The word 'reading', like the word 'literature', is far too broad to be useful for more than a few cheery generalizations, whether we are discussing the reading of adults or of children. Certainly one may begin with one familiar, necessary distinction—which can be simply, if controversially, expressed as the difference between reading conducted for its own sake and reading conducted for the sake of something else, usually learning or training. In the first category would fall the reading of what is sometimes called 'imaginative literature', including poetry, drama, fiction, certain kinds of essays and speculations; in the second category would fall all other books, juvenile and adult, which seek to tell us how things actually are or have been or ought to be. And I would think the problem of judging the excellence, the 'worthwhileness' of books in the second category—whether books on history or social questions or science or geography or religion or conduct or art itself—would simply involve determining the intelligibility, attractiveness, persuasiveness, importance, and usefulness of whatever could be learned from them. It may be very difficult to write such books—and difficult, too, to motivate children in reading them—but to assess and justify their role in the total reading experience seems relatively simple.

It is with the other type of reading, the imaginative, the reading that is pursued for its own sake, that the problems of justification and judgement become very troublesome indeed. They are, in fact, so controversial that they are precisely the questions to which critics and teachers of literature have characteristically addressed themselves during these recent decades, which some people have characterized as an Age of Criticism. Yet these questions produce answers, though never definitive ones, and they produce certain beliefs about literature, again never universally accepted, and these answers and beliefs do have a bearing on children's reading as well as adults'.

It is, in the first place, characteristic—though not by any means inevitable–that today's critic recognize that the greatest power of imaginative literature, in its various kinds, is to yield particular satisfactions—that is, unabashedly to assert that such literature is primarily read for pleasure. This may seem an unexciting, if debatable, commonplace, but I can assure you that, if so, it has only recently become one. I have dismal evidence that in classrooms—and even in recent printed curricular materials—the child's reading of a lyric poem or fantasy or even a comic short story is immediately followed by some such initial question as, 'What does the work teach us?' or 'What do we learn about so-and-so?'

Yet the primacy of pleasure as an end in reading is now quite widely accepted, and we have indeed gone further and asked some searching questions about the nature and sources of that pleasure. And because those sources properly lie in only two places—the written work before the reader and the mind of the reader himself—we have been led to concentrate upon that unique, immediate encounter between book and reader, largely and quite deliberately, neglecting such peripheral matters as the biography of the author, the circumstances under which the book was composed, its reputation, or—as I've already suggested —its 'lesson'. And in consequence we find ourselves driven to think, not primarily about authors and subject matters and 'reading' generally, but about specific books and their readers—what goes on in books, what goes on in the people, young and old, who read them.

Our thinking has prompted many of us to feel that there are

pleasures, even 'literary' pleasures, of many kinds. We recognize that certain species of work yield certain species of satisfaction. Beyond this, we have begun to suspect that there are degrees of pleasure that are largely determined by the degree of affirmative intellectual energy a reader is willing to invest. There are, we feel, the satisfactions, legitimate enough but rather flabby, that come only from a sort of effortless recognition of what is reassuringly and comfortably familiar, whether that familiarity is bred by authentic experience or by previous reading as in the case of 'series' books. There are the satisfactions of what I like to think of as 'easy fantasy'—often represented by the kind of escape-cum-identification literature one found in so many boys' books in my youth, in which, against a background of sport or youthful society that offered no challenge to the imagination, youngsters like myself enjoyed a more glamorous and triumphant life than their own. There are, again, the transient titillations afforded by flamboyant and minimally credible writings which exploit the violent or exotic or prurient or sentimental. The appeal of such work is assuredly the province of the psychologist, whose findings tend to remove these experiences from the area of intellectual—or at least aesthetic—satisfaction.

All these are pleasures, each authentic enough, frequently entirely respectable, that somehow fall short of the pleasures that can be achieved by reading, the pleasures proper to true humanistic experience. And I use the word 'humanistic' because in this kind of pleasure we inevitably make active exercise of our uniquely human gifts—the gifts of apprehension, of imagination, of discrimination, of relationship, of judgement. The humanistic satisfactions are not those of temporary, uncritical surrender (much as we like to speak of 'enchantment') but of sustained, active encounter—the kind of encounter that makes a Holden Caulfield want to telephone Old Thomas Hardy or causes a Mary Poppins to exist so vitally in the imaginations of her young admirers that, as many did, they reject her unconvincing embodiment on the movie screen.

Reading to achieve these satisfactions involves, obviously, an energetic act of the intellect—and the capacity for such an act requires cultivation which is certainly not that of mere literacy. It means, to put it bluntly, that we cannot have it two ways: if reading is to yield its deepest, most permanent, most humane satisfactions for our children, then the mere gesture of 'reading', mere uncritical pleasure in reading, is not quite enough. If we are concerned with reading for maximum satisfaction, we parents and teachers must be prepared to devise strategies, provide help, and—above all—make judgement about our children's books.

And these judgements are, of course, difficult to make. But I would suggest that, if my concept of the most satisfying reading is a correct one, we do not bother inordinately with questions such as, 'Is this a great book?' Or a wholesome one. Or an up-to-date one. Or an informative one. Or even a 'broadening' one. The questions I would ask would tend to be: Will this book call into play my child's imagination? Will it invite the exercise of genuine compassion or humour or even irony? Will it exploit his capacity for being curious? Will its language challenge his awareness of rhythms and structures? Will its characters and events call for—and even strengthen—his understanding of human motives and circumstances, of causes and effects? And will it provide him with a joy that is in some part the joy of achievement, of understanding, of triumphant encounter with the new?

All this may appear to put a somewhat pretentious light on the problem. Yet, after all, most of the special human satisfactions do require planning and training in their cultivation. Even the deepest, most appropriate satisfactions from sport—either of the participating or spectator variety—are achieved through training and practice in execution or experienced, sophisticated appreciation. And if we grant only that the satisfactions of imaginative literature are equally rich and permanent, then it seems reasonable that we think about their cultivation with equal care and responsibility. And thus, to accept the 'pleasure principle' is anything but an evasion of the duty to think about reading. It is, on the contrary, to accept the obligation to think resourcefully and carefully and devotedly in the interests of that motive which for most parents assumes the highest priority: the nature and magnitude of our children's happiness.

A second preoccupation of many critics in recent years has been with the question of literary kinds or genres—a problem that, at first glance, may seem rather lifeless and remote from the questions that should be concerning us. Yet I think it has some consequences for our thinking about children's literature. For many years, booklists, anthologies, and even literature courses and curriculums tended to classify works according to gross form—poems, plays, and novels—and, within such groups, according to 'topic' or 'subject matter'. Thus a typical anthology of poems or stories for young people might bear such headings as 'Nature', 'Foreign Lands', 'Sport', 'Other Times', 'Here and Now', 'Adventure', 'The World of Science', or whatnot. In short, classification was preceded by certain judgements—frequently not entirely accurate—as to what a work was 'about'—that is, into which very general category of human experience its contents might be pigeonholed. But the tendency of most modern criticism, especially in its educational implications, is to suggest that there are far more significant categories than these—that the structure and tone and, in particular, the peculiar effect of a literary work offer far more revealing modes for its classification. We have, that is, addressed ourselves (with, I admit, sometimes highly conflicting answers) to such questions as what is a lyric poem, a tragedy, a comedy, a naturalistic novel, an absurd play, an adventure tale, a satire—and we have recognized that such reliable old guides as subject matter or historical period have not proved very useful. For we ask, not 'What will the reader learn about?' but 'What kind of experience is he invited to undergo?'

The consequence of this for the high school and college classroom is easy to see. It is plain that *Oedipus* and *Othello* bear strong relationships, despite the 1,900 years that separate their composition; it is plain that *Gulliver's Travels* and *Catch-22* have powerful affinities, despite the disparity of their 'topics'; it is plain that *Huckleberry Finn* can afford closer comparison with the *Odyssey* than it can with *Penrod*, despite the fact that it might be lumped with the latter under some such heading as 'Books about Boys'. In short, we have become increasingly sophisticated about distinctions and relationships between literary kinds—and this has had profound effects both on criticism and pedagogy.

I would suggest, therefore, that in thinking about children's reading we relax somewhat about 'topics'. The boy whose consuming passion is the Civil War need not confine himself to century-old reprints of *Harper's Magazine* or special publications of *American Heritage*, but is likely, on the contrary, to find his way to biographies of Lincoln and Lee and the stories of Ida Tarbell and *The Red Badge of Courage* and even perhaps to 'When Lilacs Last in the Dooryard Bloomed'. The youthful baseball aficionado will quite likely come, at his own rate, to the comedy of Ring Lardner, the unique achievement of Mark Harris's *Bang the Drum Slowly*, the high art of Malamud's *The Natural*. The James Bond addict can be led on to Eric Ambler's intricate plotting and thence to Graham Greene's reflective 'entertainments' and thence, I venture to say, to Stevenson and even to Melville.

Thus, beneath the apparent uniformity of 'subject-matter' labels, there lies diversity of a far more important sort. No topic is intrinsically more 'worthwhile' than another; no topic is either a guarantee of, or a bar to, the sort of satisfactions I have mentioned previously. They can serve us as singularly useful devices by which to engage interest and by which, too, to exploit the happy diversity of literary experiences which, on the surface, they tend to obscure. In effect, if a youngster is entirely concerned with reading about the Civil War, we should view it neither apprehensively as 'obsessive' nor smugly as 'educational'. Instead, I should think we can view it as a natural and immensely promising channel, leading to a permanently rewarding diversity of humanistic encounters.

A third question that has interested many critics in recent years might be put as follows. Are there basic themes or 'motifs' whose expression and recognition in written and spoken literature help to explain the timeless appeal of certain kinds of stories and poems? I am talking here about something a little more fundamental than even such formulas as boy-meets-girl or the tale of revenge or the 'whodunit'.

The inquiries of such anthropologists as Frazer, such psychologists as Jung, and such scholar-critics as Northrop Frye have pointed to the fact that some of man's basic questions and doubts and hypothetical answers tend to take form in recurrent literary patterns—or archetypes, as they are often called.

To take an example from a field that interests me: one persuasive scholar has been able to talk about the nature of satire, even in its most sophisticated forms, by tracing its origins to certain tribal rituals, directed against hostile forces, and has gone even further back to various informal, minimally artful attempts to achieve, through extemporaneous curses, the same magical effects.[1] The work of another scholar, Philip Young, has noted the recurrence of such literary themes as the suspension of time (in stories like that of Rip Van Winkle or the many 'time machines') or the stories of kings' daughters who rescue their lovers from wrathful fathers (such as the tale of Pocahontas).[2] Not content with noting the origins of some of these literary motifs in folk literature, he has applied psychoanalytic insights into the reasons for their persistence—the needs and worries and wishes that thus find embodiment in mythic form.

In their particulars, many of these approaches still call for

---

[1] Robert C. Elliott, *The Power of Satire: Magic, Ritual, Art* (Princeton, N.J., 1960).

[2] Philip C. Young, 'Fallen from Time: The Mythic Rip Van Winkle', *Kenyon Review*, 22 (Autumn 1960), 547-73, and 'The Mother of Us All: Pocohontas Reconsidered', *Kenyon Review*, 24 (Summer 1962), 391-415.

refinement. But I am of the opinion that they are bringing us substantially closer than ever before to answering questions we have previously evaded or answered peremptorily and unsatisfactorily. They are questions, that is, that concern the unchanging appeal of certain basic kinds of literary construction.

I am not certain how thoroughly the implications of these studies have been explored with respect to children's literature—although it is plain that many of these motifs find their most uncomplicated and manifest embodiment in myths and fairy stories and folktales. What, for the moment, concerns me is their possible significance for that nagging problem, the problem that is variously defined as engagement or motivation.

I have, to be honest, been somewhat concerned with the manner in which I have discovered this problem is being handled in various curricular study centres and similar agencies designed to deal with children's reading in the schools. I have found, for example, that the principle of familiarity—of comfortable recognition—has been rather overworked in many places. It is argued that the child cannot be expected to show interest in the unfamiliar and even that literature should make no demands upon him that transcend the literal limits of his own experience. This has an odd effect on what we judge to be 'suitable'. If a story involves a city, let it be a city he knows—or knows a great deal about. If a poem involves a bird, let it be a native bird (exit nightingale). If a play is to be read, by all means let it be a play of the here and now.

Such a principle seems to me to be a pretty frail one. I believe it is in practice. Most teachers of English composition know that because a child owns a dog or has visited a farm there is no guarantee that he will write readily or enthusiastically about 'My Dog' or 'The Farm'. And most teachers of English and concerned parents soon recognize that the familiar is at best a partial handle on children's literary enthusiasm—doubtless for the very simple reason that the commonplace is the commonplace and therefore the most unexciting object to the imagination.

And one need not be a very subtle aesthetic theorist to sense the difficulties of a lopsided emphasis upon the familiar. Whether we quote Aristotle's dictum concerning the mixture of the probable and the marvelous in successful literature or Marianne Moore's lines about 'imaginary gardens with real toads in them', the principle seems pretty clear. Effective imaginative literature is an amalgam of the new and strange—what taxes credulity and complacency—with what is somehow believable, authentic, and immediate. And I should argue that if the balance is to be tipped it must be tipped in the direction of novelty, of the alien and challenging. For all genuinely memorable literary experience is, in some measure, an initiation into the previously unknown, and the overworked reviewer's phrase to the effect that after reading such and such one is 'never quite the same' is, quite literally, a criterion that may be applied to the judgement of any literary work.

The word 'romantic' is today a very unfashionable one, but it is the thrust toward romance, or at least toward the imaginative, that outruns experienced actuality and that, today as much as ever, remains a major weapon against sameness and stagnation. This is heartbreakingly apparent, for example, even in the street gangs of our cities, whose ritual and nomenclature and professed structure and self-image, it has been proven, far exceed the sordid actualities of their operations. The same phenomenon is present in the almost universal manifestations of Walter Mittyism, among the old and young, wherever the imagination is invoked in the struggle against the too familiar. Mittyism may be professionally explained as escapism or the buttressing of the *amour propre* or as protest, but, whatever its ends, the means plainly involve the enlistment of the imagination in combat against familiar reality.

I am rejecting the temptation to say that new, unfamiliar kinds of reading should be encouraged in order to 'stretch' the imagination and to 'broaden horizons'. I happen to believe that there's a good deal of truth (and some danger) in this position, but the question that immediately concerns me is that of engagement and motivation. And in this context I am simply urging that we can overdo the matter of familiarity—if it leads us to neglect the appeal of whatever strains against the boundaries of the commonplace.

But it is obvious, as I have suggested, that novelty must be balanced against the reassuring sensation of knowing where one is, that the totally alien lacks both intelligibility and consequence for any reader. As critics have always recognized, we can become engaged in literature only when it is, in some sense, 'credible', when it lays claim, in some fashion, on our sense of reality. Many writers—including writers of children's literature—have responded to this requirement by attempting to invest the familiar with the romantic, to exploit, as it were, the potential magic that is latent in everyday reality; or they seek to introduce the strange and incredible into the midst of the commonplace. This last, of course, is what has been done triumphantly in such works as *Mary Poppins* or *Stuart Little* or *Doctor Dolittle*. And the former kinds of things are worthily attempted in the familiar efforts to exploit the 'romance of coal' or the 'miracle of oatmeal' or 'the wonderful story of sewage disposal', largely for didactic reasons.

Awareness of motifs or archetypes, however, suggests that the recognizable to which we respond is not necessarily a matter of times, places, and institutions but of the basic needs we feel, questions we ask, answers we find—of the instinctive, universal challenge of the journey, tension of the conflict, the covert wish that magic mingle with reality, the complex drives of affection, the complex fears of death.

I am aware that talk of this kind breeds discomfort of sorts among parents and those who are devoted to children, professionally or otherwise. Because we love and cherish the childlike, we naturally seek to preserve it and to translate even children's reading into terms that reject many of the adult 'facts of life' as somehow corrupting. Talk of conflict and love and birth and death, of tension and terror and doubt, and even of driving curiosity seems hostile to the image some people foster of 'children's literature' as a world unsullied by the adult vision of reality —as a monument to wholesome naiveté. I am, in fact, tempted to speculate that the fatuous admiration professed by some sophisticated adults for the idyllic surroundings, the allegedly benign humour, the unworldly wisdom of *The Wizard of Oz* or *Alice* or *Winnie-the-Pooh* is not so much what it pretends to be—a recognition of 'adult' excellences in 'children's' books—as a wistful gesture of longing to recover an irretrievable, happy innocence.

It is certainly possible to view children's books as instruments for the confirmation of childishness— to rejoice in whatever preserves the guileless and ingenuous. I suspect that to do so is, in itself, an evocation of impossible magic. The child is, indeed, in all his growing faculties, the father of the man; the faculty of imagination is not a childlike gift but a faculty capable of robust, complex development. As I have mentioned archetypes, let me say that no archetype is more compelling and dangerous than that of the fall of our first ancestors, for it points to the most uncomfortable yet inevitable fact about the human condition. This fact is that the acquisition of wisdom is the loss of innocence. The fact has received ingenious evasions. From Plato, through Wordsworth, through Hugh Walpole's neglected, lovely, subversive *Golden Scarecrow* to the pubert-directed reassurances of *The Catcher in the Rye*, we have been told that the innocence of childhood somehow preserves a greater wisdom and virtue than the sagacity of adults.

Such doctrines, however attractive they may be, are mystical rather than humanistic. For the humanist, above all else, takes into account the realities of the human condition. And those realities do not lead us into a beautiful, passionless realm but are compounded of hope and fear, of doubt and reassurance, of need and the fulfilment of need. It is in encounter with these human facts that we develop uniquely human values; and they are the values we seek to develop in and share with our children.

What I have been trying to say is, first, that the problem of 'engagement' or motivation can only be met by a judicious blending of what is novel and unfamiliar with what is real and significant. And, second, I have suggested that the latter component is to be achieved, not necessarily through those overtly familiar sights and sounds and people and places we identify as what the child 'knows', but through the more basic recognitions of experienced needs and satisfactions, doubts and curiosities and preoccupations.

There is a story by Saki that may help me clarify my point. It is called 'The Toys of Peace'. In it two well-meaning, pacifically inclined parents are induced to substitute for their children's toy soldiers a set of new playthings, in which military installations and personnel are replaced by a model city hall, municipal disposal plant, figures of various worthy civic servants, and the like. The children are given these toys; but the parents return, after some absence, to discover that through the children's ingenuity the city hall has been converted into a fort, the garbage plant into another fort, and the street-sweepers, health officials, and doctors and nurses have been assigned the role of soldiers on both sides of a fierce and bloody imagined conflict. Leaving aside whatever motive was in the strange mind of Saki, the story still serves my purpose. The 'realistic', familiar, but dreary figures of civic virtue are rejected in place of the more remote, less recognizable, more 'romantic' figures of war. Yet in that act is a gesture not only toward romance but toward reality as well, toward a state of contest and dissension and uncertainty which has, in a sense, a greater authenticity than does the image of a benevolent and orderly universe.

The tendency of what I have been saying is toward the recognition of certain principles that may transcend such notions as 'maturity' and 'reading readiness' and 'suitability' and the like. It is designed to suggest that, if we don't fatuously accept children's literature as primarily a safe, sane, antiseptic device for the preservation of childishness, its most fundamental appeals are the appeals of all effective literature—it exploits our urge toward novelty as it exploits, too, our insistence on a human actuality that is an amalgam of glory and squalor, certainty and anxiety, nobility and baseness, or, for that matter 'good guys' and indubitably bad ones. And this belief, it seems to me, moves to close the gap between adults' values and children's reading. It suggests that we do not seek substitutes, in children's books, for the most cherished elements in the best adult books. It suggests the folly of 'approving' books that are mere superficial mirrors of what we think children are or ought to be, mere superficial representations of a children's world or what it ought to be. For the highest pleasures of literature to which I have already referred—whether in adults' reading or children's—combine the urgency and authenticity of life as we know it with the excitement and wonder of life as it may yet be known.

This is why I believe that 'great' children's literature, if I may use that tired term, is simply great literature. It is no accident, nor is it mere clinical curiosity, that accounts for the critics' interest in Greek myths or in *Robinson Crusoe* or *Treasure Island* or *Just So Stories* or even, for that matter, in the perennial fairy or folktales. The sources of adult curiosity, adult humour, adult suspense, adult terror, adult pity are exploited by the writers of such books with an art comparable to that of any author for any audience. If I happen to have been talking about what are called 'classics', I do not wish to be construed as believing that the existence of classics is central to any belief I have about reading by children or adults; the appetite for reading, in old and young, far outruns the capacity of a few men to produce books of transparently permanent greatness. But it seems only sensible that, when the satisfactions literature can offer are superlatively afforded by a certain, limited number of books, we should seek to experience these works. It seems equally sensible that our experience with these books should reveal, in some measure, the satisfaction that many other books are capable of affording—the satisfactions that young and old alike should seek from reading.

As great books differ from good books in degree rather than kind, so too, I think, successful children's books differ from successful adult books in degree rather than in kind. Obviously this view follows from a belief that, with respect to the faculties of understanding and the gift of appreciation, young human beings differ from older ones in degree rather than kind. Granted that youthful powers of attention and concentration are limited and thus raise real and difficult questions for us, our concern with these questions must not deter us from the recognition that neither attention nor concentration are the faculties to which literature ultimately addresses itself in children or adults.

The point of all this seems rather clear. What I have been trying to say expresses my belief that the judgement of children's literature—and all the adult efforts that proceed from that judgement—must be conducted without condescension, without turning one's adult collar in an effort to define and enforce values that are somehow uniquely juvenile. On the contrary, it seems to me that the proper satisfactions of reading, even in the newly literate child—even, indeed, in the non-literate, story-listening child—provide a robust affirmation of our common humanity, our capacity, whether we are young or old, to understand and to be moved by and to gather to ourselves the products of the creative imagination.

As I say these things I am deeply conscious of circumstances at this moment in history which may qualify my views and chasten my high hopes. Talk about rich literary experience may seem appallingly ironic in the context of the massive phenomena of minimal literacy, minimal ability to understand and communicate. A teacher of English cannot today carry on glibly about literary values without agonizing awareness of the presence of culturally deprived youngsters for whom literature can be expected to have little meaning, since such words as 'father' and 'bedtime' and even 'breakfast' have themselves virtually no meaning.

To the crushing, compelling challenge posed by such young-sters (as well as, I might add, by those ostensibly more privileged youngsters in whom parental apathy, television, and aggressive vulgarity have likewise engendered a brand of cultural privation) we must respond with whatever is relevant of our experience, our love, and our concern. Even in these instances, however, though we respond with total flexibility and undogmatic re-sourcefulness to problems of minimal communication, the imag-ination is an indispensable ally, and the awaking of the imagina-tion a relevant province of art. For there are windows to be opened, and when they are open, they must reveal a vista of more than squalor and sameness and spiritual poverty.

It is common today to insist on a distinction between mere communication, including written communication, and literary art, whether or not that art is actually practiced in writing. Because, in practical and perhaps theoretical terms, some mode of communication is always antecedent to art, communication may well demand priority in much of our educational thinking, just as minimal questions of material well-being demand priority over questions of total well-being.

But, though we distinguish communication from art and con-centrate upon the former in all its urgency, all its changes, all its opportunities, the nature and stature of literary art and its satisfactions suffer no change. Though in our folly we neglect literary art, though in our haste we seek substitutes for it, though in our complacency or cruelty we discourage access to it for many of our fellow men, art and its power remain unchanged.

The realm of the humanist (and by this time I hope it is clear that the values I have been describing are, in my view, human-istic) is the realm of what has been created by human wisdom and imagination, work that has achieved final form, work that waits to be known and savoured and remembered for the unique satisfactions it provides. And so it is that a belief in the value of reading leads to a concern, not primarily for what is desirable or appropriate, what is suitable or profitable, what is hard or easy, what can be or ought to be, but for what is *here*—here to be encountered, here to be understood, here to be responded to, here to be rejoiced in.

[1967]

Didacticism in modern dress

JOHN ROWE TOWNSEND

During most of the nineteenth century it was taken for granted that children's books had a didactic aim. The emphasis could be mainly instructional, as in the Peter Parley series or Jacob Abbott's Rollo books. It could be moral, as in Mary Butt Sherwood's alarming *Fairchild Family* or the tearful saga of Elsie Dinsmore or the novels-for-young-ladies of the impeccable Charlotte M. Yonge. It could serve other ideals: that of Empire in the boys' stories of Englishman George Alfred Henty or of self-help in the rags-to-riches novelettes of Horatio Alger. But simply giving children pleasure would have seemed too frivolous an aim to most nineteenth-century writers.

Most; not all. Didacticism began to break down with the Alice books, with *Treasure Island,* which seemed to its author to be 'as original as sin', with *The Adventures of Tom Sawyer* and *The Adventures of Huckleberry Finn*, in which, as Mark Twain said, 'persons attempting to find a moral . . . will be banished.' And today nearly all the old didactic books are dead; the survivors are those that rejected didacticism, with the addition of a few such as *Little Women* that transcended it.

Is the didactic spirit extinct in children's literature today? We tend to talk and write as though it were. It is contrary to our view of the happy, relaxed, and more-or-less-equal relationship between the generations which we now regard as ideal. Yet the urge to instruct the young is deeply built into human nature.

And if one looks at the 'quality' children's books of today, and still more at what is written about them, it is hard to avoid the conclusion that didacticism is still very much alive and that, by an engaging intellectual frailty, we are able to reject the concept while accepting the reality. We can accommodate this contradiction because of another of our frailties: we cannot extend any historical sense we may possess in order to look objectively at our own time. Years ago we threw the old didacticism (dowdy morality) out of the window; it has come back in at the door wearing modern dress (smart values) and we do not even recognize it.

The standards of those concerned with the assessment and selection of children's books are more often implicit than explicit; but in situations where these standards are being passed on they can be found stated plainly in print. Here are a few instances; I do not quote them with disapproval but only to make my point. May Hill Arbuthnot's *Children and Books* is the basic text for a great many teachers' courses, and the following passages are among a number of similar ones.

> ... *such books as* Little Women *and the Wilder stories, without referring to specific religious practices or creeds, leave children with the conviction that decent, kindly people can maintain an inner serenity even as they struggle with and master the evils that threaten them.*
>
> ... *they [children] need books that, in the course of a good story, help to develop clear standards of right and wrong.*
>
> *Above all, to balance the speed and confusions of our modern world, we need to find books which build strength and steadfastness in the child, books which develop his faith in the essential decency and nobility of life, books which give him a feeling for the wonder and the goodness of the universe.*

These views are not confined to one commentator. Charlotte S. Huck and Doris Young state in *Children's Literature in the Elementary School:*

Through reading and guided discussion of their reading experiences children may gain understanding of self and others. They may come to realize that all behavior is caused and results from individual needs. Children may gain insight into their own behavior and the process of growth by identifying with individuals or families in good literature.

Dr Bernice Cooper wrote, in an article on Laura Ingalls Wilder in a recent number of *Elementary English:*

. . . the value of the 'Little House' books is enhanced for boys and girls because Laura Ingalls Wilder's philosophy of life, without didacticism, permeates the series. That philosophy is expressed in the letter from Mrs Wilder which the sixth grade received in response to their letters to her. She wrote, 'But remember it is not the things you have that make you happy. It is love and kindness, helping each other and just plain being good.'

The use of the phrase 'without didacticism' seems to me to be a mere genuflection toward the accepted view that didacticism is out of fashion.

And here are two extracts from the excellent children's-book-selection policy of The Free Library of Philadelphia:

In the field of purely recreational reading, stress is laid upon those books which develop the imaginative faculties, promote understanding, and cultivate worthwhile ideals and values.

Recreational books of all kinds, whether story or fact, are purchased with a view towards giving pleasure in reading and developing healthy attitudes towards the family, the community, the nation, and the world.

The views of the critics and selectors of children's books are of importance because these people are so largely the ones who decide whether a children's book will be published and whether, if published, it will succeed. It is a platitude to say that when we talk of quality children's books today we are not talking about something that children buy for themselves. There is a relationship between a child's pocket money and the price of an ice cream or a root beer or a candy bar or a comic; there is no relationship between a child's pocket money and the price of a book. The child himself hardly enters into the process by which quality children's books are assessed and distributed. They are written by adults, they are read by adults for adult publishers, they are reviewed by adults, they are bought by adults. This is inevitable. But the result is that a children's book can go far on the road to success before a single child has seen it.

The expensive, approved children's book costing $3.95 or $5.50 will do well if the libraries take it and not too well if they do not. A small number of parents with taste and money will buy it too; like the librarians they will almost certainly be serious, well-meaning, conscientious people. Quality publishing for children is governed by a complex social-institutional-economic equation which replaces the law of supply and demand; and as a result the adults are uniquely able to procure on the child's behalf not so much the thing he wants as the thing they feel he ought to have.

And what the child ought to have is apt to be something that fits in with the image of our society as serious, well-meaning, conscientious people feel it ought to be. We see our ideal society as one in which everybody is thoughtful, gentle, compassionate, withal humorous and fun loving; in which everyone is integrated but nevertheless individual. We expect, consciously or otherwise, that writers for children will provide us with instruments for bringing this society into being. And if our hands are on the levers, we cannot merely expect this; we can practically insist upon it. Now is the time to recognize just what we are doing and consider the dangers we run.

The first danger is an obvious one: the child opts out of the whole procedure and reads comics or nothing. He has, after all, the ultimate veto; however much adults approve of a book, no power on earth can make him read it if he does not want to. Indeed, teachers may also opt out of the whole procedure. I have

met some—more in England than in the United States—who
are utterly cynical. They say in effect: 'It's no good trying to
wish all this highbrow stuff on us. You just spend a day with the
underprivileged kids I have in my class, and you'll see it's a
blessed miracle if you can get them to read *any* kind of rubbish.'
Even the child who is a natural reader is no longer, as in the
nineteenth century, virtually a captive audience. There is no
dearth of other reading matter or of other things that an intelligent child can do with his time.

The existence of approved books that children will not read is
a sizeable danger, though somewhat diminished by the fact that
librarians cannot afford to give space to shelf-sitters. If the reviewers like a certain author but the children do not, the news
soon gets around. The book that no child will read cannot survive—at least as a children's book—nor does it deserve to. Authors have to write books that the child can and will read, and
the effect has been to concentrate their minds wonderfully. Even
so, the danger of undercutting by the comics or formula stories is
there. The writer or publisher with an eye on the main chance has
a long start over the one who is practising or encouraging an art.

The second danger is the effect upon authorship. Writers are
human and have to eat. With a few dogged exceptions, they will
not write the kind of books that are going to be unacceptable.
The people who pay the piper can call the tune. In an article in
the spring 1966 *Author*, Philippa Pearce describes the demand
for values as insidious. If a writer has moral standards, she says,
'they will appear explicitly or implicitly in his books; or at least
their corrupting contrary will not appear. He should not need to
bother about values; his job is imaginative writing.' Arthur
Ransome, author of *Swallows and Amazons*, would not have it
that the author is responsible to anybody but himself: 'You write
not for children but for yourself,' he says, 'and if by good fortune children enjoy what you enjoy, why then, you are a writer
of children's books . . . no special credit to you, but simply
thumping good luck.' But if you write for yourself and the result

is dismissed as flippant or unwholesome, you will not feel like congratulating yourself on your luck.

The danger that the author is silenced, or more probably redirected toward producing acceptable work, must of course be seen in perspective. Plenty of good writers exist to whom the desired values are as natural as air. Ransome himself is an example. While there is no preaching in his books, they form in a sense a course for children, a powerful influence on them to look at life in a certain way—and a way that serious, well-meaning adults are likely to approve of. His children are truthful, loyal, straightforward; the things they do are sensible, constructive, character-building. And Philippa Pearce's *Tom's Midnight Garden* and *A Dog So Small* are just as firmly rooted in civilized values. Excellent authors may be found whose moral sense comes out still more explicitly in their books. One of many possible examples is Madeleine L'Engle, whose prize-winning *A Wrinkle in Time* describes a cosmic war of good against evil—evil here is the reduction of people to a mindless mass, while good is individuality, art, and love. Miss L'Engle finds it quite natural to bring in the great, and greatest, names on 'our' side:

> *'Who have our fighters been?' Calvin asked. . . .*
>
> *'Jesus!' Charles Wallace said. 'Why, of course, Jesus!'*
>
> *'Of course!' Mrs Whatsit said. 'Go on, Charles, love. There were others. All your great artists. They've been lights for us to see by.'*
>
> *'Leonardo da Vinci?' Calvin suggested tentatively. 'And Michelangelo?'*
>
> *'And Shakespeare,' Charles Wallace called out, 'and Bach! And Pasteur and Madame Curie and Einstein!'*
>
> *Now Calvin's voice rang with confidence. 'And Schweitzer and Gandhi and Buddha and Beethoven and Rembrandt and St Francis!'*

Miss L'Engle's was openly and joyfully a moral theme. I take not the slightest exception to her approach. But neither morality nor magnificent invocations will make a work of art live if the breath of life is not in it. And a moral posture assumed by an author in deference to current requirements could result in nauseating and disastrous work. A British literary editor suggested to me last year that I ought to write a children's novel 'against racial prejudice'; he was as much puzzled as disappointed when I politely declined. But it seems to me that an author will do best to write only the books that come naturally to him. Anything else is done at the peril of his soul.

A third danger, which follows closely from the second, is the evaluation of books by the wrong standards. We are, I think, getting onto critically shaky ground when books like Louisa Shotwell's *Roosevelt Grady*, which deals with the life of a Negro family of migrant workers, and Dorothy Sterling's *Mary Jane*, telling of the ordeal of a Negro girl who goes to a newly integrated junior high school, and even Ezra Jack Keats' *The Snowy Day*, a bright, cheerful picture book about a little coloured boy's day in the snow, are discussed not on their literary merits but only as representations of racial problems. It is natural if you feel as strongly as most decent people do about racial discrimination to welcome books that give it short shrift; but to assess books on their racial attitude rather than their literary value, and still more to look on books as ammunition in the battle, is to take a further and still more dangerous step from literature-as-morality to literature-as-propaganda—a move toward conditions in which, hitherto, literary art has signally failed to thrive.

I should emphasize again that I am not in general opposed to the system or standards by which children's books are chosen; it is hard to see a practical alternative, other than a lapse into commercialism with the mass production of titles aimed at the lowest common denominator. And we in the United States and Great Britain can congratulate ourselves that at least there is no official children's literature, no crude plugging of a national or party line. Authors, publishers, critics, teachers, and librarians would unite

—thank heaven—in horror at the very idea. All I am suggesting is that we should see our standards as they really are and should recognize that our emphasis on quality and on values exposes us to certain risks—which may be worth running but which we should be aware of. Let me sum them up, briefly. One is that if we are not careful the ordinary, unliterary child loses interest in books; for this problem the United States, through first-class work for children in the schools and libraries, is doing much better than England. Another is that we expect from authors what it is not right or wise to expect from them, and thus possibly stultify their creative impulse. And a third is that we judge books by the wrong standards. It is not irrelevant that a book may contribute to moral perception or social adjustment or the advancement of a minority group or the Great Society in general; but in writing there is no substitute for the creative imagination, and in criticism there is no criterion except literary merit.

[1967]

The Stratemeyer strain: educators and the juvenile series book, 1900-1980

PETER A. SODERBERGH

During the Progressive Era the question of the influence of urban-technological excesses on American children was of deep concern to parents, teachers, librarians, and social reformers. If children were the 'finest fruits of civilization' (to use Anthony Comstock's words) then the forces of seduction and spoilage had to be identified and controlled.

How character was formed had been a matter of great interest since the 1890s. It was a complex issue, but no true expert on boyhood or girlhood doubted that what a child read was a vital key to what he became. 'That the influence of reading on character is one of the most powerful is granted by every high-minded person . . .,' the editor of *Journeys Through Bookland* stated in 1909. 'We are what we read.'

And what were the youngsters reading? Not the old nemesis of earlier days, the notorious 'dime novel'. By 1900 it had declined to a state of virtual invisibility. Not 'lewd' magazines and spicy gazettes. They had not yet been passed down into children's hands. What was left to inspect? The series book. It was everywhere, it seemed. Copies of *The Rover Boys, Motor Boys, Bobbsey Twins, Frank Merriwell, Dorothy Dale,* and *Dave Porter* proliferated in bookshops, department stores, and newsstands. Young people were collecting and consuming them by the tens of thousands. Reformers began to wonder: Were reports of the death of the dime novel premature? Was the 'literary pestilence' back, masquerading as a book? Some thought so. In a February 1900 review of two *Rover Boys* tales, *Literary World* noted that 'None of these books represents the highest range of reading for boys, but all approach the dime novel order.'

Who was responsible for this new 'vulgarization of children's books?' The writers of such material, primarily: Gilbert Patten, creator of *Frank Merriwell;* H. Irving Hancock; and Frank G. Patchin, for example. But one name stood out from his colleagues, the undisputed king of the juveniles: Edward Stratemeyer. As the Pittsburgh *Dispatch* observed in 1904, 'Everybody knows that Edward Stratemeyer is the most widely-read of all living American authors for boys.' Stratemeyer was the author of 150 juvenile books and the founder of a literary syndicate that mass-produced 700 series book titles. Although he died in 1930, the residue of his work still disturbs many educators a half-century later. How professionals have reacted to his books over the years says as much about American pedagogues as it does about the series book phenomenon.

With the publication of *The Rover Boys at School* (1899) the modern phase of series book history began. Written by Stratemeyer, under the name of 'Arthur Winfield', the famous sequence sold six million copies before it expired in 1926. Stratemeyer also created *The Bobbsey Twins* (1904), *Motor Boys* (1906), *Tom Swift* (1910), *The Hardy Boys* (1927), and *Nancy Drew* (1930). Total sales of these five series alone approximate 125 million copies. He produced eighty-one distinct series in the period 1894-1930.

Early objections to series books concentrated on three features. First, the poor quality of the prose. In a time when the elevation of human thought and behavior were cornerstones of progressivism, the texts of series books were an affront. An editorial in the *Library Journal* of December 1905 asked: 'Shall the libraries resist the flood and stand for a better and purer literature and art for children, or shall they "meet the demands of the people" by ratifying a low and lowering taste?'

The second feature that evoked criticism was the series book's tendency toward exaggeration and sensationalism. Stratemeyer's fictional heroes and heroines, it was felt, were worldly, sly, and preternatural. The playful, polite, persevering juveniles in the older books by 'Oliver Optic' (William T. Adams), 'Harry Castlemon' (Charles Fosdick), and Edward Ellis had been transformed into globe-trotting, saber-rattling, wise-acreing rascals who out-foxed adults at every turn. Educators were appalled at this high degree of improbability. It was unreal, suggestive, and over-stimulating. 'The chief trouble with these books,' one of Stratemeyer's adversaries (Franklin Mathiews), wrote, 'is their gross exaggeration, which works on a boy's mind in as deadly a fashion as liquor will attack a man's brain.'

Another annoying aspect was the assembly-line manner in which series books were being produced. Stratemeyer was the main offender on this point. In 1906 he organized his system into the Stratemeyer Syndicate. From his office on Madison Avenue (1914) he presided over a 'stable of hired writers' whom he paid to complete his plot outlines. Between 1904 and 1915 he was thus able to release forty-two new series, which included 214 separate titles. Attractively bound at fifty cents a piece, Stratemeyer's books were inundating the market-place. Such an overabundance of standarized inferiority troubled educators who knew that the inexpensive, provocative books capitalized on children's 'mania for collecting things'. How could the tide of 'cheap and vicious' fiction be stemmed? No one seemed to know. Orton Lowe, a school administrator, summed up the dilemma in 1914: 'The juvenile series—the hardest problem to handle. . . . The series is always "awful long," all of the volumes are cut to the same pattern, they are always in evidence, and they are equally stupid. . . . What shall be done with them?'

The first stage of the anti-series book movement covered the years 1900-17. Unfortunately it must be described as exhortative, unscientific, punitive, and ineffective. The best organized campaigns were mounted by the American Library Association, Boy Scouts of America, and American Bookseller's Association, who kept each other informed and aroused. Classroom teachers and PTA groups joined the crusade irregularly.

In the final analysis most parties to the counter-series book movement resorted to name-calling, dire warnings, and other pressure tactics. The despised books were pronounced 'vulgar', 'pernicious', 'trashy', and 'injurious'. Series book authors were characterized as crass materialists, men of 'no moral purpose', and managers of fiction factories. Some of Stratemeyer's products (*Tom Swift, Motor Girls, Moving Picture Girls,* e.g.) were castigated publicly as samples of the current cancer. Throughout the attacks Stratemeyer proceeded with business as usual. Professional detractors did not disturb him often. He was fond of saying: 'Any writer who has the young for an audience can snap his fingers at all the other critics.' He snapped his fingers frequently in those days, and sales of his books grew with each passing year.

The First World War brought all lesser conflicts to a temporary halt. At the end of fifteen years the 'good book' forces had little to show for their pains. Collectively, *Tom Swift, Rover Boys,* and *Motor Boys* had sold 10 million copies. And how many of those had been passed from reader to reader? There were a number of reasons why the initial anti-series efforts failed to weaken the grip of the juvenile book on the popular imagination.

The educator-reformers moved on the fragile, nineteenth-century assumption that flat disapproval and informal censorship would shape mass opinion. They attacked a corporate process with moralisms. As missionaries they sought to convert people who felt no sense of sin. They attempted no serious research, preferring to protect rather than to study children. In their desire to sweep series books from library shelves they enhanced the popularity of the banished items. Most importantly, they seriously underestimated the degree to which the series book had become a cultural artifact since its origination in 1861. Many respectable citizens had fond memories of the books of their youth and could not be incited to condemn their own pasts. As one chagrined educator said at a November 1913 meeting of public school librarians, the series books were surviving because 'often they were the gift of father, mother, or Sunday school teacher' (all of whom should know better).

With one war settled, hostilities between the series book and its opponents resumed in 1919 and extended to 1931. During those post-war years the fortunes of Edward Stratemeyer and his 'army of ghosts' rose to new heights. Twenty-six new series were produced, among them being *Honey Bunch* (1923), *Blythe Girls* (1925), *Bomba* (1926), and *Ted Scott* (1927), not to mention *Hardy Boys* and *Nancy Drew*.

It is to their credit that educators in the 1920s attempted to quantify the nature of the problem Mr Stratemeyer and his peers had been causing for several decades. Research studies, informal polls, and random samplings were conducted to find answers to the questions: What is literary merit? What do children read? Why do they choose one item and not another? Underneath ran the basic issue: Why, contrary to our best advice, do children insist on reading series books? The results were predictable and exasperating. Edward Stratemeyer, of course, could not have achieved preeminence in the juvenile book field if he had not already known the answers.

A brief report of the findings of four surveys will suffice to recreate the tone of the period. Some of the studies confirmed what series authors and their publishers discovered in the 1880s. Arthur Jordan's review of *Children's Interest in Reading*, done at Columbia in 1921, proved that series writers still ruled the roost because they knew what appealed to boys (war, scouting, sports) and girls (home, school, fairy stories). In 1922 a Johns Hopkins study concluded that any given book's external appearance was a significant factor in children's choices of reading matter. The physical dimensions and complexions of the most-likely-to-be-chosen books, it happened, fit the series book perfectly.

The major undertaking of the decade was the *Winnetka Graded Book List* (1926). Over 36,000 teachers and 800 pupils in thirty-four cities were polled during the 1924-5 school year in an attempt to identify existent standards of selection, the elements of 'quality literature', and children's basic interests. Supported by the Carnegie Corporation and the American Library Association, the report elicited considerable interest and sold 3,800 copies by early 1927.

The result was both good and bad news. On the positive side, earlier findings on the correlation between appearance and selection were validated. The bad news (which was withheld for six months) was that the reading habits of fifth, sixth, and seventh graders were dominated by Edward Stratemeyer. *Bobbsey Twins, Tom Swift, Honey Bunch,* and others—'unanimously rated trashy' *a priori* by a select panel of librarians—received near-perfect interest scores from 98 per cent of the pupils. The experts were confused. The authors of the study cried out: 'Just what is "literary merit" anyhow?' Despite administrators' careful planning and coaching of the pupils, the series book came bursting through the experiment. Stratemeyer was not surprised. In June 1927, as the Winnetka list was fading into oblivion, he told a Newark *News* interviewer: 'I receive a great many letters from boys and girls who read my books. . . . It shows their hearts are with you.'

The period ended on a note of frustration. In 1930, 5,510 pupils were furnished 50,845 titles and urged by Pittsburgh educators to express their preferences. Once again junior high pupils voted for Edward Stratemeyer. They dutifully ranked the 'outstanding books' they had been alerted to, but they gave their clearest endorsements to *Tom Swift, Ruth Fielding, Baseball Joe,* and *Outdoor Girls.* Worse still, when I.Q. scores were correlated to reading choices 'about twice as many series were reported by the people with *greater* mental ability.' Nonplussed, the author of the study remarked: 'It would be interesting to find out . . . just what makes the SERIES such a favourite [with adolescents].' Florence Bamberger may have been correct. Ten years earlier she had decided that 'adults appear to estimate children's book preferences most inaccurately.'

In May 1930, one month before the Pittsburgh study was completed, Edward Stratemeyer died of lobar pneumonia at his Newark, New Jersey home. Ostensibly, the sixty-seven-year-old 'champion of juvenile series writers' was gone. He left an estate in excess of $500,000 and a literary Syndicate of momentous proportions. After several months of indecision his daughters, Edna and Harriet, decided to carry on the tradition. In November 1930 the main office was moved to East Orange, New Jersey, and the Stratemeyer Syndicate was again producing 'good series books for boys and girls'. The physical demise of Edward Stratemeyer was a matter of record, but educators would discover that he had not departed their midst entirely.

From 1931 to 1960 all was relatively quiet on the series book front. The attentions on both sides were diverted sequentially by the Depression, several wars, and the expansion of the mass media. Educators were busy reacting to charges of myopia and unpreparedness between 1945 and 1958. Radio, comic books, pulp magazines, motion pictures, and the rise of television undermined the series book's veritable monopoly of leisure time. It was only a long truce, however. The irrepressible series book, while educators were preoccupied with the new scientism, issued an old challenge.

Between 1953 and 1962 the Stratemeyer Syndicate released modernized sets of *Tom Swift, Jr.* (1954), *Honey Bunch and Norman*

(1957), *Hardy Boys* (1959), *Nancy Drew* (1959), and *Bobbsey Twins* (1961), and four new series, *Happy Hollisters* (1953), *The Tollivers* (1957), *Bret King* (1960), and *Linda Craig* (1962). Pedagogical reaction to the rejuvenation of the books was not immediate but when it did develop, it took two distinct forms. The more familiar of the two might be described as classical in mood and methodology. It was heavily populated by librarians, older teachers, English educators, and literary observers. In their statements one found attitudes identical to those expressed by their resolute antecedents of 1902-17. If they were not elitist (in that they, as adult experts, knew what was best for the reader) they were at least authoritarian. The classicists were loathe to relinquish the power of choice to the child, genuinely concerned he or she might linger too long on impoverished material. Their armory of weapons included verbal disapproval, printed criticism, and policies of exclusion.

Thus, in 1963, a respected educator, Dora Smith, wrote of Edward Stratemeyer and his 'hired hacks' who contributed to the 'tremendous spread of cheap, tawdry fiction, akin to the dime novel. . . .' In 1965 the American Library Association circulated recommendations to small libraries to aid in the elimination of *Nancy Drew, Bobbsey Twins, Hardy Boys, Tom Swift,* and other 'outmoded and poorly written series'. Dorothy R. Davis, a distinguished bibliographer, in 1967 held Stratemeyer responsible for the 'low regard' in which series books were held by 'persons in the field of juvenile literature'. In 1972 a recognized authority on children's books, Selma Lanes, used terms such as escapist, regressive, wooden, and banal with reference to *Nancy Drew, Hardy Boys,* and *Bobbsey Twins.* The librarians in the Stratemeyer Syndicate's home city of East Orange could not recall having a series book in stock since 1950. If children wanted series books they could 'get them elsewhere'. In 1978 the librarian of the Newton (Mass.) Public Library refused to stock *Nancy Drew* and *Hardy Boys* books on the basis of their poor literary quality.

In the mid-1960s an unofficial demurrer to the classicist position evolved. The developmentalists were a minority coalition of selected English educators, psychologists, and Language Arts instructors.

The developmentalists strove to direct professional and parental concerns away from a given enemy toward the particular needs of the reader. 'How to Get the Most Reluctant Reader to Read, Read, Read!' was the general battlecry. Recommendations were phrased in positive, unpatronizing language. The will to dictate and censor was absent. Debates on literary merit were forsaken as unprofitable. Parents and teachers were encouraged to view reading as a continuum, the reading habit as scrutable, and the various reading stages as identifiable elements in the total maturation process. The developmentalist attitude toward the series book was benign, as three samples from the literature indicate.

In 1966 a paper by John Rouse entitled 'In Defense of Trash' called for a revision of the abstractions formerly employed to measure literary quality. A good book, the author thought, could be one 'which gives the student a meaningful emotional experience.' Even a series book might do that, 'whether or not it is admired by the cognoscenti.' 'Teachers and librarians are sometimes too concerned with the quality of books . . .,' an English educator, Dwight Burton, said in 1968. He referred to research that allowed that 'enthusiastic readers of mature works' had often consumed 'tons' of *Nancy Drew, Tom Swift,* and *Bobbsey Twins* material. In 1971 a 239-page guide for adults, *Books and the Teen-Age Reader,* contained a chapter on 'Subliterature'. Included was the series book—still inferior, but at least a member of the literary race. In fact, 'certain benefits' might accrue to the breathless reader of the *Hardy Boys.* Series books sustained the reading habit, perhaps. That their climaxes and endings were standardized might enhance the reader's sense of security.

It is likely that the series book will remain an anathema to classicists who feel compelled to stand between the reader and low-level material. The developmentalists appear to have made a realistic (but cautious) accommodation during the 1970s to a fact of American life. They have chosen to expend their energies on the whetting of reading appetites among the young, letting the series book fall where it may. Neither group, of course, has faced the series book syndrome squarely. Both employ avoidance techniques—one traditional, the other seemingly advanced. The questions raised by their predecessors of the 1920s remain unanswered. There is still an element of astonishment that the series book captures so many imaginations but no serious attempt to discover why it does. In a manner of speaking, the will of the masses has been treated, thus far, with disdain.

That the series book persists after eighty years of condescension and coercion is adequate justification for a definite study of the phenomenon, but there may be other reasons as well.

During the last decade public interest in vintage series books increased visibly. Prices on works such as *Elsie Dinsmore* and *Frank Merriwell* have risen with the demand. Books written by Edward Stratemeyer under his own name are approaching the status of collector's items, often commanding $7.50 per volume. More articles about the juvenile book tradition have been published since 1963 than in the forty previous years. A number of university libraries (notably, Michigan State's) have sought to amass representative collections of series books from the 1868-1930 period. Transcending waves of 'nostalgia' and cyclical faddism, an awareness of the books' usefulness as a mirror of our former selves has been growing. Educators in many academic disciplines might find the nature and function of series books worthy of consideration in the classroom. Certainly this genre of book ranks with those silent films, company catalogues, and Edwardian periodicals we endorse as illuminators of the American character.

Opposition and apathy notwithstanding, the current series book moves confidently toward 2000 A.D. If the record of the

Stratemeyer Syndicate is an index, external negativity has had no demonstrable effect on its products. In 1979 *Nancy Drew* was purchased (by parents, for their children, as often as by the children themselves) at the rate of two million copies. The *Hardy Boys* and *Bobbsey Twins* sets sell one million and 250,000 titles a year respectively. Several series are available in foreign language editions. Syndicate books are well-received in Scandinavia, Great Britain, Italy, and Holland. *Nancy Drew* may be the most popular juvenile book in France. New series (*Winn and Lonny*) and modernizations of older series (*Dana Girls*) have substantial reader followings. By any standard, this is an impressive, ongoing achievement replete with implications for education.

Controversial though it may be, the ethos of Edward Stratemeyer prevails. It manifests when parents ask their local librarians why they do not make series books available to children. It manifests when an apprentice teacher wonders why her training program does not acknowledge the existence of books she collected and enjoyed. And it manifests in the thousands of letters children write to his Syndicate each year, expressing their enthusiasms for the latest story. He would be pleased to know that, as he said over fifty years ago: 'It shows their hearts are with you.'[1]

[1980]

---

[1]The spirit of this article is drawn from numerous personal and written contacts I have had with persons involved to varying degrees with the Stratemeyer family and/or Syndicate. I refer, with deepest gratitude, in particular to: Harriet Stratemeyer Adams and Edna Stratemeyer Squier (1895-1974), daughters of Edward Stratemeyer and series book writers *extraordinaire;* Irving Stratemeyer (1886-1974), cousin to Harriet and Edna; Andrew E. Svenson (1910-1975), for many years the author of the *Hardy Boys,* and other, series; Syndicate partners Nancy S. Axelrad, Lorraine S. Rickle, and Lilo Wuenn. Since 1975 the Stratemeyer Syndicate office has been located in Maplewood, New Jersey, and, by the latest (1980) accountings, is flourishing at many different levels.

'Good bunnies always obey': books for American children

JASON EPSTEIN

The boy should enclose and keep, as his life, the child at the heart of him, and never let it go . . . the child is not meant to die but to be forever fresh born. —GEORGE MAC DONALD

Ever since an eighteenth-century bookseller named John Newbery commissioned Oliver Goldsmith to compile the first Mother Goose and thus launched an industry, the publication of books for children has been, among other things, a way of making money. Lately it has become a way of making a lot of money, and as more of the nation's effort comes to be invested in educating the young, the publication of books for children promises to become a major aspect of American business. Even more, it promises to become a business of great social and political importance, for it is trafficking in nothing less than the next generation, which is to say our whole future and the future of all our technological, political, and social machinery.

In 1961 some 1,700 new children's books were published. Total sales of all children's books, not counting school texts, came to 277,420,000 copies, mainly through some 25,000 toy, department, and novelty stores, five-and-tens, and supermarkets, and to a lesser extent through the 9,000 libraries in America and the 1,804 bookstores. A growing number have also found their way into the schools—through classroom libraries, of which there are now some 25,000—to supplement the dreary and often unreadable textbooks. But schools continue to buy mainly textbooks, which are not a part of this discussion—though much of what is wrong with American textbooks is also wrong with children's books in general and for the same reasons. Children's books have increasingly become part of a bureaucratically administered sub-culture, largely cut off by a dense fog of conventional and irrelevant theory from the best literary and scientific culture of the community at large.

Such isolation is relatively recent. The great children's books of the past, though they often represented a distinct genre, were simply a department of literature, and they were commonly written by authors who, in contrast to the situation today, were not primarily writers for children. Such figures as Defoe, Swift, Blake, Coleridge, Melville, Hawthorne, Mark Twain, Kipling, Doyle, etc., wrote for children either inadvertently or out of a romantic preoccupation with childhood itself. Childhood for them was sacred and superior, in its vitality and powers of perception, to maturity, which was compromised through having accommodated itself too much to the world. In one way or another these writers believed that the recollected vitality of childhood sustained a man, if anything did, throughout his entire life and that, conversely, civilization—Wordsworth's 'prison house'—was deadly. This same belief, in political terms, led Thomas Jefferson to demand a revolution every twenty years as each new generation coming of age asserted itself against the accumulated inhibitions of the generation in being. And one finds it again, less reasonably, in today's adults who occupy themselves with cowboy heroes and perhaps among the President and his friends playing touch football.

Before the eighteenth century there were no children's books as such, except for the chap-books, though works like Aesop's fables and the story of King Arthur in its various forms interested children as well as adults. And, of course, except for the catechisms and grammars, there were no textbooks. There was only the hornbook from which children learned the alphabet and the numbers from one to ten. Lessons were usually read by the teacher and the children learned nearly everything orally and by rote or by observation and imitation (a process which corresponds somewhat to the theory of conditioned reflexes according to which modern teaching machines have been developed; the older method was, however, less passive and more social).

The use of books in the classroom is rather recent and their pedagogic value, in view of the widespread criticisms that have lately been made of them, cannot yet be taken for granted. And if one watches young children growing up, it appears that even the schools themselves tend to inflate the part that they play in educating the young. Like other young animals, children seem to learn more or less directly from their environment and by testing and observing their parents, their playmates, and perhaps their teachers. Bright children, as they grow older, traditionally have found their schools dull and confining, except for the other children they meet there, and the brighter, the more explosive and spontaneous the youngsters are, the more their classes are likely to bore them. It is at least plausible to suggest that the fault may be in the process of formal education itself. Certainly there is something wrong with the programs and books that the children are expected to put up with.

The great body of children's literature and the really vital branch of it, despite the hundreds of children's books published last year and the even greater number that will appear this year, remains within the oral tradition—carried on over the centuries by the children themselves. The rhymes and songs, the crucial bits of information, the forms of behaviour, the loyalties and friendships, the superstitions and games, the sexual discoveries that children communicate to one another as they grow older have always formed the basis of early education. It is from these that the children learn, far more than they ever do from books or in their classes, the language, its rhythm, and the fundamental principles of ethics: i.e., how to keep out of trouble, the fatal knowledge of which begins the long, painful, and inevitable movement away from childhood. As Iona and Peter Opie remarked in their brilliant study, *The Lore and Language of School Children*, 'The world-wide fraternity of children is the greatest of savage tribes and the only one which shows no signs of dying out.'

But the Opies were optimistic. The savage tribe has suddenly become a market—a big one—and the woods are full of salesmen, typically disguised as missionaries. Education is the new religion and books are among the trinkets with which to lure the children into the civilized world. As Josette Frank, Reading Consultant to the Child Study Association of America, has written, '[Today] we have an opportunity to develop better educated, better informed, increasingly cultured citizens and more of them than was ever possible in times past. There is a new public for books, and this public includes children.' And later she adds, 'Our role is to be alert to all that goes on in a child's world, ready to offer a book that further explains a motion picture; or to direct attention to a television program that amplifies a book just read, or to discover how comics may lead to new avenues for a child to explore.'

The trouble with Miss Frank's point of view is its assumption that the civilized world as she conceives it is necessarily fit for children to grow up in and that children will unquestionably take part in it on the terms she proposes. 'Today,' Miss Frank goes on, 'long before [children] are ready for higher education, the arts and sciences are there for the taking, in pictures and stories. Political campaigns are suddenly intelligible to ten-year-olds. With the turn of a dial or the riffling of a picture magazine, they may have glimpses of scientific researches and of the men and women who are grappling with them. Perhaps they would never have known what an East Indian looked like, but now the United Nations delegate from India appears on their television screen and speaks to them in perfect English. The baseball hero comes to talk to them. So does the President of the United States. The people in the news are real to our boys and girls.'

In other words, it has now become possible to alienate children from childhood in ways that would have made Wordsworth's head swim. Today's children, hardly out of their cribs, can be shoved by the children's book industry and its affiliated bureaucracy of educators, reviewers, specialists, and consultants, straight into the 'civilized' world of television, advertising, and the cold war through processes which, when we hear of them in other societies, we call brainwashing.

In America there are some four thousand experts who, like Miss Frank, concern themselves with children's reading. Their influence on the kinds of books that are published and bought for children by schools, libraries, and parents is enormous, and their power, until recently, has been enhanced by the scornful indifference with which they have been regarded by the intellectual community at large. Though the experts' inclinations tend to be widely permissive and pluralistic—having devolved from Dewey's idea that a child should be encouraged to develop along the lines in which he is strongest into the quite contrary idea that anything goes so long as the children seem interested and the community doesn't object—their effect is radically inhibiting. Most of these experts work with schools and school boards or in teachers' colleges. Many have taught school themselves, but have given it up for the more prestigious, less frustrated role of administrators. Some are book reviewers or work as curriculum directors. A number of them have been hired by publishers or are engaged as consultants to the various children's book clubs. Most of them, to judge by their own writings, have read very little and are indifferent to the rhythm of English prose.

Nevertheless, they have as a group managed to encircle the children's book business to the point where a publisher has to be very fast on his feet, or unusually indifferent to profits, to break through and confront the children with his goods directly.

In the meantime, though the business flourishes, the children themselves increasingly ignore what the experts recommend. Marie Rankin, an expert herself, has noted that the books chosen for the Newbery Medal—a sort of Pulitzer Prize for juveniles awarded annually by members of the American Library Association—are among those the children read least. And while a few of the earlier selections were of a rather high order, if one examines some of the more recent prize-winners, one's sympathies tend to be with the children. Of the four winners for 1961, which presumably are typical of what expert opinion finds admirable these days, three are contemptible by even the most relaxed critical standard, and it is almost impossible to imagine from what point of view they may be considered to have any merits at all. With respect to vitality, inventiveness, and style, they are far inferior to the *Nancy Drews and Tom Swifts* of an earlier period, which children today continue to read in great quantities though the experts dismiss them now as they did then.

One of the prize-winners, a book called *Belling the Tiger* by Mary Stolz, pointlessly enlarges on the traditional tale: the mice find that they have inadvertently belled not a cat, but a tiger, an elaboration which requires sixty-four pages to complete and which sells for $2.50. But for this price the reader also gets a moral. As the mice are about to report to their elders on their adventures, they become aware that they will not be believed by the grownups, who are clearly less intelligent than themselves. So rather than create a disturbance they suppress their interesting news, wrap their tails around each other, and fall asleep.

Another prize-winner, in this case the winner of the Gold

Medal itself, is equally without accomplishment, though it represents more explicitly than *Belling the Tiger* the preoccupation these writers have with the idea that the young had better subdue, for the sake of avoiding a disturbance within the community, whatever tendencies they may have toward rebelliousness and originality. This book, *The Bronze Bow* by Elizabeth George Speare, is a biblical novel written for a somewhat older group of children than *Belling the Tiger*. It is thickly pious and its factitious historical setting is presented in language so drab and abstract and even, occasionally, illiterate, that it is impossible to adjust one's ear to it ('Prodded on by weary drivers, the camels swayed slowly.' 'The morsels of food had not begun to whet his hunger.') But the trouble is less with the book's prose or even with its fake historical and religious paraphernalia than with the smugness of its doctrine. The hero is a young Palestinian Jew at the time of Christ. He is meant to represent a juvenile rebel of the sort who today, with a less specific enemy to confront, has become a problem for the authorities. This young man—his name is Daniel—has joined a band of marauders and with them is determined to drive the Romans from his homeland. It is clear from the start—even to those who may not be familiar with Jewish history—that his rebellion is going to fail. But miraculously, a carpenter with magical powers to heal and persuade arrives in town and prevails upon Daniel to come down out of the mountains, return to his blacksmith shop and acquiesce, like everybody else, in the Roman occupation. Eventually Daniel takes this advice and we are led to believe that he will make a profitable marriage to a pretty girl who comes from a nearby suburb.

May Hill Arbuthnot, still another expert, has tried to account for the failure of children to become interested in such stories as these by suggesting that superior literature even among adults is often less admired than trash. But if *The Bronze Bow* is what Miss Arbuthnot means by good literature, then surely there are other reasons to account for this phenomenon. One need only recall the tactics of literature that children have always found interesting to see how far off the mark this sort of product is.

In *Gulliver's Travels,* for example, the hero, bored with his wife, sets out on a series of journeys in the course of which the absurdity of human society is variously illustrated; he concludes that horses are preferable to men. Robinson Crusoe discovers that he can live successfully with an absolute minimum of human society and create a satisfactory world of his own. Alice, tired of her book, escapes the everyday world and encounters a parody of it in which the logical categories that adults claim to think in are, if carried a few steps further, seen to be absurd. The children in E. Nesbit's novels are invariably wiser and enjoy themselves more than their elders, from whom they are forever escaping. Huckleberry Finn's only friend is an outcast, a fugitive slave, and the world from which they jointly flee is filled with sanctimonious frauds, false friends, and parvenus. Holden Caulfield grows up in a world which proves to be so untrustworthy that clearly he will never take part in it, but in his case there is neither fantasy nor wilderness to which to escape; he will remain 'maladjusted'.

Nor has this theme been limited to children's literature. That organized society is hostile to growth and freedom and defeats the individual as, in the literature of an earlier epoch, nature used to do, is a dominant idea in the literary tradition, especially for those modern writers who, in the aftermath of Romanticism, have deliberately concerned themselves with questions of rebellion, privacy, and their own authenticity. It is of interest, however, that in those works which have become great children's literature, the heroes, unlike the protagonists of much modern fiction, manage to survive the environment and even, in such cases as Robinson Crusoe and Doyle's Professor Challenger, to succeed in transforming it. The affection that children have for stories of this kind seems to confirm the affinity that the Romantic writers felt between themselves and childhood and helps to explain why so much fiction of the nineteenth century appealed, and still appeals, to the young. For until recently the typical literary hero was himself, so to speak, a child growing up and testing his mettle against the world. And if one thinks of that long line of literary adolescents from Don Quixote and Hamlet to Stephen Daedalus, then the idea of childhood and the problem of growing up will appear to be representative, for many of our great writers at least since Shakespeare and Milton, of the human condition itself. All that happened to Adam when he left Paradise is that he was condemned to grow up and become civilized, to put on clothes, deny his nature, and go to work. Mankind, ever since, has been trying, in one way or another, to find its way out of this dilemma.

In proposing a closer affiliation between childhood and the 'civilized world' in which the President addresses ten-year-olds, then, the experts have undertaken not only to alienate children from their own nature but to turn one of literature's great and characteristic themes upside down. Given the refractory nature of childhood, it is not surprising that the children increasingly refuse to take part in the world that the experts are trying to sell them. One suspects that they sense the fraudulence and despair of it, and that like such writers as Joyce and Faulkner, with whom they share this view, they have retreated, some more than others, to worlds of their own, while the juvenile authorities and the Sunday book reviewers irritably wonder what can have gone wrong.

In the case of disturbed children, for whom the world makes no sense and is terrifying, it is important to do nothing that will disturb them further and gradually to convince them that the world is not so hostile after all. And even where healthy children are concerned, the problem for society and their parents is to present them with an environment that they can trust, that is credible in itself and satisfies a child's growing need for a solid reality out there. What is wrong with prize-winners like *The Bronze Bow* or with Miss Frank's picture magazines is that they are deficient in reality, so deficient indeed that it requires an entire educational bureaucracy to talk the children into accepting them. One is encouraged by the extent to which the children are able to resist such persuasion and reject such products; but it is sad that the experts have given so little advice concerning alternatives, especially since so many parents and teachers must themselves be at a loss.

In the absence of viable alternatives, the children—who, as the experts proudly tell us, avidly read—buy more than 300,000,000 comic books a year, and nightly watch men and women die on television. Comics and television have, for the children, the dubious advantage of representing, however badly, their natural aggressiveness toward those elders whom they want both to destroy and become, a function previously fulfilled for them by the Brothers Grimm and by such representatives of adult authority as Mr MacGregor who put Peter's father into a pie. But in the new version of *Peter Rabbit*, 'specially edited in vocabulary and style to meet the needs of the young child', the pie is not mentioned and over Peter's bed is the sign 'Good Bunnies Always Obey'. Beatrix Potter's little masterpiece, language and all, has fallen apart in the hands of its modern adapter. Compare, for example, the original:

> First he ate some lettuces and some
> French beans; and then he ate some
> radishes;
> and then, feeling rather sick, he went to
> look for some parsley.

with the new version:

> In the garden he saw carrots and beans
> and radishes.
> 'Mmm,' said Peter to himself, 'Carrots,
> beans and radishes are what I like best.'
> He began to eat.

> *He ate some carrots.*
> *He ate some radishes.*
> *He ate and ate and ate.*
> *Peter ate so much he got sick.*
> *He went to look for some parsley.*

The value of this inane performance is impossible to grasp. There is nothing old-fashioned or obscure about Miss Potter's version and there is nothing in the new version to make it clearer or more interesting than the original.[1] A little of it is likely to go a long way with even a slow child and none of it is likely to go anywhere at all with parents and teachers who agree with Professor Jerome Bruner of Harvard that, 'We might ask as a criterion for any subject taught in primary school whether, when fully developed, it is worth an adult's knowing and whether having known it as a child makes a person a better adult. If the answer to both questions is negative or ambiguous, then the material is cluttering the curriculum.'

Thanks to the theories of children's literature which this adaptation exemplifies, the comic book publishers can look forward to even bigger sales and the children will probably never go on to read the sequel in which Peter and his cousin, Benjamin Bunny, who in Miss Potter's original have no inhibiting signs over their beds, steal some onions and retrieve Peter's clothes from Mr MacGregor's scarecrow. And they are nearly certain to miss *The Roly Poly Pudding*, which, according to Graham Greene, who has written the only mature essay on Miss Potter's achievement, is her best work.

---

[1] The pedagogical theory that is reflected by the repetition of words in this version of *Peter Rabbit* is that a child, in learning to read, has to encounter the same few words over and over again until he has mastered them: a perfectly sensible theory except that the modern adapter in this case has misapplied it and her version is so dull that it is hard to imagine that a child would want to read it at all, whereas the original is so lively that one can easily imagine a child's reading it over and over again and encountering, as according to the theory he should, the same set of words repeatedly.

To the extent that the children's book business is not an adjunct to modern educational theory, it is a branch of the toy industry; and those few enterprising publishers who manage to break out of the encirclement of the experts have found themselves, for better or worse, in the frantic, often insane, world of infantile mass merchandising, along with the producers of breakfast food, plastic rockets, and bubble gum. In this world the product is known for what it is—merchandise—and nearly everything depends upon the package. The merchandise either sells in quantity throughout the country in chain stores and supermarkets, five-and-tens, and department stores, or it is dropped and something new is tried that is more likely to sell in the mass market.

This is not to suggest that all merchandise juveniles are bad, any more than all breakfast food or bird seed is bad. But these books do tend, necessarily, to be pretty uniform. They must strike an average quality which precludes their ever being excellent, eccentric, or bold. The risks in this business are enormous and so are the profits, and until recently there has been little time for the prissy rationalizations of the children's book experts—except where the right educational endorsement might adapt the product to a school market and thus bring in an extra profit, or where some respectability is required to take advantage of the current nervousness among parents who want their children to be on the right cultural beam. In the world of merchandise juveniles the big factors are the production men who know how to shave a penny here and there, and the salesmen who are chosen for their aggressiveness and their ability to take a $100,000 order from a chain store or a mail-order house before the competitors do.

The books themselves often reflect the latest television success or the national current worry, whatever it may be; lately it has been science. Sometimes they are historical accounts, and these, since they freqently describe heroic actions in a more or less revolutionary spirit, are often pretty effective. Though they are of doubtful value as history, they do, at their best, represent the kind of courageous and spontaneous action that used to be found in more forthrightly imaginative literature. But in the stores one pile of merchandise looks pretty much like another and the clientele is presumed to be in a hurry and not very discriminating. Except for such rarities as the works of Dr Seuss, who in his strange way is authentically a genius—a sort of supercharged Edward Lear—and whose books sell in the millions, most juveniles that are sold as merchandise can hardly be considered books at all. This is especially true of those specimens meant for children who are not yet able to read and which represent the bulk of merchandise juveniles. These products are really nursery fixtures made of paper.

Whereas the editors and publishers of books that are meant primarily for schools and libraries tend to be female, their counterparts in the merchandise lines are vigorously male, indistinguishable along Madison Avenue from their colleagues in advertising and TV, where Huckleberry Hound and Cape Canaveral are big business and where everything depends upon the package. And while the line followed by the children's specialists derives mainly from the intellectual debris of a generation or two ago—the progressivism, the liberalism, the 'social consciousness' and uplift of the thirties survive surprisingly in a stale and mindless parody in the educational journals–the producers of merchandise follow the mass culture on a more day-to-day basis. This does not, however, mean that the books aimed at schools and libraries and those sold in the supermarkets are fundamentally different. Often they are interchangeable, depending only upon adjustments of format. And some of the more enterprising experts have begun to make room for some of the drearier merchandise products in their theories. It is better, they argue, for children to read nearly anything, even if 'we' don't quite approve of it, than for them to read nothing at all—a rationalization which indicates an unlooked for area of agreement between the merchandisers and some of the experts. Both groups want to move the goods.

As the experts come more and more to work for the publishers, this area of agreement grows wider. And as the mass market gradually drifts away from the more obvious vulgarities of a generation ago toward the greater respectability of the new suburbs, and the shopping centres and the elementary schools which they create, it is an improvident merchandiser indeed who will fail to add an expert or two to his staff or to hire one to prepare modern editions of such books as *Peter Rabbit*.

The most nearly official expert publication intended for general consumption is *A Parent's Guide to Children's Reading* by Nancy Larrick, PH.D., former president of the International Reading Association and 'well known', according to the jacket, 'as a writer and lecturer on children's reading'. A wistful attempt on the part of publishers to promote the reading (i.e., the sale) of books, *A Parent's Guide* was sponsored by the National Book Committee, Inc. and prepared with the help of advisers from eighteen national organizations, including the Adult Education Association, The American Association of University Women, the Campfire Girls, the Child Study Association of America, the Children's Book Council, The Children's Services Division of the American Library Association, The General Federation of Women's Clubs, the National Council of Teachers of English, and the United States Junior Chamber of Commerce.

Not surprisingly, the *Guide* was awarded honorable mention in the competition for the Carey-Thomas Award, annually given (by the same people who offer the Newbery Medal) for the best example of creative publishing in America. We are dealing here with a rather small world. But for all these accolades it is difficult to find words that will describe Dr Larrick's book, for it is not, in fact, a book at all but a sales-talk (Shall we read aloud to them? Yes, by all means! They love it!), and a far more aggressive one than Miss Frank's. The point of Dr Larrick's exhortation is, as she says, to surround the children with books, a depressing enough thought given most of the books she has in mind, and especially when one thinks of those children, still in possession of their animal spirits, who may not feel like being surrounded by books or anything else. But books, Dr Larrick insists—and so presumably do the eighteen national organizations who helped her—can be 'fun', as much 'fun', in fact, as TV or the comics. Yet if one thinks of one's own childhood experience, the idea that books have to be 'fun' seems a little off centre. Radio was fun and the comics were great fun and so, most of the time, was playing baseball or walking in the woods or watching the trains go by, but going to the library to read a book was not primarily or even secondarily for fun. It was for the sake of learning something, or more precisely, for the sake of becoming something—something more grownup than one had been before. The impulse to go to the library was of a completely different sort from the one that led to reading the comics or going to the movies, which were, after all, more fun. Going to the library was something one did, as it were, 'for real', and the fantasies one managed to generate there among the books by Howard Pyle and George MacDonald, as one read them over and over, turned out in time to transform the idea of fun entirely. Through such books one acquired, without in the least knowing it at the time, a taste for reality and the holiness of the imagination operating at the far edges of human experience which, in later life, makes it so difficult to confront such performances as Dr Larrick's with patience.

The last forty-five pages of *A Parent's Guide* consist of lists of recommended titles, but from these lists 'Some Old Favorites, such as *Tom Sawyer* and *Little Women*, have been omitted because hardly any parent needs a reminder. The list is largely made up of books published since 1940.' But while Dr Larrick feels that most parents know all about Mark Twain and such other writers whom she fails to mention as E. Nesbit, John Buchan, and George MacDonald, she apparently doesn't feel that they know about bookcases, and she therefore devotes two pages to describing what they are and how to build one. (This seems to be a gesture on behalf of an unhappy attempt made some years ago by the publishers when they asked a famous public relations man to suggest ways of improving their business. After some thought the public relations man suggested that householders should be encouraged to build bookshelves which they would then have to fill up.)

One will not find on Dr Larrick's forty-five page list books by H. G. Wells or Howard Pyle, Jonathan Swift or Herman Melville, Frances Hodgson Burnett or Jane Austen, and one wonders if perhaps what is implied in her principle of choice may not, after all, have come to pass. Perhaps by now the great tradition is lost to most children. Perhaps only a marginal few can usefully be introduced to such authors and perhaps it is merely old fashioned to care. One wonders if the professor of education who a year or two ago advised the high school in Princeton, N.J. to get rid of 'fossilized classics' like *Ivanhoe* is not really marching forward with history, while the rest of us have, like the classics themselves, become fossilized in our affection for a dead past.

But where then do we draw the line? Do we slide all the way down to the new version of *Peter Rabbit* and those recent abridgements of the *Iliad* and *Odyssey* that have sacrificed everything to easy reading and are a waste of time to read, or to those colourful volumes which promise, in a hundred or so pages, to introduce the children to all the sciences known to man? Or do we stop halfway down and replace *Ivanhoe*, as the high school in Princeton has proposed to do, with *The Pearl* by John Steinbeck and Hemingway's *The Old Man and the Sea*, inferior works of their authors, but sexless and bloodless and therefore suitable? And if we set our standards at this level, how, when the children are older and go to college, will they deal with Shakespeare and Proust, and what will they do with a writer like

Joyce? Shall we find a way to drag these writers down so that they too can be read on the level of *The Old Man and the Sea* or perhaps even of the new version of *Peter Rabbit?* The problem is sad to contemplate and hard, and it includes the danger that the children may not grow up at all but simply grow older. For the appreciation of literature resembles the process of growing up in that they both involve the discovery of distinctions between the self and the world: the aim of both is differentiation, concreteness, and the development of a character of one's own. This is why literature is exciting and why it is, finally, inseparable from life. Where Nancy Larrick goes wrong is in her assumption that there is no particular need to distinguish one-self from the surrounding environment, that to take part uncritically in the common culture is the proper goal of growing up.

Still, it would be wrong to suggest that the level on which Josette Frank and Nancy Larrick operate necessarily represents the style in which all children's libraries and school teachers or even most experts themselves function when they are face to face with children; and it would also be wrong to suggest that *The Bronze Bow* necessarily reflects the real literary preferences of these people. Life, even in the schools, is full of its usual perplexity, and it is fair to assume that the stronger teachers consult their own experience and ideals, just as the weaker ones panic and submit, typically, to their own confusion. Though the experts on children's reading are, like experts everywhere, mis-trustful of what they do not understand, a certain tough fibre occasionally appears in their otherwise undistinguished fabric. One of the recent Newbery winners is a book called *Frontier Living* by Edwin Tunis, which is a valuable and substantial account of daily life on the edge of the American wilderness as it gradually receded toward California. This book is not only full of uncommon information; it is surprisingly candid. Unlike most books in its category, it neither patronizes nor sentimental-izes the Indians, whose side it takes against the whites where it is necessary to do so. The Kentucky settlers are described as drunken and brutal, while it is revealed that the towns farther west were often bothered by gamblers and prostitutes. The directors of the Union Pacific and Central Pacific are described as thieves and exploiters who co-operated with the California legislature to rob the public, while the United States senate is shown to have been frequently faithless in its treaties with the Indians. In its attention to detail and the cleanliness of its style, *Frontier Living* is a considerable achievement—one of those books that is likely to inspire strong feelings of social justice and patriotism in certain young readers by providing them not only with a sense of their uniqueness but with a link to the common welfare.

One is surprised to discover that such a book was chosen by the same group who also chose *The Bronze Bow* and who are usually so careful not to offend against the standard impostures of American history. But this curious thread appears to run throughout the entire fabric of the children's book industry: while the formation of natural taste and the spontaneity and explosiveness associated with childhood are largely dampened by irrelevant theory, a certain stubbornness on behalf of real literature somehow prevails. Despite their omission from Nancy Larrick's list, the standard authors are likely to be available in most public libraries, even if, in some cases, only pro forma and even if the librarians, under pressure from the schools and knowing that their budgets in some cases depend on how many books they can circulate, feature the newer books that are easier to read. Most libraries too will include the handful of modern books like Hugh Lofting's *Dr Dolittle*, Kenneth Grahame's *The Wind in the Willows*, Mary Norton's *The Borrowers*, Laura Ingalls Wilder's *The Little House in the Big Woods*, and the works of Dr Seuss—books which even Dr Larrick finds room for and which, though they represent a sort of mannerist phase of the great tradition, are generally on a very high level. The libraries themselves are frequently stimulating and their collections and personnel are impressive. To visit the Donnell Library on Fifty-third Street in New York or the Children's Room of the New York Public Library is reassuring. The mindless eclecticism, the idea that children should know less and less about more and more, that characterize the writing of such experts as we have quoted here, are absent. Absent too is the notion that the books should be adjusted to the tempers and interests of the children, which is what is implied by the idea that books 'should meet the reading needs of the young child'—an idea that would, if fully carried into practice, reduce the children to idiocy and turn the libraries into madhouses.

But if the official experts are in practice largely ignored by superior librarians, how are teachers and librarians who may not be as good as those in the Donnell to know what books to make available? It is, after all, no easier to distinguish quality among children's books than among books in general: the same critical acumen is required in either case and such acumen has never been especially abundant in any society. The criterion generally applied by the experts is: 'Is this a book for children?" But the only relevant question—and the one which, to judge by their typical preferences, the experts are incompetent to decide—is: 'Is this a book at all?' The question 'Is this a book for children?' can properly be decided only by the children themselves as they fumble and experiment among what is available. And if a child decides, as one sixth-grader whom I know of has, to read the Greek tragedies, then Greek tragedy is, for him, a suitable book. It it bores and confuses him, he will soon enough turn to something that suits him better.

We have been considering not the more or less technical problem of teaching the children to read—which is properly a branch of cognitive psychology and is within the province of qualified experts—but of helping them to find and distinguish, once they have learned how to read, those books through which they can discover themselves as individuals and discern, gradually, the nature of the world in which they must function. 'Children read, through inexperience, whatever comes their way,' Lillian Smith, who was a Canadian librarian, has written in her admirable book *The Unreluctant Years*, published by the American Library Association. 'In a time when children's books are almost a matter of mass production,' Miss Smith goes on, 'it is possible that a child may pass from infancy to maturity without encounterng one book that will satisfy him in his search for experience and pleasure; that will offer him reality in the place of a shadow of reality.' But, she adds, 'children will defend themselves against encroaching mediocrity if books of genuine quality are put within their reach.'

Thus stated, the task of teachers and librarians and the experts who advise them is simple. It has nothing to do with 'being alert to all that goes on within a child's world', or with 'surrounding him with books', or with meeting 'the reading needs of the young child'. For it is absurd to suppose that the 'reading needs' of a child who is able to read by himself are, in principle, different from those of an adult, or that a child will or should submit to being surrounded by walls of books, or that alertness to the private world of childhood is a valuable or even possible desideratum. Proposals like these are useless in themselves and serve only to rationalize and certify the industry begun by John Newbery who, significantly, sold in his shop not only books for children but quack medicines for their parents.

As the market grows larger and the rate at which new books published for children expands, and as the standards proposed by the bureaucracy of experts increasingly conform to the surrounding mass culture and the commercial requirements of the publishers, the opportunity for children to find 'books of genuine quality' will necessarily diminish. In America there are hardly more than a hundred—certainly no more than two hundred—bookstores which are able to select and carry more than a bare minimum of the standard children's classics or which can by themselves distinguish among the new books published each year those that are of any value. And the number of such stores is decreasing as more and more of them come to depend for their profits on merchandise and as the schools and libraries, in their attempt 'to meet the reading needs' of the young child, increasingly make the children unfit for the 'fossilized classics'.

Though the children themselves wrote letters strongly rejecting the proposed modification in the curriculum of the Princeton High School when it appeared in the *New York Times*, the teachers grow weary. Dickens and Scott are, after all, harder to teach than low-grade Hemingway: for many teachers they may by now be impossible; and the community, except for an unimportant fraction, no longer cares very much. Perhaps, as Edgar Z. Friedenberg recently suggested,[2] the teachers have even come to resent the brightness of their students, for as Professor Friedenberg argues, the 'free-floating ill temper' so common throughout our society is particularly endemic among those people who, defeated like so many others by the conditions of American life, must nevertheless confront the abounding and as yet uncompromised energies of the young. And so the marvelous world of George MacDonald and Conan Doyle, John Buchan and Frances Hodgson Burnett may soon vanish, except for the happy few. Perhaps, since so much else has gone—and will go—it is pointless to care. Except, of course, that the children are always there to remind us. And one naturally wonders what they will become.

[1963]

---

[2] 'The Gifted Student and His Enemies', *Commentary*, May 1962.

The child and the book

ANTHONY STORR

All day long the boy stood at the window, looking over the sea by which the princess must travel; but there were no signs of her. And, as he stood, soldiers came and laid hands on him, and led him up to the cask, where a big fire was blazing, and the horrid black pitch boiling and bubbling over the sides. He looked and shuddered, but there was no escape; so he shut his eyes to avoid seeing.

Suddenly, some men were seen running with all their might, crying as they went that a large ship with its sails spread was making straight for the city. No one knew what the ship was or whence it came; but the king declared he would not have the boy burned before its arrival.

At this point in the story the five-year-old girl burst into tears. Her mother put down Andrew Lang's *Brown Fairy Book* and hastened to comfort her.

'Don't cry. The boy was quite all right. He didn't get thrown into the cask of pitch. He was saved.'

'But I *wanted* him to be thrown into the cask of pitch,' sobbed the little girl, unable to tolerate the disappointment of finding that this exciting threat was not after all, to be put into practice.

This true story may serve to demonstrate that the effects of a book upon a child are not always easy to predict; but, unfortunately, most of our knowledge remains at this anecdotal level, and there are, so far as I can discover, no large-scale studies of the effects of literature upon children comparable with the recent survey of the effects of television.

Parents, librarians, and educators often express alarm at what their children read. They are generally concerned, firstly, that the child shall not be made frightened or unhappy; secondly, that it shall not be prematurely sexually aroused; and thirdly, that it shall not be encouraged to behave in aggressive or delinquent ways. At the back of the adults' anxiety is usually the belief that children are innocent little creatures who must not have unpleasant ideas put into their heads; a belief which should have been, but is not yet, dispelled by psychoanalytic research. There is, of course, much to be said for not frightening children—although we all enjoy being frightened a little. And no one wants a child to be made miserable—although the shedding of a sentimental tear may be a pleasurable release. Sexual excitation can, in certain instances, be premature and create problems for the child whose ego is not yet strong enough to deal with it; and delinquent behaviour is certainly not to be encouraged. But it is extremely doubtful whether books in themselves ever cause any of the dreadful effects upon children which are attributed to them by anxious adults.

Many people will remember the publicity given to horror comics a few years ago; and some will have read Dr Wertham's book *Seduction of the Innocent*. This verbose and emotional work tells us more about Dr Wertham's reaction to horror comics than about that of the children who read them; and, although he blames horror comics for almost every psychological disturbance from fetishism to theft, his claims remain unsubstantiated.

I think they are likely to remain so. The fundamental objection to horror comics is not the themes with which they deal, but the crude and vulgar way in which these themes are presented. There is no convincing evidence that horror comics corrupt, and little to be found in them which cannot be met with in earlier publications. The adventures of Jack Harkaway, for instance, contain a description of the torture of a girl with red hot stones, and of the gradual eating of a man alive: and for the last thirty years of the Victorian era Jack Harkaway was a best-selling hero. Are we to suppose that our grandfathers often indulged themselves in such activities as a result of this boyhood reading? The Victorians, though more prudish about other aspects of sexuality, seem to have been less disturbed by sadistic themes than we are today. *The Mikado* and *The Yeomen of the Guard* are generally considered suitable entertainments for children; but in both W. S. Gilbert outspokenly reveals his preoccupation with torture, and some of the short stories of Conan Doyle disclose a similar interest. It seems that adults who are alarmed by comics must feel that illustrations are more potent for harm than the spoken or written word.

Why is it that the stories which children enjoy are so often full of horrors? We know that from the very beginning of life the child possesses an inner world of fantasy and the fantasies of the child mind are by no means the pretty stories with which the prolific Miss Blyton regales us. They are both richer and more primitive, and the driving forces behind them are those of sexuality and the aggressive urge to power: the forces which ultimately determine the emergence of the individual as a separate entity. For, in the long process of development, the child has two main tasks to perform if he is to reach maturity. He has to prove his strength, and he has to win a mate; and in order to do this he has to overcome the obstacles of his infantile dependency upon, and his infantile erotic attachment to, his parents. That the erotic strand in fairy tales is less obvious than the aggressive is partly due to bowdlerization and partly to the fact that the sexual component is in childish, pregenital form. The typical fairy story ends with the winning of the princess just as the typical Victorian novel ends with the marriage. It is only at this point that adult sexuality begins; and it is for

this reason that books like *Lady Chatterley's Lover*, which describe the sexual behaviour of adults, are of little interest to
children. It is not surprising that fairy stories should be both
erotic and violent, or that they should appeal so powerfully to
children. For the archetypal themes with which they deal mirror
the contents of the childish psyche; and the same unconscious
source gives origin to both the fairy tale and the fantasy life
of the child.

Reading which produces an emotional effect rather than con-
veying information does not put things into the mind, but rather
objectifies contents which are already present. If this were not
so, we should be unable to react emotionally to a book at all.
There has to be a lock within us which the key of the book can
fit, and if it does not fit, the book is meaningless to us. The high
value which we give to the artist or writer who pleases us is
a tribute not so much to his power of invention as to his skill
in objectifying the contents of our own minds; especially those
contents which are only partially conscious, and thus unformu-
lated. The thrill is one of recognition; and if there is no recognition there is no thrill, but only the cold admiration which we
accord to some figure who achieves greatness in a field which
is incomprehensible to us.

If children have heads full of fantasies of a violent and erotic
kind, and if their delight in fairy tales and the like is due to
the thrill of recognition, why is it that they do not act upon
their fantasies, and is there not a risk that books might encourage them to do so?

A disturbed child who behaves in a delinquent way will
sometimes say that he got the idea from a book, which is one
way of disowning responsibility. But it is only the child who
is already emotionally disturbed who will act out his fantasies.
If this were not so we should all have strangled our brothers
and sisters, slept with our mothers, castrated our fathers, and
reduced to pulp all those who in any way opposed us. As a
distinguished child-analyst has put it, the individual 'is engaged

in the perpetual human task of keeping inner and outer reality separate yet interrelated.' The normal child can do this; but in the disturbed child, as in the psychotic adult, the two worlds may be confused, so that fantasies are acted upon and parents actually stolen from or pushed over cliffs. But I am sure that no book ever pulled the trigger of any gun but that upon which a finger was already quivering. Ultimately, what keeps us sane and makes us behave in a relatively civilized manner is our relationship with other people.

It is obviously quite hopeless to try and impose any kind of censorship upon children's reading, even if it were desirable to do so. If the normal child were as susceptible to the effects of literature as parents sometimes fear, we should have to proscribe reading altogether. A man told me that his masochistic interest in male slavery had been stimulated in childhood by pictures of the building of the Pyramids. Are we to ban history books on this account? Many people recall that, in early youth, they searched the pages of Leviticus for sexual information and puzzled over the mysterious sin of Onan. Should the Bible be withdrawn from all respectable households? Of course children may be sexually stimulated by their reading—just as adults are—but only when their development has reached a stage where they will look for something in a book which reflects the desires already half-formulated within them. And this they will certainly find somewhere, whatever censorship is attempted; or, if their search fails, they may write their own erotica.

It is probably reassuring for most children to read the violent tales in which they delight. We all like the comfort of finding that someone else feels as we do ourselves; nor need we be alarmed that the literature of childhood is likely to turn a child into a delinquent. For, as Gibbon remarks, 'the power of instruction is seldom of much efficacy except in those happy dispositions where it is largely superfluous.'

But although books cannot be blamed for causing either delinquency or neurosis, they do, of course, have their emotional effect; and it is probable that many adults can recall one book or one scene from a book which in childhood touched them particularly. Such scenes often stay in the mind for years, and may, like a Proustian *madeleine*, be more potent in evoking the memory of what it felt like to be child than the deliberate recollection of any actual external circumstance. My guess would be that such scenes in some way reflect a psychological situation within the child unrecognized by it at the time.

[1960]

Thoughts concerning children's books

PENELOPE MORTIMER

I strongly believe that a new look needs to be taken at the
whole idea of children's books; that the necessity for having
them at all needs at least to be questioned. I am not referring
to books for the illiterate under-fives, and have no criticism to
make of them beyond the fact that publishers and authors seem
to think that the smaller the child, the larger the book must be—
for what reason, since their arms are short and their eyesight
usually at its best, it is hard to imagine. But once these tasteful
if unwieldy volumes have lost their charm, the child begins
to be given novels which are intended to mirror what psychia-
trists and school teachers call 'the child's world'. These are
frequently sold with time limits stamped on them, like cream
cheese or Kodak film—to be read between the ages of 10 and
13, with no suggestion that this is roughly speaking. These
books are, of course, written by adults, usually selected by
adults, paid for by adults, published and printed and reviewed
by adults. Will one child pore over this Supplement, library
list in hand? Are there children who discuss, over the Ribena,
the merits of the new Nesbit or Norton?[1] Or are children's
books a form of literature which owes its continued existence
to a minority of grownups who might as well be circulating

---

[1] E. Nesbit, *Long Ago When I Was Young*, illustrated by Edward Ardizzone
(London, 1966). Mary Norton, *The Borrowers Omnibus*, illustrated by
Diana Stanley (London, 1966).

Family Planning leaflets to guinea pigs for all that they understand of the requirements of the average child?

There is, of course, no such thing as the average child—however, for the purposes of argument, I mean those children who are as far from precocity as they are from stupidity. This includes all the children I know. Apart from messages on television—addresses for sending up for things, mostly—they read H. G. Wells, Daphne du Maurier, Conan Doyle, Ian Fleming, George Orwell, and the strip cartoons in the Sunday papers. Their interest in myth, magic, and anthropomorphism of all kinds is, on the whole, slightly less than mine. They are not as sentimental as I am. They like a good laugh, particularly at other people's misfortunes; they enjoy what seems to me an immoderate amount of fear and disgust and are often, through excessive affection, very beastly to animals; they have a very strong sense of justice in regard to themselves and none whatever in regard to anyone else. They are the perfect public for Shakespeare and the more disreputable parts of the Bible. Where did we get the idea that, apart from variations in taste and experience, they are any different from us?

The segregation between children and adults began to take place around the end of the seventeenth century—up until then, apart from the necessary period of infancy, children seem to have been regarded as normal people: hard working, capable of reading Ovid and slogging about battlefields, sexy, indistinguishable from men and women except in size. In 1693 John Locke publish his *Thoughts Concerning Education* and invented the Child. Character, he said, came before learning; the educator's aim must be to instil virtue, wisdom, and good breeding into the minds of the young; this must be done by means of 'sport and play' in a cosy family environment; children must not merely be, they must be brought up. The first missionary tracts appeared in the stately nurseries of England—'books of courtesy' designed to tame the little creatures and turn them, by gentle persuasion, into domestic pets. Eagerly exploiting a new market, aware that for the first time there was a captive audience which, if it couldn't read, was going to be read to, writers took up their quills and poured out their neuroses in fiercely moral bedtime stories beside which *The History of the Rod* reads like Eleanor Farjeon. Fathers who wouldn't be seen dead with the novels of the Duchess of Newcastle or Aphra Behn resonantly rendered tales of Batman heroism from the newly published adventures of King Arthur and Robin Hood. The prototype of the Victorian fairy—no resemblance to crafty sensualists like Titania and Oberon—fluttered over from the French court and settled, simpering, in the bottom of our garden. A few lady moralists tried to suppress her, believing that she would distract the tots from the doctrines of Rousseau, but she survived—largely, perhaps, because the mamas needed someone to identify with, a glamour image, asexual, radiant with virtue, ageless, and flimsy. By the time John Newbery began the profitable publishing of his 'pretty gilt toys for girls and boys', the children's book, as distinct from the book, had arrived, and Miss Enid Blyton was on her way.

The fact that seems to have been overlooked is simply that a good book cannot possibly be written for a particular age, sex, creed, or colour—if it is, the motive and the execution must be dishonest, and the result spurious. *Black Beauty* and *The Secret Garden* are more intelligent, even sophisticated, than the average women's magazine story; *Tom Sawyer* and *Huckleberry Finn* can be enjoyed by any fairly bright executive wanting a bit of escapism between ulcers. It is as foolish to confine these books to the nursery shelves as it is to assume that your ten-year-old is incapable of enjoying Colette or Kingsley Amis.

It is absurd to say that we do not think about such things because they are so obvious—obvious attitudes, particularly if they appear vaguely progressive or humane, are the last to be questioned. The subject of children's books has not, it seems to me, been thought about since Christopher Robin said his prayers. Children, over the last two decades, have changed radically: their expectation of child life has become shorter; they are rapidly returning to the pre-Spock, pre-Locke era and ceasing to be, in the traditional sense, children. They are no longer at the mercy of their parents' tastes and opinions, but are to a large extent 'brought up' by the Ideal Parents provided for them by television: scholarly, good-looking fathers, handy around the house, knowledgeable about space, rabbit hutches, the Gobi desert; pretty, calm, independent mothers who cook, swim about in coral reefs, make their own Christmas cards, nurse pregnant cats with patience. These splendid Super-Egos can be switched on or off at will; they have no moral axe to grind, you can sit there picking your nose or worse, they just keep smiling. They provide what the modern child really wants —information. In my local children's library, books on engineering (*Let's Take A Trip To A Cement Plant*), pet-keeping, radio, magnetics, cookery, dress-making, outnumber the poetry and drama by twenty to one.

So, believing as I do that children have evolved and are now in many respects much brighter than we are, and that very few people in the literary or theatre worlds (will we, this Christmas, have Nicholas Stuart Grey *again?*) have recognized this fact —who will read these two books which I am, with infinite slowness, getting round to reviewing? For information—in the likely event of any child reading this—Miss Nesbit lived in the second great era of women novelists—the first was in the seventeenth century, the third, so the commercials say, is now —missing Charlotte Brontë by three years and dying just before the publication of *Mrs Dalloway*. Her writing had much of the wit, charm, and sense of privilege of her contemporaries. This little autobiography, so gentle and remote, adds no more than a whiff of camphor to *The Railway Children* and *The Wouldbegoods*.

'Supposing', the boy said, 'you saw a little man, about as tall as a pencil, with a blue patch in his trousers, half-way up a window

curtain, carrying a doll's tea-cup would you say it was a fairy?'
'No,' said Arrietty. 'I'd say it was my father.'

This kind of writing is good enough for anyone. The Borrowers are, it's true, Little People, living in terror of 'human beans', but they have appeared on radio and television, they are only small in relation to the gigantic hair-grips and safety-pins that they appropriate, their behaviour is in all respects entirely 'real'. This satisfactory bulk of a book contains the whole lot, *Afield, Afloat, and Aloft* as well as *The Borrowers* itself. I prefer the first, in which the family live snug under the floorboards and are very bourgeois and calm; when they become pioneers, making do in an old boot or kettle, they are less credible. There is also rather too much chat of the Archers variety, too many sympathetic human beans take over, and there are too many niggly little drawings. But I'd warmly recommend Miss Norton to any child—from, say, seven and a half to eleven and three-quarters—who has a few minutes to spare between finishing off the model railway and cooking a four-course meal.

One final thought, however: I saw a film recently in which a scientist's life was saved by 'miniaturizing' a submarine and its entire crew and injecting it into the bloodstream. Attacked by vast anti-bodies, storm-tossed inside a lung the size of Chartres Cathedral, threatened by a vast palpitating dragon of a heart, they escaped through the old boy's eye (Arrietty 'grew to know that ear quite well, with its curves and shadows and sunlit pinks and golds).' There was a spy and a blonde aboard, for good measure. The film was for adults only.

[1966]

2 Fairy tales, fantasy, animals

Where is fancy bred?

HELEN LOURIE

As Christmas inexorably approaches and the shop windows put forth their annual display of man's ingenuity to man; as red-coated Santa Clauses lurk in the recesses of the big stores, theatres are taken over by flying children, dragons, gnomes, and loquacious animals, and publishers let loose over 1,000 volumes of reading matter aimed at the population under sixteen it seems appropriate to examine the world of fantasy which the season invariably calls forth. For whose benefit is this wealth of the imagination? Why do we suppose that it is especially suitable to children? Who reads the literature of fantasy? Who writes it?

Since the age of reason set in, the wilder flights of man's fancy have had to find some framework in which to work. It was well for Sir John Mandeville to report from distant countries of men whose ears grew large enough to shield them from the sun, or who, being headless, had eyes in their shoulders. For nearly 300 years after he wrote, the extent of the earth and the laws of nature were so imperfectly understood that extraordinary events could be daily expected. Witches cast spells, alchemists searched for the philosopher's stone, scholars made pacts with the devil: at any moment one might find one's shape changed, one's status immeasurably raised, or access to infinite power within one's grasp.

The scientific discoveries of the last 200 years have altered this scene. The current image of Western man is now that of a rational creature slow to believe in anything that cannot be demonstrably proved; the password by which he gains credence, 'working hypothesis'. Travellers' tales today must be corroborated by maps and photographs, we have irrefutable means of testing gold, and if Faustus assured us that he had made a pact with Beelzebub, we could bring a battery of X-rays and expertise to disprove the authenticity of the fiend's signature. But wherever areas of ignorance remain, writers can still allow their imagination to work. It was possible in the last century for Rider Haggard to describe miraculous events, reincarnations, an immortal enchantress in the unexplored regions of darkest Africa. Conan Doyle postulated a Lost World on the high unknown plateaux of Brazil. Jules Verne, with a fecundity of invention which many better stylists might envy, populated the depths of the sea, the moon, the centre of the earth with the offspring of his fancy. Sheridan Le Fanu and Edgar Allan Poe appropriated the mysterious domains of the spirit after death. At the beginning of the twentieth century H. G. Wells explored the possibilities of unknown time; recently outer space has provided the field for the development of this particular vein of fantasy. Nature, we know, abhors a vacuum. In this she differs from man, who sees in the absence of positive knowledge a heaven-sent opportunity for invention.

This is the adult world of fantasy: a world of romance, adventure, ghosts and vampires, animals, men and machines. It is a world in which extraordinary phenomena appear, are recognized as being extraordinary, and are related to the world of scientific facts by some sort of explanation. The immortal

She learnt her magic arts from the Ancient Egyptians; the ptero-dactyls of the Lost World have escaped extinction by their geographical situation; one is able to fly through the air when one is beyond the pull of gravity. Given a primary assumption, itself often springing from a supposition difficult to disprove, these fantasies follow a logical course. It is possible to read them without forgetting one's place in society, one's moral responsibilities, one's age. They are written for the sane, the responsible, the grownup.

These books deal with a world of improbabilities. But there exists also a literature belonging to a world of impossibilities, and here one unlikely premise does not condition the rest of the story: here anything can happen at any time. In this world trunks fly, swineherds marry princesses, Jumblies go to sea in a sieve; a child is adopted by the North Wind, white rabbits carry watches in their waistcoat pockets, little boys can remain fluttering for ever between infancy and maturity, between the nursery ceiling and the wooded island in the middle of the Serpentine lake. In this world, immortality, Pobbles with or without toes, levitation, need no explanations—nor do ambition, ruthlessness, love, hate, or death. It is a world without rules, physical or moral, seen with the egoist's single eye. It is the amoral, polymorphous world of the infant. The writer who wants to express himself in terms of this world has learned to direct his appeal to the youngest readers; in some cases, but not all, he has needed the presence of a real child to enable him to reach this realm. Children pass easily from the incomprehensible adult world to the equally mysterious world of fantasy, partly because they are not steeped in the habit of convention, partly because they are still ignorant of so many of the laws by which our lives are governed that the discovery of new freedoms cannot surprise them. In their comparatively short sojourn in the world of scientific facts they have acquired less disbelief to be suspended before they can enter into the Kingdom of Never-Never.

The wilder the fantasy, the younger the reader. But who are the writers? Surprisingly it is not the very young themselves. Nor is it the sex conventionally supposed to be the more fanciful. If we exclude, as we must, the whimsy, the conscious allegory, the didactic fairies and unnatural animals who inculcate convenient moral principles into their not-so-innocent readers' minds, if we consider the unprincipled, violent, timeless, weightless, limitless literature of true magic, we find that it comes from an unexpected source. It is not the irresponsible, eccentric, or mad, not the explorers or the anthropologists, not necessarily the impractical or the dreamers. An unsuccessful dramatist of working-class origin; Queen Victoria's drawing master; an Oxford don of mathematics; a Congregationalist minister; and a flourishing writer of English stage comedy—it sounds a sober company. Yet Hans Christian Andersen, Edward Lear, Lewis Carroll, George MacDonald, and James Barrie produced, within an era of enormous respectability and veneration for order of every kind, an entry into as mad a world as could be found in any Bedlam, and achieved something that their often more accomplished contemporaries could not. While the great novelists were drawing unforgettable characters, were surveying the human scene with irony, pathos, humour, sympathy; while the Romantics were embroidering on the archetypal situations which cannot be too often restated; while innumerable gifted storytellers were entertaining the young and the old—these writers were fabricating that structure, like a spider's web at once delicate and resilient, that synthesis of the general and the particular which is the essence of the myth. For what distinguishes the story, the fable, the allegory from the myth is this: that whereas the former take an already existing shape, and embellish and enrich it with the writer's individuality and skill, the myth is the original pattern. Andersen's Ugly Duckling is as unforgettable an example of the difficulties of being undervalued as Oedipus is of another human predicament. Carroll's Red Queen, running furiously in order to stay in the same place, George Macdonald's child in the grip of the wind of inspiration too large for him to hold, Barrie's Peter Pan, an Oedipus in reverse, refusing to face the consequences of growing up: all these have taken their place in our mythology. Lear has no such striking figures to offer, but I would include him among the others for the sake of his emancipated attitude to language. He and Carroll share an art which tosses words about with as little regard for their common uses as a juggler shows for his poles and tumblers. Carroll was the more ingenious, Lear the less inhibited. In the countries they create, no event is predictable by any law of precedence. Birds mate with cats, chairs and tables promenade together, anything from a pair of tongs to a caterpillar or a playing card had its own individual voice; one can remember what is going to happen tomorrow and believe six impossible things before breakfast. These countries are not only mythological, they are themselves the myth of the freedom of the intellect.

Is it accident that all these writers and those in the same group who are writing today are men? No more, I would say, than it is by chance that the greatest works of art have been products of the male sex; and this can by no stretch of reasoning be attributed to women's want of education or of status. Women can be excellent storytellers: their powers of invention and fancy are not inferior to that of men. But what they lack is the whole-hearted abandonment to their inspiration: the power to enter the other world, whether it is through the Looking Glass or the Back of the North Wind, without keeping some conscious hold on normality. Is this why, of the incurably insane, women form over 60 per cent? Is it because those who can't voluntarily relinquish their foothold in reality run the greater risk of being involuntarily overtaken by the Eumenides? To be lunatic enough to experience the myth and to be at the same time sufficiently sane to present it to the public in the form of art, is genius; and this the great exponents of fantasy, at their best, share with the artist, the musician, and the poet.

[1962]

Children
and fairy stories

J.R.R. TOLKIEN

What, if any, are the values and functions of fairy stories *now*? It is usually assumed that children are the natural or the specially appropriate audience for fairy stories. In describing a fairy story which they think adults might possibly read for their own entertainment, reviewers frequently indulge in such waggeries as: 'this book is for children from the ages of six to sixty.' But I have never yet seen the puff of a new motor-model that began thus: 'this toy will amuse infants from seventeen to seventy'; though that to my mind would be much more appropriate. Is there any *essential* connection between children and fairy stories? Is there any call for comment, if an adult reads them for himself? *Reads* them as tales, that is, not *studies* them as curios. Adults are allowed to collect and study anything, even old theatre programs or paper bags.

Among those who still have enough wisdom not to think fairy stories pernicious, the common opinion seems to be that there is a natural connection between the minds of children and fairy stories, of the same order as the connection between children's bodies and milk. I think this is an error; at best an error of false sentiment, and one that is therefore most often made by those who, for whatever private reason (such as childlessness), tend to think of children as a special kind of creature, almost a different race, rather than as normal, if immature, members of a particular family, and of the human family at large.

Actually, the association of children and fairy stories is an accident of our domestic history. Fairy stories have in the modern lettered world been relegated to the 'nursery', as shabby or old-fashioned furniture is relegated to the playroom, primarily because the adults do not want it, and do not mind if it is misused.[1] It is not the choice of the children which decides this. Children as a class—except in a common lack of experience they are not one—neither like fairy stories more, nor understand them better than adults do; and no more than they like many other things. They are young and growing, and normally have keen appetites, so the fairy stories as a rule go down well enough. But in fact only some children, and some adults, have any special taste for them; and when they have it, it is not exclusive, nor even necessarily dominant. It is a taste, too, that would not appear, I think, very early in childhood without artificial stimulus; it is certainly one that does not decrease but increases with age, if it is innate.

It is true that in recent times fairy stories have usually been written or 'adapted' for children. But so may music be, or verse, or novels, or history, or scientific manuals. It is a dangerous process, even when it is necessary. It is indeed only saved from disaster by the fact that the arts and sciences are not as a whole relegated to the nursery; the nursery and schoolroom are merely given such tastes and glimpses of the adult thing as seem fit for them in adult opinion (often much mistaken). Any one of these things would, if left altogether in the nursery, become gravely impaired. So would a beautiful table, a good picture, or a useful machine (such as a microscope), be defaced or broken,

---

[1] In the case of stories and other nursery lore, there is also another factor. Wealthier families employed women to look after their children, and the stories were provided by these nurses, who were sometimes in touch with rustic and traditional lore forgotten by their 'betters'. It is long since this source dried up, at any rate in England; but it once had some importance. But again there is no proof of the special fitness of children as the recipients of this vanishing 'folklore'. The nurses might just as well (or better) have been left to choose the pictures and furniture.

if it were left long unregarded in a schoolroom. Fairy stories banished in this way, cut off from a full adult art, would in the end be ruined; indeed in so far as they have been so banished, they have been ruined.

The value of fairy stories is thus not, in my opinion, to be found by considering children in particular. Collections of fairy stories are, in fact, by nature attics and lumber-rooms, only by temporary and local custom playrooms. Their contents are disordered, and often battered, a jumble of different dates, purposes, and tastes; but among them may occasionally be found a thing of permanent virtue: an old work of art, not too much damaged, that only stupidity would ever have stuffed away.

Andrew Lang's *Fairy Books* are not, perhaps, lumber-rooms. They are more like stalls in a rummage-sale. Someone with a duster and a fair eye for things that retain some value has been round the attics and boxrooms. His collections are largely a by-product of his adult study of mythology and folklore; but they were made into and presented as books for children.[2] Some of the reasons that Lang gave are worth considering.

The introduction to the first of the series speaks of 'children to whom and for whom they are told'. 'They represent,' he says, 'the young age of man true to his early loves, and have his unblunted edge of belief, a fresh appetite for marvels.' ' "Is it true?" ' he says, 'is the great question children ask'.

I suspect that *belief* and *appetite for marvels* are here regarded as identical or as closely related. They are radically different, though the appetite for marvels is not at once or at first differentiated by a growing human mind from its general appetite. It seems fairly clear that Lang was using *belief* in its ordinary sense: belief that a thing exists or can happen in the real (primary) world. If so, then I fear that Lang's words, stripped of sentiment, can only imply that the teller of marvellous tales to children must, or may, or at any rate does trade on their

---

2 By Lang and his helpers. It is not true of the majority of the contents in their original (or oldest surviving) forms.

credulity, on the lack of experience which makes it less easy for children to distinguish fact from fiction in particular cases, though the distinction in itself is fundamental to the sane human mind, and to fairy stories.

Children are capable, of course, of *literary belief,* when the story-maker's art is good enough to produce it. That state of mind has been called 'willing suspension of disbelief'. But this does not seem to me a good description of what happens. What really happens is that the story-maker proves a successful 'sub-creator'. He makes a Secondary World which your mind can enter. Inside it, what he relates is 'true': it accords with the laws of that world. You therefore believe it, while you are, as it were, inside. The moment disbelief arises, the spell is broken; the magic, or rather art, has failed. You are then out in the Primary World again, looking at the little abortive Secondary World from outside. If you are obliged, by kindliness or circumstance, to stay, then disbelief must be suspended (or stifled), otherwise listening and looking would become intolerable. But this suspension of disbelief is a substitute for the genuine thing, a subterfuge we use when condescending to games or make-believe, or when trying (more or less willingly) to find what virtue we can in the work of an art that has for us failed.

A real enthusiast for cricket is in the enchanted state: Secondary Belief. I, when I watch a match, am on the lower level. I can achieve (more or less) willing suspension of disbelief, when I am held there and supported by some other motive that will keep away boredom: for instance, a wild, heraldic, preference for dark blue rather than light. This suspension of disbelief may thus be a somewhat tired, shabby, or sentimental state of mind, and so lean to the 'adult'. I fancy it is often the state of adults in the presence of fairy story. They are held there and supported by sentiment (memories of childhood, or notions of what childhood ought to be like); they think they ought to like the tale. But if they really liked it, for itself, they would not have to suspend disbelief: they would believe—in this sense.

Now if Lang had meant anything like this there might have been some truth in his words. It may be argued that it is easier to work the spell with children. Perhaps it is, though I am not sure of this. The appearance that it is so is often, I think, an adult illusion produced by children's humility, their lack of critical experience and vocabulary, and their voracity (proper to their rapid growth). They like or try to like what is given to them: if they do not like it, they cannot well express their dislike or give reasons for it (and so may conceal it); and they like a great mass of different things indiscriminately, without troubling to analyse the planes of their belief. In any case I doubt if this portion—the enchantment of the effective fairy story—is really one of the kind that becomes 'blunted' by use, less potent after repeated draughts.

' "Is it true?' is the great question children ask,' Lang said. They do ask that question, I know; and it is not one to be rashly or idly answered.[3] But that question is hardly evidence of 'unblunted belief', or even of the desire for it. Most often it proceeds from the child's desire to know which kind of literature he is faced with. Children's knowledge of the world is often so small that they cannot judge, off-hand and without help, between the fantastic, the strange (that is rare or remote facts), the nonsensical, and the merely 'grownup' (that is ordinary things of their parents' world, much of which still remains unexplored). But they recognize the different classes, and may like all of them at times. Of course the borders between them are often fluctuating or confused; but that is not only true for children. We all know the differences in kind, but we are not always sure how to place anything that we hear. A child may well believe a report that there are ogres in the next county; many grown-up persons find it easy to believe of another country; and as

---

[3] Far more often they have asked me: 'Was he good? Was he wicked?' That is, they were more concerned to get the Right side and the Wrong side clear. For that is a question equally important in History and in Faerie.

for another planet, very few adults seem able to imagine it as peopled, if at all, by anything but monsters of iniquity.

Now I was one of the children whom Andrew Lang was addressing (I was born at about the same time as the *Green Fairy Book*), the children for whom he seemed to think that fairy stories were the equivalent of the adult novel, and to whom he said: 'Their taste remains like the taste of their naked ancestors thousands of years ago; and they seem to like fairy-tales better than history, poetry, geography, or arithmetic.'[4] But do we really know much about these 'naked ancestors', except that they were certainly not naked? Our fairy stories, however old certain elements in them may be, are certainly not the same as theirs. Yet if it is assumed that we have fairy stories because they did, then probably we have history, geography, poetry, and arithmetic because they liked these things too, as far as they could get them, and in so far as they had yet separated the many branches of their general interest in everything.

And as for children of the present day, Lang's description does not fit my own memories, or my experience of children. Lang may have been mistaken about the children he knew, but if he was not, then at any rate children differ considerably, even within the narrow borders of Britain, and such generalizations which treat them as a class (disregarding their individual talents, and the influences of the countryside they live in, and their upbringing) are delusory. I had no special 'wish to believe'. I wanted to know. Belief depended on the way in which stories were presented to me, by older people, or by the authors, or on the inherent tone and quality of the tale. But at no time can I remember that the enjoyment of a story was dependent on belief that such things could happen, or had happened, in 'real life'. Fairy stories were plainly not primarily concerned with possibility, but with desirability. If they awakened *desire* satisfying it while often whetting it unbearably, they succeeded. It

---

[4] Preface to the *Violet Fairy Book*.

is not necessary to be more explicit here, for I hope to say something later about this desire, a complex of many ingredients, some universal, some particular to modern men (including modern children), or even to certain kinds of men. I had no desire to have either dreams or adventures like Alice, and the account of them merely amused me. I had very little desire to look for buried treasure or fight pirates, and *Treasure Island* left me cool. Red Indians were better: there were bows and arrows (I had and have a wholly unsatisfied desire to shoot well with a bow), and strange languages, and glimpses of an archaic mode of life, and, above all, forests in such stories. But the land of Merlin and Arthur was better than these, and best of all the nameless North of Sigurd of the Völsungs, and the prince of all dragons. Such lands were pre-eminently desirable. I never imagined that the dragon was of the same order as the horse. And that was not solely because I saw horses daily, but never even the footprint of a worm. The dragon had the trade-mark *Of Faërie* written plain upon him. In whatever world he had his being it was an Other-world. Fantasy, the making or glimpsing of Other-worlds, was the heart of the desire of Faërie. I desired dragons with a profound desire. Of course, I in my timid body did not wish to have them in the neighbourhood, intruding into my relatively safe world, in which it was, for instance, possible to read stories in peace of mind, free from fear.[5] But the world that contained even the imagination of Fáfnir was richer and more beautiful, at whatever cost of peril. The dweller in the quiet and fertile plains may hear of the tormented hills and the unharvested sea and long for them in his heart. For the heart is hard though the body be soft.

All the same, important as I now perceive the fairy story element in early reading to have been, speaking for myself as

---

[5] This is, naturally, often enough what children mean when they ask: 'Is is true?' They mean: 'I like this, but is it contemporary? Am I safe in my bed?' The answer: 'There is certainly no dragon in England today,' is all that they want to hear.

a child, I can only say that a liking for fairy stories was not a dominant characteristic of early taste. A real taste for them awoke after 'nursery' days, and after the years, few but long-seeming, between learning to read and going to school. In that (I nearly wrote 'happy' or 'golden', it was really a sad and troublous) time I liked many other things as well, or better: such as history, astronomy, botany, grammar, and etymology. I agreed with Lang's generalized 'children' not at all in principle, and only in some points by accident: I was, for instance, in-sensitive to poetry, and skipped it if it came in tales. Poetry I discovered much later in Latin and Greek, and especially through being made to try and translate English verse into classical verse. A real taste for fairy stories was wakened by philology on the threshold of manhood, and quickened to full life by war.

I have said, perhaps, more than enough on this point. At least it will be plain that in my opinion fairy stories should not be *specially* associated with children. They are associated with them: naturally, because children are human and fairy stories are a natural human taste (though not necessarily a universal one); accidentally, because fairy stories are a large part of the literary lumber that in latter-day Europe has been stuffed away in attics; unnaturally, because of erroneous sentiment about children, a sentiment that seems to increase with the decline in children.

It is true that the age of childhood-sentiment has produced some delightful books (especially charming, however, to adults) of the fairy kind or near to it; but it has also produced a dread-ful undergrowth of stories written or adapted to what was or is conceived to be the measure of children's minds and needs. The old stories are mollified or bowdlerized, instead of being re-served; the imitations are often merely silly, Pigwiggenry with-out even the intrigue; or patronizing; or (deadliest of all) covertly sniggering, with an eye on the other grownups present. I will not accuse Andrew Lang of sniggering, but certainly he smiled to himself, and certainly too often he had an eye on the

faces of other clever people over the heads of his child-audience
—to the very grave detriment of the *Chronicles of Pantouflia*.

Dasent replied with vigour and justice to the prudish critics
of his translations from Norse popular tales. Yet he committed
the astonishing folly of particularly *forbidding* children to read
the last two in his collection. That a man could study fairy
stories and not learn better than that seems almost incredible.
But neither criticism, rejoinder, nor prohibition would have been
necessary if children had not unnecessarily been regarded as
the inevitable readers of the book.

I do not deny that there is a truth in Andrew Lang's words
(sentimental though they may sound): 'He who would enter into
the Kingdom of Faërie should have the heart of a little child.'
For that possession is necessary to all high adventure, into kingdoms both less and far greater than Faërie. But humility and
innocence—these things 'the heart of a child' must mean in
such a context—do not necessarily imply an uncritical wonder,
nor indeed an uncritical tenderness. Chesterton once remarked
that the children in whose company he saw Maeterlinck's *Blue
Bird* were dissatisfied 'because it did not end with a Day of
Judgement, and it was not revealed to the hero and the heroine
that the Dog had been faithful and the Cat faithless.' 'For children,' he says, 'are innocent and love justice; while most of us
are wicked and naturally prefer mercy.'

Andrew Lang was confused on this point. He was at pains
to defend the slaying of the Yellow Dwarf by Prince Ricardo
in one of his own fairy stories. 'I hate cruelty,' he said, '. . . but
that was in fair fight, sword in hand, and the dwarf, peace to
his ashes! died in harness.' Yet it is not clear that 'fair fight'
is less cruel than 'fair judgement'; or that piercing a dwarf with
a sword is more just than the execution of wicked kings and
evil stepmothers—which Lang abjures: he sends the criminals
(as he boasts) to retirement on ample pensions. That is mercy
untempered by justice. It is true that this plea was not addressed
to children but to parents and guardians, to whom Lang was

recommending his own *Prince Prigio* and *Prince Ricardo* as suitable for their charges.[6] It is parents and guardians who have classified fairy stories as *Juvenilia*. And this is a small sample of the falsification of values that results.

If we use *child* in a good sense (it has also legitimately a bad one) we must not allow that to push us into the sentimentality of only using *adult* or *grownup* in a bad sense (it has also legitimately a good one). The process of growing older is not necessarily allied to growing wickeder, though the two do often happen together. Children are meant to grow up, and not to become Peter Pans. Not to lose innocence and wonder, but to proceed on the appointed journey: that journey upon which it is certainly not better to travel hopefully than to arrive, though we must travel hopefully if we are to arrive. But it is one of the lessons of fairy stories (if we can speak of the lessons of things that do not lecture) that on callow, lumpish, and selfish youth peril, sorrow, and the shadow of death can bestow dignity, and even sometimes wisdom.

Let us not divide the human race into Eloi and Morlocks: pretty children—'elves' as the eighteenth century often idiotically called them—with their fairy tales (carefully pruned), and dark Morlocks tending their machines. If fairy story as a kind is worth reading at all it is worthy to be written for and read by adults. They will, of course, put more in and get more out than children can. Then, as a branch of a genuine art, children may hope to get fairy stories fit for them to read and yet within their measure; as they may hope to get suitable introductions to poetry, history, and the sciences. Though it may be better for them to read some things, especially fairy stories, that are beyond their measure rather than short of it. Their books like their clothes should allow for growth, and their books at any rate should encourage it.

[1964]

---

[6] Preface to the *Lilac Fairy Book*.

The truth of fables

MICHAEL HORNYANSKY

Our own children are normal young citizens of the 1960s: addicted to television, well informed about Yogi Bear, Hercules, Robin Hood, Fireball XL-5, and so on. And yet, a cause for some surprise, they are also addicted to (even haunted by) the classic fairy stories. Why is this? Why should the old stories have such a grip, in this very different age? And why should their grip be so much stronger than the appeal of much else that has been written for children since, with our times clearly in mind—like *Tubby the Tuba, James the Red Train, Madeline,* even *Peter Pan?*

Don't imagine that our children's interest in the classics is narrow or exclusive. They read, or rather listen to, stories about machines, zoos, Saturday walks, dolls, magicians, children, and pets, without much apparent discrimination; and as I've suggested, they are avid consumers of the Hanna-Barbera products, even including such bilge as the Flintstones and the Jetsons. But the stories they want to hear last thing at night, and especially the stories they remember well enough to tell *us* (on the occasions when they decide to switch roles), are *Sleeping Beauty, Red Riding Hood, Cinderella, Snow White, Jack and the Beanstalk,* and that crowd: stories full of princes, princesses, giants, wicked witches, wolves, dwarfs, and other persons not normally encountered in modern life.

Why? The short answer, and the obvious one, is not that

such stories are 'imaginative, far from reality', and offer the child an escape into dreamland; but quite the contrary, that they do accurately reflect the child's picture of himself and his family. The father *is* king, mother *is* queen in this tiny world; and they ought to be wise, kind, and strong. The son, with light upon him from his parent's eyes, *is* a little prince; and our five-year-old daughter, for one, finds it quite natural to see herself as a princess—in fact she is prepared to look for her Prince Charming in England, because, as everyone knows, princes are scarce on this side of the water.

It is not only the royal scene that appeals to children for this reason, but also the basic situations or plots of the old-style folktale—for instance the pattern of the three princes or three princesses (it could be four, or two: but three is easier to remember, it is a magic number, with the feeling of a reliable sample), in which the two elder children miss the boat and the innocent simple-minded overlooked youngest child triumphs: what I call the Cinderella syndrome. What delight, what balm for the tiny downtrodden egotist! (And don't think I'm being scornful about egotism: it's the natural and normal place to start from.) Or take a more subtle example: *Beauty and the Beast* (or variations like 'The Frog Prince') which confirms a lesson that ought to have high priority among children: namely, you can't tell a book by its cover. *Beauty and the Beast* should be read early by every pretty girl, every girl who thinks she's pretty, and every unfortunate boy frog who knows he's a prince deep down. (Later, when you're mature enough, you can reverse the sexes in the story and watch Prince Charming learn that a hag may conceal a princess: Chaucer has already written this version in *The Wife of Bath's Tale*, which is recommended as adult entertainment.)

Stories like these are good moral propaganda. As people say, they 'teach children about life' through fables, in a way that *Tubby the Tuba* and *James the Red Train* do not, or do less successfully: because (oddly enough) these modern stories are more fantastic, farther from the child's view of life. After all, who is going to identify passionately with a tuba when he has the option of living as a prince?

But let's explore a bit further. Is this tight little kingdom (in which father is strong and just, mother kind and beautiful; the littlest prince or princess wins the day; and monsters or frogs turn into congenial mates)—is this a true picture of the world, even a child's world? We know it is not, even if we had to wait for Freud and company to tell us so. But some people have always known it—especially the tellers of stories, to men or children (as Freud was the first to admit: he recognized that most of the insights of the psychologist had been anticipated by the storyteller, the fabulist, the mythmaker). The child likewise soon learns that sometimes Daddy is not a good wise king but a fearsome giant whom the little prince or princess loves and hates at once (loves to the point of marriage, hates to the point of murder); that mother often seems cruel, tyrannical, a rival instead of a guide; and that the royal child is sometimes a forlorn waif lost in the dark wood, menaced by witches and monsters who go on being witches and monsters. We who have defeated or come to terms with these problems, at least in our waking lives, may need an effort to re-enter the child's real world, golden and pitch-dark by turns. We should recall the challenge of Al Capp, who puts it this way to the grownups: how would *you* like to be a pygmy in a world run by giants, without a dime to your name? It's a question worth pondering. Consider also that a genuine pygmy might be resolute and wholehearted even when terrified, but a child often believes, rightly or wrongly, that *he* is a monster, and deserves the dungeon.

The most haunting stories are the ones that recognize these facts and weave them into a reassuring pattern for the lost babe in the woods; the ones that accept the child's world directly, without bringing in grownup perspectives that the child doesn't know, and project it honestly, without any sentimental tidying up of the landscape. They do not distort the truth by filling the forest with cute, lovable little singing animals and motherly trees, in the manner of so many Disney cartoons; nor, at the other extreme, by filling the screen with fangs, glaring eyes, and other nightmares (as Disney used to do).

My way of putting the case is this: the fairy tales or folktales with real grip and staying power are genuine *myths* (and I trust you are grownup enough to know that myth is not an illusion or a lie: even children know better than that—it's a mistake made by foolish adults). A myth is a true story presented symbolically or indirectly instead of literally. At the moment I would distinguish two main forms of myth: one represents something that is true, but cannot or dare not be expressed directly (most of us dream this kind of myth, some time or other); the other represents something that is not always true in fact, but *ought* to be. Using these ideas as guides, I have been able to explain to myself the power of the old-time folktales, above all those of the brothers Grimm; and in a moment I'll show you what I've found.

But let me first put in a word for *some* modern myths (for it is not true, thank heaven, that we are past myth-making). Take the worlds of Hanna-Barbera, to which my children are so attached. Yakky Doodle's continuous story is a perfectly satisfactory myth: the little duck a perfect symbol (including his voice) for the lost orphan child, threatened at every turn by huge dangers (symbolized by one fox—with Jerry Lewis's voice; but that doesn't fool the kids, they know he's dangerous); and the bulldog Chopper a splendid *deus ex machina*, every child's dream of the all-powerful, kindly protector/good angel/fairy godmother, here in the comforting form of man's best friend. Or take Yogi Bear. Once you get past the adult jokes (like his name) aimed at the fourteen-year-old mind, you find another valid symbol for the child—this time a more robust child, with a timid younger brother to look after. To translate child into bear is of course comforting, because of the teddy-bear overtones;

but it is also psychologically right because it expresses the child's consciousness that he does not belong to the same species as grownups. However, the real secret of Yogi's appeal is first, his lust for food—which he must steal despite parental disapproval—and second his defiance, usually successful, of Daddy's authority—Daddy having dwindled to a rather silly park Ranger.

Now, back to the classics: the fairy tales which have lasted, and which will probably outlast Yogi Bear because they are good solid myths based in the child's own world and told directly, without archness or sentimentality or other adult nonsense. Let's start with *Snow White:* beautiful princess becomes rival of beautiful queen and is therefore ejected from family circle. This is one of those myths expressing a truth that dare not be faced directly—here, a clear case of mother-daughter rivalry (and presumably sexual rivalry, though it's presented as a straight beauty contest). The fact that the queen is called Snow White's step-mother shouldn't fool us for a moment. A child hesitates to accuse Mummy of being jealous enough to murder her, so Mummy turns into step-Mummy—which partly explains her behaviour, partly makes it okay for the child to hate *her.* The same device is useful to cover up one's normal hatred of brothers or sisters: Cinderella's sisters are so unkind that they can't be natural siblings.

What about Daddy, who ought to be the other corner of Snow White's triangle? Well, he's there, and kindly enough (we shall see this is the usual pattern: when mother is beastly father is sweet, and vice versa); but he's too much under Mummy's spell, or too busy at the office, to be very effective. Instead, the child is rescued by a father-substitute: first the woodsman or hunter who is too good-natured to obey the Queen and put Snow White to death; and afterwards the dwarfs. You may have read the other day of the latest anthropological theory about dwarfs. It's been discovered that dwarf legends all seem to originate from Roman settlements, because in the ruins of Roman towns the barbarians would find curious networks of underground passages and rooms far too small for normal folk to inhabit. Knowing nothing of Roman plumbing and heating systems, the barbarians invented the dwarf.

But that is an adult myth. To the child, the dwarf means something quite different. The seven little men who shelter Snow White are adults, but no bigger than children. She can look straight at them and see their faces instead of their knees. So Daddy has been cut down to manageable size, and split seven ways, which makes him easier to love: in fact, on this basis you can set up housekeeping with him quite cosily and never have the neighbours gossip. Unfortunately, however, Daddy still cannot cope in the long run (he has to go off to work, hi ho). Mummy breaks through his defences with poisoned fruit, Snow White falls into a deathlike sleep, and the best that little daddy can do is to build her a pretty glass coffin. It remains for a passing prince to awaken her and take her away from all that. So she finally wins the beauty contest after all (you can't fool these magic mirrors). But notice that the ending is every bit as sound, psychologically speaking, as the beginning: the only real escape from the long sleep of childhood, hemmed in by a despotic mother, is to wake up into love and ride away with a prince who prefers *you* for his queen.

Hansel and Gretel has the same kind of theme, though more strongly stated—so strongly indeed that our own children would rather not hear this one, which nevertheless has a real grip on their memories. Or perhaps they shy away from it because they perceive that *their* mother, even at her worst, isn't as bad as this?

At any rate, this time we have two children in the same boat. Their nasty mother, again disguised as a stepmother, wants to get rid of them so she can have Daddy all to herself (though the line she hands out is that there isn't enough food to go round). Poor besotted Dad actually does the ejecting by losing his children in the forest. But Hansel is a bright lad, as every elder brother ought to be; thanks to his ingenuity with pebbles, they find their way back the first time. It's really not his fault that the breadcrumb system breaks down—children can't cope with everything.

So what we have here is not mother-daughter rivalry as in *Snow White,* but a straight battle between the pygmies and the giants: or rather, between the pygmies and the female giant— for mother hasn't finished with them yet. Deep in the forest they come upon a gingerbread house, presided over by an old woman who pops them into cages for fattening and proposes later to treat them as pot roast. She is a witch, so the story goes: but don't be deceived. She is really mother again, one stage further removed so that we can make some really serious charges against her. I ask you—can you imagine a better mother-symbol than a witch who offers you gingerbread with one hand and pens you in a cage with the other? And being devoured by her is a direct symbol straight from the dreaming mind—so direct that civilized people may miss it entirely. But children are not yet civilized, and express things as truthfully as their fears will let them. The witch who eats children is their version of smother-love, the overpowering meddling that prevents them from having lives of their own. And that oven really drives the point home. As every housewife knows in this day of cake-mix commercials, the oven is a natural symbol for the womb: which every normal child wants to get out of. So *Hansel and Gretel* turns out to be the children's version of *The Silver Cord*—and it adds a neat ending. The only way to deal with such a mother is to shove her into her own oven (rough justice, I grant you; but that's life). And sure enough, when the children have eliminated the witch and found their way home, they learn that by a curious coincidence the stepmother has 'gone away'—and they have dear old Dad all to themselves, happily ever after.

Daddy gets his lumps in that marvellous myth, *Jack and the Beanstalk.* Here the focus is on a solitary boy who lives alone with his mother. Daddy is not in evidence; dead, they say—but don't you believe it, he won't be dead until Jack makes sure of him. So far, it's mere wish-fulfilment.

We need not linger over Jack's misadventures at the market, except to note that they run parallel to the Cinderella pattern—the underrated child who turns out to know better or be better than his parents: for the wretched beans that Jack brings home, to his mother's chagrin, are of course magic beans, worth far more than the cow he began with. Their value is that they provide Jack with a magic entry to the adult world. By climbing up the overnight beanstalk, Jack reaches a level where he can challenge his giant-father face to face. Of course the father must still be represented as a giant, for this is a terribly naughty thing to dream of. No wonder father roars 'Fee fie fo fun, I smell the blood of my no-good son': for the true refrain, that dare not be expressed, is 'Fee fie fo fum, Here's Jack who wants to marry Mum.'

But there is never any real doubt that Jack will win, despite the difference in size. And you'll recall that Jack's mother turns up in disguise as the giant's wife; who is significantly friendly towards the boy but terrified of her husband (a dead giveaway: now Jack can save *her* from that monster too). Technically speaking she ought to be a giant as well, but it's never mentioned, and doesn't seem to matter. Jack not only wins, he makes a grand slam. First he plunders the giant of his treasures in a series of daring raids. This is a clear example of sympathetic magic: steal your enemy's valuables and you steal his power. (I dare say one could even spell out what the various treasures stand for—but let's take the high road.) Then he chops the beanstalk so that the great lumbering idiot comes a cropper, right there in the good old marketplace. (That'll show you, Dad. Who says I'm not a businessman?) And finally Jack winds up with his dreams of glory come true: manhood, money, and mother, all to himself.

I must add a footnote. Not long ago my daughter, who was listening to one of those kindly TV uncles tell the story of Jack and his beanstalk, came pelting into the kitchen with the news that the treasures belonged to Jack's father. I was astonished. Had she gone straight to the heart of the story without any help? I hurried to the television to see who was spilling the beans. But what had happened was odder still: the TV storyteller had a cleaned-up moral version of the story, in which the giant had orginally stolen the harp and treasure from Jack's 'real' father, long before—so that in taking them back again Jack was no thief at all, but a hero of justice and property. Not very plausible, of course: why did that talking harp complain at being stolen if the giant wasn't its real owner? But it's a pretty piece of irony. As you see, in trying to tidy up the morality of the story, the bowdlerizers had unexpectedly confirmed its real moral.

Another footnote: our son Mark, who is not yet four (and who has already changed from frog to prince before our very eyes), chose to tell me this story one evening when I came to say goodnight. He got it a bit muddled, of course, but the main lines were unmistakable—until the very end, when the giant, having crashed to the ground, sat up, rubbed his hurt place, and said 'Ouch.' Then he gave Jack a chocolate bar and they lived happily ever after—because he was a friendly giant. No, I am not bragging about what a fine relationship I have with my son, or what clever things he says, or what a kindly dad I am (I do not hand out chocolate bars). I offer this simply as evidence that my son knew perfectly well what the story was about, and preferred not to hurt my feelings.

Exhibit four is *Rumpelstiltzkin:* a very different proposition indeed, and perhaps in its own way the most haunting of all (for good reasons). Who can forget the funny little man with the funny long name who spins gold for the miller's daughter and would have carried off her first-born had she not guessed his funny name? Yet he is a good deal less comfortable than the dwarfs we met in *Snow White;* and the rest of the characters are likewise a far cry from the hero-children, stepmothers, witches, and giants we've been dealing with. This time we are in an adult world—mythically treated, to be sure, but still significantly different in tone. In this world Daddy is a social-climbing miller who uses his daughter to curry favour with the local king. The king is moved purely by avarice; he will marry the girl simply to get legal title to her spun gold. No one so far has shown the least concern for her feelings—and the absence of concern is much more disturbing than hatred, for hatred is close kin to love, while callous indifference can never change. Even the funny little man who shows up to help her deliver the gold has his own axe to grind: his end of the bargain is her first child. And when he later returns to claim his rights, he is cheated—even though he has shown the only gleam of human decency in the tale, by modifying the bargain with his special name-guessing clause. Our natural sympathies lie with the young mother, but this should not disguise the fact that the dwarf has had a raw deal.

The prevailing moral climate in the story, then, is shabby—or at best ambiguous. Why is this so? One reason, already suggested, is that we have here a candid picture of the adult world, with all its shades of grey and double-dealing. But this doesn't go far enough: it doesn't account for Rumpelstiltzkin himself, who is an intruder in this everyday world, nor for the fact that we feel relieved and glad when he is defeated, despite the injustice of it. Who is this 'passionate deformed little creature' with the secret name? Consider the evidence: he pops up in a locked chamber and performs super-human tricks; in exchange he requires the dearest thing the young woman will ever own; he is accidentally overheard on a remote mountain-side, crowing over his victory and chanting his name around a campfire; and when he is beaten, he stamps his foot in rage so hard that he goes through the floor and straight on down. Where to? Why, home: where he came from. There are only two beings in the universe who have secret names, unknown to all but the adept: one of them is God, whose holy Name must not be spoken; the other, over whom mortal man may gain power by pronouncing his mysterious proper name, is the Devil. This explains why the funny little man isn't really funny, and why he is given a comic name that remains rather ominous: in German, *Rumpelstiltzchen* would appear to mean something like 'little roaring creature with strange legs'—and that is only amusing as long as you don't meet him. We can also see why we felt relieved at his defeat, however unjust: when you do business with the Devil, you have no time to worry about fair play. The story of Rumpelstiltzkin, then, is *Doctor Faustus* with a happy ending—or at least a satisfactory one.

Shall we draw general lessons in conclusion? Shall we say, for instance, that these classic fairy tales for children are in fact not children's stories at all but folktales from the half-conscious wisdom of the race, expressing in mythic form certain enduring human truths? We might say that. But we should add that this does not by any means make them unsuitable for children: far from it. And we should see once and for all the foolishness of any attempt to tamper with such tales, to pretty them up so as not to shock tender minds. I myself should prefer to take them, unaltered, as a guide to bringing up children sensibly: as examples of What Every Child Should Know, and as lessons presented in so cunning a fashion that a child can accept them before he fully understands.

If some of you should think that I've gone off the deep end, or trampled over precious flowers with my clumsy Freudian boots, I am not much worried: the evidence speaks for itself and will soon bring you round. If it doesn't, read Dr Spock. What does worry me a little is the thought that others among you will wonder why it took me so long to catch on. All I can reply is that the same uneasy thought kept occurring to me as I wrote all this down. It was all my own work, but hadn't somebody done it all before? I began to suspect that those cunning scholars, the brothers Grimm, were not at all the simpletons represented in the film, but knew exactly what they were collecting (how else could they hit the bull's-eye so often?), and that if I knew where to look, I should find that they had not only anticipated my every step, but soared far beyond my most daring guesses. Well, I have a friendly librarian working on this suspicion; and I can hardly wait to find out.

[1965]

Wells of fancy, 1865-1965

DONNARAE MacCANN

And ever, as the story drained
The wells of fancy dry,
And faintly strove that weary one
To put the subject by,
'The rest next time—' 'It is next time!'
The happy voices cry.

'Thus grew the tale of Wonderland,' Lewis Carroll continues, the tale for which happy voices still cry. During this centennial year of its publication, it is especially timely to note children's enduring enthusiasm for *Alice's Adventures in Wonderland*. Besides being a source of play and refreshment for children and a pastime for scholars, *Alice* set a precedent in children's books. The influence of such imaginative and irreverent storytelling opened the way for the development of the fantastic genre in children's literature. Before 1865, children were hardpressed in their search for imaginative stories. They might borrow Swift's *Gulliver's Travels* or Bunyan's *The Pilgrim's Progress* from their parent's library, and some were blessed with a nurse who was familiar with folktales and could tell stories. But even so skilled a writer as Charles Kingsley failed to produce a superior fantasy. *The Water-Babies*, published in 1863, contains many essential elements, but as Herbert Read points out, 'it has a subjective, or moralizing, intent, and this not only destroys its rhetorical purity but in so doing destroys its rhetorical effect.'[1] This failing was typical of children's books throughout their early history.

Fantasies improved notably after the publication of *Alice*, as seen in the works of George MacDonald, Laurence Housman, and William Hudson. In Italy *Pinocchio* was published and became available in English in 1892.

Despite the increasing distinction of fantasies, they have met with a cool reception from certain segments of the public. The genre makes a special demand upon the reader, an adjustment which is easy for children but difficult for some adults. E. M. Forster discusses this special requirement imposed by the fantasist.

. . . *other novelists say 'Here is something that might occur in your lives,' the fantasist says 'Here's something that could not occur. I must ask you to accept my book as a whole, and secondly to accept certain things in my book.' Many readers can grant the first request, but refuse the second. 'One knows a book isn't real,' they say, still one does expect it to be natural, and this angel or midget or ghost . . .—no, it is too much.'*[2]

For such a reader, there can be no communication and no appreciation of what a fantasist has achieved. Children, on the other hand, are at the height of their imaginative powers during the mid-elementary school years and often utilize supernatural characters in their play. It is not difficult for them to accept highly imaginative and unusual elements in a story. Furthermore, the fantasy's improvisations on reality are not a source of

---

[1] Herbert Read, *English Prose Style* (London: G. Bell and Sons, Ltd, 1937), p. 144.

[2] E. M. Forster, *Aspects of the Novel* (New York: Harcourt, 1954), p. 159.

confusion. By the time a child has reached the age of seven or eight, he has gained sufficient mastery of the real world, and sufficient mastery of his native tongue in particular, to enjoy the playful manipulations that literary fantasies provide.

Some adults distrust fantasies as being somehow 'unhealthy'. They raise the question, 'Won't these dwarfs and talking beasts encourage unwholesome fantasizing on the part of children or make them withdraw from the real world?' These fears result from a confusion of terms: confusion of the word fantasy when it refers to a *literary form* with fantasy as a *psychological illness*.

Fantasy, when used in the literary sense, has to do with the conception and construction of a story, its subject matter and treatment. The supernatural subject matter in the fantasy makes it an unlikely prompter of unhealthy daydreams. As C. S. Lewis has remarked:

The dangerous fantasy is always superficially realistic. The real victim of wishful reverie does not batten on The Odyssey, The Tempest, *or* The Worm Ouroboros: *he (or she) prefers stories about millionaires, irresistible beauties, posh hotels . . . things that really might happen. . . . For, as I say, there are two kinds of longing. The one is an askesis, a spiritual exercise, and the other is a disease.*[3]

One of the most characteristic features of fantasies for children is their sense of play. Although a feeling of mystery and foreboding can be the predominant mood (as in *The Jungle Book* or *The Children of Green Knowe*), more often the tone is one of playfulness. Even when the symbolic level of the story deals with social ills or philosophic questions, the writer's humour will pervade the book. His sharpest quips will be balanced by

---

[3] C. S. Lewis, 'On Three Ways of Writing for Children', *The Horn Book Magazine*, October 1963, p. 466.

his benign attitude when addressing the young.

In *Alice's Adventures in Wonderland,* the sense of play emerges primarily as word play. Alice is forever talking to herself as well as to flowers, insects, mythical beasts, and the like; and this perpetual dialogue is the means for frequent puns and verbal jokes.

> *'And how many hours a day did you do lessons?' said Alice,*
> *in a hurry to change the subject.*
>
> *'Ten hours the first day,' said the Mock Turtle: 'nine the next,*
> *and so on.'*
>
> *'What a curious plan!' exclaimed Alice.*
>
> *'That's the reason they're called lessons,' the Gryphon remark-*
> *ed: 'because they lessen from day to day.'*

By the time the reader finishes *Through the Looking-Glass,* the sequel to *Alice's Adventures in Wonderland,* he has gained considerable mastery of this game. When Alice asks, ' "Where's the servant whose business it is to answer the door?" ' many children can predict the reply, ' "To answer the door? . . . What did it ask you?" '

The Phantom Tollbooth, published nearly a century later, is the most outstanding example of word play since the two *Alice* books. Its countless verbal jokes do not imitate the word play of those volumes, but there is the same remarkable ingenuity and wit. The plot itself is greatly involved with language and communication. There is a kingdom of Dictionopolis, ruled over by King Azaz the Unabridged; and at a royal banquet, the young hero, Milo, discovers that everyone must eat his own words and that's all one will get. Thus the guests, in their speeches, are careful to say 'hamburgers, corn on the cob, chocolate pudding' or 'frankfurters, sour pickles, strawberry jam' or, in the case of the king, 'soupe á l'oignon, faisan sous cloche, salade endive, fromages et fruits et demi-tasse'. Discussing the evening's entertainment, King Azaz tells Milo of all the clever tricks his cabinet members can perform:

*'The duke here can make mountains out of molehills. The
minister splits hairs. The count makes hay while the sun shines.
The earl leaves no stone unturned. And the under-secretary,'
he finished ominously, 'hangs by a thread.'*

In Roald Dahl's *Charlie and the Chocolate Factory*[4], there are
surprising moments of word play, in addition to the nonsensical
catalogues of factory supplies:

*They passed a yellow door on which it said: STOREROOM
NUMBER 77—ALL THE BEANS, CACAO BEANS, COFFEE
BEANS, JELLY BEANS, AND HAS BEANS.*
    'Has beans?' cried Violet Beauregarde.
    'You're one yourself!' said Mr Wonka.

Fanciful inventions have a playful aspect too, and invention is
the major function of the chocolate factory, which manufactures
such new gastronomic delights as 'eatable marshmallow pillows',
'lickable wallpaper for nurseries', 'strawberry-juice water pistols',
'exploding candy for your enemies', 'luminous lollies for eating in
bed at night', and so on.

Mechanical inventions are the principal charm of William
Pène Du Bois's fantasies. In *The Twenty-One Balloons*, a family
changes the bed sheets by winding a crank which moves the
sheets across the bed, across rollers, through a sideboard, and
down through the floor to the cellar.

*There, they pass through a boiler where they are washed, then
through a drying machine. They next pass through steam-heated
rollers where they are pressed; then come up through the floor,
through the other sideboard of the bed on rollers, and back to
the top of the bed.*

When the writer himself makes a game of his storytelling, the
child is apt to return to the fantasy again and again. And this is

---

[4]Only the revised edition is recommended, an edition free of racism.

one of the most observable of the child's reactions to fantasies: he rereads them, apparently repeating his enjoyment of the game.

We readily associate play with children, but it is by no means their sole preoccupation. Inquisitiveness is perhaps an even more dominant trait in the elementary school child. On the one hand he is fascinated by the outward circumstances of experience, by action in and of itself. But it would be an oversimplification to assume that overt action in a story constitutes the limits of a child's literary enjoyment. His sympathy and curiosity are roused by all kinds of dramatic conflicts, not merely by physical feats.

Fantasies provide an ideal opportunity for observing the child's interest in inward aspects of life, in particular his fascination with the human personality. Because of its metaphorical possibilities, a fantasy is an opportune means for comment upon human nature; and for this reason, it is often more enlightening than the so-called 'realistic' forms of fiction offered to children. In many family stories, for example, characters are so idealized and incidents so contrived as to tax the gullibility of any intelligent reader. The fantasist's characters represent every conceivable human type, not just the loving family circle.

Child characters in a fantasy are often defined in quick strokes, yet with enough naturalness and distinctiveness to sustain credibility. In Edward Eager's fantasies, like *Half Magic* for example, children are endowed with the kind of contrasting personalities which invite kinship.

Jane was the oldest and Mark was the only boy, and between them they ran everything.

Katharine was the middle girl, of docile disposition and a comfort to her mother. She knew she was a comfort, and docile, because she'd heard her mother say so. And the others knew she was, too, by now, because ever since that day Katharine would keep boasting about what a comfort she was, and how

docile, until Jane declared she would utter a piercing shriek and
fall over dead if she heard another word about it. . . .
    Martha was the youngest, and very difficult.

But the writer is usually most interested in the fantastic
characters, and he uses them to create that wide diversity which
one actually encounters in human experience. The gluttonous,
self-seeking, self-pitying rat, Templeton, in *Charlotte's Web*,
provides the story with a lifelike contrast in its cast of characters.
Templeton is completely disreputable. After a characteristic
night of self-indulgence:

Slowly Templeton dragged himself across the pen and threw
himself down in a corner. . . .
    'What a night!' he repeated, hoarsely. 'What feasting and
carousing! A real gorge! Never have I seen such leavings, and
everything well-ripened and seasoned with the passage of time
and the heat of the day. Oh, it was rich, my friends, rich!'

The total effect of Templeton's charactization is comic relief,
and his role in the plot is to help produce circumstances for
a satisfying ending. Yet his nature never deviates from that of
a scoundrel.

In *The Dolls' House,* the celluloid doll, Birdie, brings a tragic
dimension to the tale. She is gay and kind-hearted, but her
mind is forever distracted by pretty sounds or objects.

Now, as she stood at the sitting-room door, the tinkling of the
musical box delighted her so much that it tinkled in her head
and she could no longer remember what anyone had said.

When a fire threatens the doll family baby, Birdie's maternal
instinct overrides 'the tinkling in her head' and she saves the
child; but she is too simple-minded to know how to preserve her
own life as well. Gradually, and sympathetically, Birdie's limited
mentality is revealed and she becomes the most memorable
character in the book. Tottie, 'with eyes . . . painted with

bright firm paint, blue and very determined', is perhaps the most attractive. Marchpane is the beautiful but malevolent doll who causes Birdie's accident, and her villainy is never glossed over. Critics sometimes have a problem with such a character; they fear that the child may imitate the wrongdoer. Such critics ignore or distrust the power of the writer, for an author who has produced strong characters is certainly capable of directing the sympathy of the reader toward one or another. Moreover, Forster's thesis applies to children's as well as adult books:

. . . novels, even when they are about wicked people, can solace us; they suggest a more comprehensible and thus a more manageable human race, they give us the illusion of perspicacity and of power.

In a novel, Forster continues, 'we can know people perfectly, and . . . find . . . a compensation for their dimness in life.'[5]

The most delightful of all pessimists, Eeyore the donkey in *Winnie-the-Pooh*, is well-known.

Sometimes he thought sadly to himself, 'Why?' and sometimes he thought, 'Wherefore?' and sometimes he thought, 'Inasmuch as which?'—and sometimes he didn't quite know what he was thinking about.

Ratty, in *The Wind in the Willows*, is the very embodiment of friendship. He never misses even the slightest opportunity to bolster the ego of his friend, the embarrassed, self-effacing Mole. When Ratty and Mole suddenly come upon Mole's long-neglected dwelling place, Mole is horrified that Ratty should see its shabbiness. Ratty, however, pays no attention.

'What a capital little house this is!' . . . So compact! So well planned! Everything here and everything in its place! We'll make a jolly night of it. . . . '

---

[5]Forster, *op. cit.*, pp. 98-9.

'No bread!' groaned the Mole dolorously; 'no butter, no—'
'No pâté de foie gras, no champagne!' continued the Rat,
grinning . . . 'what's that little door at the end of the passage?
Your cellar, of course! Every luxury in this house!'

Characterization and the interplay of personality are hallmarks
of almost any well-written fantasy. Social comment is characteristic of some. Authors can make observations about society
without indulging in direct preaching, and many writers have
undoubtedly chosen the fantasy form for just this reason.
Whatever his interest in philosophy, society, or the human
condition, the writer finds a poetic device in fantasy for its
expression. Antoine de Saint-Exupéry (author of *The Little
Prince*) and Maurice Druon (author of *Tistou of the Green
Thumbs*) are prominent examples; they are French fantasists
with many similarities in their work, but each has a unique vision
and voice.

Encounters by both the Little Prince and Tistou point to man's
habit of rationalization and circular reasoning. The Little Prince
meets a drunkard on one of his visits to a neighboring
asteroid:

*'What are you doing there?' he said to the tippler, whom he
found settled down in silence before a collection of empty
bottles and also a collection of full bottles.*

'I am drinking,' replied the tippler, with a lugubrious air.

'Why are you drinking?' demanded the little prince.

'So that I may forget,' replied the tippler.

*'Forget what?' inquired the little prince, who already was
sorry for him.*

*'Forget that I am ashamed,' the tippler confessed, hanging
his head.*

*'Ashamed of what?' insisted the little prince, who wanted to
help him.*

'Ashamed of drinking!'

The businessman on another asteriod seems just as foolish when he explains that he owns the stars in order to be rich, and the good of being rich is to be able to buy more stars, if any are discovered.

In *Tistou*, the hero questions his geography tutor about the nations of the Go-its and the Get-outs. A war is about to break out over an adjoining border country where there is oil:

'What do they want oil for?'

'They want it so that the other can't have it. They want oil, because oil's an essential material for making war.'

Tistou had known that Mr Turnbull's explanations would become very difficult to understand.

He shut his eyes in order to think better.

'If I've understood properly, the Go-its and the Get-outs are going to fight a war for oil because oil is essential material for fighting wars.' *He opened his eyes.*

'Well, its stupid,' he said.

Tistou is even more dismayed when he finds out that his father's munitions factory will supply guns to both sides: to the Go-its because they are friends, and to the Get-outs because 'that's business.'

Tistou of the Green Thumbs, although pointed in its criticism, deals primarily with the way the hero alleviates human suffering through the use of his magical thumbs. With a mere touch, Tistou can cause flowers and other plants to spring up overnight; he takes this strange power into the prison, the hospital, the homes of the poor, and finally, on to the battle-field.

That a modest wild flower should be able to create a panic among soldiers is perfectly comprehensible if you know that balsam has pods which explode at the slightest touch.

The engines were all full of it. Balsam swarmed in the carburetors of the armored cars, in the tanks of the motorcycles.

*At first contact of the selfstarter. . . . there was a growing,
spreading sound of dull explosions which, if they did no harm,
nevertheless had a shattering effect on the morale of the
troops. . . .*

*A rain of foxgloves, bluebells and cornflowers had fallen on
the Go-its' positions and they had replied, flooding the Get-outs
with buttercups, daisies and roses.*

Various professions are treated humorously or satirically in
fantasies, and in such general terms as to be easily comprehended. James Thurber makes good-natural fun of the medical
profession in *The White Deer*.

*The Royal Physician was taking his temperature, but he shook
the mercury down without looking at it.*

*'As a physician, I must take my temperature every three
hours,' he said, 'but as a patient, I must not be told what it
is.' . . .*

*'I do not believe I can cure myself,' said the sick man. 'Now,
now,' he retorted to himself, 'we mustn't lose faith in the skill
of our physician, must we?'*

The Phantom Tollbooth's commentary is devastatingly pertinent to twentieth-century urban living. It treats in symbolic
terms the problems of excessive specialization, lack of
communication, conformity, mercenary values, and other
maladies highly characteristic of our time. The story revolves
around the rescue of Rhyme and Reason (two banished
princesses) and the many villains trying to prevent it, e.g., the
Terrible Trivium, a demon of petty tasks and wasted effort, and
the Senses Taker whose business it is to 'steal your sense of
purpose, take your sense of duty, destroy your sense of
proportion.'

*'Now if you'll just tell me when you were born, where you were
born, why you were born, how old you are now, how old you
were then, how old you'll be in a little while . . . where you*

live, how long you've lived there, the schools you've attended, the schools you haven't attended. . . . '

The Senses Taker's queries fill nearly a page, but the hero can render him helpless as long as he keeps his sense of humour.

Whatever the specific area of commentary, it is the author's qualifications as craftsman, as well as philosopher, which give his work that sense of mastery which pleases and convinces children. The only notable difference in an author's stylistic treatment when he writes for the child audience is the overall tone of gaiety or sympathetic understanding pervading the story. The same writer, perhaps, may allow some bitterness to colour his communications with his peers.

If the illumination shed on social conditions is one pleasurable facet of reading, the uniqueness and totality of a fantastic conception is another. Seeing a newly created 'secondary world' is, in itself, an awesome experience. But the boundaries must be clear. In his essay, 'On Fairy Stories', J. R. R. Tolkien writes that the imaginary storyteller

. . . makes a Secondary World which your mind can enter. Inside it, what he relates is 'true': it accords with the laws of that world. You therefore believe it, while you are, as it were, inside. The moment disbelief arises, the spell is broken; the magic, or rather art, has failed. You are then out in the Primary World again . . .[6]

Without laws or boundaries the tale is both confusing and inconsequential, for 'the mind can do nothing with infinity, that most unmanageable commodity.'[7] The reader loses his sense of control. Some 'secondary worlds' which are compelling in the fullness and completeness of their conception include: the Land of Narnia in C. S. Lewis's *The Lion, the Witch and Ward-*

---

[6]J. R. R. Tolkien, 'On Fairy Stories' in *Tree and Leaf* (Boston: Houghton Mifflin), 1965, p. 37.
[7]Elizabeth Sewell, *The Field of Nonsense* (London: Chatto and Windus, 1952), p. 5.

robe; the Land Between the Mountains in *The Gammage Cup* ('It was quite untrue that the Minnipins . . . were a lost people, for *they* knew exactly where they were'); the elegant, but strangely twisted world of the Countess and the General in *Loretta Mason Potts*; the miniature, nautical world of the toy soldiers in *The Return of the Twelves*; and the island refuge of the few remaining Lilliputians in T. H. White's *Mistress Masham's Repose*.

Within the boundaries of the newly created world, a mass of corroborating detail is needed if the author hopes to inspire undeviating belief. Whether the story is about a 'hobbit' or a 'Borrower', the reader finds all sorts of data about the habits and history of their race, their domestic economy, their personality traits, etc.

The 'Borrowers' (in the book of this title) are a 'little people' race, and preventing them from becoming extinct becomes not only an adventure, but something of a game. The question is: how many real-world objects can the author utilize in a Borrowers' economy? These little people can 'borrow' and put to use only what they can carry away in their diminutive hands. In the first of four books, they have managed to tastefully decorate a tiny apartment.

> . . . the walls had been papered with scraps of old letters out of waste-paper baskets, and Homily had arranged the handwriting sideways in vertical stripes which ran from floor to ceiling. On the walls, repeated in various colours, hung several portraits of Queen Victoria as a girl; these were postage stamps, borrowed by Pod some years ago from the stamp box on the desk in the morning room. . . . There was a round table with a red velvet cloth, which Pod had made from the wooden bottom of a pill box supported on the carved pedestal of a knight from the chess set. . . . The knight itself—its bust, so to speak—stood on a column in the corner, where it looked very fine, and lent that air to the room which only statuary can give.

The discipline of working out a fantastic conception in all its vastness and detail has a bearing upon the author's style. When he conceives a story with such minute particularity as that required in a fantasy, he usually expresses it not only with clarity and euphony, but with a quality of voice which is as uniquely his own as the conception itself. His story is then a novel experience, irreplaceable by any other experience, any more than one individual is replaceable by another. This is the essence of style, and a distinguishing mark of many fantasies.

The child audience is the ideal audience to respond to this most subtle of literary gifts. Although the child doesn't know what has captured him, every line he reads or hears reveals the author's power and imaginative and expressive talent. The loyalties children exhibit toward certain authors indicate their sensitivity to the power and consistency of an individual style. There is clearly a pleasure in *how* things are written as well as *what*— a response to the writer's mode of thinking. Children refer to certain authors by name and know them as distinctive voices as well as creators of unique things. They request the C. S. Lewis books, the Edward Eager books, the Nesbit books. If the story is remembered for one dominant and striking character, the child asks for Paddington, Miss Bianca, Freddy, etc. These characters are such entertaining company children want the relationship to continue, and they persistently inquire about sequels.

But the best indicator of responsiveness to style is when the child remains unmoved by what he hears about a book's characters or incidents until the librarian says, 'Here, sit down and read two pages.' He does, and all doubt dissolves. He becomes so absorbed that he is still trying to read as he checks the book out and feels his way toward the door. From the first few lines of the story such a reader knows immediately that this tale will keep him vitally attentive and will continuously make demands upon his curiosity, intelligence, sympathy, or sense of humour. Many fantasies could be cited which fulfill this promise.

*There was once a boy named Milo who didn't know what to do
with himself—not just sometimes, but always.*

*When he was in school he longed to be out, and when he was
out he longed to be in. On the way he thought about coming
home, and coming home he thought about going. Wherever
he was he wished he were somewhere else, and when he got
there he wondered why he'd bothered. Nothing really interested
him—least of all things that should have. . . .*

*'And worst of all,' he continued sadly, 'there's nothing for
me to do, nowhere I'd care to go, and hardly anything worth
seeing.' He punctuated this last thought with such a deep sigh
that a house sparrow singing nearby stopped and rushed home
to be with his family.* (The Phantom Tollbooth)

*Maria was ten years old. She had dark hair in two pigtails, and
brown eyes the colour of marmite, but more shiny. She wore
spectacles for the time being, though she would not have to wear
them always, and her nature was a loving one. She was one of
those tough and friendly people who do things first and think
about them afterward. When she met cows, however, she did
not like to be alone with them, and there were other dangers,
such as her governess, from which she would have liked to have
had a protector.* (Mistress Masham's Repose)

*In a hole in the ground there lived a hobbit. Not a nasty, dirty,
wet hole, filled with the ends of worms and an oozy smell, nor
yet a dry, bare, sandy hole with nothing in it to sit down on or
to eat: it was a hobbit-hole, and that means comfort.* (The
Hobbit)

*If you should walk and wind and wander far enough on one of
those afternoons in April when smoke goes down instead of
up, and nearby things sound far away and far things near, you
are more than likely to come at last to the enchanted forest
that lies between the Moonstone Mines and Centaurs Mountain.
You'll know the woods when you are still a long way off by*

virtue of a fragrance you can never quite forget and never quite remember. And there'll be a distant bell that causes boys to run and laugh and girls to stand and tremble. If you pluck one of the ten thousand toadstools that grow in the emerald grass at the edge of the wonderful woods, it will feel as heavy as a hammer in your hand, but if you let it go it will sail away over the trees like a tiny parachute, trailing . . . purple stars. (The White Deer)

Are these 'special' books to be limited to 'special' children? Fantasies, because they are of necessity unique, have too often been viewed as books for a 'special' reader only, for a child considered gifted in some vague way. *Tistou of the Green Thumbs* and *The Phantom Tollbooth* received this treatment, as have many others.

But what special demands does a fantasy make upon readers? Only that they be willing to encounter the supernatural and to receive the book as a whole. Certainly the playfulness of many fantasies, the conception of something new and completely self-contained, the distinctive voice, these are pleasures to offer to all children, not just to the few. As for the social commentary, this too is usually comprehended by a wide range of readers.

In the so-called 'disadvantaged' areas especially, educators underestimate what a child can read. They claim that the children lack background, that they scarcely know the difference between a camel and a cow. Fantasies, however, do not deal with the difference between a camel and a cow! They comment upon the most universal aspects of human nature, drawing attention to things with which everyone is familiar. What child has not seen, as Tistou did in one of his lessons, how newspapers sometimes exaggerate an incident by using an oversized headline? What child has not encountered a drunkard, a self-seeking businessman, or a character like good-hearted, light-headed Birdie? Perhaps he hasn't thought about these things consciously, but there is nothing here so very foreign. He reads and he has the satisfying, lightning-quick impression: 'Yes, I've seen this happen, I've seen people like that.'

Well-written fantasies have special advantages, but little in the way of special obstacles. Besides their wit and perspicacity, they are usually marked by a felicity of style which puts them within reach of many readers, not just a gifted minority.

In an age of dreary sameness in the mass media, it is indeed cause for celebration that the 'wells of fancy' have sprung up so plentifully during the last century.

[1965]

A child's garden of bewilderment

MARTIN GARDNER

It was just a century ago this month that Macmillan in London published its first edition—two thousand copies—of *Alice's Adventures in Wonderland*. Lewis Carroll himself had arranged this date. It had been on 4 July, three years earlier, that he and a friend had taken Alice Liddell and her two sisters on a boating trip up the Isis. 'On which occasion,' Carroll later noted in his diary, 'I told them the fairy tale of Alice's adventures underground.' *Through the Looking-Glass* appeared six years later, and the two dreams soon coalesced to become England's greatest fantasy tale.

If anyone had suggested to a Victorian critic that Alice was great literature, he would have been met with an incredulous snort. Clever and amusing, perhaps, but great literature? Reviews of the first Alice book were mixed. *The Athenaeum* called it a 'stiff, overwrought story' with 'square, and grim, and uncouth' illustrations. 'Too extravagantly absurd to produce more diversion than disappointment and irritation,' said the *Illustrated Times*.

But children and adults loved it, both in England and here, and before twenty years had passed a hundred thousand copies had been printed. Warren Weaver, in his recent book *Alice in Many Tongues*, lists more than forty languages into which *Alice's Adventures* are now translated. There are several Russian versions, including one written by Vladimir Nabokov when he was a young man living in Germany. ('Not the first Russian translation,' he once told a reporter, 'but the best.') How can one explain the persistent—indeed, the still growing—popularity of this strange, outlandish dream and its even stranger sequel?

My own view is—though it arouses some Carrollians to a pitch of frenzy—that *Alice* is no longer a children's book. I do not deny that here and there a few unusual children, more in England than here, are still capable of enjoying it, but I believe their number is steadily diminishing. Like *Gulliver's Travels*, *Robinson Crusoe*, and *Huckleberry Finn*, *Alice* has joined that curious list of books that librarians call 'children's classics' but which are read and relished mostly by grownups. I myself have never met a child who said that *Alice* was one of his or her favourite books, and I have met only two U.S. adults who said they had enjoyed it as a small child. (Please don't write me an angry letter saying you have just read *Alice* to your five-year-old and she *loved* it. Try reading to her *A Midsummer Night's Dream* or Norman Mailer's *American Dream*; you'll find she loves them, too.)

The truth is that, from a modern child's point of view, the Alice books are plotless, pointless, unfunny, and more frightening than a monster movie. Let me summon a few distinguished witnesses. Katherine Anne Porter, in a radio panel discussion of *Alice* in 1942, confessed that the book had badly frightened her as a little girl. All those household things going mad and reminding her of the uncertainty and insecurity she felt in an adult world she couldn't understand! Bertrand Russell agreed. *Alice*, he declared flatly, is unsuitable for any child younger than fifteen. 'There are many objections to it as a children's book. In fact, I should like to label it "For Adults Only".'

'I wonder,' said Mark Van Doren, 'if the young these days actually do like it as much as children used to like it.'

'My experience,' replied Lord Russell, 'is that they don't, and I think this because there are so many more children's books now and because, when I was young, it was the only children's book that hadn't got a moral. We all got very tired of the morals in books.'

Another great mathematician, Norbert Wiener, tells in his autobiography how Alice's metamorphoses terrified him as a boy, and how it was not until many years later that he learned to value the book. H. L. Mencken, in his autobiography, writes: 'I was a grown man, and far gone in sin, before I ever brought myself to tackle *Alice in Wonderland*, and even then I made some big skips.'

For intelligent children over fifteen and adults who, unlike Mencken, are not bored by fantasy, the Alice books are rich in subtle humour, social satire, and philosophical depth. Both books, especially the second, are crammed with paradoxical nonsense of exactly the sort that mathematicians and logicians revel in. It is no accident that you are likely to find more references to *Alice* in a book by a modern philosopher of science than in a book by a literary critic. The central symbol in Edward Albee's Broadway enigma, *Tiny Alice*—the infinite regress of the castle in the castle in the castle—is straight out of the looking-glass. Alice dreams about the Red King but the Red King, too, is dreaming, and Alice is only a 'thing' in *his* dream. This double regress of Alices and kings, into infinitely more dreamlike levels nested in the skulls of each, is a delicious thought to philosophers concerned with separating reality from illusion. But if a small child understands it at all, he is more likely to be upset than amused.

Moreover, *Alice* swarms with jokes that no American child will catch (e.g., the Ugly Duchess's clever double pun on the proverb 'Take care of the pence and the pounds will take care of themselves'). And there are jokes not even an English child today can understand (e.g., the parodies on poems, now forgotten, that Victorian children memorized). There are even jokes that a child in Carroll's time would not understand unless he was part of the Oxford community (e.g., the three Liddell-little puns in the first verse of the prefatory poem. The last name of Henry Liddell, dean of Christ Church and the father of Alice, rhymed with 'middle'.) It is all this, from the obscure word plays to the philosophical and mathematical paradoxes, that keeps the *Alice* books alive among adults long after they have ceased to delight the average child.

It is instructive to compare Carroll with our own greatest writer of fairy tales, L. Frank Baum. On the surface, the two men seem remarkably unalike: Carroll the shy, withdrawn, stammering, prim, devout, celibate teacher of mathematics; Baum the friendly, outgoing father of four boys, a man who acted and sang in his own Broadway shows, published a newspaper in North Dakota before that area became a state, started his own movie company in Hollywood. But underneath their differences they shared a deep love for children (though on Carroll's side, only for little girls), and a genius for entertaining them with brilliantly imagined stories of outrageous comic fantasy.

Baum's first juvenile book, *Mother Goose in Prose* (it was the first book, by the way, ever illustrated by Maxfield Parrish), weaves stories around nursery rhymes in a manner comparable to Carroll's episodes about the Tweedle brothers, Humpty Dumpty, the Knave of Hearts, and the Lion and the Unicorn. The title of Baum's book, *A New Wonderland*, published in 1900, is an obvious reference to *Alice*. *The Wonderful Wizard of Oz*, issued the same year, parallels *Alice* in many ways. Like Alice, Dorothy Gale is a healthy, bright, attractive, outspoken, unaffected, supremely self-confident and courageous little girl who suddenly finds herself in a mad world where animals talk and nature behaves in a thousand unexpected ways. Alice drops into wonderland through a rabbit hole. Dorothy is blown to Oz by a cyclone. Mother and Father are conveniently absent from both stories. (Dorothy is an orphan, Alice never thinks about her parents.)

Of course there are also profound differences between the two classics, both in style and content. Baum is less interested in mathematical and word play, more in telling a straightforward adventure story. No one would expect to meet that eminent Oxford linguistic philosopher, Humpty Dumpty, in Baum's Oz; though we do meet a Humpty in *Mother Goose in Prose*, and I suppose Baum's Wogglebug and Carroll's egg have much pride and pedantry in common. (The White Knight, wearing yellow armour, turns up as Sir Hocus of Pokes in Ruth Plumly Thompson's *Royal Book of Oz*). No one would expect to find the Scarecrow or Tin Woodman behind the looking-glass. You can no more imagine the Cheshire Cat in Oz than you can imagine Bungles, the glass cat, or Dorothy's cat Eureka in Carroll's wonderland, although the White Rabbit might have strayed from Bunnybury, in the Quadling Country of Oz. This is not the place to detail differences, but surely one outstanding difference is that Baum's characters are, for the most part, as lovable as they are outlandish. They are 'Ozzy', but seldom cruel or mad. Oz is a happy utopia. Indeed, it is so attractive to Dorothy that she finally settled there permanently with Uncle Henry and Aunt Em. Both of Alice's dreams turned into nightmares.

It is a funny little irony of our culture that there are still librarians around who keep *Alice* on the children's shelves and *The Wizard* off. As recently as 1957 Ralph Ulveling, director of the Detroit Public Library, explained in a letter to the *American Library Association Bulletin* (October issue) why his library kept *The Wizard* in its adult stacks only and did not permit it in the children's room. 'More than thirty years ago', he wrote, 'the decision was made that with so many far better books available for children than was the case when *The Wizard* was first published, the library would simply let the old copies wear out and not replace them. . . . This is not banning, it is selection.'

Well, as Humpty said, words can mean whatever we want them to mean. Personally, I find it easier to believe in the Scarecrow than in Mr Ulveling. My advice is: Give *The Wizard* (in its handsome Dover paperback edition, with its bibliography of Baum's other books) to that ten-year-old; send *Alice (The An-*

notated Alice, of course) to anyone over fifteen who is bored with reading novels about psychotics in a real world.

Fantasy, said G. K. Chesterton (in his marvelous essay 'The Dragon's Grandmother'), reminds us that the soul is sane 'but that the universe is wild and full of marvels. Realism means that the world is dull and full of routine, but that the soul is sick and screaming. . . . In the fairy tales the cosmos goes mad; but the hero does not go mad. In the modern novels the hero is mad before the book begins, and suffers from the harsh steadiness and cruel sanity of the cosmos.' It is a good bet that both *Alice* and *The Wizard* will be around for many centuries after *Tiny Alice* and *The American Dream*—even that monstrous, million-punned labyrinthine dream of H. C. Earwicker's—have been forgotten by everybody except the collectors and students of twentieth-century curiosa.

[1965]

A late wanderer in Oz

JORDAN BROTMAN

I never read an Oz book when I was a child! Not for me were the earthly paradise of the Emerald City and the surrounding four Oz countries with their swarming little utopias and nightmares and the enclosing Deadly Desert, nor the fairylands beyond and the far, far country of the American middlewest, nor little Dorothy from Kansas and Betsy Bobbin from Oklahoma and the Shaggy Man from Colorado and the humbug Wizard from Omaha, nor the crowd of Oz names and Oz faces, Ozma and Glinda the Good and Ozga the Rose Queen and Polychrome the Rainbow's Daughter, the Scarecrow, the Tin Woodman, Ojo the Unlucky and the Patchwork Girl, Tik Tok and the Gump and the Private Citizen and the Incubator Baby; these and all the children and simpletons, animals and freaks and fairies that make up Oz eluded me. I must have felt the lack, because when my little boy was four I started reading him Oz books.

My little boy now has a large collection of Oz books which he reads, rereads, and ignores on his own. I found most of them in second-hand bookstores. The Oz books are still in print, but the new printings omit the lavish and fantastic colour plates that graced the early editions. There must be attics all over the country—thousands of attics in the middlewest alone—where set upon set of the resplendent original Oz books, painstakingly gathered by children of two or three generations ago, lie neglected and preserved like so many child's gardens.

Those who read the Oz books when they were children say that you can never recapture the magic of Oz on rereading them. A stranger to Oz, I was spared such disappointment. Instead I found myself fascinated by an unfolding picture of childhood which was not my own but which belonged, somehow, to the childhood of the whole country. For one thing the Oz books had a kind of California extravagance about them, and I could remember the time when California with its sunshine and its golden oranges and movies was an earthy paradise hankered after by people all over the country, certainly in the middlewest. The further I got into the Oz books, the more obvious it was that these children's stories contained a lot of the dreams, the asperities, and the hard underlay of character of Americans of sixty and seventy years ago, when most of the country—certainly the middlewest—was still in its unrealized youth.

The Oz stories are fairy tales. In the background of all good fairy tales is the hardness of real existence: the fairy tale starts from life as it is and never really escapes from it. The Oz stories begin on a poor dirt farm in Kansas and take us to a green land abundant with fruits, flowers, birds, and streams. The contrast is always there: the empty plains and severe virtues of Kansas and the pastoral, humanized landscape of Oz. 'I cannot understand why you should wish to leave this for Kansas,' says the Scarecrow to little Dorothy as she wanders through Oz in search of a way home. 'That,' replies Dorothy 'is because you have no brains. No matter how dreary and gray our homes are, we people of flesh and blood would rather live there than in any other country.' 'Of course I cannot understand it,' says the Scarecrow. 'If your heads were stuffed with straw, like mine, you would probably all live in the beautiful places, and then Kansas would have no people at all. It is fortunate for Kansas that you have brains.'

Kansas life is a harsh one in the Oz books. Dorothy's Aunt Em and Uncle Henry are gaunt people worn by sun, wind, and hard labour, fighting a losing struggle with the land and the mortgage on it. The cyclone that whisks Dorothy off to Oz is also the ruin of the family, and in a later story Dorothy is obliged to take her foster-parents to Oz to save them from an impoverished end in the city, and herself from being put out to service as a nursemaid. The old people have a hard time adjusting to the little girl's fairyland. Drudgery has been their life and lot, and the permissive climate of Oz leaves them foundering—until at the last moment Aunt Em, with a cry of 'Why, Henry, we've been slaves all our lives!' decides to make a go of it.

The lot of the Kansas child is also hard, but the child's ingenuity always dominates circumstance. In the second Oz book (*The Land of Oz*) the story is about a boy named Tip, who is parentless like Dorothy and who lives in a remote corner of Oz that resembles Kansas. Tip's guardian is a foul witch named Mombi (there are no witches in Kansas), and the 'small and rather delicate' child does farm chores all day long. Tip has no playmates, but his boy's life is eked out in fantasy and private play. He makes a pumpkinhead man for a playmate, who comes to life and escapes with Tip when Mombi decides to turn the troublesome child into an ornament for her garden.

Tip understands without illusion or self-pity that Mombi has an evil heart. Children in Oz accept the world as it is, good and bad, and the fairyland they inhabit is full of shrewdly drawn human types. The basic outlook is rural and middlewestern, because the children come from the middlewest. 'Life was a serious thing to Dorothy,' we are told, and this is true because Dorothy is both a child and from Kansas. But Dorothy also has a yearning for the pleasures of life, and this too the middlewest has echoed and acted upon, without any apparent sense of moral contradiction. One result has been the great migration to southern California—that middlewestern paradise, where Oz suddenly grew up in life.

Among the primary middlewestern attitudes ingrained in the Oz books is mistrust of and fascination for the big city. In the heart of Oz is the Emerald City, ruled by a powerful Wizard who remains invisible to his subjects. 'I am Oz, the great and terrible,' booms the Wizard from behind his screen—to whch Dorothy replies, with proper Kansas forthrightness, 'I am Dorthy, the small and meek.' The Wizard is of course humbug; Dorothy returns from her battle with the Wicked Witch of the West, and the screen falls and reveals a little old man who shamefacedly confesses that he has no magic to send her home on. 'I think you are a very bad man,' Dorothy burst out, and the humbug answers, 'Oh, no, my dear; I'm really a very good man; but I'm a very bad Wizard, I must admit.'

There is always humbug in the heart of the great city; you can fool the big city people who wear green glasses, but not the plain people from back home. It turns out that the Wizard comes from Nebraska, where he was a balloonist with a circus. This opens the way to a keener prejudice: if you are a man from the country who has made good in the city, you have to be a humbug to have done it.

Culture and higher learning, associated with city life, are also targets of the mild and simple satire of Oz. The most learned figure in Oz is H. M. Wogglebug, T. E. (Thoroughly Educated), an insect who conducts a progressive college where students take learning in pill form. H. M. Wogglebug is verbose and harmless, a featherweight. There is a place in Oz called Foxville, a fox society where animals dress gorgeously, attend concerts, and exhibit all the vanities of high fashion and culture. But the children of Oz are not immune to such pleasures, be it noted. Ozma's palace is more lavish still.

Such rural and regional sentiments in the Oz stories sometimes run together in a current of populist feeling. In *The Emerald City of Oz*, for example, the city and the surrounding farm community take on a utopian socialist character. We learn that there are no poor people in Oz, because there is no money; each person produces for his neighbour's use, and each is given what he needs. The people work half the time and play half the time, and they enjoy their labour because there are no cruel overseers.

There is a prison where wrongdoers are treated as 'sick' and cured with kindness. There are other utopian features, but the point, although it leaves its mark, is not developed in any detail —no more than is needed, perhaps, to satisfy the child's understanding of a barter economy and his keen sense of fairness. There are also contradictions and extravagances that exist side by side with the pieties of utopia, because Oz is a much more human than hypothetical paradise.

In fact there are a multitude of utopias in Oz, each one putting into effect with more or less point some logical definition about nature. They carry out in children's-story terms the middle-western appetite for creating utopias, which of course have not always been for children—Technocracy and Dianetics and Moral Rearmament came from the middlewest, and they weren't. Most of the Oz utopias are absurd, some are funny, and some are merely the private worlds of animals, monsters, or lonely eccentrics like Miss Cuttenclip, who has a menagerie of live paper dolls. There is a place called the Valley of Voe, where the people are invisible because they believe that beauty is only skin deep, and that 'good actions and pleasant ways are what make us lovely to our companions'. The only drawback to the Valley of Voe is that there are also invisible bears, who occasionally bump into the invisible people and eat them up.

The guiding philosophy of Oz is homely, practical, and inventive—adapted to the situation. On one occasion, for instance, the Scarecrow will moralize that in this world it is best to submit to fate, and on another that you must strive to overcome all obstacles. Everything depends on circumstances.

This practicality is familiar and Kansan, but Oz isn't Kansas. Oz is a kindlier place where love is reciprocated and dreams, if you work hard for them, yield a fair return. But you must work hard to achieve your heart's desire. One difference between Oz and Kansas is that in Kansas people work so hard—for nothing. Oz has a California climate, the grim uncertainties of life are lessened, and people have more time to learn about one another. In Oz, just as in idyllic California, people stop and congratulate each other about the place and the climate. In a fairyland that possesses more merely mechanical magic than any place on earth it is natural, then, that the main point should be an entirely social one: 'In this world in which we live, simplicity and kindness are the only magic that works wonders'.

If you look at L. Frank Baum's introductions to his Oz books you will find them progressively dated: the first two (1900, 1904) are dated at Chicago; the next (1907) is dated Coronado. From 1910 to Baum's death in 1919 the rest of the Oz books are sent off from a place called Ozcot, in Hollywood.

Baum, then, moved from the middlewest to southern California. In so doing he wove his own life into the design of Oz, for as an early arrival in twentieth-century California, Baum was living out an Oz dream. He was also sharing it with thousands of others to come, and anticipating by several decades the time when America at large, taking southern California as its model, would come to look more and more like Oz.

Baum got to Hollywood just before the movies did; the movies grew up around him. He lived an efflorescent California life. He bred chrysanthemums at Ozcot; he was Dahlia King of California. He wrote every day in his flower garden, seated near an enormous birdcage filled with songbirds. He read philosophy at Ozcot, played the piano, composed music, painted. He was a member of a society called The Uplifters and dedicated one of his stories to them. He turned out an Oz book a year and other books besides. In 1914 he formed his own Oz movie company. The fairyland factory at Ozcot was a private world and quite different from Disneyland, a public exploitation, but it is worth noting that Ozcot and Disneyland are pretty much in the same place.

The career that wound up in Ozcot, Cal. was as indeterminate, diffuse, and hardy as any Oz adventure. Baum was born in

Chittenango, in New York, in 1856, the son of a pioneer Pennsylvania oilman. He was educated mainly at home (it was a place called Rose Lawn, and when he was twelve Baum was putting out a paper, the *Rose Lawn Journal*). At eighteen Baum was doing reporting for the *New York Globe*; a year later he went to Bradford, Penn. and established a weekly paper called *The New Era*. In the eighties Baum took his growing family deep into the middlewest. He bought and edited a weekly in the populist stronghold of Aberdeen county, in South Dakota. (A collection of Baum's shrewd observations of middlewestern life was later gathered from his newspaper, the *Saturday Pioneer*, and published by the South Dakota Writers' Project). Baum was also a wanderer through the middlewest at various times, and worked as a 'drummer', a travelling man, peddling chinawear from farm to farm in the country. This experience is reflected in the Oz books themselves, which in part are a kind of odyssey through the middlewest; they portray the eccentricities, the hardships, the timidity, the communal longings of the country life ot the time.

Baum began sending off fiction and humorous verse to the magazines before he was twenty, and his literary output remained prolific for forty-years. In 1881, after a brief, disastrous experience as manager of an opera house in Olean, Penn., he brought out a hit play. It was an Irish melodrama called *The Maid of Arran*, and Baum quickly followed it with two other melodramas and a comedy. In the nineties—he now had four children to support—Baum wrote for the *Chicago Evening World* and edited a technical monthly for window trimmers called *The Show Window*. He founded the National Association of Window Trimmers of America, and in 1901 he wrote a book on decorating. Meanwhile he wrote fiction: when *The Wizard of Oz* appeared in 1900 Baum had already produced some twenty books for children, and some stories for adults. He became a purveyor to the fiction factories of the time, and wrote under a number of names. As Floyd Akers and Capt. Hugh Fitzgerald,

Baum wrote boys' books; as Edyth Van Dyne he wrote twenty-four girls' books. He was also Susanne Metcalf, Laura Bancroft, and John Estes Cook, and as Schuyler Stanton he wrote more-or-less grownup Gothic novels—among these, *The Fate of the Clown* and *Daughter of Destiny*.

Baum wrote most of his stories for younger children under his own name, and whatever significance we may attach to this, it was in the children's story that Baum became the great public entertainer of the era, the great moralist and prophet. In 1899 his *Father Goose, His Book* (illustrated by W. W. Denslow, who also did the pictures for the first Oz book) sold 90,000 copies in 90 days. The book was published in Chicago, and with the proceeds Baum built a summer home at Macatawa on Lake Michigan. This retreat—'The Sign of the Goose'—was a mock-up of the Californiana to come. Baum made all the furniture himself, and the heads of his upholstery tacks were in the form of brass geese. A vast stained-glass window portrayed a giant polychrome goose; the border decorations of the rooms were also geese.

By the time he wrote *Father Goose* Baum was already interested in the idea of providing a specifically 'American' fairy lore for children. *The Wizard of Oz* was the result. It was a quick success (it was made into a New York musical in 1902); it did so well, in fact, that Baum at first misunderstood its impact. He soon followed *The Wizard* with a new book, programmatically titled *Baum's American Fairy Tales: Stories of Astonishing Adventures of American Boys and Girls with the Fairies of Their Native Land*. It was not until 1904, after three other so-so children's stories, that Baum yielded to the peculiar demand for Oz.

Baum tells us what he had in mind for an 'American' fairy tale in his introduction to *The Wizard*. Here, with a brief tribute to the 'historical' European tales of Grimm and Andersen, he described the present need for a series of newer wonder tales, in which the stereotyped genie, dwarf, and fairy would be elimi-nated, 'together with all the horrible and blood-curdling incident devised by their authors to point a fearsome moral to each tale'. 'Modern education,' Baum observed, 'includes morality; therefore the modern child seeks only entertainment in its wonder-tales and gladly dispenses with all disagreeable inci-dent.' *The Wizard of Oz* was in short to be 'a modernized-fairy tale, in which the wonderment and joy are retained and the heartaches and nightmares are left out'.

This sounds like a brochure for Forest Lawn, but Forest Lawn is fake Oz. Some people I have talked to remember the night-mares they had as children over this and that episode of the real Oz stories. Even for grownups, Baum's fancy can sometimes suggest a medieval hell (in fact in one of the Oz books there is a descent to the cavernous centre of the earth, complete with monsters, satanic powers, and even a limbo). The truth is that Baum had a better instinct for his story than he knew how to say in a preface, and this goes not only for 'horrible and blood-curdling incident'—Baum knew how to pinpoint a child's nightmare—but of course for morality too. Baum knew that children are natural moralists, and the pages of Oz are full of moral instruction, drawn from experience at every turn, that has satisfied children for generations.

Nevertheless Baum did feel strongly—and rightly—that the Oz stories were a departure from the older literature. He once told his publishers that he wanted to write children's stories that had no love and marriage in them, and that got away from the 'European background'. What Baum seems really to have been objecting to was the maturity of the older stories, particularly their fatalism—the fatalism of a historical people tied to their land, their lot, their picture of heaven and earth. In Oz you can literally transform your environment, and the Oz stories though fairy stories speak to a people who are indeed about to transform their own.

Like all fairylands Oz is a land where people are immortal,

but it is also a land where mechanical ingenuity and achievement are quite as marvelous as immortality. If people are more liberated from the spell of magic in Oz than anywhere else in the world, it is simply because there is so much magic—magic has liberated them from magic. Flying machines are in the sky; a creature named Johnny Doit appears by magic and invents a machine to take you out of your difficulties; incubators, food pills, walking phonographs, a hundred contrivances are met with. Apparently the old Calvinist doctrine of work has been transformed into assurance in the power of mechanical ingenuity and faith in a paradise of leisure here and now. The deities of Oz are not the stern gods of the Kansas fathers but permissive goddesses wearing a Gibsonesque American look. And the paradise they preside over—whether in Oz or in southern California—is an emphatically democratic one: mechanical skill is not the exclusive possession of aristocracy, which for that matter has always tended to despise it.

Los Angeles itself will tell us how far away L. Frank Baum actually got from Grimm and Andersen, for Los Angeles represents Oz by as much as it represents the middlewest transformed. The later Oz books, as if authenticating the step from middlewestern myth to reality, have a pronounced southern California flavour about them. Certainly Los Angeles has been as well documented for its children, freaks, and fantasies of immortality as Oz ever was. But the resemblance does not end there. Baum today would have little difficulty in recognizing the new southern California, where the skill of the technicians has put up the aircraft plants and mass-produced Ozma's magic mirror, and where mile after mile of real-estate subdivisions, of new houses and cars and television aerials and prefabricated pools, show us that the paradisiac socialism of the Emerald City has come true, if not for people-and-people, then certainly for people-and-things. Whatever lingering traditional doubts they may carry around with them about the lot of man, Americans have discovered that through technology they can transform a society. Baum did it in the Oz books. He was the children's historian of that discovery.

The Oz books were so popular that Baum in his later career became the entertainer trapped in his creation. Others have met this fate. Charlie Chaplin never quite succeeded in shaking the tramp off his back, despite *Limelight* and the other strenuous efforts he made, under pressure from intellectuals, to upgrade his public image. Al Capp, of *Li'l Abner*, actually had to violate a public interest in order to declare his independence from his own creation. He had Li'l Abner marry Daisy Mae, and when it happened the country woke up to the shocking realization that what belonged to it was being reclaimed by one man's violence. Baum in his turn had pressing need to escape from fairyland, and not only because the children were making public property of his creation. America was catching up with Oz. It was becoming harder and harder to secure fairyland from the rest of the world.

In introduction after introduction Baum vows that each new Oz book will be his last. His readers cry for more; children and grownups by the thousands send him story suggestions— 'Why don't you bring Trot and Cap'n Bill to Oz, Mr Baum?'— and Baum gives in. Not without a struggle. From 1904 to 1907 he managed not to write an Oz book. In 1910, at the end of *The Emerald City*, he took a harsh measure and sealed off Oz forever by making it invisible—too many new airplanes, he explained, were getting across the Deadly Desert and invading Oz. The barrier held only until 1913. The children kept writing and telling Baum to get in touch with little Dorothy through the new gadget, wireless. From 1913 on Baum produced an Oz book every year. When he died he had done fourteen of them; the series was afterwards continued by others (notably John R. Neill, the great illustrator of Oz, and Ruth Plumly Thompson), but the decline of Oz in other hands was swift and sure.

Baum's appeal went further than to the children of his time

—a clergyman in England wrote to Baum in California praising him for the spiritual comfort of the Oz stories, thus reversing the moment when, only forty years earlier, a man in the wilds of California had written to George Eliot praising her for the same thing—but his appeal was also very much to the children. The sentiments of children, as Baum echoed them, naturally expressed the yearning for leisure and freedom of a country still held in a stern ethical mould; and Baum understood the sentiments of children. He gave the children a world to make and put them on their own. The children of Oz are separated from their parents; they have foster-parents or guardians, and these anyway cannot manage the world in the long run and have to be brought to Oz. In the Oz books it is the children (or the childlike adults, like the Wizard and the Shaggy Man) who are capable and effective people. They are serious too, reflecting Baum's own intimacy with seriousness of his child audience: Dorothy faces death time after time in Oz with philosophic calm, and her everyday speech, measured off in Baum's sedate literary style, is gave and sober. Oz itself, again, is not a passive fairyland but a very active one, full of arduous journeyings and doing without. A handful of blackberries is enough to satisfy Dorothy for a hard day's wandering.

The child's eye and the child's mind rule in Oz. There is continual name-making; Baum's name-fancy could range at will from erotic dreaminess (Glinda, Nimmie Amee) to the dreadful (the Long-Eared Hearer). There is constant punning and incantation, and the kind of word play that grows out of the child's sense of words as things. In one of the Oz stories Dorothy's kitten is put on trial for hiding or eating a piglet which the Wizard has given to Ozma for a gift. 'In either case,' says the prosecutor, 'a grave crime has been committed which deserves a grave punishment.' 'Do you mean,' exclaims Dorothy, 'that my kitten must be put in a grave?'

There is continual play upon the child's notions of his own identity in the world. When Tip's pumpkinhead man comes to life and learns that Tip has made him, he cries, 'Why, then, you must be my creator—my parent—my father!' 'Or your inventor,' laughs Tip, 'yes, my son; I really believe I am!' 'Then I owe you obedience,' says the man, 'and you owe me—support.' The reversal of roles between father and son provides much play through the book, at the end of which, to complicate things further, Tip becomes a girl. (He has really been Ozma all the time, but Mombi bewitched him into a boy when he was a baby.) The play on sexual character is unsentimental and childlike; Baum delighted as much as his child audience in upsetting the identity of things as given by the adult world.

Romantic love in the Oz world is, again, childlike (there are some curious and amusing romances in Oz, despite what Baum told his publishers). In *The Tin Woodman of Oz* the tin man decides, now that he has a heart, to find and woo the girl he lost long ago. On the journey he and Dorothy talk about Nimmie Amee and the married state; the exchange is ceremonial and learned. When at last the pair find Nimmie Amee, she is married to a tin soldier and has turned into a shrewish Kansas country wife. Of course pure love—love for children—is everywhere in Oz, and romantic playfulness takes place with all other adventures in an atmosphere of security. The Scarecrow, the Shaggy Man, and the other gentle Oz 'grownups' provide this atmosphere. Beyond them and beyond Ozma herself, the girl ruler of Oz, is the all-seeing sorceress Glinda the Good. Glinda has no mere temporal rule; she is the great mother, the authoress of love in Oz.

The Oz stories, clearly, have charm and variety and body enough to be real fairy tales. And for someone reading Oz books to a child—how else are you going to come across them?—there is also a familiar discovery to be made about the aspirations that have gone into the making of the American earthly paradise. The most interesting thing about Baum is that this popular writer of children's stories should have had so much to say about the most recent of the great migrations of the country's history. The move from the middlewest to southern California must now be written about as history; as an unfolding dream, Baum was writing about it in every Oz book he wrote, and his influence on the children was probably incalculable. It seems, anyway, that the new leisure that Baum was picturing belonged better in the children's story than anywhere else; in his time, and in part of the country, it was the children who were beginning to take the lead in determining what the whole country wanted.

[1965]

News
from Narnia

LILLIAN H. SMITH

'Listen', said the Doctor. 'All you have heard about Old Narnia is true. It is not the land of men. It is the country of Aslan, the country of the Waking Trees and Visible Naiads, of Fauns and Satyrs, of Dwarfs and Giants, of the gods and Centaurs, of Talking Beasts.'

The world called Narnia is the world that C. S. Lewis has created in seven stories for children, each story having a beginning, a middle, and an end, and each may be read independently of the others. Yet in these seven books, taken as a whole, we see a complete story with a beginning, a middle, and an end, in much the same way that we see, first, single stars in the sky, and then see them as a constellation which takes on a pattern our eyes can follow and recognize.

Narnia is not in our world nor in our universe. Narnia has its own sun and moon and stars, its own time. Yet the landscape is a familiar one, a green and pleasant land of woods and glades, valleys and mountains, rivers and sea. The trees, shrubs, and flowers, many birds and animals, are those we know in our own world. Even the unfamiliar, the strange and fabulous ones, are in old stories we have heard and read.

Narnia's history is brief, as we reckon time in our world, though in Narnian time it covers many thousands of years. It began when 'Sherlock Holmes was still living in Baker Street and the Bastables were looking for treasure in the Lewisham

Road'. In London, too, lived Polly and Digory who were looking for adventure. It was Digory's Uncle Andrew, a dabbler in magic, who sent Polly and Digory out of our world and into a world of darkness, which was Narnia waiting to be born.

Digory was 'the sort of person who wants to know everything' and his curiosity brought great trouble to Narnia later on. For the children had visited a dying world before coming to Narnia, and because Digory could not resist the desire to know what would happen, he broke the spell that bound an evil witch to the dying world of Charn. When the children are drawn into a new world, the witch, though against their will, comes too. And so evil enters Narnia before it is five hours old.

As the children stand in the nothingness of this new, dark, and empty world, they hear a voice singing, and with the song suddenly there were stars overhead. Soon, the sky on the eastern horizon turned from dark to grey, then from pink to gold, and just as the voice swelled to the mightiest and most glorious sound, the sun arose and the Singer, himself stood facing the rising sun. 'It was a Lion.'

The Lion's song of creation changes as he paces the waste land, and, as Polly said, 'when you listened to his song you heard the things he was making up: when you looked round you, you saw them.' 'All things bright and beautiful, all creatures great and small'—Narnia is born.

But, since evil has already entered Narnia through the curiosity of two human children, the Lion, who is called 'Aslan', decrees that 'As Adam's race has done the harm, Adam's race shall help to heal it.'

Digory and Polly are sent, over the Western Wilds and mountains of ice, to a walled garden with gates of gold. Here, Aslan tells them, must be gathered the apple whose seeds will be Narnia's safeguard against the witch in the years ahead. And this was the first of 'the comings and goings' between

Narnia and our own world as it is told in *The Magician's Nephew.*

All our news of Narnia comes from the various human children who find themselves there whenever evil times fall on the land. Centuries of peace and plenty pass unrecorded until four other children, in the story of *The Lion, the Witch and the Wardrobe,* find all of Narnia wrapped in a blanket of snow and ice. Under the witch's spell, it is 'always winter and never Christmas'. The children and the Narnians are pitted against the witch, who calls to her aid all the 'abominations': Ghouls, Boggles, Ogres, Minotaurs, Cruels, Hags, and Spectres. But Aslan, the Lion, has been seen in Narnia, and with his coming the spell of evil over the land weakens, and signs of spring are followed by budding trees and rushing brooks as the children, with the talking beaver as their guide, journey to meet Aslan at the Great Stone Table where the battle against the witch will be decided.

Although not the first story in Narnian chronology, *The Lion, the Witch and the Wardrobe* was the first to be published, and is, I think, the first for children, themselves, to read. For, from the moment Lucy opens the wardrobe, steps inside to explore, and is suddenly standing in the middle of a winter forest with snow crunching underfoot, the adventure is a magnet that draws the reader deeper and deeper into the life of Narnia and into concern for all that happens there. At the same time, the reader is aware that there is more to the story than meets the eye, phrases that set young minds and hearts pondering, overtones that set up rhythms heard not only in this book, but in all the stories as they appeared year after year until the last two, *The Magician's Nephew* and *The Last Battle.* In these the children's questions are answered and the full harmony is heard and intuitively grasped at last.

Each story has its own landscape—or seascape. For C. S. Lewis, the face of nature, its changing moods and seasons whether seen in windswept wastes or in a small mossy glade where hawthorn is in bloom, has its part in his developing theme, in shaping the sequence of events and in giving reality to the reader's imaginings as he accompanies the characters of the story on their adventures in the magical land of Narnia.

The characters, themselves, apart from the human children who come there as visitors, reflect the author's mature and scholarly interest in mythology and mediaeval romances. They reflect and communicate his abiding love for the Old Things which belonged, perhaps, to a golden age, backwards in time, when men and birds and beasts spoke to each other in a common language, a fabulous age which, it may be, lived on in myth and fairy tale as a kind of race memory of another, more innocent, world.

It is Trufflehunter, the badger, whose sense of race hints at the prehistoric antiquity of animal traits, the unchanging persistent tenacity with which they pursue their own ends. 'You dwarfs,' says Trufflehunter, are as forgetful and changeable as the Humans themselves. I'm a beast, I am, and a Badger what's more. We don't change, we hold on.'

Among the other characters who live on in memory after we have closed the books, is that valiant Chief Mouse, Reepicheep, whose code of chivalry would seem to have been learned at King Arthur's Round Table, for 'his mind was full of forlorn hopes, death or glory charges and last stands.' He is one of the company who sails in *The Dawn Treader* 'towards Aslan's land and the morning and the eastern end of the world', and, after the last battle of all the battles, he is found at the open gates of Aslan's country to bid his friends welcome.

And there is Puddleglum, the Marsh-wiggle, who takes so dim a view of every prospect, but who is the faithful, hardy guide in the children's quest for the lost Prince Rilian. Says Puddleglum: 'How a job like this—a journey up north just as winter's beginning, looking for a prince that probably isn't there, by way of a ruined city that no one has ever seen—will be just the thing. If that doesn't steady a chap, I don't know what will.' When the Prince is found, in the underworld of the witch, and when she uses her black arts to persuade the children that only the underworld exists, and that Narnia is only a myth, it is Puddleglum who stamps out the flame whose evil fumes bewilder and confuse their minds and hearts. It is Puddleglum who throws the challenge to the witch: 'Suppose we *have* only dreamed, or made up, all those things—trees and grass and sun and moon and stars and Aslan himself. Suppose we have. Then all I can say is that, in that case, the made-up things seem a good deal more important than the real ones . . . I'm on Aslan's side even if there isn't any Aslan to lead it. I'm going to live as like a Narnian as I can even if there isn't any Narnia.'

And so we come to Aslan, the Lion, who is the heart and the periphery of these stories and their reason for being: Aslan, whose pervasive influence is felt at all times, in all places, whether visible or invisible, in the world of Narnia. He says to the children, 'Remember, remember, remember the signs . . . Here on the mountain I have spoken to you clearly; I will not often do so down in Narnia. Here on the mountain the air is clear and your mind is clear; as you drop down into Narnia, the air will thicken. Take great care that it does not confuse your mind.'

We may call these books fairy tales or allegories or parables, but there is no mistake about the significance of what C. S. Lewis has to say to the trusting, believing, seeking heart of childhood. But C. S. Lewis knows well that if children are to hear what it is he has to say to them, they must first find delight in the story he tells. And so the fresh and vigorous winds of his imagination carry his readers exuberantly through strange and wild adventures, adventures that, half consciously, they come to recognize are those of a spiritual journey toward the heart of reality. This is the final quality, I think, of C. S. Lewis's writing about the country of Narnia—that above and beneath and beyond the events of the story itself there is something to which the children can lay hold: belief in the essential truth of their own imaginings.

[1958]

Babar's civilization analysed

EDMUND LEACH

It is adult rather than childish preference which from time to time awards a classic accolade to particular characters in nursery literature. Two generations back it was Alice and Peter Rabbit, then, save our souls, Winnie-the-Pooh, and today Babar. What is it that the adults find so remarkable? Why does Babar reign among the immortals?

Perhaps it is simply the author's prophetic insight into French politics: Babar, born c. 1933, is a long-nosed gentleman who returns to his devastated country in the midst of a disastrous war against the rhinoceroses; under his paternal rule as *Général-Président* the elephants achieve unheard-of prosperity; Babar, like his human counterpart, now travels in a Citröen DS19 and leads a genteel bourgeois existence in a country château remote from the turmoil of Celesteville politics.

Or should we look for Freudian symbolism? Any overdressed European male must surely derive considerable exhibitionist delight from seeing himself displayed as an elephant, whichever end you approach the matter. And no doubt there are all sorts of other possibilities as far-fetched or as obvious as you will.

But let us consider some matters of fact. The Old Lady (La Vieille Dame) recurs in all the stories. She is a direct link with mundane reality and she is the only human character of any consequence. The others such as Fernando, a circus owner, a nameless sea captain, sundry Arabs and Africans etc. make only brief appearances, usually in crowd scenes. The Old Lady has no personal name. In the earlier (Jean de Brunhoff) books the geography is a nice blend of North Africa and Southern or even Central France. Real places are never mentioned by name, but the pictures imply that it is just a short scamper from darkest Africa to the banks of the Seine. A later (Laurent de Brunhoff) volume jumbles up Arabs and kangaroos. This seems to me a mistake; it is the wrong kind of inconsistency.

Babar himself is a thoroughly civilized elephant who sleeps in a bed, reads the newspaper, drives a car, and so on. To wear no clothes is a mark of savagery. This is a characteristic both of pre-Babar elephants and of post-Babar black men ('savages'). The increasing opulence of the elephant ruling class,—the consequences no doubt of an oil strike in the South Sahara—has regularly been marked by the ever-increasing complexity of their human attire.

Elephant society is strictly on a par with that of men, and intermingles with it directly without evoking astonishment on the part of either the elephants or the humans. This land of the elephants is merely a different country, as England is to France. Other animals occupy further countries in a similar way, but it is not the case that *all* animal species are elevated to an identical para-human status. There is a definite hierarchy. Rhinos, though unpleasant fellows, are as civilized as elephants; they fight on equal terms, and an elephant airline employs a rhino as pilot. Likewise Zephir, the monkey playmate of the younger elephants, has a monkey land of his own complete with a monkey fiancée, Princess Isabel. But the other animals, which are humanized in the sense that they attend parties and generally participate in Celesteville high jinks, all seem to be on a slightly lower plane—Asiatics as against Europeans perhaps? A Michelin guide to Babar's zoology would run something like this:

FROM JEAN DE BRUNHOFF'S *Babar the King*

★★★★ CIVILIZED RULERS
   White Men, Elephants, Rhinoceroses, Monkeys
★★★ SERVILE COLONIAL POPULATIONS:
   Black Men, Dromedaries, Hippopotamuses, Kangaroos
★★ HUMANIZED ANIMALS (appearing only occasionally and then
   as individuals):
   Lion, Tiger, Giraffe, Deer, Tortoise, Mouse, Porcupine,
   Lizard. Various exotic birds (e.g. Flamingo, Ibis, Pelican,
   Marabout)
★ WILD BEASTS (hostile to elephants as they would be to
   man):
   Crocodile, Snake
   DOMESTIC ANIMALS

Domestic animals, e.g. horses, cows, sheep, goats, pigs, frequently appear in the pictures but never as 'characters' in the story; they remain domestic animals quite devoid of human qualities. Animals which rate as pets for humans (i.e. cats and dogs) are eliminated altogether with one exception: when Babar goes in search of Father Christmas—a sort of fantasy within a fantasy—he is accompanied by a talking dog (which is rather surprisingly called Duck).

The allocation of names in Babar's world has a definite pattern. The Old Lady, the only 'real' human, has no name. Babar's closest associates, that is those who are closest to being human, have names appropriate to real humans or to pets: Babar, Celeste, Pom, Flora, Alexander, Arthur, Zephir, Isabel, Eleanor (a mermaid), Cornelius.

Beyond this there is a list of Celesteville elephants who have 'real' occupations but fanciful names. Tapitor, the shoemaker, Pilophage, the officer, Capoulosse, the doctor, Barbacol, the tailor, Podula, the sculptor, Hatchibombator, the road sweeper, Doulamour, the musician, Olur, the mechanic, Poutifour, the farmer, Fandango, the scholar, Justinien, the painter, Coco, the

clown, and Ottilie, a girl friend of Arthur. The names of the
rhinos are rather similar: Rataxes, Pamir, Baribarbottom. Likewise the minor characters associated with Zephir: Huc and
Aristobel are monkeys; Aunt Crustadel and Polomoche are
'monsters' which look like nursery toys, and it is never stated
whose aunt they are. None of the three-, two-, or one-star animals have personal names except the tortoise, who on one occasion is called Martha.

It will be seen that Babar's world is very urban. The humanized animals and birds are those one might meet in a zoo, behind
bars. The list of professions suggests the atmosphere of a
small-town street.

The naming pattern has the effect of setting up class
discriminations even within the category of four-star animals.
The reader is coerced into making a self-identification with one
or the other of the members of Babar's own household; the
rest of the universe of humanized animals is then ranged round
about in categories of inferior status.

The ethnographers provide us with other evidence concerning
Babar's ideas of social class. Though Babar is elected as 'King',
he is not an hereditary aristocrat. There is no suggestion that
he is a relative of the previous monarch who died from eating
a poisonous mushroom. Nor do any of Babar's associates carry
hereditary titles such as Count; they are all Mr and Mrs plain
and simple. True, Babar has covered the walls of his new
château with portraits of sixteenth-century 'ancestors', but this
is obviously a completely fake piece of snobbery. Further evidence of class sensitivity may be seen in the fact that Babar
marries his cousin Celeste, and that the only other elephant
outsider with whom the family have intimate relations is another
cousin, Arthur. When Babar and Celeste amuse themselves in
the Celesteville Garden of Pleasure they play tennis with Mr
and Mrs Pilophage, Pilophage being a military officer. In the
same context, General Cornelius plays bowls with a sort of intellectual élite: Fandango the scholar, Podula the sculptor,

Capoulosse the doctor. But Babar does not associate with tradesmen.

All this is as it should be. It is important that the comfortable bourgeois adult readers should not have their basic assumptions about social relationships in any way disturbed. Babar has the prejudices of a middle class *colon* of the 1930s.

I have a theory about all this. I think that Babar appeals to adults because the fantasy is so carefully contrived, so fully under control. In the ordinary way we tend to categorize living creatures in terms of social distance, depending upon the degree of remoteness from 'myself', thus:

	1	2	3	4
	VERY NEAR	NEAR	FAR	VERY FAR
ME	very tame	tame	wild	very wild
		domestic	familiar	unfamiliar
	pets	animals	wild animals	wild animals
	inedible	edible	some edible	inedible
	family members	neighbours	strangers	total strangers
				savages
			some	not
	incest	marriageable	marriageable	marriageable

The categories of animals and humans falling into columns 1 and 4 are both abnormal and sacred, and the sacredness is in both cases marked by the taboo on edibility and sex relations.

This I admit is a complicated matter. The English have tended to accept biblical injunctions so that all meat-eating creatures and creeping things are inedible, also horses. But the French eat snails and frogs and horse. In Canton the restaurants serve up dog and snake as delicacies, also unborn mice and a soup made of bird saliva. Cannibal connoisseurs consider human rumpsteak delicious. But the point is that eating and sex are both matters of social convention and in all cases there is a 'very near' and a 'very far' category, *both* of which are alike inedible and sexually illegitimate.

I find it significant that almost all the humanized beasts in the Babar books belong to column 4, whereas surely the child's natural interests must lie in columns 1 and 2? Children's books in which the leading characters are humanized pets and humanized domestic animals are published with great regularity but seem to have no staying power—this can only be because the adults disapprove. But why? Might not the explanation be something like this:

For the child, fantasy is obvious. The category distinction real/unreal (true/false) is vague and unimportant; for the adult it is crucial. And in the adult's painfully constructed image of the real world the categories which are very close—those relating to the parts and excretions of the body—to family relations, to pets and familiar creatures—are the basic discriminations which serve as a rather shaky foundation for a vast superstructure of precisely defined linguistic concepts. As we get older the uncertainty of these early discriminations becomes a source of great anxiety, sex and excretion become 'obscene', they are loaded with a taboo which infects even Chanticleer and the harmless pussycat. Small wonder then that the adult finds this kind of country uncomfortable. We may blandly assure ourselves that we thoroughly approve of childish fantasy, but at the same time we want to be quite sure that the real and the unreal never get muddled up in our own imagination. Alice can do what she likes on the other side of the looking-glass or down the rabbit hole, but not too close please, not too close. If you want to see a real elephant go to the zoo: I don't want any of Mr Ionesco's rhinoceroses around here if you please.

[1962]

Only connect

P. L. TRAVERS

It was suggested to me when the Library of Congress did me the honour of asking me to address you that I should talk about how *Mary Poppins* came to be written. Now, I know that there are many people who can talk, and at great length, on subjects of which they are totally ignorant. But I'm not one of them. I can't speak of what I don't know and this is not from an excess of modesty but from lack of relevant data. Any work of fiction, any work of imagination, has inevitably something of the quality of poetry, or of those strange flashes of realization that happen for no apparent reason or rhyme—it can't be described. Words are like the notes on a piano, instruments of communication, not the poem—or the music—itself. Once a piece of work is finished, it has said all there is to be said. My instinct is always to whittle down, not to enlarge upon, and hasn't your own poet Randall Jarrell said—I forget the exact phrase for the moment— that a writer must remain silent about the way in which he writes? Even what he writes. Nothing, however, prevents a writer from speaking about the earth—the compost, as it were —from which his work arises. He can't help knowing something about that because it is, of course, his very self.

And this brings me to my title. I don't have to tell you where it comes from. When I was at Radcliffe last year students from that college and Harvard used to crowd into my small apartment once a week and the talk was so good, they were all so alive, so open to ideas, and so ready to fight me for them. I liked that. And I remember that on one occasion I said—and it still seems to me true—that thinking was linking. At that, one marvellous girl blazed out at me, 'Yes! Only connect!' and began searching for pencil and paper. But I begged her not, for the life of her, to write it down in a notebook. E. M. Forster had made the connection already, and now it was really her own. Once you write things down you've lost them. They are simply dead words on dead paper.

But 'Only connect' was the exact phrase I had been leading up to and it has been precious to me ever since I read *Howards End*, of which it is the epigraph. Perhaps, indeed, it's the theme of all Forster's writing, the attempt to link a passionate scepticism with the desire for meaning, to find the human key to the inhuman world about us; to connect the individual with the community, the known with the unknown; to relate the past to the present and both to the future. Oh, it's a marvellous phrase and I seized upon it for this lecture because—well, what else *is* there to seize upon? This question of linking is, anyway, very close to me, and since that is what I am talking about tonight inevitably I have to go back to the past.

You remember Blake's 'Little Black Boy'? 'My mother bore me in the Southern wild.' In that sense I was a little black boy, too, for I was born in the subtropics of Australia. Not that I spent all my life there, only my young years, and most of it far from cities. I lived a life that was at once new and old. The country was new and the land itself very old—the oldest in the world, geologists say, and in spite of all the brash pioneering atmosphere that still existed, even a child could sense the antiquity of it. We had also strong family traditions; we couldn't escape them, caught as we were between the horns of an Irish father and a mother of Scottish and Irish descent. It was simple, not rich, not centred at all on possessions or the search for status symbols. It seems to me that there were few *things* of any kind—furniture, of course, clothes and food, all the modest necessities. But of toys, and personal treasures, very few. If we wanted them we had to invent them, not by parental edict but from necessity. And there were few books: Dickens and Scott, of course, Shakespeare, Tennyson, and some of the Irish poets. I ate my way through these like a bookworm not because of any highbrow leanings but simply because they were books. But for the children, who as far as I can remember were seldom specially catered for, it was the grownup world that was important. There was a modest hodge-podge of good and bad: Beatrix Potter, simple—even babyish—comics, an odd book that nobody else seems ever to have heard of called *The Wallypug of Why*, Ethel Turner's stories, *Alice*, Kingsley's *Heroes*. Hawthorne I never met till I was grown up and it seems to me, as I read him now, though perhaps I wouldn't have thought so then, that he rather talks down to children, 'tinifying', if I may coin the word, and inventing dear little curly haired daughters to make people like Midas more acceptable. Kingsley doesn't do those things. He gives you the myths straight.

Then, too, we had something that no child could find today, not anywhere in the world. We had penny books. You could buy a fairy tale for a penny—that's how their lore went into me. And just as good, perhaps even better at the age, you could buy a *Buffalo Bill*. I don't know whether anybody in this audience remembers such books? Indeed, not long ago—for it seemed so unlikely—I began to wonder whether I hadn't made them up. It was a great relief to me when Rosamond Lehmann, the novelist, assured me that I hadn't. 'Of *course* we had penny books,' she said, and we dreamed over them together. Oh, why didn't I keep them? What grownup, with no eye for the future, tossed the raggedy little morsels—as I myself have done since with many a child's tattered paper treasure—into a nearby dustbin? Last year, when I was in Toronto visiting the Osborne collection of children's books that goes back to the seventeenth century, I eagerly searched the glass cases. 'If only,' I said, quite by chance, 'I could see a penny book.' A conspiratorial, Guy Fawkes sort of look passed between the librarians, and one hurried away and quickly came back with something held secretively behind her. She put it on the case before me and there was a *Buffalo Bill*—almost, it seemed, the very one, in the faded blacks and blues and reds that I had so long remembered. On the back of the cover was the advertisement for the two-and-sixpenny alarm clock that I had saved up for long ago but never quite achieved. And there, also—much more important—was the air rifle for nineteen-and-elevenpence that would kill an elephant at five yards. Alas, I never got that, either. What would I have done with it if I had, you may ask. I never had a moment's doubt about what I was saving for. It was to slay the enemies of Ireland! The sorrows of the 'most distressful country' got into me very early—how could it help doing so with my father's nostalagia for it continually feeding the imagination? My body ran about in the southern sunlight but my inner world had subtler colours, the greys and snows of England where Little Joe swept all the crossings and the numberless greens of Ireland which seemed to me to be inhabited solely by poets plucking harps, heroes lordily cutting off each other's heads, and veiled ladies sitting on the ground keening.

I think, perhaps, if there was any special virtue in my upbringing, it lay in the fact that my parents, both of them, were very allusive talkers. Neither of them ever read anything that didn't very quickly come out in conversation and from there pass into the family idiom. If my father discovered a poem he liked, even a piece of doggerel, it would presently be, as it were, on the breakfast table. Many a phrase, as ordinary to me then as the daily porridge, began its life, as I later learned, as a quotation from a poem or snatch from a ballad. As an instance, my father, who was a great lover of horses—and tricky, dangerous horses at that—would call out, whenever he returned from riding or driving, 'Bonnie George Campbell is home!' And my mother from somewhere in the house would always answer 'Thank God!' But *who* has come home, I used to wonder, for my father was neither George nor Campbell. It was not until much later, when I began to read the Scottish ballads, that I understood. You remember it?

> *Booted and saddled*
> *And bridled rade he,*
> *To hame cam' his guid horse*
> *But never cam' he.*

For all Bonnie Georges that come safely home the Lord should, indeed, be praised.

'Oh, what can ail thee, knight-at-arms?' my mother would sometimes say to a weeping child. Who was this knight, I often wondered. And yet, when you come to think of it, all children are knights-at-arms at times, alone and palely loitering. It is then they need to be comforted. But sometimes my father would prevent that. 'No, no,' he would say, 'let her weep. You know we need the rain.' Thinking of this, with hindsight, I see how really antique that was, that we cannot really escape the myths, even if we wish to. You can call it, perhaps, sympathetic magic. And it is a fact that still, in countries suffering from drought, a cup of water is poured on the ground in the hope of bringing rain. In Sumeria, the oldest civilization the world knows, the rain god was invoked by the pouring of a cup of wine. I remembered this recently when a journalist, who had been talking to people in Ireland about the assassination of President Kennedy, told me that one old man said gravely, 'We cried the rain down for him that night.' What an epitaph! The rain cried down!

Then, too, there were maxims galore and proverbs and aphorisms. I was so often told—being a passionately lazy child—to 'Make an effort, Mrs Dombey', that I began to think that Dombey was one of my own names. How could I know it was out of Dickens?

Then there were other, closer, connections with myth. In those lucky days there was always help to be had in the house. Such people are wonderful meat for children. The life they live, from the child's point of view—because to him it is strange and unknown—seems to be filled with glamour that his own dailiness lacks. One of them—Bella, or was it Bertha?—had a parrot-headed umbrella. This fascinated me. On days out, it swung besides Bella's furbelows—she was far more elegant, I then thought, than my mother—and was carefully put away in tissue paper on her return, while she told us the always fantastic story of what she had done and seen. Well, she never *quite* told—she did more, she hinted. 'Ah,' she would say, looking like Cassandra, 'if you could know what's happened to me cousin's brother-in-law!' But all too often, when prayed to continue, she would assure us, looking doomed and splendid, that the story was really beyond all telling and not for the ears of children. Oh, those inadequate ears of children! We were left to wonder, always mythologically—had he perhaps been chained to the mast because of someone's siren voice? Was his liver being slowly eaten by a baldheaded local eagle? Whatever they were, the things she didn't tell, they were always larger than life. Once, however, she spoke plain. 'I saw Paddy Liston in the gutter,' she said, 'and him as drunk as an English duke!' Well, what a sight for the inward eye! It filled out imagination to such an extent that now I can never think of our poor, probably sober, dukes without seeing then en masse under tables, robed and crowned and in the last stages of alcoholic dissolution. We didn't, as you see, need television! In a world where there are few possessions, where nobody answers questions, where nobody explains—I say this with joy not sorrow!—children must build life for themselves. One child is forced this way, one another. I went into imagination and poetry—perhaps I should more modestly say versifying—and never with grownup approbation. Come to that, I never sought it.

'Hardly W. B. Yeats,' said my father once, when my mother showed him a scrap of mine. And remembering it now I feel bound to agree with him, though at the age of seven it would have been hard even for *Yeats* to be W. B. Yeats. My father, as you see, perhaps because he was so far away from her, was in love with Cathleen ni Houlihan. Nothing that Ireland did was wrong, nothing that other countries did was completely right. Even his maxims came from Ireland. 'Never put a baby in a drawer', was one of them. But who would ever do such a thing? Even if he saw a doll in a drawer, he would pluck it out, saying 'Remember Parnell!' We had never even *heard* of Parnell, and I had to wait to make the connection till I read a life of him a few years ago. Soon after he was born his mother, called away on some pretext, put him down quickly and came back to discover that her baby had disappeared. She looked everywhere, servants searched the house, gardeners rummaged in the shrubberies—no sign of Charles Stewart Parnell. I hope I'm not inventing it, but I think the police, too, were sent for. And while they were once more searching the nursery a mewling little sound came from the bureau. And there was Charles Stewart, six weeks old and at his last gasp because his mother, absent-mindedly dumping him into a open drawer had, also absent-mindedly, shut it! I am sure my father knew this story. Where else could the maxim have come from?

So you see, I was drenched in the Celtic twilight before I ever came to it. Indeed I only came to it when it was over and had practically turned into night. I had dreamed of it all my life, and although my father was long dead, I had to test what my childhood had taught me. So the first thing I did on arriving in England was to send a piece of writing to Æ (George Russell), who was then editor of *The Irish Statesman*. With all the hauteur of youth I deliberately sent no covering letter, just a stamped addressed envelope for return. And sure enough the stamped envelope came back, as I had fully expected it to do, but inside —instead of my manuscript—was a cheque for three guineas and a letter from Æ. It said 'If you have any more, please let me see them and if you are ever in Ireland let us meet.' So, you see, even if I hadn't been already going to Ireland I would have been off on the next train.

That was how I came under the wing of Æ and got to know Yeats and the gifted people in their circle, all of whom cheerfully licked me into shape like a set of mother cats with a kitten. As you can imagine, this was blessing and far beyond my deserving. But I was not the only kitten; no young person was ever sent empty away, the riches were poured out upon all. It was strong meat, this first introduction to my father's country, among the poets and the makers of history. Perhaps it was just as well that my first contact with my Irish relatives should take me down several pegs. I needed it. They, I discovered, were not all in love with Cathleen ni Houlihan. Living cheek by jowl with her, they saw her without any trappings. Irish to the marrow, full of local lore and story, lovers of horses and the countryside, they weren't at all sure that life depended on poetry and they took the Celtic Renaissance with more than a grain of salt. 'I don't like you gallivanting around with men who see fairies,' said one. 'And the thought of you, a young girl, in Fleet Street, that terrible place—it's beyond thinking about!' From his description of it, I saw myself suffering nameless indignities at the hands of newspaper tycoons or being dragged up dark alleys by drunken reporters, and looked forward to it all with the greatest enthusiasm—though of course I didn't say so. 'And you'll meet such frightful people,' he said. 'There's one who lived down the road a way—old now, of course, but a terrible great boastful fellow. If you meet him, be courteous, but do not pursue the acquaintance. His name is Shaw, George Bernard Shaw.'

Gradually I learned to dissemble my enthusiasm for all that the elderly relatives of my father's generation found so reprehensible. One of them even remarked approvingly, 'You're not nearly so mad as you used to be.' Yet he was the one who, on his death-bed, hearing his wife asking the doctor if he was likely to last till next morning, remarked sardonically, 'I don't need to. I've seen plenty of mornings. All I want to know is, will I live to hear the result of the boat race?' Among last words this spartan, if eccentric, phrase deserves, I think, a place.

Not so mad as I used to be? Little did he know! It was coming back from visiting him that one of what he would have called my maddest moments occurred. I knew that on the way back to Dublin the train would pass Lough Gill. And I remembered that in Lough Gill lay Yeats's Lake Isle of Innisfree. So I leapt from the carriage and charged a boatman on the lapping shore to take me there.

'Ach, ther's no such place,' he said.

'Oh, but there is, I assure you. W. B. Yeats wrote about it.'

'And who would he be?'

I told him.

'Ah, I know them, those poets, always stravaiging through their minds, inventing outlandish things. *We* call it Rat Island!'

Rat Island! Well!

So we set out, under grey hovering clouds, with me in the bows and a young priest, who suddenly arose out of the earth, it seemed, joining us in the stern. At last, after a rough passage, there was Innisfree. No hive for the honeybee and no log cabin, but of course I hadn't expected them. They were only in the bee-loud glade of Yeats's stravaiging mind. But the whole island was covered with rowan trees, wearing their red berries like jewels, and the thought suddenly came to me—a most disastrous one, as it turned out—'I'll take back some branches to the poet.' In no time, for the island is diminutive, I had broken off pretty nearly every branch from the rowans and was staggering with them towards the boat. By now a strong wind had sprung up and the rain was falling and the lake was wild. Those Irish loughs beat up into a great sea very quickly. As we embarked, the waves seemed as high as the Statue of Liberty and I wished I'd had more swimming practice. Then I noticed, between one trough and the next, that the priest, pale as paper, was telling his beads with one hand and with the other plucking off my rowan berries and dropping them into the water. 'Ah, Father,' said the boatman, pulling stertorously on the oars, 'it's not the weight of a berry of two that will save us now.' He gave me a reflective glance and I got the idea, remembering that in times of shipwreck women are notoriously unlucky, that he was planning to throw me overboard, if the worse came to worst. I wished *I* had a string of beads! However, perhaps because of the priest's prayers, we came at last safely to shore. I hurried through the rain with my burden and took the next train for Dublin. The other passengers edged away from my streaming garments as though I were some sort of ancient mariner. I should never have started this, I knew, but there is an unfortunate streak of obstinacy in me that would not let me stop. From Dublin station, through curtains of cloud—taxis did not exist for me in those days—I carried the great branches to Yeats's house in Merrion Square and stood there, with my hair like rats' tails, my tattered branches equally ratlike, looking like Birnam come to Dunsinane and wishing I was dead. I prayed, as I rang the bell, that Yeats would not open the door himself, but my prayer went unheard.

For an articulate man to be struck dumb is, you can imagine, rare. But struck dumb he was at the sight of me. In shame, I heard him cry a name into the dark beyond of the house and saw him hurriedly escape upstairs. Then the name came forward in human shape and took me gently, as though I were ill or lost or witless, down to the basement kitchen. There I was warmed and dried and given cocoa; the dreadful branches were taken away. I felt like someone who had died and was now contentedly on the other side, certain that nothing more could happen. In this dreamlike state, I was gathering myself to go—out the back way if possible—never to be seen again. But a maid came bustling kindly in and said—as though to someone still alive!—'The master will see you now.' I was horrified. This was the last straw. 'What for?' I wanted to know. 'Ah, then, you'll see. He has his ways.'

And so, up the stairs—or the seven-storey mountain—I went, and there he was in his room with the blue curtains.

'My canary has laid an egg!' he said and joyously led me to

the cages by the window. From there we went round the room together, I getting better every minute and he telling me which of his books he liked and how, when he got an idea for a poem —there was a long momentous pause here: he was always the bard, always filling the role of poet, not play-acting but knowing well the role's requirements and giving them their due. He never came into a room, he *entered* it; walking around his study was a ceremonial peregrination, wonderful to witness. 'When I get an idea for a poem,' he went on, oracularly, 'I take down one of my own books and read it and then I go on from there.' Moses explaining his tablets couldn't have moved me more. And so, serenely, we came to the end of the pilgrimage and I was just about to bid him good-bye, when I noticed on his desk a vase of water and in it one sprig of fruiting rowan. I glanced at him distrustfully. 'Was he teaching me a lesson?' I wondered, for at that age one cannot accept to be taught. But he wasn't; I knew it by the look on his face. He would do nothing so banal. He was not trying to enlighten me, and so I was enlightened and found a connection in the process. It needed only a sprig, said the lesson. And I learned, also, something about writing. The secret is to say less than you need. You don't want a forest, a leaf will do.

Next day, when I was lunching with Æ, he said to me, 'Yeats was very touched that you brought him a sprig of rowan from Innisfree.' So I had to tell him the whole story. You couldn't be untruthful with Æ. 'I hope,' he said slyly, 'when you go to Dunfanaghay'—his own favourite part of Ireland—'you won't cut down all the willows for me. What about the tree spirits? Remember the dryads!' Dryads! I'd grown up on a diet of mythology and on Innisfree I'd forgotten it all. It was Æ who had to remind me, Æ whose thought was crystal-clear and hard—and still had room for dryads. These men—he, Yeats, James Stephens, and the rest—had aristocratic minds. For them, the world was not fragmented. An idea did not suddenly grow, like Topsy, all alone and separate. For them, all things had antecedents, and long family trees. They saw nothing shameful or silly in myths and fairy stories, nor did they shovel them out of sight in some cupboard marked 'Only for Children'. They were always willing to concede that there were more things in heaven and earth than philosophy dreamed of. They allowed for the unknown. And, as you can imagine, I took great heart from this.

It was Æ who showed me how to look at and learn from one's own writing. 'Popkins,' he said once—he always called her just plain Popkins, whether deliberately mistaking the name or not, I never knew, his humour was always subtle—'Popkins, had she lived in another age, in the old times to which she certainly belongs, would undoubtedly have had long golden tresses, a wreath of flowers in one hand, and perhaps a spear in the other. Her eyes would have been like the sea, her nose comely, and on her feet winged sandals. But, this being Kali Yuga, as the Hindus call it—in our terms, the Iron Age—she comes in the habiliments most suited to it.'

Well, golden tresses and all that pretty paraphernalia didn't interest me; she could only be as she *was*. But that Æ could really know so much about it astonished me, that he should guess at her antecedents and genealogy when I hadn't thought of them myself—it put me on my mettle. I began to *read* the book. But it was only after many years that I realized what he meant, that she had come out of the same world as the fairy tales.

My childish love for the tales had continued in increase in me —Tolkien says somewhere that if you are natively attached to the fairy tales (lots of people are not and there's no blame in that), that habit grows on you as you grow older. And it has certainly grown on me. 'Only connect' comes strongly into this. Not long ago I read in the *New York Times* about how the eels from America and Europe make their way to the Sargasso Sea to mate and lay their eggs, the journey for American eels taking one year, for Europeans two. Afterwards, they make their long way back to their respective homes and apparently feel, it was worth it. Well, for me the tales are a sort of Sargasso Sea and I am a kind of eel. And all these years of pondering on the fairy tale, first of all for love of it—because to learn about anything, it seems to me, you have to love it first—and later because I became enthralled by it, all this pondering has led me to believe that the true fairy tales (I'm not talking now about invented ones) come straight out of myth; they are, as it were, miniscule reaffirmations of myth, or perhaps the myth made accessible to the local folky mind. In the nineteenth century, as you know, Andrew Lang and all his fellow pundits treated them as the meanderings of the primitive intelligence—and therefore, apparently, suitable for children! Then the anthropologists had a go at them and later they descended, if I may so put it, to the psychoanalysts. But none of these seem to have been able to exhaust their meaning; there is still plenty left. They're like the magic pitcher in the Greek myth of Baucis and Philemon— you remember it retold in Hawthorne?—no matter how much milk you poured out, it was still full to the brim. This, of course, is where Jack's magic purse comes from; whenever you take out the last coin there is always another there.

Of course, you may ask—indeed, people are always asking— who invented the myths? And do you think they are true? Well, true? What is true? As far as I am concerned it doesn't matter tuppence if the incidents in the myths never happened. That does not make them any less true, for, indeed, in one way or another, they're happening all the time. You only have to open a newspaper to find them crowding into it. Life itself continually re-enacts them. Not long ago, staying with friends in Virginia, I watched from the terrace as two little girls of six and four performed the rite of burial over a dead bird. I guessed that they did not want to touch it, but they gathered all their grandfather's flowers and covered the body with them. Over these they laid branches and set a fence of sticks around them. Then they stood up and began to dance, not wildly, not gaily, not childishly, but formally, with measured steps. After that they knelt down, one on either side of the grave—were they praying? I couldn't see—and then they leaned across the sticks and gravely embraced each other. They had never been to church or a funeral, never before seen anything dead, knew nothing about the rite they were enacting out of ancestral memory, and the whole performance was true. I don't insist that you make anything out of it, but it meant something to me—the assurance that the myths and rites run around in our blood; that when old drums beat we stamp our feet, if only metaphorically. Time and the past are getting at us. The Australian aborigines have a word for this. To any happening further back than a grandmother their memories cannot go, any event further forward than a grandson, they cannot pretend to envisage. Beyond these times, when knowing is relatively possible, they can only reach by speaking of what lies there as the Dreaming. 'It is gone into Dreaming,' they say of the past. 'It will come in the Dreaming,' they say of the future.

There is a wonderful Japanese phrase, used as a Zen koan, which says, 'Not created but summoned'. It seems to me that this is all that can be said of the myths, 'They are in the Dreaming. They are not created but summoned.' But it is the fairy tale, not the myth that is really my province. One might say that fairy tales are the myths fallen into time and locality. For instance, if this glass of water is myth and I drink it, the last drop—or the lees of the wine—is the fairy tale. The drop is the same stuff, all the essentials are there; it is small, but perfect. Not minimized, not to be made digestible for children. I think it is more and more realized that the fairy tales are not entertainments for children at all. In their primal state, that is. They've been bowdlerized and had the essentials removed in order not to frighten—but to my mind it is better not to tell them at all than to take out all the vital organs and leave only the skin. And what *isn't* frightening, after all? What *doesn't* carry a stern lesson? Even the nursery rhymes present us with very difficult truths. And they, too, like the fairy tales, have long family trees, though it would not be easy, I admit, to prove it legally. Take Humpty Dumpty. All the King's horses and all the king's men couldn't put him together again. That some things are broken irrevocably, never to be whole again, is a hard truth and this is a good way of teaching it. Away back in Egypt, the myth was telling the same thing. You remember how, when the body of Osiris was cut up and scattered, his sister-wife Isis searched the world for the fourteen pieces, trying to re-member him and always unable to recover the fourteenth. I'm not trying here to suggest that whoever wrote 'Humpty Dumpty' had Isis and Osiris in mind. Of course not. I merely make the connection between them. And what about the cow that jumped over the moon? In Egypt the sky was always thought of as a cow, her body arching over the earth and her four legs standing firmly upon it. Again, it is I who make the link, not the writer of the rhyme. 'How many miles to Babylon?' What is that telling us, I wonder, with its three score and ten, the life of man? There is a gloss upon this rhyme that makes it perhaps a little clearer.

> *How many miles to Babylon?*
> *If it's three score and ten*
> *Bury me under the cold gravestone*
> *For my time is come, but make no moan,*
> *I shall be back by candle-light—*
> > *Many times again!*

You may think this is hocus-pocus and mumbo-jumbo—and well it may be, except to me—but if you look in the Oxford dictionary, you will find that hocus-pocus itself derives from *hoc est corpus* —and we are, after all, talking here about the body, if I may so put it, of an idea. Mumbo-jumbo has, alas, no known derivation. It is a figure supposed to have been invented by African chiefs in order to keep their wives properly disciplined and to give them a sense of awe. As for fee fi fo fum, you must go back to ancient Greece for that. It was the great incantation of the Erinyes, the triple furies born from the drops of blood of Cronus; and the old world rang with it as they pursued their prey. What a long and circuitous way it took before it found a home in our western nurseries!

You may, of course, feel that this is drawing a long bow. But, as I see it, what is a long bow for but to be drawn? And our phrase 'the long bow' itself comes from the great bow of Philoctetes, one of the Argonauts, who inherited it from Hercules. A man came to be a hero inwardly and outwardly to be able to draw that bow.

Or it may be that you will categorize all this as 'old wives' tales'. But I am one who believes in old wives' tales and that it is the proper function of old wives to tell tales. Old wives have the best stories in the world, and long memories. Why should we treat them with contempt? The tales have to be told in order that we may understand that in the long run, whatever it may be, every man must become the hero of his own story; his own fairy tale, if you like, a real fairy tale. Hans Andersen for me, in spite of the fact that he often used old material, is an inventor of fairy tales; so is Oscar Wilde. Their tales have an element of nostalgia in them, a devitalizing element that the true tale never has. Perhaps those that most clearly derive from myth, those that clearly show their antecedents, are the Greek stories, the Norse tales, and Grimms'. These are old trees, rooted in the folk, full of meaning and ritual; they retell the myths in terms that can be understood by unlettered people. For originally they were for the listener rather than the reader; they came long before books. Every one of these tales, it seems to me, is asking something of us, telling us something about life. Of course I am now on my hobby-horse and anyone who wishes may get up and shoot at me or at any rate ask a question. I am not here to stand and assert but to share my questioning with you.

Doesn't it seem to you, too, that there is more in the tales than meets the eye? Think of all those stories of the three brothers who go off in search of various treasures. As a child, naturally, I thought of them as separate entities—the eldest so handsome, always delayed at the crossroads, or prevented from going farther because of some temptation. He's handsome and brave, and relying on this, he assures himself that when the time comes, he'll find the treasure. Then the second, sure of his cleverness, a cleverness that proves to be groundless, also fails in the quest. Lastly, the third brother sets out, realizing his ignorance, knowing himself a simpleton. And so he is. Simple and humble, willing to accept help from anyone who will give it. You'll remember the story of 'Puddocky', a prime example of this. I always loved that youngest son. Nowadays, however, I think of the brothers, not as single adventurers, but as three stages of one man. In the beginning he sets out bravely, young and handsome, and quickly gets to the end of that; but 'I'm still clever,' he thinks to himself; yet soon he finds even that's not true. He ends by knowing he knows nothing. And once he knows nothing he begins to know something, and from there it is really only a step to happy ever after.

The fairy tales also tell us a great deal about women—or perhaps about woman and her role in life, the triple role of maiden, mother, and crone. Each one of us, of course, begins as a maiden, and whether she becomes a physical mother or not makes no difference, the role of mother is the next step, the flowering of the bud. Last of all comes the grandmother—again, not the physical grandmother, but the stage where the flower withers into seed pod. To become a crone, it seems to me, is the last great hope of woman, supremely worth achieving. An old woman who remembers, who has gathered up all the threads of life and sits by the fire with her hands in her lap—not doing anything any more—what a marvellous thing! This is what it is to become wise. There you sit in your rocking-chair as in the fairy tales—I hope I shall, anyway—aware of all you have learned and garnered and having it available in case the young ones want it. You will not force it on them, but simply tell it.

That's what the crones—all those good and bad fairies—are doing in the tales.

Of course, it is not always easy to see the relation between the fairy tale and the myth. They do not *all* insist on telling you of their great-grandparents. But many of them have lineaments that loudly proclaim their breeding. Cinderella, for instance, whose story is so ancient that she is found in one guise or another in practically every mythology known to man. She has been grossly ill-treated, however, by writers of pantomime and by illustrators who retell the tales in terms of their own illustrations. Chop off a nose or leg, what does it matter? All tellers of the Cinderella story, ever since Perrault himself retold it, make the mistake of assuming that it is because she wishes that she goes to the ball. If that were so, wouldn't we all be married to princes? No, the wishing has much more behind it; it must be so if the happy ending is to be achieved. Grimms' comes near to the true theme. There, it is not because she wishes but because she has performed the necessary rites at her mother's grave, and because, above all, she has accepted her fate, that she meets the little benevolent bird who gives her the golden gown and all the magnificent rest. And then, the story has so many sisters. There is a book—the author's name is Cox—which has over 300 versions of the Cinderella story. But I like to make my own connections. Would you not say she was the girl in 'King Cophetua and the Beggar Maid'? Isn't she, as near as makes no matter, Patient Griselda? And who but Cinderella is Lear's Cordelia, with those two monstrous sisters? Going back to myth, you will find her in the garb of Sita, the prototype of all feminine virtue in the epic of the Ramayana, in India, which is as old as history.

And what about that recurrent theme where a character in the story agrees—for a price—to give the villain the first thing that runs to greet him on his return home? It's a wonderful story. You find it in 'The King of the Golden Mountain' and 'The Singing, Soaring Lark', and it goes back to Methuselah—

or at any rate the Old Testament, in the story of Jephthah's daughter. None of the true stories was born yesterday; they all come from far and have a long way yet to go. One that was dear to me as a child—I still think it most beautiful, even though others protest that it is brutal and bloody—was 'The Juniper Tree'. There is a wicked stepmother, of course, who, when the little stepson bends down to get an apple from a chest, drops the lid and cuts his head off. Even now I never bend over a chest without making quite sure that the top won't fall on me. And so the story goes from bad to worse. Sitting the body at the table, with the head balanced on top of it, she orders the little sister to call her brother to supper. Naturally, he does not answer, so the little sister gives him a shake and down falls the severed head. And now worse hurries on to worst. The stepmother cooks the child in a stew and gives this meal to the father when he comes home from work. 'Ah,' he exclaims, 'how truly delicious. I feel as though it were all mine.' As, indeed, of course, it is. Eventually the little watching bird puts all to rights, the little sister is freed of her supposed guilt, the little boy comes alive again, the stepmother—and serve her right!—is finished off with a millstone. It sounds, I admit, like a mess of horrors. But it never bothered me at all. Knowing the power of the little bird I never doubted that the boy would be safe. If, indeed, the father ate him, it was inevitable, even natural, that the boy would somehow, and in good time, return to his proper shape. After all, hadn't Cronus, the father of the gods, eaten up his children? Son after son was born to Rhea and each time Cronus said 'He'll supplant me!' and promptly swallowed him down. But with her last child Rhea grew cunning, swaddled a stone and gave it to her husband who, feeling—though erroneously—that it was all his, let it go the way of the others. Thus Zeus was saved to become king of the gods. And, once on his throne, he himself performed the same act—or an aspect of it—when he took his unborn son Dionysus into his own thigh—his mother having been burnt to death—and at the full period of nine months brought him forth, unharmed and perfect.

And then there are the countless stories that warn against trying to see too much; of the demon lover who persuades the maiden to marry him on the understanding that she must never, once the night falls, attempt to look at him. And always the maiden—who could help it?—always the maiden fails. Either she is persuaded by her family as—again!—in the 'Singing Soaring Lark' and 'Melusine', or she is overcome by curiosity, as in 'Cupid and Psyche'. And as a result he disappears or has to go through grave vicissitudes before he comes to himself once more. This theme comes directly out of myth; it goes back to the farthest limits of time when Semele, not knowing that her bridegroom was divine, yet suspecting it, begs him to grant her one boon, that she may see him in all his splendour. Reluctantly Zeus unveils himself and she, unable to endure the lightning, is herself turned to ash. The story is a warning, repeated down the centuries, through myth, folk and fairy tale, that it is dangerous to look upon the face of the god. Seek him rather with the inward eye.

'Rumpelstiltskin' was another of my favourites, for its meaning lay very close to me. Everyone knows the story of how the miller's daughter, in order to become a queen, promises the little old man her first child if he will spin her straw into gold. Of course he does it. It is no problem. To him they are one and the same. But when the child is born she cannot bear to part with it and he agrees to let her off if she can discover his name. So for three days she tries this and she tries that, always unsuccessfully, and he warns her that when tomorrow comes he will take the child away. In despair, she sends riders far and wide, east of the sun and west of the moon. Only one comes back with a clue. 'In the land where the wolf and the hare say good night to each other, I came upon an old man jumping up and down and singing, "My name is Rumpelstiltskin." ' And so, the next day, making a great pretence of it, she asks the old man 'Is it Tom, is it Dick, is it Harry?' 'No!' 'Then is it Rumpelstiltskin?' And with that he shrieks a great 'Yes!' and stamps his foot into the earth and tears himself in two. His name is known, therefore he is finished. This role has been played out.

This idea of the secrecy of the name, the taboo against making it known, goes back to man's very early days, to the time, perhaps, when he had no name. During the war I spent two summers with the Navaho Indians, and when they gave me an Indian name they warned me that it would be bad luck both for me and the tribe if I ever disclosed it to anyone. And I never have. For one thing, I do not want to receive or give bad luck, and for another I have a strong atavistic feeling—one, I think, that is strongly shared by unlettered people all over the world—that to disclose one's name, or take another's before the time for it is ripe—well, it's dangerous. I tremble inwardly and withdraw when my Christian name is seized before I have given it, and I have the same hesitancy about using that of another person. An Indian—or a gypsy—would understand this very well. It is very ancient taboo and I relate it—though I don't suggest that anyone else relate it—to the earliest times when men built altars 'To the Unknown God'. If I were ever to build an altar, I would put that inscription above it.

In making these connections, I do not want to assert or impose. But, in fact, all things are separate and fragmentary until man himself connects them, sometimes wrongly and sometimes rightly. As far as I am concerned, it is all a matter of hint and suggestion, something seen at the corner of the eye and linked with another thing, equally fleeting. You remember Walt Whitman's poem, 'On the Beach at Night'. 'I give you the first suggestion, the problem, the indirection.' Isn't that wonderful? Turn your back on it and you'll find it! It's like Shakespeare's 'By indirection find direction out.' And with these quotations I connect Swift's dictum, 'Vision is the art of seeing things invisible.' Doesn't this relate to the unknown name?

But now let me make one last link. I was rereading recently how Aeneas came to Campania—which is now Naples—seeking some means of getting into contact with the ghost of his father, Anchises. First, for piety, he prays at the temple of Apollo, begging the god to inspire the Cumean Sybil, whose cave is at hand, to help him on his way to the underworld. Nearby is the great forest where lies the terrible Lake of Avernus over which no bird flies, and at the edge of that is the rift between the great rocks that guard the way to the realm of Pluto. You know the story. She tells him to break from one tree in the forest a small golden branch. With that in his hand he will be able to descend into the depths. So, holding the branch before him as an amulet, he begins the dreadful journey. Of course, the whole of Frazer's *Golden Bough* is about this branch and many of the fairy stories repeat it; 'The Shoes That Were Danced to Pieces', for instance, where the twelve princesses are followed each night to the underworld by a soldier who breaks off a little golden branch to bring back as a sign that he has, indeed, been there. Not for nothing, I thought, as I read again of Aeneas, were those four sites so close together—the temple of Apollo, the cave of the Sybil, the Lake of Avernus, the Land of the Dead. It is inevitable that they should touch and interpenetrate each other, not only in myth, but in life. Life, in a sense, *is* myth, one might say; the one is a part of the other. In both of them, the good and the bad, the dangerous and the safe, live very close together. And I remembered, as I thought about this, how Aeneas had begged the Sybil to speak her oracle in words and not, as was her usual practice, to write it on leaves that would blow away. That struck a chord in me, for I knew a story where this had actually happened. In this story the wind blows leaves into the hands of two children. And on each leaf a message is written. One says 'Come' and the other 'Tonight'. Now the story I'm talking about is 'Halloween'. It is in *Mary Poppins in the Park*. And there is the Sybil obeying Aeneas by writing the oracle down on leaves!

And I thought I had invented it! There's a poem by Rupert Brooke, one verse of which says:

There's wisdom in women, of more than they have known,
And thoughts go blowing through them, are wiser than their own.

Truly, I had far wiser thoughts than my own when I wrote that story. You may remember—though why should you?—that it is about a party in the park where all the shadows are free. They go out to enjoy themselves and leave their owners at home. The only one whose shadow refuses to go without her is—guess!—Mary Poppins.

I find another connection here in the fact that tonight happens to be Halloween. In ancient times this used to be the festival of the dead. I think it was one of the Popes, Boniface IV, perhaps, in the seventh century, who decided to do away with all the pagan saturnalia and turn it from what it so significantly was, into a commemoration of the saints and martyrs. But in spite of him the myth never lost its mystery: men needed the festival rites for the dead; they needed to find a way out of grieving that would ease their fear that the spirits of the dead might come back to earth and haunt them. They put on masks and disguised their faces, wrapping themselves, to cheat the ghosts, in the garments of black that became for us, their late descendants, simply mourning clothes. The wake that the Irish hold for the dead is part of this ancient saturnalia. It gives an opportunity and a justification for the living to turn their faces again to life; it also provides a propitious moment, a ritual moment one could say, a kind of crack through which some element of the unknown can be brought into the known.

Is anyone thinking of saints and martyrs on this Halloween, I wonder? And who knows, when they leave this hall, that their shadows will be with them? For me the fairy tales are abroad tonight. Good fairies and demons, Beauty and the Beast—they are all knocking at the doors, rattling their money boxes and holding out grubby hands for candy. It's a pagan festival still, be sure, swinging between trick and treat, angel and devil, yes and no. It is a night of ghosts and shadows, a night that links the past and the present, a night perhaps when that crack between known and unknown could open, and we could believe the old Greek poet, Aratus, when he declared: 'Full of Zeus are the cities, full of Zeus are the harbours, full of Zeus are all the ways of men.'

If it was true then, it is true always; time cannot change the timeless. It could be—could it not?—*this* city, full of lighted, grinning pumpkin faces; *that* harbour out on Chesapeake Bay; *we* men—if we could only connect. What do you think?

[1967]

On three ways of writing for children

C. S. LEWIS

I think there are three ways in which those who write for children may approach their work: two good ways and one that is generally a bad way.

I came to know of the bad way quite recently and from two unconscious witnesses. One was a lady who sent me the MS. of a story she had written in which a fairy placed at a child's disposal a wonderful gadget. I say 'gadget' because it was not a magic ring or hat or cloak or any such traditional matter. It was a machine, a thing of taps and handles and buttons you could press. You could press one and get an ice cream, another and get a live puppy, and so forth. I had to tell the author honestly that I didn't much care for that sort of thing. She replied, 'No more do I, it bores me to distraction. But it is what the modern child wants'. My other bit of evidence was this. In my own first story I had described at length what I thought was a rather fine high tea given by a hospitable faun to the little girl who was my heroine. A man who has children of his own said, 'Ah, I see how you got to that. If you want to please grown-up readers you give them sex, so you thought to yourself, "that won't do for children, what shall I give them instead? I know! The little blighters like plenty of good eating!" ' In reality, however, I myself like eating and drinking. I put in what I would have liked to read when I was a child and what I still like reading now that I am in my fifties.

The lady in my first example, and the married man in my second, both conceived writing for children as a special department of 'giving the public what it wants'. Children are, of course, a special public, and you find out what they want and give them that, however little you like it yourself.

The next way may seem at first to be very much the same, but I think the resemblance is superficial. This is the way of Lewis Carroll, Kenneth Grahame, and Tolkien. The printed story grows out of a story told to a particular child with the living voice and perhaps *ex tempore*. It resembles the first way because you are certainly trying to give that child what it wants. But then you are dealing with a concrete person, this child who, of course, differs from all other children. There is no question of 'children' conceived as a strange species whose habits you have 'made up' like an anthropologist or a commercial traveller. Nor, I suspect, would it be possible, thus face to face, to regale the child with things calculated to please it but regarded by yourself with indifference or contempt. The child, I am certain, would see through that. In any personal relation the two participants modify each other. You would become slightly different because you were talking to a child and the child would become slightly different because it was being talked to by an adult. A community, a composite personality, is created and out of that the story grows.

The third way, which is the only one I could ever use myself, consists in writing a children's story because a children's story is the best art-form for something you have to say: just as a composer might write a Dead March not because there was a public funeral in view but because certain musical ideas that had occurred to him went best into that form. This method could apply to other kinds of children's literature besides stories. I have been told that Arthur Mee never met a child and never wished to: it was, from his point of view, a bit of luck that boys liked reading what he liked writing. This anecdote may be untrue in fact but it illustrates my meaning.

Within the species 'children's story' the sub-species which happened to suit me is the fantasy or (in a loose sense of that word) the fairy tale. There are, of course, other sub-species. E. Nesbit's trilogy about the Bastable family is a very good specimen of another kind. It is a 'children's story' in the sense that children can and do read it, but it is also the only form in which E. Nesbit could have given us so much of the humours of childhood. It is true that the Bastable children appear, successfully treated from the adult point of view, in one of her grownup novels, but they appear only for a moment. I do not think she would have kept it up. Sentimentality is so apt to creep in if we write at length about children as seen by their elders. And the reality of childhood, as we all experienced it, creeps out. For we all remember that our childhood, as lived, was immeasurably different from what our elders saw. Hence Sir Michael Sadler, when I asked his opinion about a certain new experimental school, replied, 'I never give an opinion on any of those experiments till the children have grown up and can tell *us what really happened.*' Thus the Bastable trilogy, however improbable many of its episodes may be, provides even adults, in one sense, with more realistic reading about children than they could find in most books addressed to adults. But also, conversely, it enables the children who read it to do something much more mature than they realize. For the whole book is a character study of Oswald, an unconsciously satiric self-portrait, which every intelligent child can fully appreciate: but no child would sit down to read a character study in any other form. There is another way in which children's stories mediate this psychological interest, but I will reserve that for later treatment.

In this short glance at the Bastable trilogy I think we have stumbled on a principle. Where the children's story is simply the right form for what the author has to say, then of course readers who want to hear that will read the story or reread it at any age. I never met *The Wind in the Willows* or the Bastable books till I was in my late twenties, and I do not think I have enjoyed them any the less on that account. I am almost inclined to set it up as a canon that a children's story which is enjoyed only by children is a bad children's story. The good ones last. A waltz which you can like only when you are waltzing is a bad waltz.

This canon seems to me most obviously true of that particular type of children's story which is dearest to my own taste, the fantasy or fairy tale. Now the modern critical world uses 'adult' as a term of approval. It is hostile to what it calls 'nostalgia' and contemptuous of what it calls 'Peter Pantheism'. Hence a man who admits that dwarfs and giants and talking beasts and witches are still dear to him in his fifty-third year is now less likely to be praised for his perennial youth than scorned and pitied for arrested development. If I spend some little time defending myself against these charges, this is not so much because it matters greatly whether I am scorned and pitied as because the defence is germane to my whole view of the fairy tale and even of literature in general. My defence consists of three propositions.

1. I reply with a *tu quoque*. Critics who treat *adult* as a term of approval, instead of as a merely descriptive term, cannot be adult themselves. To be concerned about being grownup, to admire the grownup because it is grownup, to blush at the suspicion of being childish—these things are the marks of childhood and adolescence. And in childhood and adolescence they are, in moderation, healthy symptoms. Young things ought to want to grow. But to carry on into middle life or even into early manhood this concern about being adult is a mark of really arrested development. When I was ten, I read fairy tales in secret and would have been ashamed if I had been found doing so. Now that I am fifty I read them openly. When I became a man I put away childish things, including the fear of childishness and the desire to be very grownup.

2. The modern view seems to me to involve a false conception of growth. They accuse us of arrested development because we

have not lost a taste we had in childhood. But surely arrested development consists not in refusing to lose old things but in failing to add new things? I now like hock, which I am sure I should not have liked as a child. But I still like lemon-squash. I call this growth or development because I have been enriched: where I formerly had only one pleasure, I now have two. But if I had to lose the taste for lemon-squash before I acquired the taste for hock, that would not be growth but simple change. I now enjoy Tolstoy and Jane Austen and Trollope as well as fairy tales and I call that growth; if I had had to lose the fairy tales in order to acquire the novelists, I would not say that I had grown but only that I had changed. A tree grows because it adds rings; a train doesn't grow by leaving one station behind and puffing on to the next. In reality, the case is stronger and more complicated than this. I think my growth is just as apparent when I now read the fairy tales as when I read the novelists, for I now enjoy the fairy tales better than I did in childhood: being now able to put more in, of course I get more out. But I do not here stress that point. Even if it were merely a taste for grownup literature added to an unchanged taste for children's literature, addition would still be entitled to the name 'growth', and the process of merely dropping one parcel when you pick up another would not. It is, of course, true that the process of growing does, incidently and unfortunately, involve some more losses. But that is not the essence of growth, certainly not what makes growth admirable or desirable. If it were, if to drop parcels and to leave stations behind were the essence and virture of growth, why should we stop at the adult? Why should not *senile* be equally a term of approval? Why are we not to be congratulated on losing our teeth and hair? Some critics seem to confuse growth with the cost of growth and also to wish to make that costs far higher than, in nature, it need be.

3. The whole association of fairy tale and fantasy with childhood is local and accidental. I hope everyone has read Tolkien's

essay on fairy tales,[1] which is perhaps the most important contribution to the subject that anyone has yet made. If so, you will know already that, in most places and times, the fairy tale has not been specially made for, nor exclusively enjoyed by, children. It has gravitated to the nursery when it became unfashionable in literary circles, just as unfashionable furniture gravitated to the nursery in Victorian houses. In fact, many children do not like this kind of book, just as many children do not like horsehair sofas: and many adults do like it, just as many adults like rocking-chairs. And those who do like it, whether young or old, probably like it for the same reason. And none of us can say with any certainty what that reason is. The two theories which are most often in my mind are those of Tolkien and of Jung.

According to Tolkien the appeal of the fairy story lies in the fact that man there most fully exercises his function as a 'sub-creator'; not, as they love to say now, making a 'comment upon life' but making, so far as possible, a subordinate world of his own. Since, in Tolkien's view, this is one of man's proper functions, delight naturally arises whenever it is successfully performed. For Jung, fairy tale liberates the Archetypes which dwell in the collective unconscious, and when we read a good fairy tale we are obeying the old precept 'Know thyself'. I would venture to add to this my own theory, not indeed of the Kind as a whole, but of one feature in it: I mean, the presence of beings other than human which yet behave, in varying degrees, humanly—the giants and dwarfs and talking beasts. I believe these to be at least (for they may have many other sources of power and beauty) an admirable hieroglyphic which conveys psychology, types of character, more briefly than novelistic presentation and to readers whom novelistic presentation could not yet reach. Consider Mr Badger in *The Wind in the Willows*—that extraordinary amalgam of high rank, coarse manners, gruffness, shyness, and goodness. The child who has once met Mr Badger has

---

[1] [See pages 111 to 120 for a long extract from this essay.]

ever afterwards in its bones a knowledge of humanity and of English social history which it could not get in any other way.

Of course as all children's literature is not fantastic, so all fantastic books need not be children's books. It is still possible, even in an age so ferociously anti-romantic as our own, to write fantastic stories for adults—though you will usually need to have made a name in some more fashionable kind of literature before anyone will publish them. But there may be an author who at a particular moment finds not only fantasy but fantasy-for-children the exactly right form for what he wants to say. The distinction is a fine one. His fantasies for children and his fantasies for adults will have very much more in common with one another than either has with the ordinary novel or with what is sometimes called 'the novel of child life'. Indeed the same readers will probably read both his fantastic 'juveniles' and his fantastic stories for adults. For I need not remind such an audience as this that the neat sorting-out of books into age-groups, so dear to publishers, has only a very sketchy relation with the habits of any real readers. Those of us who are blamed when old for reading childish books were blamed when children for reading books too old for us. No reader worth his salt trots along in obedience to a time-table. The distinction then is a fine one; and I am not quite sure what made me, in a particular year of my life, feel that not only a fairy tale, but a fairy tale addressed to children, was exactly what I must write—or burst. Partly, I think that this form permits, or compels, you to leave out things I wanted to leave out. It compels you to throw all the force of the book into what was done and said. It checks what a kind but discerning critic called 'the expository demon' in me. It also imposes certain very fruitful necessities about length.

If I have allowed the fantastic type of children's story to run away with this discussion, that is because it is the kind I know and love best, not because I wish to condemn any other. But the patrons of the other kinds very frequently want to condemn it. About once every hundred years some wiseacre gets up and tries to banish the fairy tale. Perhaps I had better say a few words in its defence, as reading for children.

It is accused of giving a false impression of the world they live in. But I think no literature that children could read gives them less of a false impression. I think what profess to be realistic stories for children are far more likely to deceive them. I never expected the real world to be like the fairy tales. I think that I did expect school to be like the school stories. The fantasies did not deceive me: the school stories did. All stories in which children have adventures and successes which are possible, in the sense that they do not break the laws of nature, but almost infinitely improbable, are in more danger than the fairy tales of raising false expectations.

Almost the same answer serves for the popular charge of escapism, though here the question is not so simple. Do fairy tales teach children to retreat into a world of wish-fulfilment— 'fantasy' in the technical psychological sense of the word—instead of facing the problems of the real world? Now it is here that the problem becomes subtle. Let us again lay the fairy tale side by side with the school story or any other story which is labelled a 'Boy's Book' or a Girl's Book', as distinct from a 'Children's Book.' There is no doubt that both arouse, and imaginatively satisfy, wishes. We long to go through the looking-glass, to reach fairyland. We also long to be the immensely popular and successful schoolboy or schoolgirl, or the lucky boy or girl who discovers the spy's plot or rides the horse that none of the cowboys can manage. But the two longings are very different. The second, especially when directed on something so close as school life, is ravenous and deadly serious. Its fulfilment on the level of imagination is in very truth compensatory: we run to it from the disappointments and humiliations of the real world; it sends us back to the real world undivinely discontented. For it is all flattery to the ego. The pleasure consists in picturing oneself the object of admiration. The other longing, that for fairyland, is very different. In a sense a child does not long for fairyland as a boy longs to be the hero of the first eleven. Does anyone suppose that he really and prosaically longs for all the dangers and discomforts of a fairy tale?—really wants dragons in contemporary England? It is not so. It would be much truer to say that fairyland arouses a longing for he knows not what. It stirs and troubles him (to his lifelong enrichment) with the dim sense of something beyond his reach and, far from dulling or emptying the actual world, gives it a new dimension of depth. He does not despise real woods because he has read of enchanted woods: the reading makes all real woods a little enchanted. This is a special kind of longing. The boy reading the school story of the type I have in mind desires success and is unhappy (once the book is over) because he can't get it: the boy reading the fairy tale desires and is happy in the very fact of desiring. For his mind has not been concentrated on himself, as it often is in the more realistic story.

I do not mean that school stories for boys and girls ought not be written. I am only saying that they are far more liable to become 'fantasies' in the clinical sense than fantastic stories are. And this distinction holds for adult reading too. The dangerous fantasy is always superficially realistic. The real victim of wishful reverie does not batten on *The Odyssey, The Tempest*, or *The Worm Ouroboros*: he (or she) prefers stories about millionaires, irresistible beauties, posh hotels, palm beaches, and bedroom scenes—things that really might happen, that ought to happen, that would have happened if the reader had had a fair chance. For, as I say, there are two kinds of longing. The one is an *askesis*, a spiritual exercise, and the other is a disease.

A far more serious attack on the fairy tale as children's literature comes from those who do not wish children to be frightened. I suffered too much from night-fears myself in childhood to undervalue this objection. I would not wish to heat the fires of that private hell for any child. On the other hand, none of my fears came from fairy tales. Giant insects were my specialty, with ghosts a bad second. I suppose the ghosts came directly or indirectly from stories, though certainly not from fairy stories, but I don't think the insects did. I don't know anything my parents could have done or left undone which would have saved me from the pincers, mandibles, and eyes of those many-legged abominations. And that, as so many people have pointed out, is the difficulty. We do not know what will or will not frighten a child in this particular way. I say 'in this particular way' for we must here make a distinction. Those who say that children must not be frightened may mean two things. They may mean (1) that we must not do anything likely to give the child those haunting, disabling, pathological fears against which ordinary courage is helpless: in fact, *phobias*. His mind must, if possible, be kept clear of things he can't bear to think of. Or they may mean (2) that we must try to keep out of his mind the knowledge that he is born into a world of death, violence, wounds, adventure, heroism and cowardice, good and evil. If they mean the first I agree with them: but not if they mean the second. The second would indeed be to give children a false impression and feed them on escapism in the bad sense. There is something ludicrous in the idea of so educating a generation which is born to the Ogpu and the atomic bomb. Since it is so likely that they will meet cruel enemies, let them at least have heard of brave knights and heroic courage. Otherwise you are making their destiny not brighter but darker. Nor do most of us find that violence and bloodshed, in a story, produce any haunting dread in the minds of children. As far as that goes, I side impenitently with the human race against the modern reformer. Let there be wicked kings and beheadings, battles and dungeons, giants and dragons, and let villains be soundly killed at the end of the book. Nothing will persuade me that this causes an ordinary child any kind or degree of fear beyond what it wants, and needs, to feel. For, of course, it wants to be a little frightened.

The other fears—the phobias—are a different matter. I do not believe one can control them by literary means. We seem to bring them into the world with us ready made. No doubt the particular image on which the child's terror is fixed can sometimes be traced to a book. But is that the source, or only the occasion, of the fear? If he had been spared that image, would not some other, quite unpredictable by you, have had the same effect? Chesterton has told us of a boy who was more afraid of the Albert Memorial than anything else in the world. I know a man whose great childhood terror was the India paper edition of the *Encyclopaedia Britannica*—for a reason I defy you to guess. And I think it possible that by confining your child to blameless stories of child life in which nothing at all alarming ever happens, you would fail to banish the terrors, and would succeed in banishing all that can ennoble them or make them endurable. For in the fairy tales, side by side with the terrible figures, we find the immemorial comforters and protectors, the radiant ones: and the terrible figures are not merely terrible, but sublime. It would be nice if no little boy in bed, hearing, or thinking he hears, a sound, were ever at all frightened. But if he is going to be frightened, I think it better that he should think of giants and dragons than merely of burglars. And I think St George, or any bright champion in armour, is a better comfort than the idea of the police.

I will even go further. If I could have escaped all my own night-fears at the price of never having known 'faerie', would I now be the gainer by that bargain? I am not speaking carelessly. The fears were very bad. But I think the price would have been too high.

But I have strayed far from my theme. This has been inevitable for, of the three methods, I know by experience only the third. I hope my title did not lead anyone to think that I was conceited enough to give you advice on how to write a story for children. There were two very good reasons for not doing that. One is that many people have written very much better stories than I, and I would rather learn about the art than set up to teach it. The other is that, in a certain sense, I have never exactly 'made' a story. With me the process is much more like bird-watching than like either talking or building. I see pictures. Some of these pictures have a common flavour, almost a common smell, which groups them together. Keep quiet and watch and they will begin joining themselves up. If you were very lucky (I have never been as lucky as all that), a whole set might join themselves so consistently that there you had a complete story without doing anything yourself. But more often (in my experience always) there are gaps. Then at last you have to do some deliberate inventing, have to contrive reasons why these characters should be in these various places doing these various things. I have no idea whether this is the usual way of writing stories, still less whether it is the best. It is the only one I know: images always come first.

Before closing, I would like to return to what I said at the beginning. I rejected any approach which begins with the question 'What do modern children like?' I might be asked 'Do you equally reject the approach which begins with the question "What do modern children need?"—in other words, with the moral or didactic approach?' I think the answer is Yes. Not because I don't like stories to have a moral: certainly not because I think children dislike a moral. Rather because I feel sure that the question 'What do modern children need?' will not lead you to a good moral. If we ask that question we are assuming too superior an attitude. It would be better to ask 'What moral do I need?', for I think we can be sure that what does not concern us deeply will not deeply interest our readers, whatever their age. But it is better not to ask the question at all. Let the pictures tell you their own moral. For the moral inherent in them will rise from whatever spiritual roots you have succeeded in striking during the whole course of your life. But if they don't show you any moral, don't put one in. For the moral you put in is likely to be a platitude, or even a falsehood, skimmed from the surface of your consciousness. It is impertinent to offer the children that. For we have been told on high authority that in the moral sphere they are probably at least as wise as we. Anyone who *can* write a children's story without a moral, had better do so: that is, if he is going to write children's stories at all. The only moral that is of any value is that which arises inevitably from the whole cast of the author's mind.

Indeed everything in the story should arise from the whole cast of the author's mind. We must write for children out of those elements in our own imagination which we share with children: differing from our child readers not by any less, or less serious, interest in the things we handle, but by the fact that we have other interests which children would not share with us. The matter of our story should be a part of the habitual furniture of our minds. This, I fancy, has been so with all great writers for children, but it is not generally understood. A critic not long ago said in praise of a very serious fairy tale that the author's tongue 'never once got into his cheek'. But why on earth should it?—unless he had been eating a seed-cake. Nothing seems to me more fatal, for this art, than an idea that whatever we share with children is, in the privative sense, 'childish' and that whatever is childish is somehow comic. We must meet children as equals in that area of our nature where we are their equals. Our superiority consists partly in commanding other areas, and partly (which is more relevant) in the fact that we are better at telling stories than they are. The child as reader is neither to be patronized nor idolized: we talk to him as man to man. But the worst attitude of all would be the professional attitude which regards children in the lump as a sort of raw material which we have to handle. We must of course try to do them no harm: we may, under the Omnipotence, sometimes dare to hope that we may do them good. But only such good as involves treating them with respect. We must not imagine that we are Providence or Destiny. I will not say that a good story for children could never be written by someone in the Ministry of Education, for all things are possible. But I should lay very long odds against it.

Once in a hotel dining-room I said, rather too loudly, 'I loathe prunes.' 'So do I' came an unexpected six-year-old voice from another table. Sympathy was instantaneous. Neither of us thought it funny. We both knew that prunes are far too nasty to be funny. That is the proper meeting between man and child as independent personalities. Of the far higher and more difficult relations between child and parent or child and teacher, I say nothing. An author, as a mere author, is outside all that. He is not even an uncle. He is a freeman and an equal, like the postman, the butcher, and the dog next door.

[1952]

The animal story: a challenge in technique

WILLIAM H. MAGEE

In art realistic animals are as old as the caveman drawing on his stone wall, but in the novel and short story they are as new as the theory of evolution. A direct if minor effect on literature of the controversy over that theory appeared in the sudden creation of animal heroes in the closing quarters of the nineteenth century. Although a consciousness of such an inspiration would probably have shocked some of the first modern writers with four-legged heroes, particularly moralists who made a cause of the prevention of cruelty to animals, Sir Charles G. D. Roberts made the connection. He also described the first consistently realistic animals in literature, thus giving Canada a founding influence in this development in modern literature.

Ancient and medieval writers who had used animals in fiction usually had had purposes which discouraged or even prevented realistic characterization. Primitive storytellers used animals as antagonists of human heroes to depict man's struggle for survival against nature. Those animals might possibly have been created as true to life as had those in the cave drawings, but in fact the temptation of making them almost human antagonists, of having them think human thoughts and speak, beguiled the storytellers away from the simple truth of the cave artistry. In contrast, didactic stories called for animal figures that were strictly human except for some single superficial characteristic. For classical writers Aesop's *Fables* provided virtually the archetype for animal heroes. Likewise medieval writers used animals to point up human morals for human readers, in allegory as well as in fable. Bestiaries perhaps partook no more of the fantastic than did most medieval literature, but the animal characters were easier to pervert than the human ones. Medieval romance encouraged fantasy still more, with dreamland dragons and questing beasts. None of these classical or medieval literary purposes encouraged the depicting of animals as characters leading independent lives.

Renaissance and neo-classical writers showed much less interest in using animals as characters. For although their object in writing remained essentially didactic, the new spirit of representational art controlled their technique. In their man-oriented world, too, new literary uses for animals were not likely to develop, and even stories in earlier forms touched on the animal characters more lightly. Romances used considerably fewer animals, pastoral heroes and heroines ignored their sheep, and La Fontaine forced a satire of his human contemporaries on animals in the Aesop tradition. Indeed the customary bent towards satire made neo-classical animals still less realistic, for they were required to expose this or that human foible. Perhaps it was unconscious remorse for this falsification, together with increased knowledge of geography, that sent the fanciful beasts migrating to the then much smaller unknown world. Although the temper of the times encouraged such writers as Swift to make such creatures conform to common sense, with the houyhnhnms a didactic aim still thwarts realism in the characterization of animals. Before animals could again come into general use in literature, two changes had to occur. First, the nonhuman heroes had to live for their own ends, not just to echo the concerns of human readers. Second, some new techniques had to be found for drawing in words a truly representational character study of animals. Neither their primitive use as daily antagonists of man nor their medieval use for allegory or romance appealed to writers in the early nineteenth century, and no new one developed. Only single lesser writers who watched them with objective interest, such as Mrs Catharine Parr Traill, or who hunted, like Robert Surtees, thought of building simple stories around them.

The widespread use of animals in modern literature dates from the last quarter of the nineteenth century. In 1877 Anna Sewell began the vogue with *Black Beauty*, the best selling horse story which pleaded for more humane treatment of domestic animals. Through her philanthropy Miss Sewell had hit on a purpose for her story which distinguishes animal characters from man, instead of stressing similarities. The artistic appeal for human readers is genuinely indirect, a good will based perhaps on the misery and cruelty suffered by all living creatures and caused by bad men. For the first time in literary history it was no longer desirable or even artistically sensible to draw manlike animals. Any failure to make the domestic animals credible on the part of Anna Sewell or her followers is the result only of failures in technique.

Pets can beguile readers into tears even more readily than horses can, and so it is that the Canadian contribution to Anna Sewell's type of animal story is even more sentimental than *Black Beauty*. When Margaret Marshall Saunders wrote her famous dog story, *Beautiful Joe* (1894), she won a competition for a companion piece to *Black Beauty*. Again the animal is at the centre of the scene, and again the author stresses needs peculiar to it rather than common with man. Indeed *Beautiful Joe* seems for chapter at a time to be less a story than a manual in the care of animals. Chapter headings read 'Training a Puppy', Goldfish and Canaries', 'A Neglected Stable', 'A Talk about Sheep'; but these at least avoid the sentimentality and melodrama of the rest of the book. At first the dog hero is, as he puts it, merely a dumb animal, but he quickly finds a way to communicate the author's message to younger puppies, such as Billy the fox terrier: 'I used to tell him that he would kill himself if he could eat all he wanted to.' The characterization of Beautiful Joe takes on a clarity of outline through its new, nonhuman perspective, and some continuing credibility results from the marked simplicity of the dog's reflections and its lack of dialogue. Miss Saunder's failure came in the more advanced challenge of devising a credible plot for her dog hero. Confronted with the need to develop a conflict, she borrowed a melodramatic villain and weeping young woman from the traditions of nineteenth-century human fiction. The cruel master Jenkins not only demonstrates man's cruelty to animals by disfiguring the hero, he also destroys the initial authenticity of the story when he tries to rob and burn a house which the hero dog is defending. The constant Christian didacticism in the book suggests another literary tradition of the times. As a result, the story which begins from a distinctive and credible nonhuman point of view ends in a medley of long popular conventions of fiction. They sufficed to make *Beautiful Joe* the most popular Canadian best seller to date, as well as to launch Miss Saunders on a career which ran to nearly a dozen domestic animal novels, none of which shows any advances in technique.

Also in 1894, Rudyard Kipling introduced a different widespread use of animals in modern literature with his first *Jungle Book*. It is a pure romance of man living among the beasts of the jungle, with the boy Mowgli as the typical hero of an adventure which differs from the hackneyed only because of the rest of the cast. Sometimes Kipling reverted to the primitive use of animals as antagonists of man, sometimes his characters echo human virtues and vices. The animals would suit Kipling's purpose at least as well if they were characterized realistically. As with Miss Sewell and Miss Saunders, the old hybrid characters no longer were essential to the purpose, and the incredible humanness is merely a difficulty of technique. The chief literary advance in Kipling's animal stories results from the more unified atmosphere provided by his romantic approach. Kipling subdued the attendant artistic dangers of triviality, sentimentality, and melodrama, although his sprawling progeny of Tarzan and other yarns of men living among somewhat nonhuman beasts has carried the art of fiction close to its nadir. Sir Charles G. D. Roberts objected to the falsified animals of both traditions and started a third and accurate one in *Earth's Enigmas* (1896).

When Roberts turned to the animal world to populate his stories, he tried to look at life from the animals' point of view. To do so he would choose an animal or animal family going about its daily business of searching for food, the most common concern of such creatures, Roberts felt. Their chief obstacle is the threat of danger or death from the intended victim or from another hungry animal. Consequently the typical character has a serious outlook on life, with no time for fun, no concern for outsiders, and the stories seethe with this solemnity. When the simple wants of two such hungry animals clash, when the one eats the other, or more often the young of the other, the irreconcilable conflict creates an effect of stark tragedy. Roberts usually increased the poignancy of this effect by making the animals either pregnant or starving from trying to feed their young. In 'The Young Ravens That Call upon Him' *(Earth's Enigmas)*, a starving eagle seizes a newborn lamb to feed the starving eaglets, bringing momentary contentment to the nest but leaving the wandering ewe utterly forlorn. Such a juxtaposition can make the animal story a profound comment on the tragedy of life on earth.

Having focused his animal characters on the central concern of their lives, Roberts went on to draw them as convincingly nonhuman. Anna Sewell and Miss Saunders had chosen a special rather than a central problem of animals in the world, one in which man plays a unique and godlike rather than a similar role. Without any men at all in some of his stories, Roberts was driven back to consider the first principles of animal characterization. His animals do not talk, and their thoughts are single, immediate, and simple. Most of the time their behaviour is habitual or instinctive, as when the male eagle always hunts the

Squatook Lakes and his mate hunts the Tuladi in 'The Lord of the Air' (from *The Kindred of the Wild*). When the environment changes, as when an Indian trapper regularly leaves food for the male eagle, and later a net under the food, the eagle comes to accept the change as habitual too. After being captured, the bird can think of one quick move to escape, but only pride provides the continuing urge to escape, and an unexpected ferocity makes it succeed. As the story closes, the eagle has returned to its habitual perch over the Squatooks. The dominion of the eagle, and his determination, make the character heroic, but the simplicity of his outlook helps retain the conviction of reality.

At best Roberts developed a powerful new literary form out of the simple stories of such realistic animals. The climax of two stories of starving animals in the same incident lends depth to the view of the world, and the joining at the climax turns their innocent wants into pathetic tragedy. A rare irony deepens the effect still further at the end of 'When Twilight Falls on the Stump Lots' (*Kindred of the Wild*), after a mother cow has fatally gored a bear looking for food for its cubs:

The merry little cubs within the den were beginning to expect her, and getting restless. As the night wore on, and no mother came, they ceased to be merry. By morning they were shivering with hunger and desolate fear. But the doom of the ancient wood was less harsh than its wont, and spared them some days of starving anguish; for about noon a pair of foxes discovered the dead mother, astutely estimated the situation, and then, with the boldness of good appetite, made their way into the unguarded den.

As for the red calf, its fortune was ordinary. Its mother, for all her wounds, was able to nurse and cherish it through the night; and with morning came a searcher from the farm and took it, with the bleeding mother, safely back to the settlement. There it was tended and fattened, and within a few weeks found its way to the cool marble slabs of a city market.

The curtailed lives of both groups in the conflict, dams and offspring alike, add a perspective of the futility of survival that makes this Robert's most moving story. Perhaps a less conscious irony underlies the treatment of man as just another animal with the same hunger to satisfy. In 'Savoury Meats' *(Kindred of the Wild)*, a man shoots a doe to give his invalid father the red food to live, but a wildcat eats the abandoned fawn. In 'Wild Motherhood' *(Kindred of the Wild)*, which tells three parallel stories, a man with a meat-hungry wife and son shoots not only a wolf who is trying to feed a pregnant mate who cannot hunt because of missing a paw, but also the moose that the wolf is hunting. In stories like these man is an animal competing with his fellows in satisfying the same wants, and succeeding because he is the most fit.

Other variations on the basic characters and plots proved less rewarding. Stories of men trapping tended to distract Roberts into sentimental studies of tender-hearted human beings. 'The Moonlight Trails' *(Kindred of the Wild)* ends with a boy, who has excitedly been snaring rabbits, repenting at the sight of dead rabbits hanging in the noose. Even more sentimental is the longing of a goose that has been raised on a farm from a wild egg to be off with the migration ('The Homesickness of Kehonka', *Kindred of the Wild)*. The young goose, with his wings clipped, falls easy prey to a red fox, but by then his untamable spirit has no doubt done its intended work on the reader. Once in a while man even enters as a god looking after animals like a puppet master. In 'The Watchers of the Camp-Fire' *(Kindred of the Wild)*, the man shoots a hungry panther just to save a doe which has been attracted to the site by the light of his campfire. In casting around for the necessary variety in the development of his plots, Roberts fell back more and more on the repertoire of human fiction, particularly in his later volumes. Roberts also had an instinctive bent towards romantic justice which clashed with the air of objectivity so important to his best effects. In 'The Haunter of the Pine Gloom' *(Kindred of the Wild)*, the animal-loving young boy of 'The Moonlight Trails' turns out to hate lynx while loving all other creatures. With romance entered nostalgia, with nostalgia sentimentality. A heightened scene produces a heightened emotion, and so melodrama was pressed in service.

Ultimately Roberts was unable to develop a general repertoire of fresh characters and situations for his new genre. Deliberately giving up the dialogue, the extended descriptions, and the casual plotting of traditional fiction, he found it difficult to fill up his stories without repetition. The juxtaposition of two or even three parallel searchers for food, climaxing in tragedy for at least one, eked out the material for several well-rounded stories, but it did not provide a pattern which was repeatedly reusable and fresh. The restriction to simple wants also worked against variety. In effect Roberts seldom wrote well with any other want for his heroes than food. In 'The King of the Mamozekel' (*Kindred of the Wild*), the long biography of a bull moose from birth to adult domination of a herd is tied together only by the dubious psychological dread of bears suggested as unique to this moose. The wintertime longing of a young ox for the dream pastures of the previous June makes 'Strayed' (*Earth's Enigmas*) an untypical romance of minimal interest. Roberts developed a new literary form, but then he found no reliable means to give it variety.

'Alike in matter and in method, the animal story, as we have it to-day, may be regarded as a culmination.' When Roberts began his essay on 'The Animal Story' (in *The Kindred of the Wild*) with these words, he was recording his technical frustration. He was also rejoicing in the sense of his own accomplishment and his new recognition of the significance of the history of animals in literature. He saw that the keys to his discovery were the recent advances in psychology and the biological sciences, declaring that 'the animal story at its highest point of development is a psychological romance constructed on a framework of natural science.' Consequently he sets his own stories and those of

Ernest Thompson Seton against those of Anna Sewell, Marshall Saunders, and Kipling, pointing out their errors in the representation of animals. Although he is rather distressed that Christianity with its 'Dispensation of Love' had not stimulated this advance long before, he rejoices ultimately that his stories appeal to the heart and the spirit of evolutionary man after 'the long upward march of being'. Perhaps the delight in this 'potent emancipation' provided the stimulus for Roberts to produce a score of animal story books despite his conviction that he had reached the culmination of the genre: 'There would seem to be no further evolution possible.'

The example provided by Roberts in *Earth's Enigmas* stimulated several kinds of animal stories, but neither the naturalists nor the romancers succeeded in discovering any other distinctive patterns in plots. Naturalists and wild-animal lovers like Ernest Thompson Seton and Grey Owl tried using the form to make natural history memorable, but they also made it bizarre. Explaining the choice in the prefatory 'Note to the Reader' in *Wild Animals I have Known* (1898), the first of more than a dozen volumes, Seton applies hero worship to the animal world as the most memorable device for informing the reader about a species. In the stories themselves, however, he stresses individual rather than representative aspects or heroism. Lobo the wolf organizes a pack in deliberate opposition to man, and Lobo proves his superiority to man in incident after incident ('Lobo, the King of Currumpaw'). Vixen the fox eludes a watch at both the hen house and the kennel, to bring freshly killed chickens to his captured cub night after night ('The Springfield Fox'). At best these stories create a dramatic tension comparable with Roberts's, and Seton can deepen them with a similarly tragic vision: 'No wild animal dies of old age. Its life has soon or late a tragic end. It is only a question of how long it can hold out against its foes' ('Raggylug, the Story of a Cottontail Rabbit'). Thus Vixen the fox counters every human attempt to thwart her feeding her cub, but when she concludes that she can never free the cub she kills it, in a particularly moving climax. Most of Seton's stories, however, are too episodic to build up such drama. Without a representative unifying drive like the constant search for food in Roberts's stories (in these stories the animals seldom eat), Seton's animals usually drift from crisis to unrelated crisis. Silverspot the crow learns many separate things in his recounted life ('Silverspot, the Story of a Crow'), and Redruff the partridge sees his young die one by one ('Redruff, the Story of the Don Valley Partridge'), and then each is by chance eaten by an owl. Even less promising are the stories in which Seton turned desperately to conventions of human fiction, which are not only trite but gratuitous in the animal world. Lobo the wonder wolf abandons its fight against man and lets itself be trapped when its mate is caught. Seton was unable to expand the genre of the animal story with any new patterns of plot or characterization.

The many romances of wild animals in our century share the general interest of Roberts and Seton in animal psychology, but for unity and emotion they rely on trite models of human fiction. Individual incidents can dramatize conflicts peculiar to the animal world, as in Jack London's *The Call of the Wild* (1903), when Buck wins the leadership of the dog team in a fierce fight for survival. For London as well as Seton, however, survival or simple leadership proved insufficient material for a worthy plot. The chosen animal must be a hero, and with heroism enters villainy, moral insight, and active affections. These animals typically move more and more from the simple, single thoughts reminiscent of Roberts's stories the further the author ekes out their lives.

As well as centring animals in fiction, modern writers have sometimes adopted the methods and even the attitudes of the tradition for animals in secondary roles. Then animals can draw off the point of view for observing human characters and situations to an unusual perspective, either serious or amusing. Stories of sports which climax in the killing of an animal, like bullfighting or fox hunting, have gained intense poignancy through a sensing of the beast's plight. John Masefield carries the emotional identity to its ultimate in *Reynard the Fox* (1919), when he forsakes the hunters and pants ahead of the chase with the fox. Among the humorists, authors who deal in the comedy of human manners can gain from the startling perspective of how loving ones look to pets. Tobermory, the infamous talking cat of Saki's story, says only what would sound trite or obvious from a human being. Yet what Tobermory says seems in keeping with the nastiness suggested by a cat's smug face. Other writers have found animals useful in fixing human characterization. The impudent, loud parrot of *Jalna* helped Mazo de la Roche to her most memorable character study, grandmother Adeline, reinforcing the image with repetitive traits. Galsworthy's atmosphere of beautiful old age in 'Indian Summer of a Forsyte' draws impressively from the dog Balthasar. The dog shows how admirable Old Jolyon's repose is, and reflects his security. Steinbeck exploited symbolic beauty and security still more in 'The Red Pony'. Here the elemental dramas of death and birth in the lives of horses catch a romantic vision of life lost by the farmer amid his daily chores and cares. Animals convincingly drawn can lend a tangible reality to everyday associations.

The successful representation of animals in modern fiction, developing rapidly since the beginnings in *Black Beauty, Beautiful Joe*, and *The Jungle Books*, has added to literature a huge range of possible character long ago exploited by sculptors and painters. In the careful inner studies as prompted by zoology and psychology, writers have found the means to a success denied to ancient, medieval, and Renaissance writers alike. Animals, who live in nature and even in the house for themselves and not for man, are credible in fiction only so long as they care about themselves first. The early modern stories, in which animals plead for human kindness or support romances of men raised by beasts, ventured on the new animal hero through special, nontypical applications of this care. From them Roberts developed the wider exploitation of animal heroes for general stories in which conflicts outside the repertoire of human fiction are centred on animals. No matter whether they were emphasizing science or adventure, Roberts and his followers depended for their artistic appeal on the universality of the earthly challenges facing man and animal alike. They ask their readers to feel at one with their heroes in contrast to the myriad enemies to both. They also expose the limits as well as the vastness of the expanded range of characters and topics for fiction. Art and life may be one, but stories of animals living only for themselves must still appeal to readers that are human.

[1964]

3 Some writers and their books

Hans Christian Andersen

ALAN MORAY WILLIAMS

Since 1835, when the first of his *Eventyr Fortalte for Boern* were published in Copenhagen, Danish writer Hans Christian Andersen's fairy tales have been translated into eighty-two languages. In England alone more than five hundred different editions have appeared, by twenty-five different translators. For generations of children *The Tinderbox, The Ugly Duckling, The Little Mermaid, The Emperor's New Clothes, The Staunch Tin Soldier,* and the rest have held a magic which they have never quite forgotten.

Yet comparatively few know the story of Andersen's life, which, as he was fond himself of saying, was as colourful and romantic as any of his stories. Few realize, either, that the fairy tales—'those trifles', he first called them—were only a by-product of his inventive mind and that he was disappointed that his fame rested on them rather than on the novels, plays, travel books, poetry and prose sketches which compose the bulk of the thirty-three volumes of his posthumous collected works.

Born in Odense, a country town of 7,000 inhabitants, then

twenty hours' journey from Copenhagen, the capital, he was the only child of an unsuccessful cobbler who loved books and an illiterate washerwoman eight years older than her husband. His parents were so poor that they lived, worked, and slept in a single room (today charmingly preserved as a museum). There was a streak of lunacy in the family and the boy himself sometimes had fits. As a small child he was dreamy and reclusive, and, teased for his oddness by other children, spent much time playing on his own with a home-made puppet-theatre. Sent to a school for poor men's sons, he received almost no education; but his imagination was spiced by avid reading (*The Arabian Nights*, Holberg's and Shakespeare's plays, and Scott's novels), relished theatre-visits, and tales of ghosts and goblins told him by superstitious old women.

When he was eleven, his father died. Two years later his mother remarried. At fourteen he decided to be an actor and told his mother (who wanted him to be a tailor): 'I am going to Copenhagen and I'm going to be famous. First one must go through all kinds of hardships and *then* one becomes famous.' Local worthies, who had counselled him to 'learn a trade', tapped their heads ominously; but he was fortified in his 'craziness' by an old fortune-teller, who had told his parents that some day he'd be something great and fine and 'all Odense would be illuminated for him.'

In September 1819 he arrived by mail-coach in Copenhagen with nothing but a bundle of clothes, twelve silver pieces from his clay savings pig, and a vague letter of introduction to an actress. Disproportionately lanky and thin, rather ugly, and with comically ill-fitting clothes, he was ill-equipped to realize his dreams. In three years Copenhagen's Royal Theatre gave him, as a pupil, only one part—as an anonymous troll. A petition for aid which he sent to the king, 'equipped only with a fervent desire for the theatre and a trust in noble souls to help him', was turned down. A callow tragedy he submitted to the directors was returned after six weeks' hopes as showing 'absolute lack of elementary culture and necessary education.'

Three things sustained him in the hungry garret-existence he led: an unshakable determination, a deep though unorthodox religious faith which he maintained all his life, and an ingratiating naivety which made people of all walks of life want to help him, even if they secretly laughed at him a little.

Of the many writers, officials, and others who kept him going with gifts of money or clothes, meals at their homes, useful introductions, etc., the most important was Jonas Collin (pronounced *Colleen*), a state councillor and one of the Royal Theatre's directors. One of the great patrons in the history of literature, he early sensed the boy's possibilities and not only got him free schooling, at state expense, at Slagelse Grammar School, but took him into his cultured middle-class home and made him one of the family.

His five years at school were, according to his autobiography, the blackest in his life. Though he had already written and published (at his own expense) a story in imitation of Walter Scott, he knew no Latin, Greek, history, geography, or arithmetic, and had to start from scratch. The headmaster, who lashed boys as viciously with his tongue as Wackford Squeers did with his cane, nicknamed him 'Shakespeare with the vampire eyes' and humiliated him in every way, telling him his writings were only fit for the wastepaper-basket and that he'd end up in an asylum.

But his five years' cramming proved a precious bane, for soon after matriculation in 1827 he managed to produce three books: a travel journal which achieved some success, a comedy which was performed at the theatre, and a book of poems. These established him as a professional author, but brought him little money. For five years he floundered in the muddy waters of freelance writing, painfully dependent on the life-belt of his friends' charity.

It was not until 1832, when Collin secured him a travel-scholarship to visit Italy for two years, that his genius expanded in the warm south and he wrote a novel, *The Improvisator*, which gained international fame and led to his being given a small state pension. From then on, honours and fame piled on him and his work till in 1869—fifty years after his arrival in Copenhagen— his native Odense was duly illuminated for him at a ceremony in his honour.

His first tales (Andersen always distinguished carefully between his 'fairy' tales—concerned with the supernatural—and the rest) were written as a kind of afterthought, mainly to make money. They were a logical outcome of his childhood puppet-plays. In a letter to the poet Ingemann in 1843 he described how he wrote them:

The first ones were, of course, some which I had heard in my childhood and re-told, but then I found that those which I created myself such as The Little Mermaid *got the most applause, and that has started me off. Now I dip into my own bosom, find an idea for the older people and tell it to the children, but remembering that father and mother are listening! . . . I have masses of material, more than for any other kind of work; often it seems to me that every fence, every little flower said: 'Just look at me, then you'll know my story,' and if I so desire, the story is mine.*

If Danish was a world-language like German, a handful of Andersen's poems, lyrics, and patriotic songs would probably be as well known as Goethe's. An opera he wrote, *Little Kerstin*, is still performed in Denmark. But apart from the tales and his autobiography, *The Fairy-Tale of My Life*, little of his prose work is read today. Two of his novels, *The Improvisator* and *Only A Fiddler*—romantic projections of his own early struggles —can still be read with enjoyment, however.

The tales combine the freshness of vision and the innocence of childhood with the gentle ircny and knowledge of human psychology that only hard experience can produce. They are racy with the homely speech of the Danish common people and warm with the simple beauty of the countryside. There are 158 of them, not all equally good. A few seem potboilers, and some are marred by what Mr W. H. Auden has called the 'Sensitive-Plantishness and Namby-Pamby Christianity of their heroes'. But most are little masterpieces, as perfect in their way as Tanagra statuettes. One wishes they were available singly in Britain, like the Beatrix Potter books, with the original illustrations by Vilhelm Pedersen.

Like Kierkegaard, Andersen was celibate. Like Oliver Goldsmith (with whose gawky, ungainly personality he had something in common) he was able to travel very widely between 1838 and his death in 1875 and feel himself a citizen, if not of the world, at least of Europe. He twice visited England, was given a great reception (you *need* no introductions, the Danish Ambassador, Count Reventlow, told him) and stayed with Dickens at Gad's Hill—but the Dickens family, it must be recorded, found him 'a bony bore' and Dickens, though he admired Andersen's work greatly, stuck a notice on the dressing-table in the room he'd occupied: 'Hans Andersen stayed in this room for five weeks—which seemed to the family AGES!'

Andersen was a man with a chronic inferiority complex. All his career was a struggle to compensate for his lowly origins and early humilations and snubbings. Hence his faults: his vanity, morbid sensitiveness to criticism, inverted snobbery, and neurotic quirks. But unlike that all-too-familiar figure, the self-made man who, success's mountain once climbed, scorns or ignores those still toiling at its base, he never lost touch with the humble and the handicapped. Though in his years of fame counts and princes competed for the honour of his celebrated company, he never, one feels, belonged to their privileged world, but remained a part of ordinary suffering humanity. This is what makes him sympathetic and lovable.

[1963]

The publication of *Alice in Wonderland*

JOHN PUDNEY

The Revd C.L. Dodgson both enjoyed the fame and also revelled in not enjoying the fame of being Lewis Carroll. He was a great one for having his cake and eating it. Himself a relentless pursuer of celebrities, he rejected a request from *Vanity Fair* for a sitting for a Spy cartoon—'nothing would be more unpleasant for me than to have my face known to strangers.'

He almost obsessively supervised the illustration, production, and publication of *Alice in Wonderland,* which sold some 110,000 copies in his lifetime. He was enthusiastically committed to the promotion of the *Alice* stories, by cheap, nursery, facsimile editions, by tableaux and operatic adaptation, and by such gimmicks as the Wonderland postage-stamp case. He could, however, be very tetchy about being Carroll. To Edith Rix, a child friend, he wrote: 'Would you tell your mother I was aghast at seeing the address of her letter to me: and I would much prefer "Rev C.L. Dodgson, Ch. Ch., Oxford". When a letter comes addressed "Lewis Carroll, Ch. Ch.", it either goes to the Dead Letter Office, or it impresses on the minds of all letter-carriers, &c., through whose hands it goes, the very fact I least want them to know.' He continued to fulminate about correspondence reaching him addressed Lewis Carroll. Yet to another child friend, Kathleen Eschwege, he subscribed his letter, 'Your affectionate friend, Charles L. Dodgson (*alias* "Lewis Carroll").'

In spite of such quixotics he set about his literary affairs with all the thoroughness of a mathematician, and with a promotional flair which would have served him well among the media of this century. The first draft of 18,000 words of *Alice's Adventures Under Ground* was not only lovingly handwritten for the little girl, but was garnished with thirty-seven illustrations by the author. He finished writing in February 1863, but it was not sent to Alice at the Deanery until November 1864. Between those two dates Carroll, from having 'no idea of publication', had by May 1863 been persuaded by various friends to let it be published, and this meant his getting in touch with the Clarendon Press at Oxford to print the work at his expense. But first he made an enlarged draft of 35,000 words, and placed it in the hands of John Tenniel, introduced to him by Tom Taylor, the dramatist and future editor of *Punch*. Tenniel had established himself as a draughtsman with his illustrations to *Aesop's Fables* (1848), the drolleries of which brought him into lifelong association with *Punch*.

When he died in 1914, aged ninety-three, Sir John Tenniel left 2000 *Punch* cartoons—including a biting anti-sweatshop work of 1863, and the famous 'Dropping the Pilot' on the Kaiser's dismissal of Bismarck in 1890. His greatest gift to posterity was the illustrations immortalized in the two *Alice* books. The world has never seen a matching of word with drawing to equal the Carroll/Tenniel collaboration. For Tenniel it was the least agreeable task in his long life. He took on the first *Alice* book mainly because there were plenty of animals in it and he liked doing animals. Though his own reputation was much enhanced by the *Wonderland*'s success, he refused for a long time to tackle *Through The Looking-Glass*. He was persuaded only by the most urgent entreaties of his tyrannical author to undertake the work. In spite of this, Carroll confided to another illustrator, Harry Furniss, that out of the ninety-two drawings in *Wonderland* he had liked only one. Tenniel was reported by Furniss to have said, 'Dodgson is impossible! You will never put up with that conceited old Don for more than a week!'

Examples of Carroll's notes to Tenniel: 'Don't give Alice so much crinoline', and, 'The White Knight must not have whiskers: he must not be made to look old.' Tenniel sometimes fought back, and sometimes won: 'A wasp in a wig is altogether beyond the appliances of art. . . . Don't think me brutal, but I am bound to say that the "wasp" chapter doesn't interest me in the least, and I can't see my way to a picture. . . .' Carroll omitted the chapter.

In May 1864 he sent Tenniel the first of the slip (galley) proofs from the Clarendon Press: and Tenniel was already at work when Macmillan agreed to publish the work on a commission basis. This was the beginning of an even more politely abrasive— and profitable—relationship. According to Charles Morgan, in his history of Macmillan's: 'There never was an author more elaborately careful than Lewis Carroll for the details of production, or one that can have more sorely tried the patience of his publisher.' He bore the expense of his own fussiness and perfectionism, which extended to every aspect of the business. He 'never allowed himself to be far absent from the minds of publisher, printer or binder. . . . Books, ingenuities and trouble poured from him.'

Not even the packers escaped his attention. He sent in a diagram showing how parcels were to be stringed and how the knots were to be tied. This hung for years in the Macmillan post-room. He soon came to regard his publisher also as a general factotum. For many of his frequent forays to London theatres, Macmillan's were given the task of buying his tickets, and making sure that the seats were on the extreme right as he was deaf in his right ear. They were also required to send a 'trusty and resolute messenger' to retrieve watches when he sent them to be mended.

In December 1864, only just after he had given Alice Liddell her manuscript copy (sold in 1928 for £15,400), Carroll sent off to Macmillan 'the whole of my little book in slip. It is the only complete copy I have. . . . I hope you may not think it unfitted to come under your auspices.' If Macmillan's supposed they were

BY JOHN TENNIEL FROM *Through the Looking-Glass*

BY JOHN TENNIEL FROM *Alice's Adventures in Wonderland*

dealing with a naïve mathematical cleric they were soon disillusioned. They sent Carroll a specimen volume in May 1865 which he liked and passed, saying that he wanted publication of the edition of 2000 copies quickly for his young friends, who 'are all grown out of childhood so alarmingly fast'. On 15 July he went to the publisher's office to autograph some twenty copies, and everything was sunny. Five days later he reappeared with gloom in the shape of 'Tenniel's letter about the fairy tale—he is entirely dissatisfied with the printing of the pictures, and I suppose we shall have to do it all again.'

And that is what they did. Carroll declared in his diary that the 2000 copies, for which he had paid the Clarendon Press £135, 'shall be sold as waste paper'. He sent out a circular letter recalling the personal copies he himself had already given away. These—the few survivors have fetched £5000 a piece—were redistributed free to hospitals. The remaining 1,952 unbound sheets were not sold as waste, but shipped to the United States where they were bought, bound and sold by Messrs Appleton of New York—Carroll on this and several other occasions indulging a snobbish contempt for American cultural standards. A new

English edition was printed by Richard Clay and published by Macmillan in November 1865. That Tenniel's complaint had been ridiculously sensitive, and that Carroll had been absurdly fussy in acting on it, may be gathered from a study of the respective texts in the British Museum.

The book's reception was good, but fell short of acclamation. The *Pall Mall Gazette* called it 'a children's feast and triumph of nonsense'. The *Athenaeum* said, 'This is a dream story, but who can in cold blood manufacture a dream? . . . We fancy that any real child might be more puzzled than enchanted by this stiff, over-wrought story.' Among his appreciative friends, Christina Rossetti thanked him for 'the funny pretty book'.

The book's fame spread by word of mouth, and Lewis Carroll's name, though not the identity of the mathematics don Dodgson, was established as a curiosity in the Victorian scene. There was a new edition each year from 1865 to 1868. In two years he had made a profit of £250 on his original outlay of £350—which included Tenniel's payment. From 1869 to 1889 there were twenty-six reprintings.

Queen Victoria, widowed four years before the book's appearance, was undoubtedly one of his readers. Walter de la Mare, writing in 1932, quotes an old lady who, at the age of three and a half, and too young to read, had sat on a footstool looking at Tenniel's pictures in the presence of the Queen. 'Noticing this rapt doubled-up little creature in the fire-light so intent over her book, the Queen asked her what it was. She rose and carried it over, and standing at the royal knee opened it at the page where tinied Alice is swimming in the flood of her own tears. . . . This little girl, pointing at the picture, looked up into the Queen's face, and said: "Do you think, please, *you* could cry as much as that?" ' The old lady did not remember the Queen's precise reply, though it expressed great enthusiasm for Carroll. It was followed next day by a locket sent from Windsor by special messenger.

[1976]

Andrew Lang
in fairyland

ROGER LANCELYN GREEN

The name of Andrew Lang is more closely connected with fairy tales than that of any other writer who used the English language, and indeed it seems that he now holds as secure a place as historian of fairyland as do Perrault, Grimm, and Andersen. Although he did not collect folktales from the peasants like the brothers Grimm, Lang occupies an important niche among those folklorists and anthropologists whose researches are carried on with the aid of printed sources, and he is remembered among scholars as the author of the first full refutation of Max Muller's theory of mythology derived from 'a disease of language' stemming from the Aryans, as well as for the more controversial suggestion that the 'lower mythology' derived from the 'higher' and even perhaps from monotheism.

Lang's long and gruelling studies as a folklorist and desk-anthropologist, like his Classical studies which resulted in the finest prose translations of the *Iliad* and *Odyssey* and three important books on the Homeric Problem, supplied the solid foundations on which his more famous collections of fairy tales were built. His own personal background also contributed to the turn which his genius was to take, and his character and the chances of his career gave him a ready 'pass' into fairyland.

He was born at 'Viewfields', Selkirk, on 31 March 1844, the eldest son of John Lang, Sherriff Clerk of Selkirk, whose father

Andrew had held the same position under and become a trusted friend of Sir Walter Scott.

Andrew Lang had several brothers and one sister, and passed a happy boyhood in the Border Country, fishing in the burns, digging for hidden treasure among the ruined keeps and peel-towers, and playing cricket for the Selkirk team against those of the neighbouring townships.

He was always, however, a bookish and imaginative child, and took particular pleasure in the tales and legends of the Borders. He and other boys would seek out an ancient shepherd learned in fairy tales; Nancy Hall, the old nurse at 'Viewfields', had all the local legends of magic, ghosts, and hidden treasures at her finger-tips—and they lost nothing in the telling. Scott's poems opened a new world of enchantment to him, and the good laird of Abbotsford was a living memory wherever he went by Tweed and Yarrow and Ettrick.

Apparently Lang was always delicate, shy, and hypersensitive —always ready to escape from the rough and tumble of everyday life in some literary or legendary fairyland of the imagination. His early schooldays at Selkirk Grammar School gave him the right leavening of solitude and society, but when at the age of ten he proceeded to Edinburgh Academy he found his contemporaries less to his taste and read more and more voraciously. Inspired Classical instruction turned him from a loathing of Greek to his life-long devotion to Homer, and a scholarly career was already opening before him when he entered St Andrews University in 1861.

He spent almost two years at 'the college of the scarlet gown' and always looked back on them as the happiest of his life, though they closed with the death of the college friend, Henry Brown, on whose account he wrote of

> *St Andrews by the northern sea*
> *That is a haunted town to me.*

Lang's earliest surviving writings date from 1862 when he

edited *The St Leonard's Magazine* (a manuscript affair produced in his hall of residence, of which a selection was printed the following year), and contributed to the more formal *St Andrews University Magazine* articles on such subjects as 'Scottish Nursery Tales' and 'Spiritualism Medieval and Modern'.

He was already reading any volume on ancient medieval magic he could find in the university library, and the more accessible collections of folktales; but his Classical studies did not suffer, and he was moved to Glasgow University in 1863 to qualify for a Snell Exhibition to Balliol College, Oxford, which he obtained in 1864. At Balliol he took Firsts in Classical Moderations and Literae Humaniores, and won an Open Fellowship to Merton College in December 1868, which he held for seven years.

The academic career so auspiciously started did not prosper, however. The period at Merton proved that it was contrary to Lang's temperament and talents. Dons in those days were expected to stick rigorously to the normal fields of scholarship and not to flirt with each of the Muses in turn. After staying with Lang at Merton in 1874, Robert Louis Stevenson in his poem to 'Dear Andrew of the brindled hair' described Oxford as 'The abhorred pedantic sanhedrin', and Lang, though he wrote that there 'Youth an hour came back to me', also realized that 'at last, if men linger there too late, Oxford grows a prison.' Outside influences also came to upset him: his parents died within a few days of one another in September 1869, there was perhaps an unhappy love affair, and certainly in 1872 Lang's health broke down completely and he spent two winters in the south of France in danger of his life through lung trouble.

When he won back to something like health in 1874 he became engaged to Leonora Blanche Alleyne, whom he married the following year. He resigned his Fellowship and they settled at 1 Marloes Road, Kensington, their home for the rest of his life.

Already at the beginning of 1874 Lang was writing reviews for a newly founded weekly, *The Academy*; and on settling in London he plunged into journalism, writing regularly for many years for *The Daily News* and *The Saturday Review*, besides an astonishing number of contributions on all kinds of subjects to numerous other papers and magazines, popular or learned. He published over a hundred books, and it has been reckoned that his uncollected works would fill more than that number of volumes over again.

It would be possible to write of Lang in many other fields besides journalism. He began as a minor poet of some distinction and considerable promise, though disappointment over the poor reception of his narrative poem *Helen of Troy* (1882) turned him towards light verse and parody. He wrote two amusing and absolutely distinctive novels which were popular only with a minimum of more literary readers; and historical romance, which he also essayed, proved in his own words 'too bitterly historical' for readers glutted with more thrilling works of Stanley Weyman, Conan Doyle, S. R. Crockett, and A. E. W. Mason. As a literary critic he was for many years the most popular and influential of his time; but criticism is transitory, though he left several volumes of permanent interest. In more academic fields his book on folklore, totemism, Homeric scholarship, Scottish history, and 'historical mysteries' are still remembered by specialists in each; and all that he wrote in prose or verse is still readable on account of the charm and individuality of his style, through which shines the illusive, yet strangely attractive mind and character of their author.

Lang wrote no masterpiece in the accepted sense, and only those who fall captive to the magic of his personality as glimpsed through his writings will follow him now beyond an odd volume or two appealing to some special interest.

Yet by an odd irony of fate he is remembered and known throughout the world for a group of books which contain little of his actual writing—the Fairy Book series. For of the twelve volumes of fairy tales, named according to colour, though he was the collector and presiding genius, hardly any were actually retold by him.

His early interest in folklore took a strictly scientific bent while he was at Merton, and he wrote most learnedly on the origin and diffusion of popular tales. 'There was a time,' he recalled, 'when I considered all *contes,* except *contes populaires,* as frivolous and vexatious.' He was never enthusiastic about literary fairy stories, though he had a special affection for *The Rose and the Ring* and was an early admirer of George MacDonald's *Phantastes.*

This did not however prevent him from trying his hand at a little fairy story, which he called *The Princess Nobody,* in 1884 at the suggestion of his friend and publisher Charles Longman. This pleasant trifle (recently reprinted in Dent's *Modern Fairy Stories*) was written to fit a series of pictures of fairyland by Richard Doyle, and Lang showed great ingenuity in arranging them and fitting together a number of the stock incidents of folklore for them to illustrate in such a way that *The Princess Nobody* appears to be a completely spontaneous tale written simply in the traditional vein, rather as Mrs Ewing did in her *Old Fashioned Fairy Tales.*

The success of this effort broke down Lang's resistance to the literary use of the fairy *genre,* and he ventured still further with *The Gold of Fairnilee* in 1888, for which the inspiration was drawn from the Border Ballads and the old superstitions that still lingered by Tweedside when he was a boy, and the setting was the ruined house near Selkirk where he and his brother had dug for the fabled treasure in vain.

This is the most completely original of Lang's own fairy stories, and the most perfectly written. That it was not the most popular is due mainly to the unfamiliar background among the evil fairies of the north, so alien to the English nursery tradition derived from Perrault, Madame d'Aulnoy, and Grimm.

By far his most successful venture came the following year when Lang first introduced his readers to the Kingdom of Pantouflia, situated on the borders of fairyland in a region not far from Thackeray's Paflagonia, where the adventures of *Prince Prigio* take place. This book was at once recognized as a classic, the leading American critic, Brander Matthews, for example, writing that he 'unhesitatingly proclaimed it the most delightful of modern fairy-tales since *The Rose and the Ring*', and it has been constantly reprinted ever since, the last edition, in company with its sequel, *Prince Ricardo* (1893), being in Dent's *Children's Illustrated Classics* in 1961. Lang's attempt at a return to Pantouflia, *Tales of a Fairy Court* in 1907, could not recapture the spontaneity and irresistible charm of the earlier adventures, though it contains authentic echoes. But the original *Prince Prigio* can stand comparison with all but the greatest children's books, even of that golden age which began with *The Rose and the Ring* and *Alice* and ended with *The Wind in the Willows* and the Nesbit series.

It is not, however, so well known as another book with Lang's name on the title page which also appeared in 1889. *The Blue Fairy Book* was a daring venture at a time when even the traditional fairy tales were in eclipse and the child-novels of Mrs Ewing and Mrs Molesworth held the centre of the stage. Its only important predecessor, *The Fairy Book* prepared by Mrs Craik, had appeared as early as 1863, and was drawn almost entirely from the obvious French sources and from Grimm.

Lang's collection, 'made for the pleasure of children, and without scientific purpose, includes nursery tales which have a purely literary origin'—as he was careful to explain in the introduction to the limited large-paper edition. This accounts for the unexpected appearance in it of a shortened version of 'Gulliver in Lilliput', three tales from *The Arabian Nights* and five from Madame d'Aulnoy, besides three from the *Cabinet des Fées*; but of the truly traditional tales Lang included seven from Perrault, seven from Grimm, four Norse tales, two Scottish, one from Asia Minor, and his own brilliant version of the ancient Greek story of Perseus recast in its original fairy-tale form.

The book was published in an edition of 5000 at six shillings, with numerous illustrations by H. J. Ford and P. Jacomb Hood, and was very much of an experiment. It was certainly not intended as the first of a series. But its success was immediate and amazing: it changed the whole trend of children's literature and brought back the fairies in full force.

A sequel was called for, and *The Red Fairy Book* followed for Christmas 1890—now in an edition of 10,000 and containing only traditional fairy tales (except for Lang's retelling of the *Volsunga Saga*)—eleven French, eleven Norse, eight German, two Russian, two Romanian, and one English. By the time *The Yellow Fairy Book* arrived in 1894, the first edition was of 15,000 copies, and the contents included Norse, Estonian, German, French, Modern Greek, Hungarian, Russian, Polish, Red Indian, Chinese, and Icelandic folktales.

In the preface to *The Green Fairy Book* (1892) Lang wrote: 'This is the third, and probably the last, of the Fairy Books of many colours . . . If we have a book for you next year, it shall not be a fairy book.' But the demand for fairy tales showed no sign of slackening, and in the end the series ran to twenty-five annual volumes (1889-1913), of which twelve were Fairy Books, though several others such as *The Arabian Nights*, the two *Romance Books*, and the final *Strange Story Book* hail almost entirely from the realms of faerie.

'There is no story quite so worth reading as a fairy story,' wrote G. K. Chesterton when *The Violet Fairy Book* appeared in 1901. 'A fairy story is, perhaps, more artistic in the strict sense of the word than any other form of art.' That adults should admit to reading and enjoying the old fairy tales was a great triumph for Lang who, in 1889, was fighting against the critics and educationists of the day who considered their unreality, brutality, and escapism to be harmful for young readers, while holding that such stories were beneath the serious consideration of those of mature age. Already the accolade of a truly 'adult' taste was the appreciation of Henry James, Ibsen, and the Russians, to the exclusion of anything that might be termed romantic as a sign of escapism or arrested development.

Lang insisted, however, that fairy tales contain more fundamental truth than the most 'realistic' novel by Tolstoy or Thomas Hardy, and 'unobtrusively teach the true lessons of our wayfaring in a world of perplexities and obstructions'. He had already, in a more apologetic vein, preached from the same text in the introduction (for adults) to the large-paper edition of *The Blue Fairy Book*, pointing out, for example, that 'when the Princess wakens, after her betrothal to the Yellow Dwarf, and hopes it was a dream, and finds on her finger the fatal ring of one red hair, we have a brave touch of horror and of truth. All of us have wakened and struggled with a dim evil memory, and trusted it was a dream, and found, in one form or other, a proof, a shape of that ring of red hair.'

Nevertheless, as he grew old, Lang longed more and more to escape from the changing age which had outgrown him. Like his friend's Dr Jekyll, he found himself more and more inclined to slip out of his own personality without meaning to—though it was to the fairylands of legend and literature.

His later literary criticism suffers from this form of escapism —in his case a kind of melancholia which caused him to take events both private and public more and more to heart; when he died suddenly of angina pectoris on 20 July 1912, his wife wrote: 'It was the Strikes that killed him.' But it increased his understanding of fairy tales and the romances of the past. The later Fairy Books are better than the more famous earlier ones. Though Mrs Lang was responsible for most of the writing, Lang 'superintended' them to an extent which it is now impossible to discover—but he left his touch on nearly all of them.

One of the best things he ever wrote appeared in 1907: *Tales of Troy and Greece*, of which two-thirds consists of *The Adventures of Odysseus* (reprinted in Dent's *Children's Illustrated Classics* in 1962). The retelling is entirely by Lang, and into his re-creation of the Old Greek legends he put all the love and understanding of a life-long devotion to Homer, besides the underlying realization of the fairy world behind the adventures of Theseus, Perseus, and Jason—as well as of Odysseus when he wandered among one-eyed giants, beautiful witches, fairies on magic islands, and princesses in kingdoms beyond this world on his way from the cruel reality of fallen Troy to the final happiness of the simple, everyday world of his home in Ithaca.

Among all retellers of Greek myth and legend, Lang best understood 'how a child's mind worked' and alone succeeded in capturing the necessary simplicity of style without losing any of 'the old original magic', as an anonymous writer in *The Times Literary Supplement* put it recently in reviewing some modern retellings; and he went on 'How one longs for Lang's *Tales of Troy and Greece* to be reprinted; in their chosen field they were, and remain, unequalled.'

The Fairy Books are also, in their own way, still unequalled. Even in the new editions, lacking the inspired illustrations by Henry Justice Ford, which seemed an essential part of the original volumes, they capture and hold new generations of children. And those who, like Lang himself, enjoy the best of the old fairy tales at any age, turn back to them again and again—to pick out one story, perhaps, but then to fall under the spell and read tale after tale, forgetful of all but the eternal world of fairyland when led into its magic purlieus by that great enchanter, Andrew Lang.

[1962]

Meg, Jo, Beth, Amy, and Louisa

ELIZABETH JANEWAY

Meg, Jo, Beth, and Amy are a hundred years old on 3 October, and except for Natasha Rostova, who is almost exactly their contemporary (*War and Peace* appeared over the years 1865 to 1869), the Marches must be the most read about and cried over young women of their years. In my time we read *Little Women* of course, but we liked to think it was because our sentimental mothers had loved the book so and urged it on us. For all I know, this is still the cover story today, but just the same, the answer to 'Have you read *Little Women*?' is still 'Of course.' In the last week I've heard it from three Americans, an Italian, and an English girl, all in their twenties—the English girl quoted the whole opening: 'Christmas won't be Christmas without any presents', it begins, in case you've forgotten—and a mother of teenagers assured me that her daughters were even now devouring the works of Miss Alcott. Read *Little Women*? Of course.

Why? It is dated and sentimental and full of preaching and moralizing and some snobbery about the lower classes that is positively breathtaking in its horror: that moment, for instance, when old Mr Laurence is improbably discovered in a fishmarket, and bestows his charity on a starving Irish woman by hooking a large fish on the end of his cane and depositing it, to her gasping gratitude, in her arms. It is as often smug as it is snug, and its high-mindedness tends to be that peculiar sort that pays.

Brigid Brophy, writing in *The New York Times Book Review* a few years ago, called it a dreadful masterpiece, and the judgement stands (though not, I think, quite on Miss Brophy's grounds). And yet here it is in a new and handsome centennial edition, as compulsively readable as it was a century ago when publisher Thomas Niles's nieces overrode their uncle's doubts and urged him to bring it out.

Its faults we can see in a moment. They cry to heaven, and when Miss Brophy dwelt at length on the literary sin of sentimentality which falsifies emotion and manipulates the process of life, she hardly had to cite evidence. *Little Women* does harp on our nerves, does play on our feelings, does stack the cards to bring about undeserved happy outcomes here and undeserved come-uppance there. But that is not the whole story, and couldn't be, or there wouldn't be all those girls with their noses in the book right now and all those women who remember the supreme shock of the moment when Jo sold her hair; when Beth was discovered on the medicine chest in the closet with scarlet fever coming on; when Meg let the Moffats dress her up; when Amy was packed off, protesting and bargaining, to Aunt March's stiff house.

No, *Little Women* does manipulate life but it is also *about* life, and life that is recognizable in human terms today. Miss Alcott preached, and the conclusions she came to are frequently too good to be true; but the facts of emotion that she started with were real. She might end by softening the ways to deal with them, but she began by looking them in the eye. Her girls were jealous, mean, silly, and lazy; and for a hundred years jealous, mean, silly, and lazy girls have been ardently grateful for the chance to read about themselves. If Miss Alcott's prescriptions for curing their sins are too simple, it doesn't alter the fact that her diagnoses are clear, unequivocal, and humanly right. When her girls are good, they are apt to be painful; but when they are bad, they are bad just the way we all are, and over the same things. It must have been a heavenly relief a hundred years ago to learn that one's faults were not unique. Today I suspect that it is a relief to be told to take them seriously and struggle with them; that it is important to be good.

This general background of human interest makes *Little Women* still plausible, but it is hardly enough to keep it a perennial classic. The real attraction is not the book as a whole, but its heroine, Jo, and Jo is a unique creation: the one young woman in nineteenth-century fiction who maintains her individual independence, who gives up no part of her autonomy as payment for being born a woman—and who gets away with it. Jo is the tomboy dream come true, the dream of growing up into full humanity with all its potentialities instead of into limited femininity: of looking after oneself and paying one's way and doing effective work in the real world instead of learning how to please a man who will look after you, as Meg and Amy both do with pious pleasure. (So, by the way, does Natasha). It's no secret that Jo's story is the heart of *Little Women*, but just what that story represents has not, to my knowledge, been explored, and I think it is worth looking at.

We shall have to work back and forth from Louisa May Alcott's life to her book, but no one has ever denied that Jo is Louisa and that a great deal of her story is autobiographical. The very fact that *Little Women* was written so quickly makes that conclusion inescapable: two and a half months for the first part and two months for the second. More clearly in life, but clearly enough in her book, Louisa-Jo wanted to become the head of the family. In part, this was necessity. Bronson Alcott suffered from a kind of obsessional generosity that appears at times to have verged on *folie de grandeur*, and his wife and daughters learned early to shift for themselves, for Papa's plans not only went astray, they were apt to ignore the existence of his family completely.

Then there came a time—Louisa was eleven—when Bronson Alcott all but deserted his wife and daughters and went off to join a Shaker colony with his English friend, Charles Lane, who (as his wife put it) had almost hypnotic power over him. In the end he did not go, but suffered so powerfully from the crisis that he did in fact abdicate the father's role in the family. In that frequent nineteenth-century gesture of despair, he took to his bed and turned his face to the wall. None of this was hidden from Louisa. She and her older sister Anna made part of the family council which discussed Mr Alcott's decision to go off with his friend to the celibate Shakers or to stay.

This clumsy agony is glossed over in *Little Women*, where absent Mr March is away as a chaplain during the Civil War. But the pressure on Jo to hold her family together by working and earning is all there, and so is the emotion of the one who aspires to play the role of responsibility when it has become vacant. When Meg is falling in love, Jo blurts out in fury, 'I just wish I could marry Meg myself, and keep her safe in the family.' This is of course treated as a joke, though sociologist students of the incest taboo in the nuclear family would find it of interest. It is, at any rate, indicative of Jo's desire to become the responsible head of the household, and the last half of the book is devoted to her effort to achieve this end, which in her life she did achieve.

This aim explains her refusal to marry handsome Laurie, the next-door hero. Their relationship has always been that of two equals, which in nineteenth-century America (and in some places today) implies two equals of the same sex. Twice at least Laurie suggests that they run off together, not for love-making but for adventure, very much in the manner and mood in which Tom Sawyer and Huck Finn plan to run away from comfort and civilization. Again when Jo speaks to her mother about the possibility of marriage to Laurie, Mrs March is against it 'because you two are too much alike.' So they are, and so—with no explanations ever given—Jo refuses Laurie, and the reader knows she is right, for Jo and Laurie are dear friends, competitors and not in the least a couple. It is worth noting that the two other adored nineteenth-century heroines who say 'No' to the hero's proposal give way in the end, when circumstances and the hero have changed: Elizabeth Bennet and Jane Eyre. But Jo says 'No' and does not shift.

The subtlety of Miss Alcott's character drawing (or self-knowledge, if you will) comes through here, for Jo is a tomboy but never a masculinized or lesbian figure. She is, somehow, an idealized 'New Woman', capable of male virtues but not, as the Victorians would have said, 'unsexed'. Or perhaps she is really archaic woman, re-created out of some New-World-frontier necessity when patriarchy breaks down. For Jo marries (as we all know! Who can forget that last great self-indulgent burst of tears when Professor Bhaer stops, under the umbrella, and asks 'Heart's dearest, why do you cry?'). Yes, Jo marries and becomes, please note, not a sweet little wife but a matriarch: mistress of the professor's school, mother of healthy sons (while Amy and Laurie have only one sickly daughter), and cheerful active manager of events and people. For this Victorian moral tract, sentimental and preachy, was written by a secret rebel against the order of the world and woman's place in it, and all the girls who ever read it know it.

[1968]

Beatrix Potter

GRAHAM GREENE

'It is said that the effect of eating too much lettuce is soporific.'
It is with some such precise informative sentence that one might
have expected the great Potter saga to open, for the obvious
characteristic of Beatrix Potter's style is a selective realism, which
takes emotion for granted and puts aside love and death with a
gentle detachment reminiscent of Mr E. M. Forster's. Her stories
contain plenty of dramatic action, but it is described from the
outside by an acute and unromantic observer who never sacri-
fices truth for an effective gesture. As an example of Miss Potter's
empiricism, her rigid adherence to what can be seen and heard,
consider the climax of her masterpiece *The Roly-Poly Pudding*,
Tom Kitten's capture by the rats in the attic:

> *'Anna Maria,' said the old man rat (whose name was Samuel
> Whiskers), 'Anna Maria, make me a kitten dumpling roly-poly
> pudding for my dinner.'*
> *'It requires dough and a pat of butter, and a rolling pin,' said
> Anna Maria, considering Tom Kitten with her head on one side.*
> *'No,' said Samuel Whiskers. 'Make it properly, Anna Maria,
> with breadcrumbs.'*

But in 1908, when *The Roly-Poly Pudding* was published,
Miss Potter was at the height of her power. She was not a born
realist, and her first story was not only romantic, it was historical. *The Tailor of Gloucester* opens:

> *In the time of swords and periwigs and full-skirted coats with*

FROM BEATRIX POTTER'S *The Tale of Tom Kitten*

flowered lappets—when gentlemen wore ruffles, and gold-laced waistcoats of paduasoy and taffeta—there lived a tailor in Gloucester.

In the sharp details of this sentence, in the flowered lappets, there is a hint of the future Potter, but her first book is not only hampered by its period setting but by the presence of a human character. Miss Potter is seldom at her best with human beings (the only flaw in *The Roly-Poly Pudding* is the introduction in the final pages of the authoress in person), though with one human character she succeeded triumphantly. I refer of course to Mr MacGregor, who made an elusive appearance in 1904 in

The Tale of Benjamin Bunny, ran his crabbed earth-mould way through *Peter Rabbit*, and met his final ignominious defeat in *The Flopsy Bunnies* in 1909. But the tailor of Gloucester cannot be compared with Mr MacGregor. He is too ineffective and too virtuous, and the atmosphere of the story—snow, and Christmas bells and poverty—is too Dickensian. Incidentally in Simpkin Miss Potter drew her only unsympathetic portrait of a cat. The ancestors of Tom Thumb and Hunca Munca play a humanitarian part. Their kind hearts are a little oppressive.

In the same year Miss Potter published *Squirrel Nutkin*. It is an unsatisfactory book, less interesting than her first, which was a good example of a bad *genre*. But in 1904, with the publication of *Two Bad Mice*, Miss Potter opened the series of her great comedies. In this story of Tom Thumb and Hunca Munca and their wanton havoc of a doll's house, the unmistakable Potter style first appears.

It is an elusive style, difficult to analyse. It owes something to alliteration:

Hunca Munca stood up in her chair and chopped at the ham with another lead knife.

'It's as hard as the hams at the cheesemonger's,' said Hunca Munca.

Something too it owes to the short paragraphs, which are fashioned with a delicate irony, not to complete a movement, but mutely to criticize the action by arresting it. The imperceptive pause allows the mind to take in the picture: the mice are stilled in their enraged attitudes for a moment, before the action sweeps forward:

Then there was no end to the rage and disappointment of Tom Thumb and Hunca Munca. They broke up the pudding, the lobsters, the pears, and the oranges.

As the fish would not come off the plate, they put it into the red-hot crinkly paper fire in the kitchen; but it would not burn either.

It is curious that Beatrix Potter's method of paragraphing has never been imitated.

The last quotation shows another element of her later style, her love of a precise catalogue, her creation of atmosphere with still-life. One remembers Mr MacGregor's rubbish heap:

There were jam pots and paper bags and mountains of chopped grass from the mowing machine (which always tasted oily), and some rotten vegetable marrows and an old boot or two.

The only indication in *Two Bad Mice* of a prentice hand is the sparsity of dialogue; her characters had not yet begun to utter those brief pregnant sentences, which have slipped, like proverbs, into common speech. Nothing in the early book equals Mr Jackson's, 'No teeth. No teeth. No teeth.'

In 1904 too *The Tale of Peter Rabbit*, the second of the great comedies, was published, closely followed by its sequel, *Benjamin Bunny*. In Peter and his cousin Benjamin Miss Potter created two epic personalities. The great characters of fiction are often paired: Quixote and Sancho, Pantagruel and Panurge, Pickwick and Weller, Benjamin and Peter. Peter was a neurotic, Benjamin worldly and imperturbable. Peter was warned by his mother, 'Don't go into Mr MacGregor's garden; your father had an accident there; he was put in a pie by Mrs MacGregor.' But Peter went from stupidity rather than for adventure. He escaped from Mr MacGregor by leaving his clothes behind, and the sequel, the story of how his clothes were recovered, introduces Benjamin, whose coolness and practicality are a foil to the nerves and clumsiness of his cousin. It was Benjamin who knew the way to enter a garden: 'It spoils people's clothes to squeeze under a gate; the proper way to get in is to climb down a pear tree.' It was Peter who fell down head first.

From 1904 to 1908 were vintage years in comedy; to these years belong *The Pie and the Patty Pan*, *The Tale of Tom Kitten*, *The Tale of Mrs Tiggy Winkle*, and only one failure, *Mr Jeremy Fisher*. Miss Potter had found her right vein and her right scene. The novels were now set in Cumberland; the farms, the village shops, the stone walls, the green slope of Catbells became the background of her pictures and her prose. She was peopling a countryside. Her dialogue had become memorable because aphoristic:

'I disapprove of tin articles in puddings and pies. It is most undesirable—(especially when people swallow in lumps).'

She could draw a portrait in a sentence:

'My name is Mrs Tiggy Winkle; oh yes if you please'm, I'm an excellent clear-starcher.'

And with what beautiful economy she sketched the first smiling villain of her gallery! Tom Kitten had dropped his clothes off the garden wall as the Puddle-Duck family passed:

'Come! Mr Drake Puddle-Duck,' said Moppet. 'Come and help us to dress him! Come and button up Tom!'

Mr Drake Puddle-Duck advanced in a slow sideways manner, ad picked up the various articles.

But he put them on himself. They fitted him even worse than Tom Kitten.

'It's a very fine morning,' said Mr Drake Puddle-Duck.

Looking backward over the thirty years of Miss Potter's literary career, we see that the creation of Mr Puddle-Duck marked the beginning of a new period. At some time between 1907 and 1909 Miss Potter must have passed through an emotional ordeal which changed the character of her genius. It would be impertinent to inquire into the nature of the ordeal. Her case is curiously similar to that of Henry James. Something happened which shook their faith in appearances. From *The Portrait of a Lady* onwards, innocence deceived, the treachery of friends, became the theme of James's greatest stories. Mme Merle, Kate Croy, Mme de Vionnet, Charlotte Stant, these tortuous treacherous women are paralleled through the dark period of Miss Potter's art. 'A man can smile and smile and be a villain'—that, a little altered, was her recurrent message, expressed by her gallery of scoundrels: Mr Drake Puddle-Duck, the first and slightest, Mr Jackson, the least harmful with his passion for honey and his reiterated, 'No teeth. No teeth. No teeth', Samuel Whiskers, gross and brutal, and the 'gentleman with sandy whiskers' who may be identified with Mr Tod. With the publication of *Mr Tod* in 1912, Miss Potter's pessimism reached its climax. But for the nature of her audience *Mr Tod* would certainly have ended tragically. In *Jemina Puddle-Duck* the gentleman with sandy whiskers had at least a debonair impudence when he addressed his victims:

'Before you commence your tedious sitting, I intend to give you a treat. Let us have a dinner party all to ourselves!
'May I ask you to bring up some herbs from the farm garden to make a savoury omelette? Sage and thyme, and mint and two onions, and some parsley. I will provide lard for the stuff—lard for the omelette,' said the hospitable gentleman with sandy whiskers.

But no charm softens the brutality of Mr. Tod and his enemy, the repulsive Tommy Brock. In her comedies Miss Potter had gracefully eliminated the emotions of love and death; it is the measure of her genius that when, in *The Tale of Mr Tod*, they broke the barrier, the form of her book, her ironic style, remained unshattered. When she could not keep death out she stretched her technique to include it. Benjamin and Peter had grown up and married, and Benjamin's babies were stolen by Brock; the immortal pair, one still neurotic, the other knowing and imperturbable, set off to the rescue, but the rescue, conducted in darkness, from a house, 'something between a cave, a prison, and a tumbledown pig-sty', compares grimly with an earlier rescue from Mr MacGregor's sunny vegetable garden:

The sun had set; an owl began to hoot in the wood. There were many unpleasant things lying about, that had much better have been buried; rabbit bones and skulls, and chicken's legs and other horrors. It was a shocking place and very dark.

But *Mr Tod*, for all the horror of its atmosphere, is indispensable. There are few fights in literature which can compare in excitement with the duel between Mr Tod and Tommy Brock (it was echoed by H. G. Wells in *Mr Polly*):

Everything was upset except the kitchen table.

And everything was broken, except the mantelpiece and the kitchen fender. The crockery was smashed to atoms.

The chairs were broken, and the window, and the clock fell with a crash, and there were handfuls of Mr Tod's sandy whiskers.

The vases fell off the mantelpiece, the canisters fell off the shelf; the kettle fell off the hob. Tommy Brock put his foot in a jar of raspberry jam.

Mr Tod marked the distance which Miss Potter had travelled since the ingenuous romanticism of *The Tailor of Gloucester*. The next year with *The Tale of Pigling Bland*, the period of the great near-tragedies came to an end. There was something of the same squalor, and the villain, Mr Thomas Piperson, was not less terrible than Mr Tod, but the book ended on a lyrical note, as Pigling Bland escaped with Pig-Wig:

They ran, and they ran, and they ran down the hill, and across a short cut on level green turf at the bottom, between pebble-beds and rushes. They came to the river, they came to the bridge —they crossed it hand in hand—

It was the nearest Miss Potter had approached to a conventional love story. The last sentence seemed a promise that the cloud had lifted, that there was to be a return to the style of the earlier comedies. But *Pigling Bland* was published in 1913. Through the years of war the author was silent, and for many years after it was over, only a few books of rhyme appeared. These showed that Miss Potter had lost none of her skill as an artist, but left

the great question of whither her genius was tending unanswered. Then, after seventeen years, at the end of 1930, *Little
Pig Robinson* was published.

The scene was no longer Cumberland but Devonshire and the
sea. The story, more than twice as long as *Mr Tod*, was diffuse
and undramatic. The smooth smiling villain had disappeared
and taken with him the pungent dialogue, the sharp detail, the
light of common day. Miss Potter had not returned to the great
comedies. She had gone on beyond the great near-tragedies to
her *Tempest*. No tortured Lear nor strutting Antony could live
on Prospero's island, among the sounds and sweet airs and
cloudcapt towers. Miss Potter too had reached her island, the
escape from tragedy, the final surrender of imagination to safe
serene fancy:

*A steam of boiling water flowed down the silvery strand. The
shore was covered with oysters. Acid-drops and sweets grew
upon the trees. Yams, which are a sort of sweet potato, abounded
ready cooked. The breadfruit tree grew iced cakes and muffins
ready baked.*

It was very satisfying for a pig Robinson, but in that rarefied
air no bawdy Tommy Brock could creep to burrow, no Benjamin pursued his feud between the vegetable-frames, no Puddle-
Duck could search in wide-eyed innocence for a 'convenient dry
nesting-place'.

[1933]

NOTE. On the publication of this essay I received a somewhat acid letter
from Miss Potter correcting certain details. *Little Pig Robinson*, although
the last published of her books, was in fact the first written. She denied
that there had been any emotional disturbance at the time she was writing
Mr Tod: she was suffering however from the after-effects of flu. In conclusion she deprecated sharply 'the Freudian school' of criticism.

Huckleberry Finn: a critical essay

T. S. ELIOT

The Adventures of Huckleberry Finn is the only one of Mark Twain's various books which can be called a masterpiece. I do not suggest that it is his only book of permanent interest; but it is the only one in which his genius is completely realized, and the only one which creates its own category. There are pages in *Tom Sawyer* and in *Life on the Mississippi* which are, within their limits, as good as anything with which one can compare them in *Huckleberry Finn;* and in other books there are drolleries just as good of their kind. But when we find one book by a prolific author which is very much superior to all the rest, we look for the peculiar accident or concourse of accidents which made that book possible. In the writing of *Huckleberry Finn* Mark Twain had two elements which, when treated with his sensibility and his experience, formed a great book: these two are the Boy and the River.

Huckleberry Finn is, no doubt, a book which boys enjoy. I cannot speak from memory: I suspect that a fear on the part of my parents lest I should acquire a premature taste for tobacco, and perhaps other habits of the hero of the story, kept the book out of my way. But *Huckleberry Finn* does not fall into this category of juvenile fiction. The opinion of my parents that it was a book unsuitable for boys left me, for most of my life, under the impression that it was a book suitable only for boys. Therefore it was only a few years ago that I read for the first time, and in that order, *Tom Sawyer* and *Huckleberry Finn*.

Tom Sawyer did not prepare me for what I was to find its sequel to be. *Tom Sawyer* seems to me to be a boy's book, and a very good one. The River and the Boy make their appearance in it; the narrative is good; and there is also a very good picture of society in a small midwestern river town (for St Petersburg is more western than southern) a hundred years ago. But the point of view of the narrator is that of an adult observing a boy. And Tom is the ordinary boy, though of quicker wits and livelier imagination than most. Tom is, I suppose, very much the boy that Mark Twain had been: he is remembered and described as he seemed to his elders, rather than created. Huck Finn, on the other hand, is the boy that Mark Twain still was at the time of writing his adventures. We look at Tom as the smiling adult does: Huck we do not look at—we see the world through his eyes. The two boys are not merely different types; they were brought into existence by different processes. Hence in the second book their roles are altered. In the first book Huck is merely the humble friend—almost a variant of the traditional valet of comedy and we see him as he is seen by the conventional respectable society to which Tom belongs, and of which, we feel sure, Tom will one day become an eminently respectable and conventional member. In the second book their nominal relationship remains the same; but here it is Tom who has the secondary role. The author was probably not conscious of this when he wrote the first two chapters: *Huckleberry Finn* is not the kind of story in which the author knows, from the beginning, what is going to happen. Tom then disappears from our view; and when he returns, he has only two functions. The first is to provide a foil for Huck. Huck's persisting admiration for Tom only exhibits more clearly to our eyes the unique qualities of the former and the commonplacess of the latter. Tom has the imagination of a lively boy who has read a good deal of romantic fiction: he might, of course, become a writer—he might become Mark Twain. Or rather, he might become the more commonplace aspect of Mark Twain. Huck has not imagination, in the sense in which Tom has it: he has, instead, vision. He sees the real world; and he does not judge it—he allows it to judge itself.

Tom Sawyer is an orphan. But he has his aunt; he has, as we learn later, other relatives; and he has the environment into which he fits. He is wholly a social being. When there is a secret band to be formed, it is Tom who organizes it and prescribes the rules. Huck Finn is alone: there is no more solitary character in fiction. The fact that he has a father only emphasizes his loneliness; and he views his father with a terrifying detachment. So we come to see Huck himself in the end as one of the permanent symbolic figures of fiction, not unworthy to take a place with Ulysses, Faust, Don Quixote, Don Juan, Hamlet and other great discoveries that man has made about himself.

It would seem that Mark Twain was a man who—perhaps like most of us—never became in all respects mature. We might even say that the adult side of him was boyish, and that only the boy in him that was Huck Finn was adult. As Tom Sawyer grown up, he wanted success and applause (Tom himself always needed an audience). He wanted prosperity, a happy domestic life of a conventional kind, universal approval, and fame. All these things he obtained. As Huck Finn he was indifferent to all these things; and being composite of the two, Mark Twain both strove for them and resented their violation of his integrity. Hence he became the humorist and even clown: with his gifts, a certain way to success, for everyone could enjoy his writings without the slightest feeling of discomfort, self-consciousness, or self-criticism. And hence, on the other hand, his pessimism and misanthropy. To be a misanthrope is to be in some way divided; or it is sign of an uneasy conscience. The pessimism which Mark Twain discharged into *The Man That Corrupted Hadleyburg* and *What is Man?* springs less from observation of society, than from his hatred of himself for allowing society to tempt and corrupt him and give him what he wanted. There is no wisdom in it. But all this personal problem has been diligently examined by Mr Van Wyck Brooks; and it is not Mark Twain, but *Huckleberry Finn*, that is the subject of this essay.

You cannot say that Huck himself is either a humorist or a misanthrope. He is the impassive observer: he does not interfere, and, as I have said, he does not judge. Many of the episodes that occur on the voyage down the river, after he is joined by the Duke and the King (whose fancies about themselves are akin to the kind of fancy that Tom Sawyer enjoys), are in themselves farcical; and if it were not for the presence of Huck as the reporter of them, they would be no more than farce. But seen through the eyes of Huck, there is a deep human pathos in these scoundrels. On the other hand, the story of the feud between the Grangerfords and the Shepherdsons is a masterpiece in itself; yet Mark Twain could not have written it so, with that economy and restraint, with just the right details and no more, and leaving to the reader to make his own moral reflections, unless he had been writing in the person of Huck. And the *style* of the book, which is the style of Huck, is what makes it a far more convincing indictment of slavery than the sensationalist propaganda of *Uncle Tom's Cabin*. Huck is passive and impassive, apparently always the victim of events; and yet, in his acceptance of his world and of what it does to him and others, he is more powerful than his world because he is more *aware* than any other person in it.

Repeated readings of the book only confirm and deepen one's admiration of the consistency and perfect adaptation of the writing. This is a style which at the period, whether in America or in England, was an innovation, a new discovery in the English language. Other authors had achieved natural speech in relation to particular characters—Scott with characters talking Lowland

Scots, Dickens with cockneys—but no one else had kept it up through the whole of a book. Thackeray's Yellowplush, impressive as he is, is an obvious artifice in comparison. In *Huckleberry Finn* there is no exaggeration of grammar or spelling or speech, there is no sentence or phrase to destroy the illusion that these are Huck's own words. It is not only in the way in which he tells his story, but in the details he remembers, that Huck is true to himself. There is, for instance, the description of the Grangerford interior as Huck sees it on his arrival; there is the list of the objects which Huck and Jim salvaged from the derelict house:

We got an old tin lantern, and a butcher-knife without any handle, and a bran-new Barlow knife worth two bits in any store and a lot of tallow candles, and a tin candlestick, and a gourd, and a tin cup, and a ratty old bedquilt off the bed, and a reticule with needles and pins and beeswax and buttons and thread and all such truck in it, and a hatchet and some nails, and a fish-line as thick as my little finger, with some monstrous hooks on it, and a roll of buckskin, and a leather dog-collar, and a horseshoe, and some vials of medicine that didn't have no label on them; and just as we was leaving I found a tolerable good curry-comb, and Jim he found a ratty old fiddle-bow, and a wooden leg. The straps was broke off, but barring that, it was a good enough leg, though it was too long for men and not long enough for Jim, and we couldn't find the other one, though we hunted all round.

And so, take it all round, we made a good haul.

This is the sort of list that a boy reader should pore over with delight; but the paragraph performs other functions of which the reader would be unaware. It provides the right counterpoise to the horror of the wrecked house and the corpse; it has a grim precision which tells the reader all he needs to know about the way of life of the human derelicts who had used the house; it (especially the wooden leg and the fruitless search for its mate) reminds us at the right moment of the kinship of mind and the sympathy between the boy outcast from society and the Negro fugitive from the injustice of society.

Huck in fact would be incomplete without Jim, who is almost as notable a creation as Huck himself. Huck is the passive observer of men and events, Jim the submissive sufferer from them; and they are equal in dignity. There is no passage in which their relationship is brought out more clearly than the conclusion of the chapter in which, after the two have become separated in the fog, Huck in the canoe and Jim on the raft, Huck, in his impulse of boyish mischief, persuades Jim for a time that the latter had dreamt the whole episode.

'. . . *my heart wuz mos' broke bekase you wuz los', en I didn' k'yer no mo' what become er me en de raf'. En when I wake up en fine you back agin', all safe en soun', de tears come en I could a got down on my knees en kiss' yo' foot, I's so thankful. En all you wuz thinkin' 'bout wuz how you could make a fool uv ole Jim wid a lie. Dat truck dah is trash; en trash is what people is dat puts dirt on de head en dey fren's en makes 'em ashamed.'* . . .

It was fifteen minutes before I could work myself up to go and humble myself to a nigger—but I done it, and I warn't ever sorry for it afterwards, neither.

This passage has been quoted before; and if quote it again, it is because I wish to elicit from it one meaning that is, I think, usually overlooked. What is obvious in it is the pathos and dignity of Jim, and this is moving enough; but what I find still more disturbing, and still more unusual in literature, is the pathos and dignity of the boy, when reminded so humbly and humiliatingly that his position in the world is not that of other boys, entitled from time to time to a practical joke; but that he must bear, and bear alone, the responsibility of a man.

It is Huck who gives the book style. The River gives the book its form. But for the River, the book might be only a sequence of adventures with a happy ending. A river, a very big and powerful river, is the only natural force than can wholly determine the course of human peregrination. At sea, the wanderer may sail or be carried by winds and currents in one direction or another; a change of wind or tide may determine fortune. In the prairie, the direction of movement is more or less at the choice of the caravan; among mountains there will often be an alternative, a guess at the most likely pass. But the river with its strong, swift current is the dictator to the raft or to the steamboat. It is a treacherous and capricious dictator. At one season it may move sluggishly in a channel so narrow that, encountering it for the first time at that point, one can hardly believe that it has travelled already for hundreds of miles and has yet many hundreds of miles to go; at another season it may obliterate the low Illinois shore to a horizon of water, while in its bed it runs with a speed such that no man or beast can survive in it. At such times it carries down human bodies, cattle, and houses. At least twice, at St Louis, the western and the eastern shores have been separated by the fall of bridges, until the designer of the great Eads Bridge devised a structure which could resist the floods. In my own childhood, it was not unusual for the spring freshet to interrupt railway travel; and then the traveller to the east had to take steamboat from the levee up to Alton, at a higher level on the Illinois shore, before he could begin his rail journey. The river is never wholly chartable: it changes its pace, it shifts its channel, unaccountably; it may suddenly efface a sandbar and throw up another bar where before was navigable water.

It is the River that controls the voyage of Huck and Jim, that will not let them land at Cairo, where Jim could have reached freedom; it is the River that separates them and deposits Huck for a time in the Grangerford household; the River that reunites them and then compels upon them the unwelcome company of the King and the Duke. Recurrently we are reminded of its presence and its power.

When I woke up, I didn't know where I was for a minute. I set up and looked around, a little scared. Then I remembered. The river looked miles and miles across. The moon was so bright I could a counted the drift-logs that went a-slipping along, black and still, hundreds of yards out from shore. Everything was dead quiet, and it looked late, and smelt late. You know what I mean—I don't know the words to put it in.

. . . It was kind of solemn, drifting down the big still river, laying on our backs looking up at the stars, and we didn't ever feel like talking loud, and it warn't often that we laughed, only a little kind of a low chuckle. We had mighty good weather as a general thing, and nothing ever happened to us at all, that night, nor the next, nor the next.

Every night we passed towns, some of them away up on black hillsides, nothing but just a shiny bed of lights, not a house could you see. The fifth night we passed St Louis, and it was like the whole world lit up. In St Petersburg they used to say there was twenty or thirty thousand people in St Louis, but I never believed it till I see that wonderful spread of lights at two o'clock that still night. There warn't a sound there; everybody was asleep.

We come to understand the River by seeing it through the eyes of the Boy; but the Boy is also the spirit of the River. *Huckleberry Finn*, like other great works of imagination, can give to every reader whatever he is capable of taking from it. On the most superficial level of observation, Huck is convincing as a boy. On the same level, the picture of social life on the shores of the Mississippi a hundred years ago is, I feel sure, accurate. On any level, Mark Twain makes you see the River, as it is and was and always will be, more clearly than the author of any other description of a river known to me. But you do not merely see the River, you do not merely become acquainted with it through the senses: you experience the River. Mark Twain, in his later years of success and fame, referred to his early life as a steamboat pilot as the happiest he had known. With all allowance for the illusions of age, we can agree that those years were the years in which he was most fully alive. Certainly, but for his having practised that calling, earned his living by that profession, he would never have gained the understanding which his genius for expression communicates in this book. In the pilot's daily struggle with the River, in the satisfaction of activity, in the constant attention to the River's unpredictable vagaries, his consciousness was fully occupied, and he absorbed knowledge of which, as an artist, he later made use. There are perhaps only two ways in which a writer can acquire the understanding of environment which he can later turn to account: by having spent his childhood in that environment—that is, living in it at a period of life in which one experiences much more than one is aware of; and by having had to struggle for a livelihood in that environment—a livelihood bearing no direct relation to any intention of writing about it, of *using* it as literary material. Most of Joseph Conrad's understanding came to him in the latter way. Mark Twain knew the Mississippi in both ways: he had spent his childhood on its banks and he had earned his living matching his wits against its currents.

Thus the River makes the book a great book. As with Conrad, we are continually reminded of the power and terror of Nature, and the isolation and feebleness of Man. Conrad remains always the European observer of the tropics, the white man's eye contemplating the Congo and its black gods. But Mark Twain is a native, and the River God is his God. It is as a native that he accepts the River God, and it is the subjection of Man that gives to Man his dignity. For without some kind of God, Man is not even very interesting.

Readers sometimes deplore the fact that the story descends

to the level of *Tom Sawyer* from the moment that Tom himself reappears. Such readers protest that the escapades invented by Tom, in the attempted 'rescue' of Jim, are only a tedious development of themes with which we were already too familiar —even while admitting that the escapades themselves are very amusing and some of the incidental observations memorable.[1] But it is right that the mood of the end of the book should bring us back to that of the beginning. Or, if this was not the right ending for the book, what ending would have been right?

In *Huckleberry Finn* Mark Twain wrote a much greater book than he could have known he was writing. Perhaps all great works of art mean much more than the author could have been aware of meaning: Certainly *Huckleberry Finn* is the one book of Mark Twain's which, as a whole, has this unconsciousness. So what seems to be the rightness of reverting at the end of the book to the mood of *Tom Sawyer* was perhaps unconscious art. For Huckleberry Finn, neither a tragic nor a happy ending would be suitable. No wordly success or social satisfaction, no domestic consummation would be worthy of him; a tragic end also would reduce him to the level of those whom we pity. Huck Finn must come from nowhere and be bound for nowhere. His is not the independence of the typical or symbolic American Pioneer, but the independence of the vagabond. His existence questions the values of America as much as the values of Europe; he is as much an affront to the 'pioneer spirit' as he is to 'business enterprise'; he is in a state of nature as detached as the state of saint. In a busy world, he represents the loafer; in an acquisitive and competitive world, he insists on living from hand to mouth. He could not be exhibited in any amorous encounters or engagements, in any of the juvenile affections which are appropriate to Tom Sawyer. He belongs neither to the Sunday school nor to the reformatory. He has

---

[1] *e.g.* '*Jim* don't know anybody in China.'

no beginning and no end. Hence, he can only disappear; and his disappearance can only be accomplished by bringing forward another performer to obscure the disappearance in a cloud of whimsicalities.

Like Huckleberry Finn, the River itself has no beginning or end. In its beginning, it is not yet the River; in its end, it is no longer the River. What we call its headwaters is only a selection from among the innumerable sources which flow together to compose it. At what point in its course does the Mississippi become what the Mississippi *means*? It is both one and many; it is the Mississippi of this book only after its union with the Big Muddy—the Missouri; it derives some of its character from the Ohio, the Tennessee, and other confluents. And at the end it merely disappears among its deltas; it is no longer there, but it is still where it was, hundreds of miles to the North. The River cannot tolerate any design to a story, which is its story, that might interfere with its dominance. Things must merely happen, here and there, to the people who live along its shores or who commit themselves to its current. And it is as impossible for Huck as for the River to have a beginning or end— a *career*. So the book has the right, the only possible concluding sentence. I do not think that any book ever written ends more certainly with the right words:

> *But I reckon I got to light out for the Territory ahead of the rest, because Aunt Sally she's going to adopt me and sivilize me, and I can't stand it. I been there before.*

[1950]

Professionals and confessionals: Dr Seuss and Kenneth Grahame

CLIFTON FADIMAN

I've been thinking lately about two writers of children's books who, both first-rate, are interestingly contrastable. One, Kenneth Grahame, who wrote *The Wind in the Willows*, was born in 1859. His centenary was fittingly marked by an excellent book by Peter Green: *Kenneth Grahame: A Biography*. The other is Dr Seuss, 1951 winner of an Academy Award for the screenplay of the now-classic animated cartoon *Gerald McBoing-Boing*, and perhaps the most successful current writer of juvenile literature.

I learn from the new Grahame biography that since its first appearance in 1908 *The Wind in the Willows* has sold an average of 80,000 copies a year. I find this figure difficult to believe. I suspect, though I would enjoy being refuted, that today it is read mainly by grownups. Perhaps it also pleases that small minority of American children in whom reflection is not too severely discouraged—for it is a most thoughtful book.

Not only is it thoughtful. It is even in its dulcet way polemical. And above all it is confessional. Like Andersen, Louisa Alcott, and Mark Twain, Kenneth Grahame put into what he claimed was a children's book his deepest sense of the meaning of his own adult life. Dr Seuss on the other hand is not in the least confessional; he is professional. He writes and draws his books, not as envelopes of covert or unconscious self-revelation, but to please and entertain himself and his young readers.

I believe that into one of these two classes—the confessional or the professional—any notable children's classic is apt to fall.

Kenneth Grahame, born a Scot in 1859 lived most of his life in England, dying in 1932. He was reared by his maternal grandmother. The older Grahame (the mother had died) coolly abandoned the four little Grahames, an action which was forever after to influence Kenneth's views on the character of grownups. The young Grahame, had he been properly educated, would have made an excellent backwater don, and we should probably be minus *The Wind in the Willows*. But his heavy-Victorian uncle would not pay the fees for Oxford and instead arranged for Kenneth to take a post in the Bank of England. His charm, natural intelligence, and physical attractiveness helped the dreamy young man to rise in the bank until in 1898 he became its secretary, and his financial future was assured.

Like many men he possessed no talent for that most exacting of professions, marriage; and like most men he married. (Someday, ten thousand years from now, the race will have advanced to the point where it will perhaps be one-tenth as exigent before granting a marriage licence as it is today before granting a plumber's licence.) Mrs Grahame was an impossible creature, affected, demanding, at bottom a fool. They had one child, Alastair, an unhappy, physically handicapped boy who, the evidence is now virtually all in, committed suicide at twenty by arranging to have a train run over him. There is no reason to suppose that the Grahames had any more ability at child-rearing than at making a harmonious marriage.

As was the case with so many eminent Victorians and Edwardians, Grahame led two lives. The first was imposed on him by his class: the Bank of England job, marriage, money-getting, paternity, respectability. The second was his dream life, the long, sad, halfhearted flight from what is called responsibility.

This dream life was his redress for many things: his father's cruelty; his dissatisfaction not so much with the Bank of England as with the England the bank stood for; his unhealthy relationship with his wife; his bohemian detestation of 'progress', industry, and trade; his aversion from the whole adult world, finding expression in a courteous misanthropy, an excessive love of nature, and an excessive idealization of animals.

Out of the conflict between the imposed life and the buried life came four slim books. One, *Pagan Papers*, is Stevenson-and-water: arty, wistful essays, perfectly in the *fin de siècle* mood of the nineties. *The Golden Age* and *Dream Days* are re-creations of the life of childhood, oddly mingling an affectionate sympathy for the young and a restrained bitterness toward grownups—the 'Olympians', as he ironically termed them.

The only one of Grahame's books that will last is *The Wind in the Willows*. This story of the riverside adventures of the Mole, the Water Rat, the Badger, and the Toad is generally received as a delightful animal fantasy. Indeed it can be so read, particularly by children. But many readers have often vaguely felt it to be more than that, just as they know *Gulliver* to be more than a story about little people and big people. Some of us perhaps find ourselves wondering about the conceited Mr Toad, in many ways an odd character for a child's book. By making Mr Toad a rich man was not Grahame quietly expressing his opinion of his money-making era, as Dickens did more explicitly? By making Mr Toad motor-mad was he not suggesting that the nineteenth century was to its own cost abandoning a life lived simply and naturally?

And then the book is not of one piece. Part of it seems simple and pleasant enough: the conversion of Mole to the delights of river life; the dangers Mole and Rat run in the Wild Wood and their rescue by Badger; Toad's transgressions and his final rehabilitation by the sorely tried but loyal friends. But other parts of the book are allegorical, even philosophical, and young readers will almost surely pass over them lightly. With the chapter called

'The Piper at the Gates of Dawn' and at several other points the
tone alters. What was a humorous fancy about talking animals
turns into a pagan hymn or a sly but not trivial commentary on
the inferiority of humans to beasts.

All these matters are at last fully illuminated in the pages of
Mr Green's biography. I found it admirable, if a mite solemn—
for occasionally the author loses sight of the fact that after all
Grahame is a one-book author, and a minor one at that. He is
almost over-perceptive. Poring over Grahame with a magnifying
lens he discovers more than a few things not open to the natural
vision. What remains once these qualifications are registered is
a fascinating exploration of a life that was a fiasco, in which all
the major problems were side-stepped, the life of a charming,
talented but essentially weak man. Yet out of his very failure,
his hidden resentments, his reluctance to face up to the demands
of his hard century, Grahame drew *The Wind in the Willows*.
The sources of the little masterpiece are traced by Mr Green in
his subject's conscious and unconscious life, much as John Livingston Lowes, that supreme literary sleuth, tracked down in *The
Road to Xanadu* the operations of the mind that produced *The
Ancient Mariner*.

Mr Green's conclusions are subtle and various, but one can
sum them up by saying that in all his work, and particularly in
The Wind in the Willows, Kenneth Grahame was revenging himself on the adult world which he had been forced to join and on
the century whose materialism his sensibility could not accept.
He said once that he was 'not a professional writer'. It is true;
he was a confessional one. The book that he stoutly protested he
wrote for children was a letter written in invisible ink to himself.

On the other hand there is Dr Seuss. I have known Ted Geisel
for many years. (The 'Seuss' is his mother's maiden name, the
'Dr' represents the PH.D. he never quite managed to collect.) I

do not care to infuriate him by suggesting that he has no unconscious and that those extraordinary animals he draws are not symbolic but merely the consequence of his liking to draw extraordinary animals. He may have a complete set of private despairs that he fondles lovingly in the dark—I would be the last man to deprive him of them. He may have a dandy buried life. I wish to state, however, that if he has one it is not reflected in any of the delightful children's books he has written and drawn during the last twenty-five years. While it may not be quite the decent thing these days to say of a friend, I believe Dr Seuss has not only added to the general store of happiness but that he is himself a happy man.

He is also—which such greater artists as Kenneth Grahame were not—a professional writer of juveniles. I do not mean that he writes with cold calculation for a shrewdly gauged market. On the contrary, he writes and draws as he does because he feels that way. But he knows exactly what he is doing. He aims to create nothing more than what meets the eye or ear. He is not *using* his books for any purpose beyond entertaining himself and his readers. *The Wind in the Willows* is a dream. But *On Beyond Zebra* (which deals with the letters of the alphabet after z, such as YUZZ, UM, and HUMPF) and *Horton Hears a Who!*, though far more extravagant, are not dreams. They are ingenious solutions, exploited with unique humour and slyness and absurdity, of the standing problem of the juvenile-fantasy writer: how to find, not another Alice, but another rabbit hole.

The Geisels have no children ('You make 'em—I amuse 'em,' says Dr Seuss), and while he likes youngsters well enough, he does not claim any transcendental understanding of the juvenile mind. (Grahame, it might be noted, did not particularly care for *real* children, only for his dream children, just as Lewis Carroll detested boys and didn't care much for girls once they got beyond Lolita's age.) The sordid fact is that to be a good writer of juveniles you don't have to love children, any more than you have to love criminals to write *Crime and Punishment*.

Ted Geisel turned into Dr Seuss more or less accidentally. Early in his career his absurd animals began to brighten the pages of the old *Judge*. But they did not pay dividends until they were transferred to the world of the Flit advertisements. He might have pursued his career of extermination indefinitely had it not been for his wife, who has all the qualities Elspeth Grahame lacked. Once, returning from Europe on the *Kungsholm*, Mr Geisel, like the man in Mark Twain's story (Punch in the presence of the passenjare!), found himself mumbling over and over to the beat of the ship's engines:

> *And that is a story that no one can beat,*
> *And to think that I saw it on Mulberry Street.*

In order to prevent their lives from being darkened by the continued repetition of this couplet, Mrs Geisel persuaded him to invent a story in which it might reasonably appear. The result was his first book, *And To Think That I Saw It on Mulberry Street*. It was rejected by twenty-seven publishers, on four grounds:

1. Fantasy doesn't sell.
2. Verse doesn't sell.
3. It had no 'pattern', whatever that meant.
4. It wasn't 'practical'—that is, it didn't teach the child how to become a better child, or grownup, or mortician.

The twenty-eighth publisher was densely ignorant of the juvenile market. He published the book for a fantastic reason—he liked it. Since then Dr Seuss's books (according to my calculations there are twenty of them) have sold something in the neighbourhood of four million copies. His *The Cat in the Hat* should be within sight of the million mark. It is probably the most influential first-grade reader since McGuffey. Using only 223 different words, it manages to tell a story that for the first time in the history of beginners'-grade education actually amuses the tot, and so persuades him that reading is a worthwhile experience.

Dr Seuss is a craftsman, not an allegorist, or a satirist in disguise. He modestly ascribes much of his success to the fact that he is his own illustrator, permitting him to make every page pull double weight. In his own way he is as mad about language as Flaubert was. Once he spent five hours in his publisher's office working over a single line of verse until he had removed an extra beat that bothered his ear. In the next room he overheard the editor trying to persuade a lady novelist, whose talents tend to the copious, to remove 75,000 words from her new book. (The editor lost.)

Dr Seuss also believes that children (and grownups too—there's quite a serious Seuss cult) like him because he *bucks* the trend in children's books, supplying oddity instead of wholesome instruction, wild humour instead of mere pleasantness, and the unbelievable instead of a duplication of the child's familiar environment. Whatever may be the good Doctor's secret, there is no doubt that he is the most successful writer in his field today, and a true professional. Whether his work will last, as *The Wind in the Willows* has lasted, is another matter. Possibly the absence of that very ambiguous element you find in Kenneth Grahame, that teasing sense of other meanings and under-meanings, destine it to a shorter life than children's classics saturated with the confessional element. At the moment Dr Seuss is single-handedly changing the reading habits of hundreds of thousands of American children. That's enough for any one man. Somebody ought to give him that PH.D. he's always hankered after.

[1962]

Combined ops

ROSEMARY SUTCLIFF

Once, and only once to date, my Daemon has completely taken over the making of a book for me, telling me what to write and how to write it, and presenting me with a set of ready-made characters who only required putting down on paper, as though they were people I had known and loved rather than creations of my own imagination. The result was *The Eagle of the Ninth*, for which I have had a very special affection ever since. All my other books, save for the very early ones which came lightly and with ease, have been laboriously spun out of my own being, like spider's silk—but probably with considerably more effort and discomfort, stress and exasperation than any spider has to put up with. My Daemon, however, still decides what each book is to be about, which is to say that it is the subject which chooses me and not the other way round. No good for me, having finished one book, to look round anxiously for an idea for the next, even if I know the kind of idea I should like. (I have always wanted to write an eighteenth century story with smugglers in it, but my Daemon says No, and the thing turns to mere cloak-and-dagger in my hands.) I have to wait, keeping, as it were, my doors and windows open; and one day something comes along—a paragraph in a book of local history, a few lines of a poem, a stretch of country that catches my imagination, or simply an idea out of the blue for no apparent reason at all—and my Daemon says, small but unmistakable, 'All right, this is It. Now let's begin.'

The Lantern Bearers was one of these ideas out of the blue.

Not even an idea really, just a thought drifting around and looking for somewhere to settle. I was making the toast and tea for breakfast one morning and thinking of nothing in particular, when it occurred to me (that is the undisciplined way my mind works) how very wide of the mark the usual history book accounts of the withdrawal of the Roman Legions must be.

One leaves school with a vague idea that the Romans came, remained in Britain as a military occupation force—never becoming mingled with the native population—for approximately the same time as lies between the accession of the first Queen Elizabeth and the present day, and were then recalled to defend their native land against the Goths and Vandals. The truth is of course far otherwise. The Legionaries were forbidden to marry while still with the Eagles; but being far from home, with twenty years or so of military service in front of them, they overcame the difficulty by taking unofficial wives from the native population, and making honest women of them when they retired. They then settled in the land of their long service, and their sons joined the Legions after them. There was no marriage ban on the civilian officials, nor on officers above the rank of centurion, and they intermarried freely from the first. So by the time the empire fell to pieces and the order for withdrawal came in 410, the matter had become a far more complicated and tragic one than the mere withdrawing of an occupation force. Many of the men who now made up the three Legions in Britain were native born and bred, they had British mothers and grandmothers and anything up to four hundred years of British roots behind them. They were not being called home from occupied territory, they were being ordered to leave their own country to the Barbarians and go off to die in defence of a concept called Rome that no longer meant very much to them. For many of them there must have been a heartbreaking conflict of loyalties before the transports sailed; and suddenly, standing over the grill and waiting for the kettle to boil, I wondered how many of them went 'wilful missing' at the last moment.

With rising excitement I began to see the situation personified in one young soldier faced with that appalling choice. A boy bred (to make it as hard as possible for him) in the Service tradition of the type of family which in later years sent its sons for generation after generation into the Ghurka Rifles or an English County regiment. I began to wonder what he would feel like if he chose Britain, took the way of a deserter and let his comrades sail without him; and what would happen to him afterwards. While I was wondering, the kettle boiled over and the toast went up in flames.

I dealt with the crisis, and later consumed charred toast and marmalade with my mind in fifth-century Britain, my family wondering the while whether I was overcome with remorse for past sins, trying to remember the name of something, or had merely been taken worse with an idea.

I began by going through any books of my own that might provide a page or two on the end of the Roman era. Arthur Weigell's *Wanderings in Roman Britain* and *Wanderings in Anglo-Saxon Britain* gave me a little; so did *The Romans in Britain* by Bertram Windle, Collingwood's *Roman Britain*, and volume 1 of the *Pelican History of England*. Arthur Bryant's *The Makers of the Realm* yielded only a few words, but they were written in fire. One of the first things I discovered was that although the last regular Legions were withdrawn in 410, the last Auxiliary troops did not follow them until about forty years later. That pushed the start of my story on to 449 and made my hero an Auxiliary and not a Legionary officer; for if there were imperial troops of any kind still in Britain after he made his choice, the story lost most of its force. It also opened up the tremendously exciting possibility that he might have come in contact with the historical hero who stood behind the legends of King Arthur; for it is, I think, generally accepted now that the fighting years of that hero, chieftain or war lord or whatever he was, lay in the second half of the fifth century and the beginning of the sixth.

I turned to Gildas, Nennius, William of Malmesbury, and Geoffrey of Monmouth. They made enchanting reading, save for Gildas who was too busy telling everybody what he thought of them to be pleasant, but they either didn't mention Arthur at all or seemed too full of dragons to be really reliable.

After that I started on the county library. I wanted books about the Roman withdrawal, the coming of the Saxons, the Dark Ages in general, Arthur in particular. I didn't know the names of any of the books I wanted, but that was what they had to be *about*. The county library, as always, rose nobly to the occasion and after a frustrating delay while they searched the rest of the United Kingdom on my behalf, produced, among other books, the *Battle for Britain in the 5th Century* and *The Rise of Wessex*, both by T. Dayrell Reed. These proved to be treasure trove. They provided a possible and coherent reconstruction of the years between the fall of Roman Britain and the rise of Saxon England—desperate and heroic years when the British people, far from lying down passively to be slaughtered, as was at one time believed, were fighting to the last ditch. Also, in the first volume the author had a good deal to say about the historical Arthur, even a theory to offer as to who he might have been by birth. And the theory seemed to me a good one.

So gradually the background grew and took shape, and against this more or less fixed background my own particular young soldier, his character and his fortunes and his reactions to those fortunes, began to develop.

He was another decendant of Marcus's, and therefore he had to be called by one of Marcus's names or a name derived from one of them. I had already used Flavius for the hero of *The Silver Branch*, so he became Aquila and developed a character to suit his name. His home was the farm that Marcus had made below the South Downs three hundred years before, and Marcus's signet ring with its flawed emerald was still in the family.

But if the story was to deal with the Romano-British resistance to the Saxons as well as with the fortunes of Aquila, that aspect of it, as well as Aquila's private affairs, must be brought to a fit ending-off place; one of those places where history reaches a climax or pauses for breath. The only place for the ending of *The Lantern Bearers* (the name had come already) was the Battle of Wallop, where the Romano-British won the first of a series of resounding victories over the Saxon hordes. It was, for the time being, the turning of the tide. But it did not happen until 472. So if Aquila was nineteen, which seemed a likely age, at the start of the story, he was going to be forty-three by the end. Since it was supposed to be a children's book, that meant a son to carry on the interest, and presumably a wife to produce the son. I gave him Ness and an 'arranged' marriage ripening slowly into something else; and I gave him Flavian, called after his father but commonly known as The Minnow because of one of those family jokes so small that viewed from outside the family they are almost invisible. I gave him the tragedy of his greatly loved sister because it was the kind of thing that must have happened so often; as Flavia herself says, 'Isn't it always so? The men fight, and after the fighting, the women fall to the Conquerors.' And having done that, I knew (for I was beginning to understand him reasonably well by that time) what effect it would have on him: the hard defensive shell of bitterness and the fear of being hurt more than he could bear a second time that would maim his relationships with other people, especially anyone he loved, from that time forward; and that it would take the rest of the book, and the help of most of the other characters in it, for him to work out his salvation.

At which point my Daemon, ignoring the existence already of a large red exercise book dropsical with notes, and a vast number of hieroglyphics on the back of envelopes, said 'Enough! Now come down to earth and start writing.'

And so, on a clean new sheet of foolscap, *The Lantern Bearers* was begun.

[1960]

4 *Illustration*

Creation of a picture book

EDWARD ARDIZZONE

I am not an expert. I am a man with a family who has made up stories for his children. For the past thirty-four years I have been a practising artist, during which time I have painted many hundreds of pictures, illustrated over eighty books by various authors, written and illustrated ten of my own books, taught at the Royal College of Art in London, and done many other things. After so long a time, it is inevitable that one should have developed some ideas about one's craft.

The story of *Little Tim and the Brave Sea Captain*, the first of the Tim books, was invented twenty-four years ago. It did not spring ready-made to the mind, but started as a rather brief little tale made up on the spur of the moment to amuse my children. Luckily it did amuse them, so it was told again the next day and then the day after that and so on, and each time it was told again it grew somewhat in the telling until I finally found I had a story which I felt was worth illustrating and sending to the publisher.

Now this process of telling and retelling until it grows into something worthwhile has two major advantages. The first is that the script will inevitably be cast in a mould which is easily read aloud; and this is important, because the poor parents may

well have to read the story over and over again. Secondly, and
probably more important, the children will often make their
own suggestions. They will add those wonderful inconsequential
details which only children can think of and which, if incorpor-
ated in a tale, so greatly enrich the narrative.

When it comes to making the drawings for one's tale and
writing down the tale to match the drawings, then a number of
special problems arise, problems which are peculiar to the production of picture books. In picture books the drawings, of
course, are as important as, or more important than, the text. The
text has to be short, not more than two thousand words. In fact,
the text can only give bones to the story. The pictures, on the
other hand, must do more than just illustrate the story. They
must elaborate it. Characters have to be created pictorially because there is no space to do so verbally in the text. Besides the
settings and characters, the subtleties of mood and moment have
to be suggested.

Now this is where the old convention of the balloon coming
out of a character's mouth, with writing in the balloon, can be
invaluable. Take a passage like this from *Tim to the Rescue*. The
situation so far is that Ginger, who has anointed his hair with the
Mate's hair restorer and whose hair is growing alarmingly,
comes up before the ship's barber to have his hair cut for the
umpteenth time. In the drawing, there is poor mop-headed Ginger with the tears streaming down his face, the barber with his
scissors, and the Bosun. The text reads as follows: 'Seaman
Bloggs, the ship's barber, said he was sick and tired of it, that
his fingers were worn to the bone and that he ought to have
extra pay.' But in the drawing, a balloon comes out of Bloggs's
mouth in which is written, 'Blimey, Mr Bosun. I just can't, my
thumb aches simply 'orrible.' While out of the Bosun's mouth
comes another balloon in which is written, 'Mutiny, eh Bloggs!'

You will see at once that what is said in the balloon pinpoints
the characters of Bloggs and the Bosun for us, as well as describing the tension in the ship due to the deplorable growth of

Ginger's hair. This would take a page or more of text to describe, and in picture books, with only sixty words to a page, there is not the room to spare. Balloons, however, must be used sparingly; otherwise one's book might take on the character of a strip cartoon, which would be sad indeed.

Now to make drawings which tell a story clearly and in which characters are portrayed convincingly and subtleties of mood conveyed is difficult. It demands some professional ability, more ability even than the writing of the text. There is an idea that the work of an amateur or inexperienced artist is suitable for books for little children, provided they have a certain spurious brightness of colour. Though there may be exceptions, I think this idea a bad one. Little children should have the best possible pictures to look at, and I think too that good or bright colour alone is not sufficient to make a good picture. Drawing is of paramount importance. The well-known picture-book classics by Kate Greenaway, Randolph Caldecott, Beatrix Potter, William Nicholson, and, nearer our own time, Jean de Brunhoff, are all impeccably drawn.

Writing the text for a picture book also has its particular difficulties, the main one being that the tale has to be told in so few words yet must read aloud easily and sound well when read. Another difficulty is that at the turn of each page, and one rarely has more than one hundred and twenty words between the turns, the text must end with a natural break, a note of interrogation or suspense. With rare exceptions, the professional writer who is no artist finds this extremely difficult, if not impossible, to do. Not being visually minded, he cannot leave out enough; he must elaborate; he cannot visualize how the picture will tell the story. And this, I think, is why the best picture books have been created by artists who have written their own text. It is a one-man job.

In what I have said I seem to have suggested that a good picture book should contain certain elements which can be defined and enumerated. Yet if somebody asked what made a good picture book, I would be hard put to say. Some genius might easily come along and break all the rules and produce a work of enduring delight. All the same, I feel sure that there is a basic quality or virtue common to all the finest work and, rather hesitatingly, I suggest it may be the quality of enjoyment. The author-artist must enjoy the act of creating his book. It must be fun for him and he must believe in it. Or rather, he must create a world in which, in spite of all sorts of improbabilities from an adult point of view, he can believe in one part of himself, the childish part.

Characters in the books must also have life. Tim, or Ginger who is not very clever and rather jealous, the disgruntled Bloggs, or the respectable Mrs Smawley must all act their parts and never act out of character. This is particularly so in the drawings. One must be able to believe in them.

To repeat what I have said, the author must enjoy creating this book and must believe in it. Put another way, one might say that, for the childish part of him, the story must be both possible and true, and of course in its childish framework it must have its own formal logic. You will notice in the splendid kingdom of Babar the Elephant how all the animals act quite logically in the given framework. Then, I think, the story might have that enduring appeal which makes it a classic. It will be a story that may well appeal to the childish element in the adults, as well as to the child.

However, let's take this question of the author's enjoyment of his work somewhat further and say the following, which sounds something of a paradox: the author-artist does not primarily create his books for children, but rather to amuse that childish part of himself. If this is so, and he may not always admit it, he will never be in danger of committing that cardinal error of writing and drawing down to children. Instead he will be writing up to himself. I am sure we are all agreed that this question of writing up or down for children is of the greatest importance. Little children love all books. They have no taste, and rightly so, and of course will read and look at anything with pleasure. All the more reason, therefore, that we should give them the best.

But what is the best, what sort of books should be given to children, what kinds of subject dealt with? I don't know, nor have I the courage or the knowledge to discuss the subject. This is surely the province of the educationalist and the child psychologist. All the same, I will be brave enough to say that I think we are possibly inclined, in a child's reading, to shelter him too much from the harder facts of life. Sorrow, failure, poverty, and possibly even death, if handled poetically, can surely all be introduced without hurt. After all, books for children are in a sense an introduction to the life that lies ahead of them. If no hint of the hard world comes into these books, then I am not sure that we are playing fair. In this respect, I think the old nursery rhymes are splendid. Their fine jingling rhymes, their words, sometimes cruel and sometimes gay and often meaningless to fit the jingle, are never sentimental. They seem to express a sort of racial experience which is the very stuff of life itself. Then again, take the beautiful stories of a writer like Hans Andersen. What a wonderful introduction they are to the poetry of the emotions, with the implication that children can enjoy sadness and the pleasure of tears at some sad tale as well as grownups.

Now in all this I may be wrong. But what I do find when I read to children, and what indeed I can be sure of, is that children, particularly little children, love the sounds of words for their own sake, which is why they so often love listening to verse. One should therefore be choosy as to the quality of the verse and prose one gives them. The prose in particular should not only be simple and lucid but should have a poetic cadence which will appeal to the ear. Long and difficult words can be used as long as they are explained as the text unfolds. Notice how cunningly Beatrix Potter does this. Children, in fact, love strange words, and I don't think it matters much if at first they don't understand them.

I am often asked why the Tim books are about the sea and

FROM EDWARD ARDIZZONE's *Tim All Alone*

not about animals or fairies or other possibly more suitable themes. The answer, of course, is they are what they are because of the kind of artist I am. An artist's work is not really divisible into compartments. I like drawing people and creating characters visually and therefore the Tim books are primarily about people. They are about the sea because where else can one find a more splendid gallery of characters than on the little ships that sail around our coasts?

The scenes in the books are, to a great extent, drawn from old half-forgotten memories of past experiences. Not that I have suffered shipwreck or collision or fire at sea or any such adventures; but I made, as a child, the long sea voyage from China to England and have been at sea much since then and seen a gale or two. Now for me, these old half-forgotten memories are far the best to work from. Time has removed the inessentials, while nostalgia has given them a poignancy which no close or too well remembered thing can have. For instance, Tim's house by the sea was one we stayed in long ago. The beach that ran in front of it and stretched away as far as the eye could see we knew in all weathers. I dare say that the imperfections of memory and nostalgia have caused me to make this house with its odd balcony and the beach with its steep pebble bank and wooden greyness look more romantic in my drawings than they really are. But what of that! Surely for the purpose of illustration they are better for it.

The little ships that are pictured so often in the Tim books are based on very old memories indeed. I used to play on them as a child before the 1914 war. In those days we lived in Ipswich, a small seaport town on the east coast of England. It was a rough, tough, and lively little town and no bad place for boys to be in. Being a seaport town, there were the docks, and the docks were always full of a variety of craft—small coastal steamers carrying grain or china in their holds; Dutch boats, with their high bows and sterns, which sailed across the North Sea from Rotterdam and Antwerp; and barges with their great red sails. These barges carried cargo from port to port along the coast.

My cousin Arthur and I would play truant and spend many happy hours on these docks. The sailors were kindly men and we were given free run of their craft. The decks and the rigging were ours to play on, and we were allowed to explore both engine room and hold. The mates and bosuns and ordinary seaman—I knew them all. Changed they may be in my drawings. All the same, when I look over London Bridge and see the ships lying in the Pool of London below, they look little different from those of nearly fifty years ago and the men seem little different too from the men I used to know.

I have, in the course of years, illustrated many books by various authors, and many of these books have been for children. Illustrating other people's books is never quite as easy or so pleasant as illustrating one's own. If one has no feeling for a book, neither for its language nor imagery, then the task can be a difficult and weary one. As a professional, to get a book like this is all in the day's work and no excuse for making bad drawings, though I fear it sometimes leads to indifferent ones. On the other hand, when it comes to illustrating for a fine and poetic writer, then it is a different matter. To illustrate Walter de la Mare's *Peacock Pie* was sheer delight, and sheer delight it was, too, to illustrate the poems and prose of such writers as James Reeves and Eleanor Farjeon.

In all these books the very sound of the words is evocative of pretty pictures. It is as if the poems or stories take charge and illustrate themselves and one's pen is only a medium for their self-expression. In truth, I have found that all works by good authors, especially poetic ones, have this in common, whether they were written in prose or verse. That is, that the meaning of the words plus the sound of the words always produce a precise visual image. There is no ambiguity about them, and therefore the illustrator's task is made an easy one. For example, let's take the first verse of Walter de la Mare's 'Song of Enchantment':

> *A song of enchantment I sang me there*
> *In a green wood by waters fair*
> *Just as the words came up to me*
> *I sang it under the wildwood tree.*

Or take this poem of James Reeves's called 'The Street Musician':

> *With plaintive fluting, sad and slow*
> *The old man by the woodside stands.*
> *Who would have thought such note could flow*
> *From such cracked lips and withered hands?*
>
> *On shivering legs he stoops and sways,*
> *And not a passer stops to hark;*
> *No penny cheers him as he plays;*
> *About his feet the mongrels bark.*

But piping through the bitter weather,
  He lets the world go on its way.
Old piper! Let us go together,
  And I will sing and you shall play.

Now what more can an illustrator want than to have such verse to illustrate! The work of creation is done for him and all that remains is to make the drawings, and that is the easiest part of his task.

Before I finish, I would like to mention one book which is not strictly a children's book and which is by the author of some of the greatest prose ever written in the English language. The book is *The Pilgrim's Progress*, and I cannot resist including a short passage from the opening page: 'I dreamed, and behold I saw a man clothed in rags, standing in a certain place, with his face from his own house, a book in his hand, and a great burden upon his back. I looked, and saw him open the book, and read therein; and as he read, he wept and trembled; and not being able longer to contain, he brake out with a lamentable cry, saying, "What shall I do?" '

This is noble language, but to me the genius of Bunyan is shown in the phrase 'with his face from his own house'. This phrase instantly visualizes the scene for us. Christian has his back to his house. The house is obviously visible but must be some way off on the edge of a distant town, and the town itself must be surrounded by a flat, sad, and somewhat open landscape.

I illustrated the wonderful book about twelve years ago. But for twenty years before that it had been my ambition to do so. In fact, my first acquaintance with it came earlier still. I was a schoolboy when I was given a tiny pocket edition illustrated with many thumbnail engravings which delighted me. On looking back, I think it was this book, and particularly these little engravings, which started me off on my career. In a way, it crystallized in me the desire to become an illustrator and a painter.

It was many years before I could achieve this. I had to earn my living in various jobs in the city of London until I was twenty-six and it was only then that I could break away. Of course this long period of office work had its influence. It meant that I had little art school training. It also meant that I turned to the more exacting medium of watercolour, since oils took too long, and also, of course, to the graphic arts. If I had not had this long period as a clerk I might have been, for better or for worse, a very different sort of painter. Therefore I have no regrets.

To conclude, let me return for a moment to my own children's books. They were, of course, primarily written and illustrated to amuse the children, and I hope that the poor grownups who have read them over and over again do not find them too irksome. But all the same, they were still written largely to amuse that childish part of myself. I am afraid this is an awful confession to make, but alas I am not only incorrigible but also unrepentant, and so will go on concocting new works merely for the fun of it.

[1961]

Children's book illustration: the pleasures and problems

ROGER DUVOISIN

When I was offered the honour of speaking here for 'one full hour' about children's books, I worried a bit. The letter of invitation was clear: 'We want you to speak for one full hour.' This was flattering. To speak for one full hour without interruption is an opportunity never offered to most people. But it meant also, I took for granted, a formal *serious* talk. A formal serious talk, when 'amusing and fun' is probably more appropriate to describe the making of children's books. In the actual work of making a child's book, the artist had better keep his sense of humour and pleasure about him: if he forgets to do so, he may well end up with a book which will bore children. Therefore, I will mix fun and seriousness in trying to tell about my personal pleasures and problems in this delightful occupation of illustrating children's books.

First, I must say I have a suspicion that more than a few artists who write and illustrate children's books have not deliberately chosen the occupation: they discovered its pleasures accidentally while doing some sort of stories with drawings as a form of play with their own children. It does not take long when playing in this fashion to have the rough form of a lively story, and all done with the participation of the children themselves. In executing this little feat the artist may be astonished to discover a previously unknown talent in himself.

Everyone who has improvised stories and pictures in the presence of a few children knows the fun one can have in that game. When this act has life and humour, the children's eager eyes and laughter are pleasant rewards. Even the bored looks which come to the children's faces when the story and the pictures lack inventiveness are part of the amusement. Bored looks spur one to higher feats of imagination in order to bring back the laughs.

The making of children's picture books is indeed like playing with children. The game is on even when the author-illustrator sits alone at his drawing table. For he is really not as lonely as he seems to be. He has his abstract public with him, as have artists in every field. In his case it is a public made up of two kinds of children. First, there is the child *he* was, a child who is very much present and who inspires him and helps him understand the other children. Second, there are the abstract children who are watching over his shoulder.

From his own childhood, he remembers the things, impressions, attitudes which impressed him most. He remembers his childhood conceptions of people, of animals, of scenes, and of books which were part of his world.

From the abstract children watching over his shoulder, he will have the fresh, unexpected, imaginative conceptions which they have expressed during games or conversations. In this give and take with his abstract public of children the illustrator will learn to let his imagination flow more freely.

There is in the maker of children's books what is in most adults in their relations to children: that little sneaking desire to teach and to moralize, to pass on to children what we think of our world. A picture book is such a fine medium for this exercise that it is difficult to resist the temptation. Even if these sentiments are carefully hidden in the book they are generally there, and so much the better. The children's-book maker has the added pleasure of believing that he has done more than merely entertain. Personally, I like to think that while children read my books they do not waste their time on the hundreds of toy trucks, cars, tractors, and bulldozers which fill most children's rooms nowadays, or on some of those books of useless facts.

The modern picture book with its large pages, its wealth of colour made possible by modern processes of reproduction, is a tempting invitation to the artist to play with his brush and pen. The fine books which have been published in recent years prove that more and more artists of talent are eager to join in the fun.

This fun is apparent to anyone who walks into public or school libraries or into bookstores. And it is fun which is spreading far and wide, for the modern picture book has invaded the world. I have seen picture-book stores all over Europe, east and west. I have seen a few in Iran. In an Iranian bookstore, a clerk brought out a book which he said was the outstanding picture book in Iran. I told him that I had seen two better ones in the office of a Teheran publishing firm. 'I do not think that could be,' he answered, 'this one was chosen by the American Institute of Graphic Art for their book *The Children's Books of Asia.*' And indeed, he brought me the book which, until then, I had never seen. It was a most interesting book. This indicated that in Asia there were bookstores with children's-book departments such as the one I was visiting. There are very few of these stores in poor countries, however.

One might ask where all this is taking the children's-book creators. What standing have they won in our society? Who will take seriously artists who spend so much of their time playing with children and children's books? Not many people, in my own experience. Not even their own children. When I filled out an application for a passport last year, I wrote 'Children's book illustrator and writer' in the space for 'occupation'. When the clerk saw this he looked up with a wink and a smile

FROM ROGER DUVOISIN'S *Petunia*

and said, 'Hm, children's books, eh?' There was absolutely no doubt that he meant, 'Hm, harmless fellow.' Or at a party of serious business people, a lady friend is liable to introduce you to a grave-looking gentleman and say, 'This is Roger Duvoisin; he is the author of *Petunia the Silly Goose.*' This is sure to bring another wink and a smile. A third example is that of my granddaughter, who was asked when she was nine, 'Well, Anne, do you write stories for children as does your grandfather?' 'Oh yes,' she replied, 'I do write children's stories, but when I grow up I will write grownup stories.'

Anne can be forgiven for she did not know that generally speaking one has to be a grownup to write and illustrate stories which children will enjoy. But as for those grave, practical grownups, I know it is they who are foolish, they who should be smiled and winked at. Their attitude does not give me the slightest inferiority complex. I have no apologies to offer for being part of a zoo of imaginary animals, geese, hippopotamuses, rabbits, lions, raccoons, bugs, crocodiles, and others. These animals are my loyal friends and my wife's too. We have much affection for them. Together we do our best to make the imaginative stories and fantasies which children need to develop their imagination and to learn about reality.

Instead of living in a zoo I could just as well live among fairies, dragons, dwarfs, and giants. They are just as necessary to children. But I love my zoo and I prefer to draw animals. Besides, animals have been used as symbols of men and to represent the gods and the world of magic ever since men could talk.

But there is also a serious aspect to the making of children's books, an aspect which at times demands very much hard work. This other aspect of children's books concerns the illustrations from an artistic point of view. That is to say that while the artist desires to communicate his own pleasure to children, he wants to do so with illustrations that are original in their conceptions, that are well composed in their designs and colours. In this he is driven by his own need to experiment and to try to improve his art, and he is encouraged by the importance the art in children's books has acquired as an art form.

The two aspects of illustrating children's books—the fun aspect and the serious artistic aspect—should not be separated really, for they are part of one overall effort to make a book as good and as beautiful as possible. But I will separate them here for the purpose of making it easier to explain, if I can, what an illustration is and what makes it beautiful.

The modern picture book, then, must be considered as more than a vehicle to carry stories and pictures to children in order to amuse them and give food to their imagination—and to amuse their authors at the same time. It is also a most interesting medium for artists to experiment in with colours and design—to invent to their heart's content. This is why many talented artists have been attracted to the picture book, not only for the fun of it but also for the opportunities it offers for their art. The result is that the best children's books have become art creations without losing the particular qualities which give pleasure to children.

Imagine a layman listening to one artist as he explains to another artist what he is trying to do in working on a new book. What he may hear will make him wonder whether the poor child has not been completely overlooked in the problems the artist is trying to solve. These problems may pertain only to the proportions of margins to the interest of the white spaces and coloured shapes, to the inventiveness of the design, to the relationship of the various colours, and other such problems.

Where is the child in all these things? Has he been sent to bed to leave the grownups to discuss serious things without being disturbed? The answer is that the child is very much present indeed. One of the reasons for making a page which is well designed is to tell the story with more simplicity, more verve, clarity, and impact; to give importance to what is important; to eliminate what destroys the freshness, the originality of the page; in other words, to make a page which will be more easily read by the child. A well-designed page will also educate the child's taste and his visual sense. A beautiful book is a beautiful object which the child may learn to love.

The modern children's-book illustrator is not isolated from the turmoil of the art world around him. Instinctively or consciously, sometimes too consciously, he tries to swim in the current with varying degrees of success, depending on his talent. He wants to present to children books which reflect what he has learned from the new developments in art.

What these developments are everyone interested in painting and the graphic arts knows very well, but it seemed to me that it would be interesting to speak about them here and to tell how they are affecting the making of children's books.

Roughly, the extraordinary things which happened to painting during the nineteenth and twentieth century—its evolution away from representation and toward pure abstraction—have made the art of illustration what it is today. Illustration in some of its forms has long been confused with painting, and it is this evolution of painting toward abstraction which has helped clarify the difference between the two. However some confusion still exists. Illustration, in its narrow meaning, is an art whose purpose is to complement a text in a book or a magazine, to tell the story pictorially. But an illustration can tell a story without the help of a text. In this wider meaning, an illustration is a form of independent writing. It is pictorial literature.

It can even be said that illustration antedates the written word, for many of the prehistoric paintings or drawings were illustrations. For instance, those of the Tassili region in North Africa often describe scenes of the material or religious life of the people who made them: hunting, war, dance scenes, etc. The religious frescoes and paintings of the medieval period and the Renaissance were, for the people who could not read, what the illustrations in a picture book are for the child who has not yet learned to read. They told pictorially the stories and legends the people had heard.

A painting can be an illustration. A large painting which describes a battle scene can be merely a painted illustration and not a true painting. That is, its end may be strictly literary: to tell the story of a battle. Two well-known French painters of the nineteenth century—the historical painter Detaille and the great painter Delacroix—serve well as examples of this. When Detaille did a battle scene his purpose was simply to tell a highly sentimentalized, romanticized version of that battle. He painted the figures, the arms, and the uniforms down to the last button with a precise realism, like a storyteller who can't help putting in all the details. To Delacroix, however, the battle scenes he chose to paint were but subjects on which to work out abstract problems of painting. Even if, superficially, one will see only romantic pictures of battle scenes in the works of these two painters, the fact remains that Delacroix painted a painting while Detaille painted an illustration. This is how paintings can be confused with illustrations and illustrations with paintings.

Painting is the independent, abstract creation of an artist—abstract whether the subject which started it on its way remains or disappears in the process of creation, or whether there ever was any subject to begin with.

The arbitrary division between abstraction and representation in a painting has sometimes been explained by replacing a painting by a page of Chinese writing. To a person who cannot read Chinese, such a page is simply a beautiful abstract design. It means nothing, it only satisfies the visual senses. If, by some magic, the person admiring the abstract design of the page could suddenly understand the Chinese language and Chinese writing, the page would automatically cease to be a beautiful abstract design affecting the visual sense. It would become a poem about a lake, or a Chinese tale, or any other piece of writing. Only the trained artist may continue to admire the beauty of the abstract design.

Now, the point where a representational painting ceases to be a painting and becomes an illustration is not a well-defined one. The layman can take comfort in the fact that painters themselves do not always agree on the matter.

Up to the nineteenth century, no artist had left in writing his opinion of what makes a painting a true painting. We have only the opinions of writers who, for centuries, have considered that painting was an imitation of nature. In other words, a painting was a picture or illustration or literature.

The Greeks—for example, Aristotle—had expressed this opinion. The Greek paintings, the drawings on the Greek vases, all their art and sculpture were imitations of nature. They were representations of mythological figures or of everyday scenes. Unfortunately, we do not know what the artists thought of their art.

The paintings of the Romans reached an astonishing degree of realism. Many are pure illustrations painted on walls. They reveal to us the most intimate details of everyday life and the Roman's pictorial conceptions of their mythology.

The art of Byzantium was an interlude. Its almost abstract art ended realism and literature in art for several hundred years.

But toward the end of the thirteenth century the famous painter Giotto brought back realism and literature in painting. Whatever the value of his paintings as true paintings, their realism was the reason for his very success. People of his day flocked to see his paintings. Never before had the figures and scenes of the church seemed so alive to them. His realism and illustrative talent were highly praised by the writers of his day and of later periods. For them Giotto had liberated painting from the conventions of Byzantine art.

With the discovery of the laws of perspective in the fifteenth century, painting became more than ever illustration for most everyone, even for some painters. It is probable that most of the

princes who ordered these paintings saw in them masterful illustrations of religious, mythological, or historical literature, and
illustrations of their personal feats.

The problem went on during the next centuries and is well
demonstrated in the art criticism which has been written all
along. Paintings were almost continuously judged for qualities
which were literary ones. A quotation from an eighteenth-
century writer will give a good example. It was written about a
painting by the French painter Greuze which was titled 'The
Death of a Wicked Father':

*The death of a wicked father, abandoned by his children, tears
the soul of the spectator. It is hair raising. Everything expresses
the despair of the dead, the disorder and horror of his condition.
The strong, deep, revolting impression made by the painting
repulsed many spectators. There is here a sublimity, as well as a
beauty which few souls could bear.*

In this case the painter was expressing human feelings which
could be expressed in words. This made his painting a piece of
literature. So we can forgive the writer for wanting to put it
down in writing.

But the great painters of every period most certainly knew
that the representation of a subject was not what mattered most
in a painting even though they could not have discussed abstraction in the way it is discussed today.

It was in the nineteenth century that painters began to be
articulate about the problem. Delacroix seems to have been the
first to write on the subject. He was not only a great painter, he
could also write well about painting. His diary and his letters
make extremely interesting reading for artists. As far as we
know, he was the first to express concern because people misunderstood paintings. When he painted he was not writing, he
said. He had nothing to tell in mind. His paintings were only

meant to reach the senses. In other words, what was of value in them was felt and could not be expressed in words. He also seems to have been the first to question the necessity of the subject. Its elimination was, of course, the most effective way to clear the misunderstanding. It is ironical that Delacroix ended up by being the victim of the subject. The subjects he chose for his paintings were so romantic that the paintings have not been popular in our century. But painters still see the true art in his paintings under their romantic dress.

More and more painters toward the end of the last century expressed the opinion that painting was a creation, an abstraction, not an imitation of nature, not literature. This led to twentieth-century painting, to pure non-representational art.

But painting also ceased to appeal to the layman. Spectators were so accustomed to considering painting as pictures or illustrations that their reactions were ones of revolt and anger when they first saw the paintings whose subjects were beginning to break up. They were frustrated at not recognizing their illustrations and accused the painters of mocking them. I remember the indignation that was created by a poster when I was a child. It represented a large horse done in stone lithography. The horse was not particularly distorted, but it was green. A green horse! Who had ever seen a green horse! That slight departure from realism was enough to bring a wave of protests.

While the painters were slowly effecting the divorce of illustration from painting, dismembering the subject, planning its final murder, the professional book illustrators had a good time.

Illustrated books were popular during the nineteenth century. There were many professional illustrators of talent who were often accomplished craftsmen in wood or copper engraving and in the new reproduction process of stone lithography. These illustrations were printed in black, but were sometimes coloured by hand. During the second half of the century the printing of colour overlays was perfected. But illustrators generally followed the tradition of realism and of closely following the text with exact literalness.

Children's-book illustrators were also busy during this time. What is remarkable is how some of these illustrators remained solidly wedded to the contemporary literature they illustrated. *Alice in Wonderland* and Tenniel comes to mind first as the classic example. When we think of Alice, we think of Tenniel's conception of her, and if we read the book without Tenniel's illustrations something is missing. At the turn of the century, *The Wind and the Willows* and Arthur Rackham is another example. We may not like now the mannered style of Rackham but his illustrations are well wedded to the story.

Even when an illustrator was not the contemporary of the author whose books he illustrated, his name could be closely associated with these books. Doré was such an illustrator. His drawings were not particularly distinguished, nor was he concerned with well-composed pages, but he had enormous verve and imagination. His name was for long identified with some of the classics he illustrated. Among these are masterpieces which are loved by children. They are Perrault's *Mother Goose Tales* and La Fontaine's *Fables*. In *Mother Goose Tales* Doré added to the fantasy of the tales; his forests were as dark, frightening, and mysterious as fairy-tale forests should be, and the romanticism of his castles lingered for a long time in the minds of readers.

But one of the most important things that happened to illustration during the nineteenth century was the interest that some major painters began to take in the work of illustrating books. It was a modest beginning at first, in the sense that few of these painters illustrated books. But it was the beginning of an interest which continued to grow and became extremely important during our century.

By a strange coincidence, the first of the major painters to express concern that his paintings were being mistaken for literary work was also the first to put his hand to the literary work of illustrating a book. He was Delacroix. Delacroix illustrated the *Faust* of Goethe on lithographic stones. It was, of course, the very personal creation of a great artist. Goethe himself was pleased with the vigour and power of these illustrations and was generous enough to say that they were superior to his text in the conception of some scenes. The book became a classic example of the combination in one book of a great writer and a great artist. Delacroix also illustrated *Hamlet* and other dramas.

A few more nineteenth-century artists, such as Turner, Manet, Rodin, did book illustrations. But it was in the twentieth century that their number really became important: Toulouse-Lautrec, Picasso, Matisse, Derain, Dufy, Miro, Redon, Juan Gris, Maillol, Klee, Chagall, even Calder and others. Recently, Rauschenberg did pages for Dante. Picasso himself illustrated a long list of books: poetry by his friends, novels, Greek classics, even Buffon's *Natural History*.

These painters who, little by little, led painting to non-figurative art also brought new conceptions to book illustration. They were often in their own art the equals, if not the betters, of the writers whose works they illustrated. With their creative powers, they could not simply see their illustrations as the servants of a text and illustrate with literalness and realism. They did away with these conceptions. They illustrated on their own terms though they kept within the spirit of the particular piece of literature they chose to illustrate.

What interested them in this literature was that it offered their creative imaginations a base from which to invent graphic ideas.

There has been much criticism expressing disapproval of the liberties these artists took with the literature they illustrated, but it was these liberties as well as the greatness of their art which make their work in book illustration valuable and defensible.

Literature is an art which has its own conceptions and its own means of expressions. It does not need help from another art, unless the writer himself has planned it that way. Illustrations which impose the artist's conception of a novel with definitiveness and precise literalness come like a screen between the author and his readers. The illustrations interfere in a very unpleasant way with the readers' own dreams.

But illustrations as done by the superior artists are related to the text in a free, loose, subtle way; they leave the reader free to interpret the writing with complete freedom. And he has the added pleasure of doing the same with the illustrations.

One can see the difference between the two conceptions by comparing the illustrations done for the same literary work by two artists. Doré illustrated an edition of Rabelais's *Gargantua* which had much success in his time. His illustrations had verve and boisterousness, but they fixed the scenes and personages of the book with such realism and definitiveness that the reader had no choice but to see Gargantua as Doré saw him. Derain's illustrations, half a century later, had much success also, but they are only free suggestions of Renaissance art and styles and of Rabelais's figures. They make fine pages which leave the reader free to see his own Gargantua. Thus, just as painters were extricating painting from illustration, they gave illustration some of the abstract features of painting.

It is worth saying here, also, that the pure abstract painters, that is the painters who have completely eliminated the subject in conceiving their paintings, have never illustrated books. Illustrative art and abstract art are too opposed to each other.

Now, after this very simplified history of the confusion between illustration and painting, we are back where we started: our modern picture book.

It may seem irrelevant to spend so much time speaking of the relationship between illustration and painting and of the evolution of painting toward abstraction in a talk about the minor art of children's-book illustration; it may also seem preposterous to imply that children's picture books have such noble ancestry.

But all these things are what makes our picture books what they are now.

In eliminating the representational from painting, painters were better able to examine what painting was. All the graphic arts profited from the discoveries the painters made.

Illustrators were able to learn the importance of the design which holds the narrative elements together in a page and gives order and visual qualities to that page. They could reflect over the conception that what makes a painting beautiful is not what it represents, a conception which to some extent is applicable to illustration. What makes an illustration beautiful is not its descriptive qualities but its underlying graphic inventions. Even in children's-book illustrations it is worth while to think of the narrative elements as materials with which to build a beautiful page instead of concentrating on them for their own sake.

Then there was the realization that literalness and realism were to the illustrator what the cage is to the bird. Having gotten out of the cage, illustrators found the most pleasant freedom in relating illustrations to a text, in composing pages, and in using colours.

Illustration profited much from abstract painting in spite of the opposition between the two. The treatments of surfaces, the use of space, the colour relations, the free, dramatic forms and lines, etc., of abstract paintings teach much to the illustrator.

However, the children's-book artist must think about all this within the very special art of picture books. Because making a picture book is like playing with children, the particular way children react to the world around them cannot be forgotten. This need not be a limitation; on the contrary, limitations are a challenge and a source of inventions.

With their uninhibited vision, children do not see the world as we do. While we see only what interests us, they see everything. They have made no choice yet. We do not see what sort of buttons a man we pass in the street has on his coat or how many there are, unless we are a button maker. But a child cares and will count the buttons if he can. He will care just as much about the tiny ladybug which falls accidentally on the dining-room table as about the grownups who sit around it. More, in fact. The child's interests are infinite and he sees the tiniest details of his world as well as the biggest forms. And he does not say, 'I do not understand.' He looks and sees. He lives among wonders and the children's book artist only has to take him by the hand, so to speak, to lead him toward the most imaginative adventures.

The child also has the tendency to enjoy this detailed world of his in terms of happenings, of things being done, in other words, in terms of stories.

In their own art, the children are not aware of abstract considerations. They are not concerned with colour harmony or colour contrast, with composition and design. Their art is only a sort of writing, however beautiful it might be sometimes. With it they tell a story. If a child is asked to explain a painting he has made, he will most likely tell what is happening in it. 'This is a woman going to the market to buy fruit. This is a truck driver climbing on his truck. This is the sea, full of fish which the fisherman will catch.'

I still remember an experience I had with my elder son when he was four. It illustrates what I have just said. One day his mother took him up the Hudson River to Nyack. When they returned I asked him if he had liked the beautiful river with hills on both sides. He thought for a while and said, yes, he did. There was a boat on it which smoked and which had a little house in the middle. A door opened and a man came out of the house and went to look into the water. The only thing which struck him was an action, a little story. So let's give the child all the stories he wants.

Another quality children possess is their love and understanding of the humorous side of things. This also can be a rich source of ideas for the maker of children's books. Not only can he laugh with the child as he makes his books, but he can tell the most serious and important things while he laughs.

I have said enough, I think, to show that the artist and author cannot complain that the making of children's books has limitations. Those limitations rather resemble a jail whose windows and doors open wide into a beautiful paradise. The degree of talent of the children's-book maker may be the only limitation.

In the art itself, I think we will see artists taking more and more liberties. Even abstract art can have a place in a child's book under certain circumstancees. If the artist is inclined to search for his page designs and for his colours by using the elements of the story in rough, free, almost abstract forms, he will be tempted to leave his page almost in the rough abstract condition. The forms, the bright colour surfaces which are not cut or soiled by details, the white spaces which remain pure have a freshness, a force, and an interest which they may lose when details and precisions are brought in. The artist may then be searching for a simpler and more ingenuous way of telling the necessary story.

When the artist writes his own story, he can conceive both his text and illustrations simultaneously, thus making the text and pictures help each other as they develop the story. He even can make his illustrations first with great freedom and get ideas for the text from them. In this case, the text may be like the threads the dressmaker uses to hold the pieces of material which will form the dress.

This matter of abstraction and illustration recalls to my mind a fascinating experience I had with a friend of mine, a well-known abstract painter. He wanted to illustrate a charming story he had invented for his children, but never having illustrated before, he came to live with us for a few days to work out the problem. In spite of his talent for drawing, making illustrations was for him like speaking the language of an unknown country. He could no longer see the story in literary terms when he tried to imagine the various scenes with his brush on the paper. To see visually the sequence of these scenes as they were described in his own story and translate them pictorially proved impossible for him. After several days a pile of nice miniature abstract paintings had been made, none telling any story. Yet when I think of this now, it seems to me that a few well-placed details drawn with the pen might have transformed the abstractions into story-telling pages. This experience demonstrates, however, how difficult it is to join two art conceptions which are so opposed to each other. It demonstrates also that in picture books, as in every art form, everything is worth trying.

As I come to the end of the 'one full hour' I see that I could ramble on for another hour, but I think you can see now that the making of children's books can be as great a source of satisfaction for the artist as the finished book can be a source of pleasure for the child.

[1965]

Randolph Caldecott

FREDERICK LAWS

The kind of books we give to children are an indication of what we think and feel about childhood, and these beliefs and emotions lie close to the heart of our national culture. Mr F. J. Harvey Darton's history of *Children's Books in England* is a more serious history of England than most volumes which recite the names of battles and Acts of Parliament. It is no simple story of progress. Broadly speaking, in the eighteenth century parents and publishers fussed little about the young. They were presumed to be small adults and dressed as such. They could read such grownup books as interested them, but like the lower classes they found their pleasure in books mainly in the fairy tales, songs, and stories of adventure crudely printed in chapbooks from the pedlar's pack. One publisher of genius, John Newbery, began catering especially for children, and by the end of the century he had a host of followers. Newbery called himself 'the friend of children', and his books were friendly and entertaining. But in the early nineteenth century children's books became both a flourishing business and a very serious matter. Their authors, though benevolent, edifying, and even understanding, were scarcely *friendly* to the child reader. The books had to save children's souls and to stuff their minds with suitable facts. According to the author of *The Fairchild Family*: 'All children are by nature evil, and while they have none but the natural evil principle to guide them, pious and prudent parents must check their naughty passions in any way that they have in their power, and force them into decent and proper behaviour and into what are called good habits.' Story books might help to frighten them into virtue. But fairy tales and nursery rhymes were irrational, uninformative and even immoral. Cinderella, for instance, 'paints some of the worst passions that can enter into the human breast, and of which little children should, if possible, be totally ignorant; such as envy, jealousy, a dislike to mothers-in-law and half-sisters, vanity, a love of dress, etc., etc.' Fortunately this dreary and barbarous attitude to the young was not universal, and great writers who *liked* children came along. Gaiety, poetry, nonsense, and the ancient heritage of folklore were brought to the nursery by Edward Lear, Lewis Carroll, Hans Andersen, and the translators of Grimm in the 1840s, 50s, and 60s. When Walter Crane, Kate Greenaway, and Randolph Caldecott began drawing for children they were under no public compulsion to be morally edifying or factually informative. Children were no longer supposed to be 'young persons' whose taste would be much the same whether they were five or fifteen. So long as they pleased children they were free; indeed Crane wrote that 'in a sober and matter-of-fact age Toybooks afford perhaps the only outlet for unrestricted flights of fancy open to the modern illustrator who likes to revolt against the despotism of facts.'

Since the eighties books for children have grown steadily in prestige and numbers and our attitude to children has altered immensely. The child is anything but downtrodden. His innocent eye is the final court of appeal for many aesthetic extremists. A pack of writers from Barrie downwards have envied his dream world. A contemporary illustrator might well seek to escape from the despotism of fantasy. Educational extremists say that 'the wisdom of the child' should decide what he ought to learn. The severest criticism of a children's book now is that it might frighten its readers.

In 1878 when Caldecott published his first picture book the

child had not become such a domineering father of the man. But the social and aesthetic importance of the baby's book was well established. Ruskin had denounced the pious ugliness of 'the literature which cheap printing enables the pious to make Christmas presents of for a penny . . . full of beautiful sentiments, woodcuts and music . . . Splendid woodcuts, too, in the best Kensington style, and rigidly on the principles of high, and commercially remunerative, art, taught by Messrs Redgrave, Cole, and Company.' He felt it would lead to: 'Ruin—inevitable and terrible, such as no nation has yet suffered . . . Yes—inevitable. England has to drink a cup which cannot pass from her—at the hands of the Lord, the cup of His fury;—surely the dregs of it, the wicked of the earth shall wring them and drink them out.'

The illustrations of the old chapbooks had been coarse in colour and vulgar in design. Even decently produced books as late as 1850 had the colour added to them in patches by children working in large groups. About 1868 the processes of colour printing took a leap forward in convenience and potential beauty. Walter Crane was inspired by Japanese colour prints: 'Their treatment in definite black outline and flat brilliant as well as delicate colours, vivid dramatic and decorative feeling struck me at once.' And as he worked with Edmund Evans, a printer of rare skill and taste, he was able to experiment successfully in adapting his ideas to mass colour printing. Evans printed the work of Caldecott and Kate Greenaway too, and played a considerable part in setting good standards of quality as the new mechanical processes developed.

Walter Crane's *The Baby's Opera* is a remaining classic of the nursery, and when he illustrated the same nursery rhymes as Caldecott he could excel him in beauty of design. But his vein of humour was not strong, and his elegant figures in Pre-Raphaelite attitudes were more decorative than illustrative. He tried to make his books train the taste of their readers, and made them a vehicle for his ideas about furniture and decoration.

Kate Greenaway was Caldecott's other chief rival. She drew beautiful children in costumes which she said were of the eighteenth century but which, in fact, came from her own imagination. Her gracefully sentimental work was so popular that the fashions she invented for children of the past became real. Kate Greenaway dresses and bonnets, made uglier of course, were worn by children here, in France, and in America. Ruskin alternated between grossly overpraising her work and cramping her style by trying to make her draw correctly.

Caldecott illustrated two or three books for Mrs Juliana Ewing —the best of them being *Jackanapes*—and was evidently sympathetic to her lively though elevating storytelling. His real reputation with infants, however, rests upon the picture books whose texts are either nursery rhymes or songs or ballads of the eighteenth century. The origins of the nursery rhyme are unquestionably ancient, but splendidly obscure. Theorists have claimed to find sources and parallels for them in anthropology; others hold that they are linked with popular political satire. It is all quite inconclusive, and the rhymes remain, magical fragments which add to nobody's store of knowledge, improve no infant characters, but persist in giving delight. Caldecott's affection for the late eighteenth century has been mentioned before. His idea of the period has nothing in common with the rational, elegant, witty, unregenerate *dix-huitième* in which Lytton Strachey discovered a spiritual home. It was almost as reliable as history, however. The poems which Caldecott raised almost to the true fame of anonymity included two by Oliver Goldsmith—the *Elegy on the Death of a Mad Dog* from *The Vicar of Wakefield* and his *Elegy On The Glory of Her Sex Mrs Mary Blaize*. It may be worth noting that the *Vicar of Wakefield* itself was nostalgic and pastoral—an escape from sophisticated London to old-fashioned country people. The 'good old days' seem to be progressively recessive. Neither of these poems were meant for children though Goldsmith, through his friendship with Newbery, wrote more for children than for adults. They are nonsense in a way, but the verbal nonsense of paradox and anti-climax rather than the image-nonsense of dream poetry. Caldecott made them live by ignoring their critical wit and exploiting every 'sympathetic' touch for all it was worth. The Mad Dog himself is a famous charmer:

> *The dog and man at first were friends*
> *But when a pique began,*
> *The dog, to gain some private ends,*
> *Went mad, and bit the man.*

In three drawings Caldecott makes it clear that the friendship was based on the gift of bones, that the pique was a matter of jealousy of a cat, and that the madness was an unfortunate private matter which 'the wondering neighbours' were impertinent to discuss.

Caldecott's choice of Robert Bloomfield's *Farmer's Boy* needs no explaining. It illustrates itself with a new animal on every page which those young persons who have learnt few words can nevertheless greet with appropriate noises. *John Gilpin* by William Cowper is more an older child's book. The riding and the misfortunes make active pictures, but babies may agree with Miss Greenaway that the accidents and sufferings of a nice old man are more distressing than funny.

Samuel Foote's *Great Panjandrum* is queerest of all. Foote wrote it to annoy the actor Macklin, famous for his Shylock. Macklin retired from the stage to keep a coffee-house and hoped to attract custom to it by giving lectures. Foote knew that sooner or later he would boast of his actor's skills in memorizing anything at a single hearing, and attended his lecture armed with *The Great Panjandrum*. This was a piece of nonsense from which each vestige of consecutive thought, every memory aid of association, and all sane meaning had been carefully excluded. Where Caldecott found it I cannot imagine. Foote's witty though scurrilous farces had been off the stage since his death in France after a prosecution as notorious in its time as that of Oscar Wilde. *The Life and Bonmots of Samuel Foote*, which contains the Panjandrum, was not a common book. The life was scandalous and the bonmots often regrettably coarse. But he *did* find it, and in no time dons and clergymen were sending translations of it into the Greek or Hebrew to *Notes and Queries*, and the young had adopted it is an excellent difficult thing to learn by heart.

His illustrations for this Dadaist masterpiece are an extreme example of the method of work and the peculiar fitness of his sort of imagination for the entertainment of small boys and girls. It is clear that he did his first drawings while telling a story to a child on his knee. The book of *Lightning Sketches For The House That Jack Built* proves that. So, obviously, did Edward Lear, and we are told the same of Lewis Carroll. It keeps your story moving at a proper pace. You find out when you are permitted to elaborate or digress and when you *must* have pictures to carry you over an unknown word or an ambiguous phrase.

Caldecott had kept the severely literal visual imagination which I believe to be characteristic of young children. The thing imagined for them is not of another order of reality from the thing seen. After all, you can see it in your head. They are willing to accept flexible conventions in imagining, will grant for the sake of fun that a cloud is very like a camel or Father like a bear. Yet their fancy has hard edges and is not at home off the solid earth. Until corrupted by whimsical elders, they prefer what they know or can see to fanciful inventions.

In picturing the Panjandrum, Caldecott leaves no point unsharpened and no bridgeable gap unbridged. 'So she went into the garden to cut a cabbage-leaf to make an apple-pie; and at the same time a great she-bear, coming down the street, pops its head into the shop. What, no soap? So he died, and she very imprudently married the Barber; and there were present the Picninnies, and the Joblillies, and the Garyulies, and the

FROM RANDOLPH CALDECOTT'S *Sing a Song for Sixpence*

great Panjandrum himself, with the little round button at top; and they all fell to playing the game of catch-as-catch-can, till the gunpowder ran out at the heels of their boots.' The she-bear goes down a real streeet—in Whitchurch. The regrettable shortage of soap directly causes death. The round button at top of the Panjandrum proves him a schoolmaster, and the gunpowder which ran out at the heels of the boots of the dancers, though unexplained, is clearly drawn in.

He brought the same thoroughgoing habits of realistic visualization and explanation to nursery rhymes, and the purist may object to such hard-and-fast interpretation. His most elaborate piece of exposition comes in *Sing a Song of Sixpence* which he changed to a Song *for* Sixpence without authority. The lines

> *Sing a song for sixpence*
> *A pocketful of rye*
> *Four-and-Twenty blackbirds*
> *Baked in a pie.*

are given eight pictures. An old lady gives a little girl sixpence, presumably for having sung. The girl gives it to a man chopping wood. The man buys or acquires a poacher's pocketful of rye which he takes home. His children set a blackbird trap in the snow, and evidently catch twenty-four birds which their mother bakes in a pie. This *looks* a likely story, but it is more probable that the first two lines of the song mean nothing at all. However, parents with children who ask Why? are fully covered. And the birdtrap picture is a very charming colour design. Humanitarians may disapprove of the whole blackbird incident. I can only report that at the age of three a kindly daughter of mine found the picture with the birds beginning to sing a sad one, on the grounds that the little girl with the spoon might get no dinner.

Another piece of rationalizing one might regret is the lowness of the moon jumped over by the cow. But no parent will regret the introduction of pigs to explain what fun the little dog laughed at. An insufficiency of pigs is one of the great faults of modern children's books.

The most famous of all Caldecott's drawings came in his first picture book—*The House That Jack Built*. The Dog that Worried the Cat sits there exhausted by his effort but happy in the consciousness that that effort has been virtuous, while behind him threatens the unsuspected, inevitable cow. Tragic irony and the madness of pride could not be more precisely expressed.

Story and picture have merged so closely in these books that to pick out a single page as a specimen of drawing is like removing a line from a sonnet. Each sketch depends on what went before and what comes after. The girls opening the gate here have been eavesdropping on the proposal scene just ended and will join the indignant heroine in chasing the kind gentleman. The dog slinking off on the right has been making up to the milkmaid's dog before and will be driven away by it afterwards. His set pieces in colour sometimes achieve dignity—the fine lady on a white horse is unquestionably handsome—and they have vigour and gaiety always. But his great achievement is the creation of a fluid style of pictorial storytelling which is as natural and as pleasant as friendly conversation.

[1956]

An interview with Maurice Sendak

WALTER LORRAINE

How do you think an illustration functions in a book?

It's either a mere decoration, or it's an expansion of the text. It's your version of the text as an illustrator, it's your interpretation. It's why you are an active partner in the book and not a mere echo of the author. To be an illustrator is to be a participant, someone who has something equally important to say as the writer of the book—occasionally something more important, but certainly never the writer's echo.

Do you feel there are different categories of illustration?

I could make up categories, but I'll tell you only about the one I'm interested in and do well—interpretive illustration. It involves a kind of vigorous working with the writer. Sometimes you're the writer, too, so you're working with yourself; then the difficulty and strain and joy of that particular work is the balancing between the text and pictures. You must not ever be doing the same thing, must not ever be illustrating exactly what you've written. You must leave a space in the text so the picture can do the work. Then you must come back with the word, and the word does it best and now the picture beats time.

It's a funny kind of juggling act. It takes a lot of technique, a lot of experience, to really keep the rhythm going between word and picture. It's a kind of muscular rhythm, though the reader isn't aware of it. You have worked out a text that is so supple it stops and goes and stops and goes, and the pictures are shrewdly interspersed. The pictures become so supple, too, that there's this interchangeableness between them and the words, and they're both telling two stories at the same time.

How would you define a picture book?

A picture book is not only what most people think it is—an easy thing to read to very small children with a lot of pictures in it. For me, it is a damned difficult thing to do, very much like a complicated poetic form. Some poets really like to get into difficult forms because they're the most challenging things in poetry. I think a picture book is one of those beautiful, challenging forms, which demands so much that you have to be on top of the situation all the time to finally achieve something that seems so simple and so put together—seamless if you will— that it looks like you knocked it off in no time.

It's like a good poem. You shouldn't be aware of the pastings together. You should only be aware of the work as a complete and total entity; and it should look as breezy as a moonlight night if that's what the poem's about. A picture book has to have that incredible seamless look to it when it's finished. One stitch showing and you've lost the game. I don't know of any other form of illustrating that is so interesting to me.

Grimm's fairy tales are obviously not picture-book material, but they do allow for interpretive illustration. The illustrations have as much to say as the text; the trick is to say the same thing, but in a different way. It's no good being an illustrator who is saying a lot that is on his or her mind if it has nothing to do with the text. But to say the same thing that the story is saying in your own *personal* way, so that you heighten the meaning of the original tale, contributes dimension to the story.

You're not out to do your own 'shtick'—you're out merely to do your shtick within the confines of the story you're illustrating. Whatever the story happens to be—Hansel and Gretel, Snow White—you have made it bigger than it was because you have had insight into the story as an artist. The illustrator is doing a tremendous job of expansion, of collaboration, of illumination. But he must be discreet. The artist must override the story, but he must also override his own ego for the sake of the story. It's more fun than any other kind of illustration.

Is there a particular style of writing that encourages a good picture book?

It can't be the pedantic form of writing where every nail is knocked in, every fact is obvious. For my taste, it has to be ambiguous—it has to allow for a number of meanings to shine through. It can't be a heavy-handed text that says little Johnny goes from the left to the right, because then the illustrator doesn't have any choice but to make little Johnny go from the left to the right. The text has to be less precise, less obvious. You can have facts, but the facts have to allow the artist to move the characters in any direction.

An example of what I mean is a nursery rhyme of Mother Goose, which might have meant something quite specific in an earlier century, but means nothing now. One of my own books, *Hector Protector*, is a good instance. You can make up your own story.

> *Hector Protector was dressed all in green,*
> *Hector Protector was sent to the Queen.*
> *The Queen did not like him, no more did the King,*
> *So Hector Protector was sent back again.*

Now what the hell does that mean? Maybe a bit of a joke in Elizabeth the First's day. It means nothing to us now, but it's a super text. It's a very funny rhyme, the meter is lovely, and the language is peculiar. What is going on—well, that's the illustrator's game. You have a nice little piece of Mother Goose text that allows you to rearrange the characters in any way you like and make up a story, any story you want; it just has to spring from those words. Whatever imaginative tale you tell must begin with *Hector Protector* dressed all in green, but you can interpret that in new ways. He can be a boy in China, in Alaska, in

Israel, but somehow or other he has to be dressed all in green. That's all you have to show. You can invent the rest. The whole book is your story as an illustrator.

How important is technique to the illustrator?

There is a need for only a rudimentary grasp of drawing or graphic technique in my opinion. Edward Lear—not one of my favourite illustrators—is someone who had sufficient technique, incredibly sufficient technique, to convey concepts in a very few untrained lines. I think the better the illustrator is technically, the better off she or he will be—but it isn't essential. The peculiar gift in being an illustrator is that one has an odd affinity with words, that it's natural to interpret words, almost like a composer thinking music when reading poetry.

Arthur Hughes is one of my favourite illustrators, but he couldn't draw people in three-quarter view! He did beautiful paintings, he worked from models, and you wonder, why couldn't he draw people in three-quarter view? Well, he couldn't. You can see how wooden they look, you see how awful they look—like their noses have been chopped off. It doesn't take an inch away from *The Princess and the Goblin*—it doesn't take anything away at all. I noticed it because I am a craftsman, but I wish I had his gift. It doesn't matter that he didn't have the prowess of a Norman Rockwell. (I don't mean to put Mr Rockwell down, but that's not what Arthur Hughes is all about.)

Arthur Hughes was an interpretive illustrator. He used whatever technique and craft he had at hand. It's not necessary to do elaborate and refined drawings, because elaborate and refined drawings with fantastic technique don't mean a hill of beans if you're not a good illustrator. Now, I suppose as Arthur Hughes got older, he learned to draw better. But alas, he also became a weaker illustrator, so that the last pictures he did look more graphically polished, but have nothing of the magic and power of those earlier clumsy drawings.

I'm saying this clumsily, too, because it's so hard to put this into language. I've seen so many gifted people who were natural illustrators who didn't have technical facility, but to me they had a great treasure. They had what you can't learn. You can draw better by practicing, but you can never learn that other intuitive quality.

What do you think of the quality of picture books today?

Well, I'll have to make a very generalized statement because I don't see that many of them. Much of what I do see is bad, and I think the form of the picture book has been, in large part, debased. It is overused, it is overdressed, it is garish, it is vulgar, it is despoiled. Somehow we've forgotten along the way how difficult it is to make a good picture book. Why don't we look at the major works around? Why don't we look at the little books of William Nicholson, *The Pirate Twins* and *Clever Bill*, which are seemingly so simple they run through your fingers, you can't catch them fast enough. Most of the picture books I've seen are pedantic, obvious, and overcoloured, overtechniqued, and over-written. Very few have excited me. There are exceptions. Many of the young people I teach have a fresher, simpler approach to the form. They give me hope for the future.

Was there a time that you feel picture books were better than today?

Yes. Of course there was Wanda Gág. There's always *Millions of Cats*. And we did have a very good period in the 1950s and '60s. I think we were influenced by the books that were coming from other countries. Remember the '50s when Hans Fischer's books were first published here, and *Finders Keepers* won the Caldecott Award? That book was so influenced by European illustration. I remember my excitement when I first saw it. It had an international flavor, which was something new in American children's books. The '50s was a very exciting time. Many of the books that were being done were influenced by what we were seeing from abroad. And there was Tomi Ungerer and a lot of us just beginning. We had about a decade's worth of terrific stuff, then we started getting very rich on it. We started shutting the door in the face of new talent—or so it seems to me.

Do you think there is a lack of talent in the picture book area today?

I did think that for a long time. I thought that historically and socially there was a wasteland, that the creative soil was infertile. But since I've been teaching I know that's not true. Believe me, I don't see many brilliant people, but I do see some very talented people. And I can say without any hesitation that a small number of my best students are quite ready to be published. They have an ethical approach toward the picture book, a vital and serious approach; and it has made me realize that my original view that talent wasn't there was probably false.

If talent is around but nobody is using it, what *is* wrong? It seems to me that the system is at fault. If you speak to publishers, every one of them will say, 'We're always looking for new people.' But I wonder why they aren't publishing them. I have, in all fairness, seen some books by new people, but there are far too few being published. I've had great difficulty in placing some of my gifted students. What's the risk? It seems to me that publishers are less ambitious than they used to be, in general less brave, less willing to go out on a limb. Now if you say this aloud, you get the response: 'But we are publishing young people.' Well, where are they?

My suspicion is that publishers are afraid to take risks. In the old days they did take chances. Nothing's happening now. I'm nearly 50 and when I turn around I see very few young people climbing up the mountain. When I was young, in the '50s, we were given all the encouragement in the world.

Do you think a new and truly innovative book, by a new talent, can reach an appropriate audience today?

I don't know, because I really have lost touch with how the books go out and where they go to. I mean that. Now, my only feedback is the letters I get from children.

Do you think there are others besides publishers who encourage this conservatism?

I think there must be. I hear about this dearth of talent and the wailing about where is the talent coming from, which bewilders me—because I see some of it, and I say, it's over there and it doesn't get published. There's some jarring disharmony some-where. It seems to me, to make a very general statement, that the way the industry is now, very few people would be willing to go out on a limb with a very different kind of book.

Do you think that critical reaction today does encourage superior books?

No. There are exceptional publishers, and there are a few exceptional critics—some very few exceptional critics—who take the trouble to evaluate a children's book in an intelligent way. They're not burdened with boring, tedious attitudes, such as whether a book is good for kiddies or not good for kiddies. They take an overall view of it aesthetically. Does it stand up as a work of art?

I think, from my own personal experience, I have not learned anything from reviews of my books. I've not seen reviews of other people's books that I ever thought did real justice to a book's special qualities. These statements are too general, because there are some few intelligent reviewers who do take their job very seriously—who are trying to encourage talent and can distinguish between the real and the phony. They take the larger view and escape the fatal 'Kiddiebookland' disease that most reviewers suffer from. But they are exceptional, very exceptional. Too often, children's books are nailed down by whether they conform to the rules of the kindergarten, of what children ought or ought not to be reading. Hardly ever is the American children's book seriously or intelligently reviewed.

What do you mean by Kiddiebookland?

Kiddiebookland is where we live. Didn't you know? It's next to Neverneverville and Peterpanburg. It's that awful place that we've been squeezed into because we're children's book illustra-

MAURICE SENDAK'S ILLUSTRATION FOR 'HANSEL AND GRETEL'
FROM *The Juniper Tree*

tors or children's book writers. Yes, we are! But isn't our work meant for everybody? How infuriating and insulting when a serious work is considered only a trifle for the nursery!

When you've worked a year on a book, when you've put your life into it, you expect the point of view of the professionals (editors, teachers, librarians) to be somewhat larger, more expansive. You expect the book to be read by people of all ages. When someone says, 'Well, don't you like doing children's books?' I say, 'Yes, apparently I do, I've been at it for a long time. But it also is a major part of my life, and I'm talking about all kinds of things in my work, which only happens to take the form of a picture book.'

Do you think critics should react differently to the illustrations in picture books?

I think they should try to learn what picture books are all about. There is some fine mystery in this difficult form (I am aware of this and struggle with it), a mystery that is the artist's business. Any serious artist's work is never just one thing. What I'm objecting to is that picture books are judged from a particular, pedantic point of view vis à vis their relation to children—and I insist that any serious work of art is much more.

I think when people are reviewing our books, a collision inevitably occurs with preconceptions concerning children. There is a whole theory about children that everybody works from, and people look for whether a picture book has followed the 'rules' about what is right for children, or what is healthy for children, or what we *think* is right and healthy for children. This comes into conflict all the time with those things that are mysterious. Children don't need a pedantic approach to the book. Children are much more catholic in taste; will tolerate ambiguities, peculiarities, and things illogical; will take them into their unconscious and deal with them as best they can.

The anxiety comes from the adults who feel that the book has to conform to some set ritual of ideas about childhood, and unless this conforming takes place they are ill at ease. A very important conflict occurs because the artist really doesn't go by any specific rules. The artist has to be a little bit bewildering and a little bit wild and a little bit disorderly. That's the art of being an artist. Artists run into difficulty because they're dealing with our most upright, uptight business, which is the industry called childhood.

Most people are out to protect children from what they think is dangerous. The genuine artists have the same concern. Their work, however, may not conform to what the specialists think is right or wrong for children. The artists are going to put elements into their work that come from their deepest selves. They draw on a peculiar vein of childhood that is always open and alive. That is their particular gift. They understand that children know a lot more than people give them credit for. Children are willing to deal with many dubious subjects that grownups think they shouldn't know about.

If a book doesn't follow the course of what a childhood specialist considers right, then it's a bad book for children. So picture-book people are more easily condemned than almost any other artists in creation because we're dealing with such a volatile subject—children. We must protect the children, and yet children are unprotected in every other way. No one protects them from terrible television. No one protects them from life because you cannot protect them from life, and all we're trying to do in a serious work is to tell them about life. What's wrong with that? They know about it anyway.

What elements make up a good children's book?

The basic ground-floor element is honesty. Whatever you're doing—a realistic story or fantasy or far-out science fiction— must begin with a basis of honesty. You must tell the truth about the subject to the child as well as you are able without any mitigating of that truth. You must allow that children are small, courageous people who have to deal every day with a multitude of problems, just as we adults do, and that they are unprepared for most things, and what they most yearn for is a bit of truth somewhere.

Now if you honestly start with that, then you can proceed in whatever form you like, tell it whatever way you like. If it's a bitter pill that children don't want to swallow, give them the opportunity of saying no. Let there not be guards in front of children who decide what they should or shouldn't be reading. Why are children kept in ghettos, and why are there guards in front of the doors telling them what is right and what isn't right? We have the opportunity of choosing what we like to read. Why shouldn't children have the same opportunity?

A woman once said to me: 'I've read *Where the Wild Things Are* ten times to my little girl, and she screams every time.' And I said, 'Why are you reading it to her?' She said, 'But it's a Caldecott book, she ought to like it.' I said, 'That's absurd. You're a sadist. If the kid doesn't like the book, throw it away.' What's wrong here is that the mother insisted that the child should like the book. Why? Children don't give a damn about the Caldecott award. Why should they? We should let children choose their own books. What they don't like they will throw away. What disturbs them too much they will not look at. They're not going to fall apart if they look at the wrong book. It isn't going to do them that much damage. We treat children in a very peculiar way, I think. We don't treat them like the strong creatures they really are.

What should we look for in a picture book?

Originality of vision. Someone who has something to say that might be very commonplace, but who says it in a totally original and fresh way, who has a point in view, who has a genius for expressing the prosaic in a magical way. Do not look for pyrotechnics, for someone who can make a big slambang picture book out of very little, but look for the genuinely talented person who thinks originally.

Can you define what a picture book is for you?

Well, I think I have; it's everything. It's my battleground. It's where I express myself. It's where I consolidate my powers and put them together in what I hope is a legitimate, viable form that is meaningful to somebody else and not just to me. It's where I put down those fantasies that have been with me all my life, and where I give them a *form* that means something. I live inside the picture book: that's where I fight all my battles, and where hopefully I win my wars.

[1977]

5 *The modern scene*

'**W**hat is real?' asked the rabbit one day

PATRICK MERLA

PLOT ONE
'Never shall his side touch a woman's of the race that now dwells upon this earth.' Thus Llew Llaw Gyffes is condemned to loneliness by his mother, the enchantress Arianrhod. But Gwydion, the boy's uncle and heir to the throne of Gwynedd, fashions with the High King Math a bride of flowers for Llew, summoning through magic a soul for the maid. The bride betrays Llew, however, and contrives with her lover a foul death for the boy. Llew's spirit takes the form of an eagle, hovering with an arrow in its breast in the branches of a tree above his human body. Unable to accept his nephew's death, Gwydion searches the world for the eagle and woos the boy's spirit back into his decaying corpse. Restored to life and health, Llew destroys his rival. Arianrhod's magic turns back upon her, and she is swallowed up by the sea. Unrepentant, Llew's bride is transformed by Gwydion into an owl, a bird of darkness, called ever afterward by her own name—Blodeuwedd, the Flower-Like.

PLOT TWO

Morag, having spent most of her life unwanted in foster homes, runs away. It is spring when she arrives in the mountains. Managing to befriend a mountain goat and its kid, she finds a cave to live in, sustaining herself by stealing from nearby farms. She teaches herself to kill game and to make cheese from the goat's milk. Finding a human skeleton in the woods above her cave, she decorates it with flowers and worships it. One day she happens upon the scene of an accident. A young man has been killed in a fall, his head cracked open on a rock. Another is barely alive. Morag nurses him back to health. In return, he rapes her, becomes her lover briefly, then deserts her to return to civilization. Pregnant, Morag realizes that she will not survive the winter in the mountains. Seeking help, she is attacked by the irate villagers she has robbed. Wounded, Morag makes her way to the seashore. There she miscarries and dies, becoming finally a skeleton herself, her bones 'merely a part of the white sand.'

Most readers, if asked to choose, would state confidently that the first of these plots was for children and the second for adults. They would be wrong. Plot One is from *The Island of the Mighty*, an adult fantasy; Plot Two is from a children's book, *A Wild Thing*. Children are forsaking innocence in their reading habits to peruse stark realities, while adults, paradoxically, are wandering more and more into fictional never-never-lands.

Eleven years ago in New York my high school circle of friends included a bunch of precocious teen-agers. We made weekly pilgrimages to the Gotham Book Mart to purchase British editions of the early novels of Hermann Hesse (there were no American editions in print then); and shortly thereafter we discovered the *I Ching*. For music we had Bach and Vivaldi, Buxtehude and Josquin des Prez, Ruth Etting, and the film scores of *Jules et Jim* and *La Dolce Vita*. But not all of our interests were esoteric. We devoured Salinger's *Frannie and Zooey* as soon as it came out. (Of course, Salinger's book sent us scurrying back to the Gotham for little green-bound volumes of *The Way of the*

Pilgrim, the religious book that Frannie is always reading.) We studied avidly the works of Gide and Fitzgerald, and also John Knowles's *A Separate Peace.* We listened seriously to rock-and-roll as an expression, if not of ourselves, then of many of our peers. And we thought of Joan Baez as an older sister.

One day, while we were studying T.H. White's *The Once and Future King,* our middle-aged English teacher casually recommended that we read what she called (hyperbolically, we thought) 'the greatest novel of the twentieth century'—a three-part book by J.R.R. Tolkien, a British philologist, called *The Lord of the Rings* (not to be confused with Golding's gruesome parable, *Lord of the Flies,* which was then the rage of American college campuses and which we had already digested). Little did we realize that our mentor was a Hobbit-cult member of long standing and that *she meant what she said.* Be that as it may, those of us inspired by the White masterpiece wrote down the name of the trilogy and bought it on our next trip to the Gotham. Thus began our search for fantasy.

Our circle has been broken many times since then. We have gone our separate ways into Tibetan Buddhism, Surat Shabd Yoga, mental institutions, motherhood and song writing, macrobiotic restaurants and progressive schools in New Hampshire, marriage with childhood sweethearts, vegetarianism, and death. For some of us the search for fantasy has ended. For the rest it has continued on and off over the years, being handsomely rewarded in the last few with the advent of the vogue for adult fantasy fiction.

For myself the search at first led directly and inevitably to children's literature, since there was so little adult fantasy that we either knew about or could find when we first began looking for it. Only occasionally did we discover in secondhand bookshops works such as poet Elinor Wylie's novel *The Venetian Glass Nephew.*

It was only three years ago, however, that I became aware of the 'problem' of realism (or lack of it) in children's literature. As a panel member of New York's now defunct WBAI-FM *Kid Stuff* program, I heard my colleagues complain about the lack of 'relevant' books for children in ghettos, children from broken homes, disturbed children, and so on. What do they think now, I wonder, about the current rash of sex, drugs, death, and violence in children's books? Certainly, there are 'relevant' books now. What are some of them, and what are they *about?*

Many of them deal with coping. Coping with: alienation (*The Dream Watcher, Run Softly, Go Fast);* premarital sex and abortion (*My Darling, My Hamburger*); unwed motherhood (*The Longest Weekend*); drugs (*Go Ask Alice*); death (*Grover*); suicide (*A Blues I Can Whistle*); mental retardation (*Hey, Dummy*); senility (*The Pigman*); and poverty (*Where the Lilies Bloom*). There are books about runaways (*The Runaway's Diary*); books about the Depression (*Somebody Will Miss Me*); innumerable books with black protagonists or racial themes (*Sounder, Zeely, The Almost Year, The Cay, The Soul Brothers and Sister Lou, Viva Chicano*). Recently there have been books about the plight of the American Indians (*Retreat to the Bear Paw, Only the Names Remain*). There are even books about wars: Vietnam (*War Year*) and World War II (*Fireweed, Ceremony of Innocence, From Ice Set Free*).

More specifically, in John Donovan's *Wild in the World,* readers are introduced to the Gridleys, a thirteen-member family of homesteaders in the hills of New Hampshire. At the outset we're informed that only three brothers remain. The first pages of the book detail the deaths of the others from fire, scarlet fever, rattlesnake bite, suicide, childbirth, and a few unspecified causes. On page 5 Abraham rips a fishhook out of his hand, contracts an infection, and dies two days later. Page 6 sees Amos kicked by a cow and 'dead in a day or so'. 'This left John,' the author states succinctly, closing Chapter One. Shortly thereafter John befriends an animal that is either a wolf, a wolf dog, or a large dog that resembles a wolf. (Donovan carefully avoids telling us which). John teaches the animal tricks and makes plans to join a circus. Bitten by a rattlesnake, the pet hovers near death for days but lives. John is less fortunate. A good part of this ninety-four-page novel details John's slow death from pneumonia.

Jean Renvoize's *A Wild Thing* (Plot Two above) is full of passages such as this one:

> . . . The rabbit was a perfect target . . . She swallowed, aimed and shot.
>
> . . . The rabbit screeched, jumped up into the air kicking wildly, somersaulted over backward, and fell down heavily to the ground. . . .
>
> . . . it began to jerk wildly and scream out. Thrashing around in violent convulsions all the time it let out those piercing screams that filled the wood and sent the birds crashing through the young leaves in their alarm. . . .
>
> Finally pity gave her strength to summon herself, helped her to grab the frenzied thing, swing it up high and bring it down like a chopper onto the edge of the stump, so that its neck broke and at last it lay still, bloody and lifeless.

Both *Wild in the World* and *A Wild Thing*, though excellently written, present an *extreme* realism in which, although specific details are scrupulously, even meticulously, rendered, the situations are so extraordinary as to be out of the range of average experience. Similarly, Chingiz Aitmatov's *The White Ship* presents a small boy's suicide; the book's folk-tale-like narrative, beautiful as it is, and its foreign setting might make it inaccessible to some, almost too 'fantastic' to be believed.

Of course, there is no rule that a book must be about everyday occurrences for an audience to be able to identify with it. As James E. Higgins has pointed out in his excellent *Beyond Words*, a child's reality is not necessarily bounded by time and space; most children can, by *imagining*, identify with situations they might never face in their own lives. (Higgins is referring to works of fantasy, but his observation is still applicable. In fact, much of the most astute commentary on realism for children comes from writers talking about fantasy.) The lever for determining whether a particular child will be able to identify with these books must be that child's sensitivity to the material at hand.

But if adults, parents in particular, are shocked by any one element of the 'new realism' in children's literature, it is likely to be the liberal treatment of drugs and sex. More than one-third of the titles I've listed deal primarily with drugs and/or sex in some fashion. Take this passage from Barbara Wersba's *Run Softly, Go Fast*:

> . . . *Marty was a dealer in dope. . . . I was in the midst of Marty's entourage. . . . Guys like Valiant who made cookies laced with pot and sold them in schoolyards. Girls like Happytime who balled anyone who would give her speed. Pale sick people who lived in communal pads and caught each other's lice and washed each other's backs in a dirty communal tub. . . . Who got busted and went to jail for possession, and got sprung, and made the scene again. Who lived like paupers but had the best stereo systems in the world. Who lay around evenings on mattresses as the joint was passed from hand to hand, and the music blared, and the incense wafted from paisley wall to paisley wall. And whose parents . . . were looking for them all over America. . . . Clever Martin Brooks. . . . Playing father to little street junkies and fourteen-year-old derelicts because they put out for him, in more ways than one. . . .*

Powerful and *accurate*. Yet for some reason parents—and perhaps adults in general—become upset when they think that children (their own or somebody else's) may be reading this sort of thing. Are they being naive? Could it be that the sexual revolution and the counterculture have not yet made an impression on Middle America? I doubt it. There have been far too many nationally broadcast television programs dealing with these 'problems' for me to believe it. California had such a problem with girls dropping out of high school to have babies that a special program was initiated to enable them to continue in school; the same state seems well on its way to liberalizing its drug laws. California may be unusual in its solutions but not in its problems.

But I have other reasons for suspecting that many adults are being ingenuous. Recently a ceremony was held in a church near my home. It was a wedding, and it was held behind closed doors. The bride was fifteen years old and very pregnant; the groom was eighteen. They had obtained special court permission to marry. The pastor of the church locked the doors 'to prevent a scandal'. I know about it because the child bride is the daughter of my neighbor and friend. Only a year ago an acquaintance of this child died of an overdose of heroin—and she was not the first. Then there are the two boys who ran away from home. The pretty one was quickly discovered by a minority group—all 'respectable citizens', mind you—and initiated into the mysteries of drugs and sex. That was four years ago, when he was fifteen. Since then he has 'worked' as a prostitute and a dealer but manages somehow to spend his winters in Puerto Rico. When his younger brother, who is less pretty, arrived on the scene a year after him, *another* minority group discovered *him*. He's been a heroin addict ever since.

Books like *Run Softly, Go Fast* and *Go Ask Alice* (which deals even more graphically with the world of drugs and sex) are presenting real situations in true-to-life terms and deserve to be read. Were they written solely as moral lessons or to teach, these books would be rejected as dishonest and meaningless by the very people who can get the most from them. When they are good, they speak for and to the people they are about. William Armstrong's *Sounder* (about a sharecropper family's struggles after the father has been imprisoned), Eleanor Clymer's *We Lived in the Almont* (about a young girl in the city whose father is a tenement superintendent), Mary Stolz's *By the Highway Home* (about a family's heartbreaking attempts to come to terms with a son's death in Vietnam), and John Neufeld's *Lisa, Bright and Dark* (about a teen-aged girl's futile efforts to get help from her parents as she descends into insanity)—books such as these are intensely moving, unforgettable accounts of people we can care about. At their best they are open-ended, like life itself. They do not pretend to have answers to questions that puzzle even adults. In some ways they are among the most advanced books available today. Isabelle Holland's *The Man Without a Face,* dealing *positively* with a difficult subject—homosexuality—through complex, believable characters and situations, and E.L. Konigsburg's *(George)*, which presents a young boy who has a 'double personality' and retains it even after psychoanalysis, are books that must be considered enlightened works. And, occasionally, as with Barbara Wersba's books, *Run Softly, Go Fast* and *The Dream Watcher,* they are masterpieces, books that are likely to be read and loved by adults as well as children for years to come.

But not all of the books being published for children these days are violent or full of drugs and sex. There are the superb and funny books of E.L. Konigsburg, which portray a 'fanciful' realism; the historical novels of Rosemary Sutcliff, Hester Burton, and Patricia Beatty; the fantasies of Lloyd Alexander, Ursula K. LeGuin, and Alan Garner; the period (real or imaginary) mystery/adventure stories of Joan Aiken and Leon Garfield—all of them excellent. There are a variety of poetry anthologies, ranging from collections of nineteenth-century narrative poems through volumes of contemporary poems and poems relating in some way to rock music, as well as collections of poems by young people themselves. There are S.E. Hinton's books, which are important because they were written *by* a young person (my friends had *Harrison High* by teen-aged John Farris, which was published as an adult book). There are a number of excellent biographies and even some Gothic romance novels.

The important question about these strange new books is: Just who is reading them, are they being read at all, and why? One would have to conduct a survey of the entire reading public to get a definite answer because the 'experts'—people in and out of the field of children's literature—disagree among themselves.

I would say that the average reader of these books is fourteen years old or younger, in spite of the fact that the books may be written for slightly older 'young adults'. Children, I think, tend to read about people who are older than themselves; at least, this was true of my friends. Also, I think that older children are well into reading adult books, usually paperbacks that they buy and circulate among themselves. These are books such as Claude Brown's *Manchild in the Promised Land,* or Eldridge Cleaver's *Soul on Ice,* Mario Puzo's *The Godfather,* or Jacqueline Susann's *The Love Machine;* one might even find a few copies of Alan Watts's *The Book* floating around. (This is by no means a new phenomenon; Leon Uris's *Exodus* was making the rounds of high schools eleven years ago.)

But are these new books actually being read? I am satisfied that they are. Librarians such as Ruth Rousen, Manhattan Borough young adults specialist of the New York Public Library, have told me that children *do* ask for these books; and 80 to 90 per cent of all sales are made to schools and libraries. But what of the children who do not use libraries? some might ask. Most of the publishers of children's books have gone into paperback publication of their young-adult titles. One might well find these volumes in bookstores among other paperbacks, sometimes in the adult stacks. In fact, when established paperback publishers, such as Avon, Signet, and Bantam, bring out young-adult titles, they often do so in adult book formats. Such is the case with *Fireweed, The Soul Brothers and Sister Lou, Lisa, Bright and Dark, My Darling, My Hamburger,* and *Run Softly, Go Fast,* to mention just a few.

Which brings us to *why* these books are being read. A sociologist friend has suggested to me that young people have basically romantic natures and want to know what's in store for them—good or bad. Librarians and editors have stated that today's young people are more sophisticated than young people were ten years ago. Another friend, who is studying to become a school administrator, has pointed out that America's educational system is a desert for most young people and the new books may constitute a meaningful oasis for them—materials from which they can learn in their own fashion.

One magazine editor hazarded the opinion that our concept of childhood—and, therefore, childhood itself—is changing, that we are beginning to think of childhood less as a state of innocence and more as a period of greater maturity. The rule for *all* children's books is that they appear to fill a need. If such a change of concept has occurred, it would be most evident in picture books, since picture books are the literature of the very young. But, aside from *The Feral Child* and *The Boy Who Tried to Cheat Death* (with their startling depictions of sexuality and death) and occasional books such as *Joseph and Koza* or *Harriet and the Promised Land,* which have frightening illustrations, books that attempt to deal with difficult subjects for very young children are usually oversimplified manifestoes of moral lessons. There are notable exceptions: Nancy and Myron Wood's *Hollering Sun;* John Steptoe's *Stevie, Uptown,* and *Train Ride;* Tom Feelings's *Black Pilgrimage;* Judith Viorst's *The Tenth Good Thing About Barney* (illustrated by Eric Blegvad); Elizabeth Bishop's *The Ballad of the Burglar of Babylon* (illustrated by Ann Grifalconi); and Cheli Durán Ryan's extraordinary *Hildilid's Night* (illustrated by Arnold Lobel).

There are those who say that art echoes the experience of society at large and that the current trend toward grim realism is the natural result of a society that has been fighting an undeclared war for so many years.

And, finally, some people believe that these new books are a means to bridge the much-discussed 'generation gap'—a way to help young people overcome their alienation.

Beyond all this speculation, however, one might ask: *Should* these books be read? And, if so, *by whom?* Any parent in a quandary about what kind of book to purchase for a particular child need only watch that child's reactions to what is offered. Children of all ages usually have good notions of what they like and dislike and can decide for themselves what they want to read.

This brings us to the second half of our paradox: What are adults reading?

One need not travel too far to discover the answer to that question. A short visit to any neighborhood drug, candy, or stationery store that sells paperbacks, or to a local bookstore, will reveal that most of the books that are making money are escapist literature. (Gothic romances, fantasies and science fiction, horror stories, occult-oriented books, novels about thinly disguised celebrities, historical novels, and so on.)

The appearance in 1965 of the paperback edition of Tolkien's *The Lord of the Rings* undoubtedly served as the impetus to the vogue for adult fantasy; a vogue that, when related to the other 'escapist' writings already mentioned, must be called a publishing trend. The hardcover edition had first appeared in its entirety in 1956. But, except to members of the Tolkien Society (such as my high school English teacher), it remained relatively unknown until its appearance as a paperback. Before *LOTR* (as it is known to fans) publishers were certain that fantasy titles would not sell; consequently, not much was published. But, after the enormous success of *LOTR* (it sold 250,000 copies in its first ten months as a paperback and has, to date, been through thirty printings), Ballantine Books ventured into the publication of a few other titles (E.R. Eddison's *The Worm Ouroboros* and David Lindsay's *A Voyage to Arcturus*). These also sold fairly well. Perhaps the 'rule' about fantasy was a myth?

At about this time Lin Carter, a science fiction writer, submitted to Ballantine a manuscript that traced Tolkien's sources and showed clearly that *LOTR* was not the first or only work of its kind, as many then believed. *Tolkien: A Look Behind 'The Lord of the Rings'* contained so much information, so many names of works no one had ever heard of, that, after agreeing to publish it, Ballantine asked Carter to serve as consultant for a projected series of adult fantasy titles—a series that has had a remarkable career.

LOTR's first success was with college students, but its popularity soon spread. There have been other, earlier and later, 'campus sensations', but only Tolkien's book started a trend and received so much news coverage. *LOTR* continues to be popular, and not just with college students. Lin Carter tells me that, since Ballantine inaugurated its program, he's received letters from readers of all ages. Old works, such as William Morris's *The Wood*

Beyond the World (which Carter has brought back into print), are now being discovered by readers from eight to eighty years old. Given this large audience, many publishers in addition to Ballantine are now issuing adult fantasy titles.

What makes a book fantasy? According to Carter, fantasies are works in which the settings are either completely enchanted and purely imaginary, imaginary prehistoric realms such as Atlantis or Lemuria, or recognizable worlds with imaginary histories. In his essay, 'On Fairy-Stories' Professor Tolkien speaks of the creation of a Secondary World, produced by the author through 'enchantment', into which 'both designer and spectator can enter, to the satisfaction of their senses while they are inside.' I would add that fantasies are often concerned with the nature of Good and Evil and how they manifest themselves in individuals, sometimes with an heroic quest, and sometimes with the power of love and the amazing transformations brought about by it.

But the essential element of any true work of fantasy is magic—a force that affects the lives and actions of all the creatures that inhabit the fantasist's world. This magic may be innate or manifest; it may be used by the characters who live with it, or come from 'gods' of the author's contrivance. Always it is a *supernatural* force whose use, *mis*use, or *dis*use irrevocably changes the lives of those it touches. Thus, such excellent books as Roger Zelazny's *Lord of Light* (with its karma machines), Fritz Leiber's *Gather, Darkness* (with its biological explanation of witchcraft), or Zenna Henderson's books about 'The People' (whose powers derive from their alien orgins) are not fantasies. Nor is Frank Herbert's abominably written, enormously popular *Dune* a fantasy (with its fascinating ecology and bogus drug-induced mysticism). The 'magic' in these books is not Real Magic. Real Magic cannot be explained in material terms, nor manufactured with mechanical devices, nor achieved through ingested substances.

Now magic is like religion and politics: few people agree about it. Surprisingly enough, many of those who write about fantasy or create it themselves do not believe in it. When I asked Lin Carter if he did, he answered: 'Definitely not. If I believed in it or any part of it, I couldn't write it, any more than a devout Catholic could write a new gospel.' I see his point but find his analogy debatable.

Why all this fuss about magic?

Essentially there are three kinds of science fiction/fantasy readers. There are the cultists, whose major interest is these books and who are familiar with everything that has been written. Many are writers themselves and know one another. They have a historical, specialized perspective that can immediately categorize any given work by origins, influences, and originality. Lin Carter is one of these. Then there are the enthusiasts, whose reading interests may be very broad, but who more or less consistently keep abreast of what is available in science fiction and fantasy. They have some knowledge of the comparative history of the field but nothing comprehensive. And there are those who read only occasional works of science fiction or fantasy and judge them solely on their literary merits. They may not care at all about a book's history. Naturally these groups overlap. But magic, and whether or not one believes in it, is what determines any reader's reaction to these books, as well as the manner in which one measures the books' authenticity—at least where fantasy is concerned.

I believe in magic. Not as mystic mumbo jumbo, but as a way of life. I do not pretend to have Lin Carter's overwhelming familiarity with the field of fantasy writing. Like all fans of this genre, I am indebted to Carter for the many hours of reading pleasure his erudition has made possible. But I do know magic. Having long been a student of mysticism (Oriental and Occidental), I have observed that a magical substructure underlies the best fantasies. A book's setting may be Khendiol (*Red Moon and Black Mountain*), King Arthur's England (*The Once and Future King*), or ancient Wales (*The Mabinogion*), but its magic is Real Magic, an archetypal life-giving quality, consistent with magic as it has always been. (In a way this 'cosmic uniformity' is similar to the astonishing similarity of the poetry of Kabir, Rumi, and St John of the Cross—three mystics from different eras and cultures, all of whom wrote about their religious experiences in almost identical terms.)

There are as many ways of enjoying fantasy books as there are volumes. A comparison of works derived in some way from *The Mabinogion* (the Druidic book of legends of the Welsh people)—both from a literary standpoint and as magical expositions—may give readers an idea of the nature of successful fantasy. J.R.R. Tolkien and Joy Chant have both made use of magical archetypes found in *The Mabinogion* to enrich their own books; Evangeline Walton's books, on the other hand, are actual retellings of these diverse legends in novel form. Each of these works deals with the struggle between the forces of Good and Evil. Each of them presents some form of quest. Three of them deal with the nature of love.

So much has been written about *LOTR* that I'm reluctant to add even a line. But necessity demands it. Structurally, the book is a failure; philosophically, it is materialistic in the extreme. I wonder if Tolkien believes in magic; I think he must. His fairy beings—elves, dwarves, trolls—are too faithful to Celtic sources to be purely imagined by the author. (Although scholarship might supply the clue. Readers should refer to E.Y. Evans-Wentz's *The Fairy Faith in Celtic Countries*.) But I do not believe that Tolkien has ever *experienced* magic himself. Not Real Magic, at any rate.

Joy Chant's *Red Moon and Black Mountain* is a far more successful book. Ironically, Tolkien's work was obviously one of Chant's major influences. She, too, presents an evil magician who has broken his banishment and returned to his 'Black Mountain' of power. But Chant realizes that Good and Evil must confront each other if they are to do battle, which Tolkien seems to have overlooked. There is a cosmic order to Chant's Khendiol that is completely lacking in Tolkien's Middle Earth. She knows that there are levels of magic, both good and evil. She also knows that the order that sustains all magic—call it what you will—is benevolent.

If *Red Moon and Black Mountain* is in any way flawed, it is that the book is too short. But this is a minor fault. Fantasy is most successful when it plucks its magic images from the reader's own mind, and Chant has given us just enough to do that. This is precisely where Tolkien fails most dismally. He shows us too much. Lacking the sure knowledge that there is more magic in any reader's mind than ever could be committed to paper, he leaves nothing at all to the imagination.

If I appear determined to denigrate the achievement of *LOTR*, I do not mean to. The book has great successes. Many readers—perhaps most—will have no difficulty losing themselves in Tolkien's world. It is certainly complete enough to get lost in. There is even one area of 'magic' in which Tolkien succeeds almost totally—the naming of names. As Lin Carter has pointed out so well in talking about Lord Dunsany (whom Carter considers the master of this genre), the proper naming of characters and places is crucial to the effectiveness of any fantasy. A name must be evocative to the point of instilling a sense of magic in the reader. 'Mithrandir', 'Smeagol', 'Elendil', 'Galadriel', 'Lothlorien', 'Aragorn', 'Celeborn', 'Eowyn of Rohan', —these names are Tolkien's triumphs in *LOTR*. Which is as it should be: Tolkien is, after all, a philologist. No one—not even Lord Dunsany—has done so well with the naming of names. Dunsany does come up with some marvelous names ('Ziroon-derel', 'Lirazel'), but more often than not they are inconsistent and, like most of Dunsany's work, seem 'made-up': *unreal*. (No work of fantasy is successful if the reader does not believe it to be 'true', even if only for the book's duration.)

But these are imagined names. Not even Tolkien can create names more magical than those found in *The Mabinogion* itself. (Of course, the Druids were wielders of Real Magic.) In one sense, therefore, Evangeline Walton had some of her work already done for her before she began to write her as yet unfinished tetralogy based on the four 'branches' of *The*

Mabinogion. These three books (*The Island of the Mighty, The Children of Llyr,* and *The Song of Rhiannon*), together with C.S. Lewis's *Out of the Silent Planet, Perelandra,* and *That Hideous Strength* and T.H. White's *The Once and Future King,* are not only the best fantasies of the twentieth century. They are also great works of fiction.

The wonders of Walton's books are manifold. The brief sample I have included at the beginning of this article as Plot One is but a small part of *The Island of the Mighty.* Before it there have been other human betrayals and magical transformations. I suspect that Evangeline Walton knows something about magic from personal experience. Her books are so thoroughly steeped in mysticism that mere anthropological knowledge of Druidical lore is insufficient to explain their authority. Only C.S. Lewis (in the graveyard search for Merlin in *That Hideous Strength*) has matched Walton's subtle depiction of the forces of Good and Evil.

Evangeline Walton presents us with an enchantress (Arianrhod) who is not evil but whose obsessive vanity and lack of wisdom cause her to bring great evil upon those she loves and whose thoughtless use of power destroys her in the end. We are shown Gwydion (called in other chronicles 'the Good'), whose desire for an heir inadvertently triggers Arianrhod's wrath and precipitates a tragedy. Walton succeeds in creating an imaginary world that we believe *actually existed* in this world's history. She is able to do what few writers of worth would dare attempt: to predict a future we have already witnessed—this century's wars —and to make that prediction credible in the context of the past she presents.

In Walton's realm of Gwynedd magic does not disappear when materialism enters the scene—as it does in Tolkien's book and in most of the works drawn from *The Mabinogion*. It merely becomes invisible to men who would not wish to see it if they could.

When I asked Lin Carter why he thought adult fantasy has become so popular, he replied that since World War II people have come to want the 'better worlds' that fantasy provides. But there is something about worlds like Evangeline Walton's Gwynedd that is not at all fantastic.

Can children's fantasies, then, provide these 'better worlds'? That's an interesting speculation, especially since there is really no boundary between children's fantasy and adult fantasy these days. Richard Bach's *Jonathan Livingston Seagull*—published two years ago as a children's book—has been at the top of the *Times* Best Seller List for half a year now. Ballantine books is planning a possible series of children's fantasy publications to parallel its adult fantasy program. Such books as Ursula K. LeGuin's *A Wizard of Earthsea* and Andre Norton's novels, published originally as juvenile titles, appear in paperback as adult fantasies. *The Day the Earth Stood Still* by Poul Anderson, Gordon Dickson, and Robert Silverberg, a juvenile title, is a fall selection of the adult Science Fiction Book Club. Many devoted readers of the Ballantine series are also admirers of George MacDonald's children's story *The Day Boy and the Night Girl* (anthologized by Carter as 'The Romance of Photogen and Nycteris').

Perhaps there is some veiled link between adult fantasy and children's realism that we have yet to fathom. Can it truly be that only young people listen seriously when John Lennon sings?—

> *Imagine there's no countries*
> *It isn't hard to do*
> *Nothing to kill or die for. . . .*
> *Imagine all the people*
> *Living life in peace*
> *You may say I'm a dreamer*
> *But I'm not the only one. . . .*

Indeed not. Thirty years earlier, in his book *The Once and Future King*, T.H. White had his beloved Wart—King Arthur—standing on a battlefield, remembering how Merlin once transformed him into a gander as a child:

> . . . *He remembered Lyo-lyok and the island which they had seen on their migration, where all those puffins, razorbills,*

guillemots and kittiwakes had lived together peacefully, pre-serving their own kinds of civilization without war—because they claimed no boundaries. He saw the problem before him plain as a map. The fantastic thing about war was that it was fought about nothing—literally nothing. Frontiers were imagi-nary lines. There was no visible line between Scotland and Eng-land, although Flodden and Bannockburn had been fought about it. It was geography which was the cause—political geography. It was nothing else. Nations did not need to have the same kind of civilization, any more than the puffins and the guillemots did. . . . Countries would have to become countries—but countries which could keep their own culture and local laws. The imagi-nary lines on the earth's surface only needed to be unimagined. The airborne birds skipped them by nature. How mad the fron-tiers had seemed to Lyo-lyok, and would to Man if he could learn to fly. . . .

Imagine. . . .

If we truly want to understand what the present literary trends are about, we must ask ourselves a very simple question:

'What is REAL? . . . Does it mean having things that buzz inside you and a stick-out handle?'

Given our industrialized society, the question is oddly appropriate, especially when couched in such terms. Ironically enough, it does not come from either a 'new realism' children's book or an 'adult fantasy'. The question is asked by a toy rabbit, in a fairy tale that was first published in 1922. *The Velveteen Rabbit* has sold more copies in the last two years than it did in its entire printing history prior to that. (Friends of mine at Harvard inform me that it was a cult book there a year or so ago.)

Young and old alike are suddenly finding the strangest books meaningful. Why? Because they ask, in some fashion or other, *What is REAL?*

Of course this is only one person's view of a complex situation; a view not necessarily shared by the many friends and associates I have so freely mentioned. But it is a view arrived at out of concern for what the current literary trends may signify.

I am part of the first generation to grow up threatened with nuclear extinction, having been born just a few months before the bombs fells on Nagasaki and Hiroshima. (The shadow of that threat was never so palpable, perhaps, as during the Cuban crisis, when it became clear that the United States was not unassailable.) This is not the place to raise questions about the ramifications of that threat and its effect on today's youth, or to dissect America's moral anatomy. But it seems to me that we are living at a moment in history when people are consciously seeking answers to problems of existence, not out of idle philosophical speculation, but because it is imperative to find them if we are to continue to live. We have not found any answers yet. But the current literary trends may be indicative of that search, and the paradox of 'reality' for children versus 'fantasy' for adults may be double-edged—children looking for facts to help them cope with an abrasive environment while adults probe a deeper, archetypal reality that can transform society altogether. A paradox not merely bemusing or amusing, but one that betokens a renascence of the wish to live humanely: a wealth of profound possibilities for mankind.

[1972]

The problem novel

SHEILA EGOFF

There has been more distinguished fiction written for children since 1960 than in any previous two decades—perhaps even in the whole history of children's literature. *A Sound of Chariots* by Mollie Hunter, *What About Tomorrow* by Ivan Southall, and *The Planet of Junior Brown* by Virginia Hamilton exemplify the heights reached by modern realistic fiction for children. They compel belief by the extraordinary strength of their literary qualities: the logical flow of their narratives, the delicate complexity of their characterizations, their style, and the insights they convey about the conduct of life as their protagonists move from childhood to adolescence or from adolescence to adulthood. They provide an experience that transcends such objectives as entertainment, information, or catharsis. They touch both the imagination and the emotions.

In popularity, however, such books are quite overshadowed by the publications of a legion of writers, chiefly American, who have remodelled and narrowed realistic fiction to the extent that a new name has been coined for their creations: the 'problem novel'. While most of these books could be destroyed on literary grounds, or challenged as amateurish forays into the disciplines of psychology and sociology, as a group they are formidable in their popularity and influence. Just as the series novels (*The Hardy Boys, The Bobbsey Twins* et al.) swept North America sixty years ago, so problem novels are the great addictive publications today.

The convenient handle seems a bit of a misnomer because almost all realistic fiction written today deals with problems children face in a time of physical, psychological, intellectual, and emotional maturation. Taking the approach that maturity can be attained only through a severe testing of soul and self, most realistic fiction being written today for young people features some kind of shocking 'rite of passage', such as the uprooting of a child's life by war, the death of a close friend or parent, an encounter with sex. Realistic fiction and its sub-genre, the problem novel, both use similar themes having to do with conflict and crisis in children's lives. But while the realistic novel may have conflict at its heart, this is integral to plot and characterization, its resolution has wide applications, and it grows out of the personal vision of the writer. In problem novels the conflict stems from the writer's social conscience: it is specific rather than universal, and narrow in its significance rather than far-reaching.

It is easy to recognize this genre of children's fiction.

1. Problem novels have to do with externals, with how things look rather than how things are. They differ from the realistic novel in their limited aim, which is to tell rather than show. Indeed, the titles alone often tell all—*My Father Lives in a Downtown Hotel; My Name is David, I am an Alcoholic; Philip Hall Likes Me, I Reckon, Maybe*—and the narratives are simply elaborations of them. One- or two-word descriptions can be affixed to them—*Dinky Hocker Shoots Smack!* (obesity—not drugs), *Hey Dummy* (mental retardation), *Grover* (death), *The Man Without a Face* (homosexuality)—as if the writers had begun with the problem rather than with plot or characters.

2. The protagonist is laden with grievances and anxieties that grow out of some form of alienation from the adult world, to which he or she is usually hostile.

3. Partial or temporary relief from these anxieties is received from an association with an unconventional adult outside the family.

4. The narrative is almost always in the first person and its confessional tone is rigorously self-centred.

5. The vocabulary is limited and the observations are restricted by the pretence that an 'ordinary' child is the narrator.

6. Sentences and paragraphs are short.

7. Locutions are colloquial and the language is flat, without nuance, and often emotionally numb.

8. There is an obligatory inclusion of expletives.

9. Sex is discussed openly.

10. The setting is urban—in most cases New York city, New Jersey, or California.

In retrospect it can be seen that the formula was established by Emily Neville's *It's Like This, Cat* (1963). The first-person narration by a young teenager is glibly confessional and features alienation from parents, a New York apartment setting, a refuge outside the home with an older person who is not a relative, and stereotyped characters that are almost caricatures: a stuffy New York lawyer-father, a helpless mother, an eccentric recluse who lives with cats. The problem of alienation is resolved when the square father helps the boy's new-found friends. The basic formula was to be maintained even when everyday and relatively uncontentious family 'problems' gave way to social topics such as drugs, alcoholism, contraception, abortion, and homosexuality.

It's Like This, Cat, and all subsequent problem novels, were seminally influenced by Salinger's *Catcher in the Rye* (1951). Holden Caulfield is an intelligent, sensitive teenager trapped, as he feels, in the 'phoniness' of the adult world, which he describes with irony and bitter humour. Though he suffers a breakdown, he comes to terms with the world and there is assurance of his recovery. But while *Catcher in the Rye* inspired many writers of juveniles, it was Holden's alienation from adult society and the glory he found in criticizing it with unrestrained frankness that attracted them, not the novel's depth and insight, its credible eccentricity, or its stylistic brilliance. The earthbound confessions and banal reflections that make up the problem novel bear little resemblance to Salinger's first-person narrative, which is not only incisive and sometimes poetic, but is also refreshingly colloquial. The Salinger book spawned thin fiction, without weight or resonance, whose total significance seems to be on the surface of the narrative.

Problem novels can be divided into two groups: those that deal with normal problems of family life—sibling rivalry, moving, adjusting to a step-father—and those that focus on social or emotional topics like drugs, alcoholism, abortion, or sexual experimentation. The former are usually read by a younger age-group, seven-to-ten, though some 'heavy' problems filtered down into these junior books.

Among those who write for the younger group, Judy Blume is by far the most popular. One of her early books, *Are You There God? It's Me, Margaret* (1970), is typical in its childlike concern with the effect of an action on 'me'—rarely on 'us', never on 'them'. It is about eleven-year-old Margaret, whose anxiety is aroused because her family moves from New York to a small community in New Jersey. An added 'problem' is her decision to choose her friends from among classmates who belong either to the Y or to the Jewish community centre. Yet another arises at home: her grandmother wants her to be Jewish and her parents, partners in a mixed marriage, want her to decide about a religion when she is older (while wanting her to be like them—agnostic). Taking precedence over these worries—certainly where readers are concerned—is Margaret's concern over the fact that she is slower than some of her friends in her physical development: she has not begun to menstruate. She discusses these things casually and often with her confidant, God, as in the opening paragraph:

Are you there God? It's me Margaret. We're moving today. I'm scared God. I've never lived anywhere but here. Suppose I hate my new school? Suppose everybody there hates me? Please help me God. Don't let New Jersey be too horrible. . . .

It might be thought that the problems dealt with are to be given a moral or ethical dimension, but this is not the case. Religion has provided the book with its arch title and little else. In Margaret's homework project on the subject, God's surrogates on earth are found wanting, and God Himself is chastised when He does not obey Margaret precisely and immediately—though He is given the credit when her physical development takes its natural course. But the possible significance of religion in her life is not confronted—nor need it be to satisfy readers. The novel's immense popularity with young girls (and some boys) has been gained solely by the reassurance it conveys about pubescence.[1]

The greatest problems in problem novels are adults, usually parents, who contribute to them, frequently cause them, but rarely offer a believable or loving solution. Parents—the main alienating presence in these books, which are essentially about alienation—are often viewed as 'the enemy'.

Generally speaking, between 1900 and 1960 parents were removed from children's books in any serious, participative way: the young were thus given a taste of freedom, but still within a secure family setting. In the problem novel, however, parents figure prominently, as in the days of the moral tale, but they do not necessarily interact with the child protagonists. They are usually objects in space, mercilessly described as confused, inept, insecure, self-centred, cynical, violent, sadistic—or otherwise unsympathetic or damaging to the child's psyche. 'My mother's a dumb one. My father's a mean one,' says a runaway girl in Paul Zindel's *I Never Loved Your Mind* (1970). In contrast to parents in nineteenth-century fiction who could do no wrong, parents in the modern problem novels can do no right.

Unlike books of the past, almost every problem novel gives ample external information about parents, prejudiced though it may be—their clothes, lovers, views of life, and temperaments. In most cases, however, these adults are significant for their well-documented absence. This is sometimes physical—they have died, deserted, divorced, or are kept away on business—but in many books the absence is psychological: parents are too busy with their own concerns to pay attention to their children. Not only do they not know what's going on in their children's lives, they don't care. In Jeanette Eyerly's *Escape from Nowhere* (1969) Carla, whose businessman father is often absent and whose mother is an alcoholic, experiments with drugs. Lisa's parents in

---

[1]While boys do not disregard problem novels—particularly if word of sensational content has reached them — it is girls who read them voraciously.

John Neufeld's *Lisa, Bright and Dark* (1969) refuse to acknowledge that she is mentally ill, though she and her friends come to see this. In S.E. Hinton's *Rumble Fish* (1975), Rusty-James's mother has deserted the father, a drunken ex-lawyer on welfare, and is living in a tree-house with a movie-producer. When Rusty-James is injured in a knife fight, his father says:

> '*Are you ill?*'
> '*Got cut up in a knife fight,*' I told him.
> '*Really?*' *He came over to take a look.* '*What strange lives you two lead.*'
> '*I ain't so strange,*' I said.
> *He gave me a ten-dollar bill.*

In Paul Zindel's *My Darling, My Hamburger* (1969), teachers and parents fail miserably in every incident. The book opens with the female gym teacher telling Liz, Maggie, and their class that the way to stop a guy who wants to go all the way is to suggest going to get a hamburger. When Dennis feels destroyed because Maggie has broken a date to the prom, his parents spend the dinner hour talking about the correct way for him to handle the kitchen garbage. While Liz at various times considers suicide, abortion, or forcing Sean to marry her, her mother gives her long lectures on smiling or on being sweeter to her stepfather at the dinner table. In school Sean writes a story called 'The Circus of Blackness' about a young circus couple who commit a ritualistic murder of their child in front of an audience. The teacher's comment: 'You have a remarkable imagination.'

Moreover, adults are shown to be insensitive and callous about anything outside the norm. In Kin Platt's *Hey Dummy* (1971) not one adult shows even ordinary humanitarian concern for a retarded child. Neil wants to bring the boy to his house for dinner:

> '*Brain-damaged, did you say?*' *my mom said. She threw herself into a grotesque pose, arms and hands at awkward angles, making her face look stupid and drooly.* '*One of those kind?*'

As a result of the attitude of unconcern, even loathing, of adults towards the handicapped child, Neil develops an 'altered personality'. He prefers to withdraw psychologically rather than be part of the so-called real world.

As the sixties moved into the seventies, the sexual content became more explicit. John Donovan's *I'll Get There, It Better Be Worth The Trip* (1969) contains one suggested, quickly passed-over homosexual incident, but in Isabelle Holland's *The Man Without A Face,* published three years later, there is no doubt about the homosexual relationship. And 1977 saw the publication of a problem novel by Judy Blume, *Forever,* that is as explicit as a sex manual. The treatment of such topics as abortion and contraception indicates that these subjects are no longer even controversial, much less taboo. In Paul Zindel's *My Darling, My Hamburger* Liz is quite upset at the idea of an abortion. But Norma Klein's *It's Not What You Expect* (1973), which appeared four years later, describes Ralph and Sara Lee nonchalantly arranging to have an abortion in New York. They return, according to Ralph, with 'no problems'. Sara Lee does not tell her mother and carries on as if nothing unusual has happened.

The matter-of-fact explicitness of problem novels is accompanied by unrestrained language. Back in 1959 Karl Bjarnhof, in an adult novel, would not have surprised readers by having one of his youthful characters remark: 'But Hamsun. . . . He's the one who swears in his books. I don't mind people swearing, but in a book!'[2] By 1973 a child in John Neufeld's *Freddy's Book* could ask the librarian for 'a book about fucking'. In an article written in 1975 Norma Klein said she would 'like to see four-letter words used as frequently in realistic books for children as they are in the everyday lives of what I would consider respectable, middle and upperclass people.'[3] The spirit of linguistic liberation does not extend to departing from a style that is undemanding and serviceable at best—combining banality and flatness, in an attempt to suggest the speech of children, with a certain

---

[2]Karl Bjarnhof, *The Good Light,* tr. by Naomi Walford (London, 1960), p. 157.
[3]'More Realism for Children', *Top of the News,* XXXI (April 1975), p. 309.

narrative efficiency that bespeaks the adult writer.

> *I walked into the lobby of my apartment building, thinking how good a big, cold drink would taste. I pushed the Up elevator button and waited. When the elevator got to the lobby Henry opened the gate and I stepped in. Just as he was about to take me upstairs Peter Hatcher and his dumb old dog came tearing down the hall.*
> —Judy Blume, *Otherwise known as Sheila the Great* (1972)

> *'What do you think of Mom's new boy friend?' she asked suddenly.*
> *I thought for a second and shrugged. 'He's okay, I guess.'*
> *Chloris frowned, . . . 'He's not okay,' she said angrily. 'He's a creep.'*
> *'How do you figure that?'*
> *She pushed back her long brown hair and scowled.*
> *'You don't have to figure it. A creep is a creep.'*
> *'Yes, but . . .'*
> —Kin Platt, *Chloris and the Creeps* (1973)

> *I'd better begin this story by telling you that until a month ago I was quite a mess. I mean, I was such a mess that my mother wanted to send me to a psychiatrist but backed down when she discovered that it would cost twenty-five dollars an hour.*
> — Barbara Wersba, *The Dream Watcher* (1968)

After a book-length recital of grievances and 'problems' in these books, their resolution becomes a matter of some interest. A consideration of the endings alone strengthens the impression that it is the problems themselves—or rather the cool, anecdotal explication of them—that are the *raison d'être* of problem novels, for psychologically convincing resolutions seem to be neither required by readers nor demanded by the conventions of the genre. Reflecting the fatalism and resignation of adolescents who see their lives as compounded of one 'problem' after another, none of them with any hope of resolution, some of these novels are almost existential in not having a conclusion. 'Then again, maybe I won't,' Tony says, at the end of Judy Blume's book of that title (1973), about whether he will cease his practice of spying on a girl undressing. And Ox in John Ney's *Ox, The Story of a Kid at the Top* (1970), after a wild trip with his wealthy father from whom he feels estranged, simply decides that 'nothing ever changes'. In novels for older children, the conclusions suggest that the long road to recovery has not even started, or is only just beginning. Sean in Paul Zindel's *My Darling, My Hamburger* deserts Liz, who is pregnant, after a conversation with his crude and cynical father. Roger in Kin Platt's *The Boy Who Could Make Himself Disappear* (1968) undergoes psychiatric treatment, the outcome of which is not at all clear. And the ten-year-old in Marilyn Sachs's *The Bear's House* (1971), who has tried to take care of a younger brother and newborn baby while hiding her mother's breakdown, appears at the end to be about to enter a classroom playhouse of the three bears—psychologically, at least, never to emerge. In books for younger children the endings tend to be predicated on arbitrary and sudden psychological changes or to appear as band-aids applied to a serious wound rather than as genuine cures achieved through a more mature outlook or some kind of rehabilitation. Overweight Dinkey in *Dinkey Hocker Shoots Smack!* is taken off to Europe by her parents to encourage her to stick to her diet, leaving the impression that her psyche and body will be put in shape without any major effort on her part. Antonia in Norma Klein's *Confessions of an Only Child* (1974) grudgingly comes to terms with having a baby sister, and Brett in Klein's *Mom, the Wolf Man and Me* (1972)—in an unexpected reversal—accepts the fact of her mother's marriage.

There is one event that turns up over and over again to effect a miraculous change in the outlook and circumstances of the troubled protagonist, and that is death. The preponderance of deaths (though not death scenes) is astonishing, considering that ninety-five per cent of us reach adulthood without experiencing a family death.[4] The death is usually that of a *deus ex machina*—an older eccentric outside the family with whom the child has had a

---

[4] World Book Encyclopedia (1978), vol. V, p. 53.

close relationship and the support that had not been forthcoming from parents. The janitor in Constance Greene's *A Girl Called Al* (1969), Mr Pignati in *The Pigman*, the alcoholic schoolteacher in Barbara Wersba's *The Dream Watcher* (1968), the lonely, middle-aged homosexual in Isabelle Holland's *The Man Without a Face* all have to die in order that the children who have become attached to them may come to terms with themselves. Death is treated as a 'soft', only moderately disturbing problem—the edge is taken off it; the child's ego and self-absorption are hardly affected by the experience. In *A Girl Called Al* the death of the janitor is portrayed as 'a good death, a happy death'; it is the turning-point in Al's self-acceptance. In other books the children are left by adults to bear their grief alone (Constance Greene's *Beat the Turtle Drum*, 1976), or they come to terms with death more quickly than adults, as Grover does in Vera and Bill Cleaver's *Grover* (1970). But however the deaths of these stray mentors are presented, they provide the dénouement that resolves insecurities and self-doubts. They enable the children to 'find themselves'—for most young readers a totally expected resolution.

In all fields of writing there are the good and the bad and the mediocre. A rare problem novel successfully avoids the land-mines of a clichéd form to become something else: a novel that employs all the stylistic and thematic devices of the genre while maintaining an emotionally charged credibility. Ursula Le Guin's *Very Far Away from Anywhere Else* (1976) and M.E. Kerr's *Is That You, Miss Blue?* (1975) are two such novels. They both use a brief time span and a circumscribed setting — Le Guin a few months of friendship in the closed world of two teenagers, and Kerr a term in a girl's boarding school. These books succeed because the protagonists are intelligent, well educated, and have an ardent curiosity about life, and their main thrust is not an unburdening of the soul but concern for another person. They are not exercises in egotism. In cleanly written, controlled prose Le Guin shows the friendship between two teenagers (neither of whom has a terrible home life) and how they delicately adjust to a loving relationship without the pressure of sex. They genuinely care for one another. Owen says:

And so the next time we met, it was entirely different. I had decided that I was in love with Natalie, I hadn't fallen in love with her, please notice that I didn't say that; I had decided that I was in love with her.

The ending is as low-keyed as the relationship: both go off to their respective colleges. But this novelette (94 pages) still manages to convey a whole life story. One knows what kind of adults Owen and Natalie will become.

The 'Miss Blue' of *Is That You, Miss Blue?* is an elderly, brilliant schoolteacher driven from her job because of her eccentricities —she converses with Jesus. The group of teen-aged girls in the Episcopal boarding school, with whom the story is concerned, have problems of their own, and they express them in the breezy, sophisticated terms that are typical of the problem novel with older protagonists. Carolyn Cardmaker explains why she is at Charles School:

'A Preacher's Kid!' She was tracing the initials PK in the soot on the train window with her finger. 'I'm a preacher's kid with a high I.Q., which means I won a scholarship. There are only four reasons why anyone is ever shipped off to Charles School, and I qualify as a Number One. Number One is Bright and Piti-ful. I could be Bright and Black, or Bright and Oriental, or Bright and a Migrant Worker's daughter. But I'm worse than all of those because I'm bright and a preacher's kid, which means that I'm practically a pauper. I'm even wearing a secondhand school blazer.'

Flanders Brown, the fifteen-year-old narrator with recently divorced parents, also had adjustments to make in her life. But all the girls can see outside themselves. They have an affection for eccentricity and feel strongly for a person driven to pain and disgrace. And their realization that remarkable people, no matter how briefly known, can have an effect on one's life is made convincing.

Both books are closer than most other problem novels to the concepts imaginatively expressed in Salinger's *Catcher in the Rye*, especially his bitter-sweet view of growing-up. These novels are self-defining; they possess a tough clarity of thought and language. Most problem novels give their protagonists a voice that is too shrill and garrulous for enlightenment. They are merely laments, couched in the language of the day, that are glib and self-centred. One thinks of Aunt Susan's remark in Penelope Lively's *The House in Norham Gardens:*

> *'It's only those who have never listened who find themselves in trouble eventually.'*
> *'Why?'*
> *'Because it is extremely dull'* said Aunt Susan tartly, *'to grow old with nothing inside your head but your own voice. Tedious, to put it mildly.'*

Alienation, hostility, egocentricity, the search for identity, the flouting of conventions—these things have evoked instant interest and sympathy from the young since the sixties. That was a period of general reaction against authority, which expressed itself in protest movements and various forms of rebellion that focused on a multitude of injustices and inequalities and revealed a hitherto unexpressed need for honesty and openness in relationships—instinctively and tacitly yearned for by young people, actively sought by adults. They brought into question power structures of all kinds—in government, in education, in the family itself. The stability of family life was taken for granted in children's literature until changes in life-styles and the liberated attitudes of the sixties made this convention seem mythical. A society where roles and standards are clear and consistently supported offers a form of security for children. Autonomy, though stimulating, can bring with it insecurity, and this is the generating force behind problem novels. The reassurance they provide in dealing openly with issues that had heretofore been hidden is perhaps the main reason for their popularity. Another is the hostility to adults they reflect. They play on frustrations and resentments—increased where there is lack of attention or sympathy—that every child feels throughout the process of socialization. Not only are the main characters impotent and often angry, but they feel alone in a hostile world;

they rarely have the support of parents, relatives, teachers, or spiritual advisors. On the other hand, they consistently oppose their parents' values (when they have any) as being oppressive and archaic. Combine these ingredients with parents who are responsible for all injustices—reversing the childhood syndrome that anything bad that happens in the family is somehow the child's fault—and you have a mixture of fictional elements that is irresistible to the older child or early adolescent.

There are numerous secondary reasons for these books' popularity. In cases where readers suffer from the very difficulties featured, it is presumably good for them to know that they are not alone in their anxieties. Conversely, for those children who cannot identify themselves with the protagonists, there is the appeal of the exotic in the sordid events described, or of having one's curiosity and even prurience satisfied by matter-of-fact discussions of sensitive subjects. Another attraction is that the language and style—or rather the simple 'with it' language and the absence of a 'literary' style—make the content totally accessible. Eschewing any such distractions as formal literary conventions and linguistic niceties, these books face their problems head-on by means of a convention of their own: the colloquial first-person narration of a knowing child, with its appearance of verisimilitude and confidentiality.

Yet another factor in their popularity is the conditioning provided by television—its mesmerizing delivery of words and pictures flooding the unselective viewer with both images of real life and facile simulations of it. Problem novels, with their clear-cut topical subjects, their lack of background and depth, and the prevalence of dialogue, require little adjustment from the inveterate TV watcher. Indeed, more than a few of them have been dramatized for television.[5]

Shallow and narrow though they may be, problem novels have made their influence felt in the more creative realm of

---

[5]John Neufeld's *Lisa, Bright and Dark* (1969), Richard Peck's *Are You in the House Alone?* (1976), and *Go Ask Alice* (anonymous, 1971) are three problem novels that have been adapted for television.

imaginative fiction for children. In freeing children from an idealized conception of childhood, they have demythologized it (possibly while creating a few myths of their own). They confront children with problems that are not of their own making—unlike the crises that issued from the spirited adventure stories of the past—but with which they have to come to terms. And these concerns, both social and psychological, have individualized characters to a degree that was formerly unknown. It was the writers of the 1960s who began to emphasize the way in which personality and the sense of self alter when a psychological chasm is reached. Some protagonists find a bridge and cross it; others fall in. In either case the characters are changed to an extent and with a finality quite different from the rather simple and lighthearted 'growing up' that the children in earlier books experience. This approach of treating characters as individuals and making them sensitive to their environment colours all recent fiction for children, so that even a historical novel about the American Civil War, Betty Cummings's *Hew Against the Grain* (1977), focuses not on external events but on the introspective main character and her personal problems resulting from the war; it is non-partisan and includes a rape scene. And Mollie Hunter's *A Sound of Chariots* (1972) is about a young girl's obsession with death. (An atmosphere of bleakness pervades recent fiction for children—another legacy of problem novels.)

Children's literature has always responded to changes in social attitudes and values, but the mass production of problem novels, and their quick acceptance, speeded up the process of change. What new trend will manifest itself for children today who, we are told, are much more accepting of their parents' middle-class values than their immediate predecessors? However this shift in attitude is confronted by writers, we can be sure that in one and a half decades the world of children's fiction has already changed fundamentally—and forever.

[1980]

Perspective on the future: the quest of space-age young people

SYLVIA ENGDAHL

Those of us who work with literature for youth have many things in common, whether we are writers, librarians, or teachers—and I believe that one of them is a very strong and basic interest in the future. I have been fascinated by ideas about the future, and particularly about space exploration, since I myself was in my teens; for the past five years I have devoted my full time to writing about it. While educators may not have such specific enthusiasm for the subject of the distant future, all are deeply concerned with preparing young people to live in the world of tomorrow. None of us can predict just what that world is going to be like, but I think there is much we can do to equip the next generation to cope with whatever tomorrow brings.

I suppose every author is asked how he came to write what he writes, but I think the question is raised more frequently with authors of science fiction than with others. People are always curious about why anyone would choose to write about imaginary things instead of the things we know. Each author has his own reasons, and mine are not really typical; perhaps an explanation of them will make clear why I feel that stories that deal with the future are important, and are of interest even to those for whom neither science fiction nor science itself has any special appeal.

First of all, I should mention that my books are more for a general audience than for science fiction fans. Although I think science fiction fans will enjoy them, I aim them principally toward people—especially girls—who normally do not read science fiction, and I avoid using esoteric terminology that only established fans can understand. Actually I am not what one would call a fan myself, at least not in the sense of keeping up with the adult science fiction genre. I use the science fiction form simply because my ideas about man's place in the universe can best be expressed in the context of future or hypothetical worlds.

This is not to say that my books are wholly allegorical. I have been rather dismayed to find that some people interpret them that way, because although there is indeed a good deal of allegory in them, they also have a literal level. For instance, what is said in *Enchantress from the Stars* and *The Far Side of Evil* about how a truly mature civilization would view peoples of lesser advancement is meant to be taken literally; scientists are beginning to ask why, if civilizations more advanced than ours do exist in other solar systems, they haven't contacted us, and that is my answer as to why.

Of course, one of my main reasons for writing science fiction is that I believe very strongly in the importance of space exploration to the survival of mankind. I have held this belief since the days when all space travel was considered fantastic, and indeed I developed the theory of the 'Critical Stage', on which my book *The Far Side of Evil* is based, in unpublished work that I did before the first artificial satellite was launched. I am entirely serious about the choice between expansion into space and human self-destruction being a normal and inevitable stage of evolution; the fact that when I came to write the book, our establishment of a space program had made it impossible for the story's setting to be Earth, as it was in my original version, is to me the most encouraging sign of our era. In the early fifties I had been afraid that the Space Age would not begin soon enough.

But apart from my commitment to the cause of space exploration, I think there is good reason to set stories in the future when writing for teenagers. Today's young people identify with the future. Many of them find it a more pertinent concept than that of the past. If we are going to make any generalization about the human condition, any convincing statement that evolution is a continuous process in which the *now* that seems all-important to them is only a small link, we stand a better chance of communicating when we speak of the future than when we describe past ages that—however mistakenly—the young have dismissed as dead and irrelevant. Teenagers are far more serious-minded than they used to be, yet they don't consider anything worth serious attention unless they see its relationship to problems they have experienced or can envision.

This has become more and more evident during the past few years. It so happened that I began writing in a period when young people's involvement with matters once thought too deep for them was increasing. I was not at all sure that there would be a place for the kind of novels I wanted to write, because they were too optimistic to fit the gloomy mold of contemporary adult fiction, yet too philosophical, I thought, to be published as junior fiction. Fortunately I directed them to young people anyway, and quite a few seem to like them. I don't think this would be the case were it not that the boys and girls now growing up are more mature in their interests than those of former generations.

It is apparent today that the young people of our time are searching desperately for something that they are not getting in the course of a standard education. They are searching in all directions: some through political activism; some through 'dropping out'; some through renewed interest in religion in both traditional and novel forms, or even in the occult; and all too many through drugs or violence. Misguided though some of these attempts may be, I feel that they all reflect a genuine and growing concern on the part of our youth for a broader view of the universe than our present society offers them. Some can find meaning in the values of their elders; others cannot. There would seem to be a wide gulf between the two attitudes. There is a great deal of talk about polarization. Yet underneath, whatever their immediate and conscious goals, I believe that all young people are seeking the same thing: they are seeking a perspective on the future.

The need for such perspective is not new. It is a basic and universal human characteristic. What is different now is that the perspective inherent in the culture passed automatically from one generation to the next is no longer enough. Perspective implies a framework, a firm base from which to look ahead, and in this age of rapid change the old framework is not firm. Many of its components are still true and sound, but it has become so complex that as a whole it must necessarily invite question, if only because of the contradictions it contains. Scarcely anyone today is so naive as to suppose that all aspects of our current outlook are valid. There is much controversy, however, as to which are valid and which are not, and among free people the controversy will continue, for we live in an era when man's outlook is constantly shifting and expanding.

Whether this is occurring because—as I believe—the time of our first steps beyond our native planet is the most crucial period in mankind's history, or whether its basic cause is something else, the fact remains that it is happening. It is a confusing time for all of us, but especially for our young people, the members of the first Space Age generation, who are so aware of change and of the need for change that they can find nothing solid to hold to. They haven't the background to know that problems have been solved in the past, that present and future problems will in turn be solved, that the existence of problems is not in itself grounds for bitterness. They hear their disillusioned elders speak of the future with despair and they have no basis for disbelief. Yet instinctively, they do disbelieve—and I wonder if this, as much as the world's obvious lack of perfection, may not be why they find it so hard to believe anything else their elders tell them. They cannot accept the now-fashionable notion that the universe is patternless and absurd; they are looking for answers. Inside, they know that those answers must exist.

Young people cannot be blamed for thinking the answers are simple. Earlier generations have thought the same. But nowadays one's faith in a simple answer cannot survive very long; what the Space Age generation needs is awareness that one must not expect simple answers, and that man's progress toward solutions is a long, slow process that extends not merely over years, but over centuries. Knowledge of past history alone does not give such awareness because most of today's teenagers just don't care about the past. Significance, to them, lies not in what has been, but in what is to come. I believe that only by pointing out relationships between past, present, and future can we help them to gain the perspective that is the true object of their search.

One might wonder how I can consider this need for perspective so fundamental when for years, psychologists have been saying that people's basic need is for security. Yet I think our young people are showing over and over again that they do not want security, at least not security as it has commonly been defined. A great deal of effort has been devoted to making them secure, yet many turn their backs and deliberately seek out something dangerous to do. The security they need cannot come from outside; it must come from within, from experiences through which each person proves that he is capable of handling himself in an indisputably insecure world. But no one can handle a situation in which he sees no pattern, no meaning. There can be no security without direction. Thus a perspective on the future is implicit in the very concept of inner security.

One's view of the future is, of course, a highly personal thing. Our beliefs can differ greatly as to the direction we are going, or ought to go. In my books I naturally present my own opinions, and I don't expect all readers to agree with them. But I hope that even those who do not agree will gain something by being encouraged to develop their private thoughts about the topics I deal with. I hope that they will be convinced that we are going *somewhere*, and that this will help to counter the all-too-prevalent feeling that human evolution is over and done with. It is this, more than anything else, that I try to put across: the idea that there is continuity to history, that progress—however slow—does occur, and that whatever happens to us on this planet is part of some overall pattern that encompasses the entire universe. We are not in a position to see the pattern. We can only make guesses about it, and many of those guesses are bound to be wrong. Still, I do not believe that guessing, either in fantasy or in serious speculation, is a futile task; for when we ignore the issue, we are apt to forget that the pattern exists whether we see it or not. That, I think, is the root of many young people's turmoil. They have no conviction that there is any pattern.

A common reaction to the space flights so far undertaken seems to be that we had better appreciate Earth because it's the only good planet there is. It is quite true that it is the only one in this solar system that is suitable for us to live on at present, and that those of this system are the only ones we have any immediate prospect of reaching. But the attitude that no other planet is worth anything strikes me as a new form of provincialism. Our solar system is merely a small part of a vast universe that contains billions upon billions of stars. People sometimes ask me if I really believe that there are inhabitable planets circling those other stars; the answer is that I do, and that most scientists now do also. Not everyone seems to realize this; several acquaintances have told me rather shamefacedly that they themselves think that there is life in other solar systems, although they are sure that scientists would laugh at them. As a result, I am now writing a nonfiction book that will explain to young people not only what modern scientists do believe, but what many philosophers of past ages believed about an infinity of worlds. The idea is not new, and it has not been confined to science fiction. Giordano Bruno was burned at the stake in the year 1600 for holding it.

Of course, I do not believe that the inhabitants of other solar systems are as much like us in the physical and cultural sense as I have depicted them in my novels. Most serious science fiction does not make them so similar, and I think that many potential readers are thereby turned away. They are put off by the weird element inherent in any attempt to imagine what sentient species other than ours would be like. I feel that this is distracting. Since we don't know what they are like and my aim is to show essentially identical spiritual qualities, it seems to me best to portray them in our terms, just as I have to make them speak in our language. Also, in *Enchantress from the Stars,* I wanted to leave open the question of which, if any, of the people were from Earth. Only in that way could I make my point about various levels of advancement.

This point, which is further developed in *The Far Side of Evil,* concerns evolutionary advancement, not mere cultural advancement. My intent was to comment upon relationships between eras of history, and between peoples at different stages of evolution, not relationships between societies here on Earth. We of Earth, whatever our nationality or our color, are all members of the same human race. We are one people, one species. Someday, generations hence, we may encounter other sentient species. It is not too soon for us to begin thinking about our identity as a people, our place in a universe inhabited by many; the young are better aware of that than most adults.

To those who do not believe that there will ever be contact between the stars, I would like to suggest that as far as contemporary youth's perspective is concerned, it makes no difference whether there is or not. The mere idea is, in itself, of consequence. I am troubled by science fiction's usual portrayal of advanced aliens either as hostile, or as presumptuous meddlers who take it upon themselves to interfere with the evolutionary process. The dangers of the first attitude are obvious; those of the second are perhaps less so. Maybe the whole issue seems remote and insignificant when we have so much else to worry about. Yet if young people acquire the idea that some extrasolar civilization could solve our problems for us if its starships happened to come here, or that it would consider our failings evidence that our whole human race is wicked instead of merely immature, will that not add to their already-great sense of futility? Will it not interfere with whatever perspective on human history they have managed to absorb? I think it will; and furthermore, whether there really are any alien civilizations is immaterial. Science fiction may be fantasy, but that young people like it and are affected by it is fact. It is also a fact that the Jupiter probe recently launched by NASA carried a plaque designed to communicate its origin to any intelligent beings who recover it after it passes out of our solar system. It may be that no aliens will ever see that plaque, but our children saw it on television; their attitude toward its hypothetical viewers is bound to influence their attitude toward our own civilization.

Their view of civilization is already confused and inconsistent enough. On one hand, many believe that only scientific knowledge is factual, and that advancement is merely a matter of inventions and technical skill. On the other, during the past few years some people, especially the young, have come to distrust science, to blame it for our problems and even to question the value of technological advance—which, I believe, is the greatest distortion of perspective I have yet seen.

Today, in their quest for meaning, young people are challenging the materialistic outlook many scientists have held in the past—and rightly so. At the same time, however, some of them are rejecting not only inadequate theories, but the whole idea of scientific progress. They seem to feel that in so doing they are defending spiritual values against some implacable enemy. They imagine that they seek a wider truth. Yet actually this viewpoint is equally narrow and in fact self-contradictory, for truth is precisely what science seeks, and has always sought from its very beginnings. There has never been any conflict between the real scientific attitude and spiritual values, where there appears to be; the trouble is with the particular theory involved and not with science as such. Truth is truth; science is simply the name given to the part we have attempted to organize and verify.

I think the current misunderstanding is the result of our tendency over the past hundred years or so to compartmentalize science, to separate it from the rest of life in the same way that some people separate religion. There was a time when the major scientific thought of an era could be understood by every educated person; but for many years now specialization has been necessary, and this has led to an unfortunate conception of what science is. Non-scientists have gotten the idea that it is some kind of esoteric cult that stands apart from other human endeavors, while both they and the scientists themselves have felt that its realms have been charted and need only to be conquered. When young people observe that there are things worth investigating outside these realms, and that some of our current scientific theories are questionable, it often doesn't occur to them that the answer lies not in abandoning science but in expanding it: refuting its dogmatic portions as dogma has been refuted countless times in the past. This, perhaps, is why some of them are turning in desperation to supernaturalism, astrology, and the like. Yet science is distinguished from superstition not by the subject matter with which it deals, but by the maturity of its explanations; it is distinguished from philosophy not by content, but by the availability of data to which objective scientific methods can be applied. All the phenomena now dealt with by science were once explained by superstition and, as an intermediate step, all our sciences were once divisions of philosophy. For that matter, there are advanced theories in all fields that are philosophic in that they are not yet subject to empirical proof. Because nowadays the men who hold such theories are called scientists and not philosophers, we get the impression that the theories are authoritative; but actually some are no more so than theories of the Middle Ages that have been disproven.

The point to be made is that this process of progression is by no means finished or complete. There is no area of truth that is outside the province of science in principle, though there are many that science lacks the practical means to investigate at its present stage of development. It is thus a great mistake to identify science with materialism, and to assume that it inherently deals only with the material aspects of the universe, when the fact is merely that these aspects can be more readily studied than other aspects that we are just beginning to rescue from the realms of the 'supernatural'. There is no such thing as the supernatural, since 'natural', by definition, includes all aspects of reality. But too many of us have shut out parts of reality. We have discarded not only superstition, but also the areas with which superstition presently deals, forgetting that the superstition of today is merely an immature explanation of the science of tomorrow. We have failed to recognize that there are natural laws that cannot be explained in terms of the ones we know because they are, in themselves, equally basic.

Worse, our society has tended to assume that there is a firm line between science and religion. It has outgrown trust in superstition, and many have identified faith with superstition, discarding that also. Yet the fact that the physical aspects of natural law are the most readily analyzed does not mean that there isn't a spiritual reality that is just as real, just as much a part of the universe, as the material reality that science has so far studied objectively. I don't wonder that young people have difficulty in viewing the world with perspective when they have been led to feel that it is necessary to reject one or the other. The young today sense that moral and spiritual values are important, though they will not accept dogma in religion any more than in any other field, and it is understandably hard for them to reconcile their innate idealism with a science that is seemingly opposed.

To me, science itself can never be opposed to truth in any form whatsoever, no matter how many specific theories may be mistaken, and no matter how dogmatic certain scientists may be in support of their own era's beliefs. This is how I have viewed it in *Enchantress from the Stars,* and I think one of the book's appeals for young people is that it does take seriously certain things outside the traditional bounds of science, such as extrasensory perception, without putting a materialistic interpretation on them. I hope readers notice that nowhere have I suggested that advanced peoples, in progressing beyond a materialistic orientation, would give up any of their technology; because I feel strongly that as they matured, they would improve their technology and learn to put it to better use.

I am convinced, therefore, that the solution to future problems lies not in de-emphasizing science, but in advancing it, as well as in an outlook that recognizes that the science of any given age is imperfect and incomplete. For instance, I believe that while there is much that can and should be done now to slow the rate of population growth, the only permanent answer to overpopulation is the colonization of new worlds. I have been asked how I can approve of our colonizing planets in other solar systems if other sentient species exist. Certainly I don't think we should colonize planets that are already occupied; I trust my books make that very clear. What I do think is that there are many worlds on which no intelligent life has evolved that can be made livable by advanced technology, and that in the normal course of a sentient species' evolution, it expands and utilizes such worlds. There is nothing less natural in that than in our ancestors building the ships and other equipment needed to colonize America. Pioneering is a basic human activity; that's the comparison I have tried to draw in *Journey Between Worlds*.

This question of what is natural for us seems to need a good deal of examination right now. There is a feeling prevalent today, particularly among young people, that we ought to get 'back to nature. Insofar as this means preserving and enjoying the beauties of our world, it is a good thing. But those who say that we as a species should *live* in a more 'natural' way are, I think, overlooking what 'natural' means as applied to human beings. It is the nature of animal species to remain the same from generation to generation, evolving only as adaptation to physical environment may demand. It is the nature of man, however—and whatever other sentient races may inhabit this universe—to learn, to change, and to progress. There is no point at which it is 'natural' to stop, for to cease changing is contrary to the mental instincts that are uniquely human. If it were not so, all learning, from the discovery of fire to the conquest of disease, would be unnatural, and I don't think anyone believes that—least of all the young, who are more eager for change than their elders. It is the nature of man to solve problems. It is the nature of man to grope continuously toward an understanding of truth. There may be disagreement as to means, disagreement as to what is true and what is not, but never on the principle that to search for truth is an inherent attribute of mankind.

In my most recent novel *This Star Shall Abide* and its forthcoming second volume *Beyond the Tomorrow Mountains,* I have said quite a bit about the search for truth, from both the scientific and the religious standpoints; and I have also tried to say something about the importance of faith. Yet the people of these stories are stranded in a desperate situation where only advanced technology, and an eventual major advance in scientific theory, can prevent their extinction. To achieve this advance, they are dependent on the kind of creative inspiration that has underlain all human progress since the beginning of time. Their religion is central to their culture, and it is in no way a materialistic religion; but the hope it offers them can be fulfilled only through faith in the ultimate success of their scientific research.

I wrote a description of the books not long ago in which I defined science as the portion of truth that no longer demands faith for acceptance. That's the way I look at science: it is part of a larger truth. I believe that if we can give young people that sort of attitude toward it—if they can be helped to view its failure to provide all the answers overnight with neither hostility nor despair, but with the willingness to keep on searching—we will go a long way toward building their perspective on the future. And I believe that it is such perspective, more than anything else, that will fit them to take their place in tomorrow's world.

[1972]

Are children's books racist and sexist?

JOHN ROWE TOWNSEND

Hugh Lofting, who wrote the Doctor Dolittle books, was allegedly 'a white racist and chauvinist, guilty of almost every prejudice known to modern white Western man'. William H. Armstrong's *Sounder*, which won the principal American children's book award in 1970 and has been made into a successful film, is denounced as 'emasculating' the black man and 'destructuring' the black family. Beatrix Potter's *Tale of Peter Rabbit* is described as 'perhaps one of the most sexist animal fantasies in children's literature': it 'keeps selling and influencing young boys and girls to believe that only males have great adventures and are excitingly "naughty".' In *Watership Down*, Richard Adams is said to have 'grafted exalted human spirits to the rabbit bodies of his male characters and has made the females mere rabbits. The males are superhuman and the females sub-human'.

The first two of these charges are made in articles reprinted in *Racist and Sexist Images in Children's Books*, published by the Writers and Readers Publishing Co-operative and obtainable from Children's Rights Workshop, 73 Balfour Street, London, S.E. 17. The third comes from *Sexism in Award Winning Picture Books*, by Suzanne M. Czaplinski, which is also available from CRW. The fourth is from an article by Jane Resh Thomas in America's leading magazine on children's literature, the *Horn Book*, for August 1974.

I will come back to these accusations later. They are just a few among scores of similar charges levelled at well known children's books. The supposedly innocent pastures of children's literature are beginning to look like minefields as one instance after another of alleged racism or sexism is detected and exploded. Why is this happening? How far are such allegations justified? What, if anything, ought authors and publishers to be doing about them?

The campaigns against racism and sexism appear to have got most of their early impetus from the United States. Two articles—not, I think, the first in their fields, but the first to be widely known and quoted, and to make a powerful impact— were one by Nancy Larrick in *Saturday Review* for 11 September 1965, on *'The All-White World of Children's Books'* and one by a collective of 'Feminists on Children's Media' in *School Library Journal* for January 1971, called 'A Feminist Look at Children's Books'.

Nancy Larrick drew attention to the almost complete omission at that time of Negroes, from books for children. Although in some American cities more than half the schoolchildren were black, she found that over a three-year period only four-fifths of one per cent of trade books for children from 63 leading publishers told a story about American Negroes today: and that many children's books which did include a Negro showed him as a servant or slave, a sharecropper, a migrant worker or a menial.

Nancy Larrick's article noted incidentally the formation in New York of the Council on Interracial Books for Children. This council has been the source of many studies, ten of which make up the booklet already mentioned on *Racist and Sexist Images*. (Actually, the title is somewhat misleading, as there is only one study of sexism, and that relates to books about Puerto Ricans, few of which books are likely to be found in Britain.)

In 1971 the Feminists on Children's Literature presented what they themselves called a 'merciless analysis' of some of the more highly praised children's books, and concluded that there were proportionately far too few books with girls as central characters. They also found that most of the books they examined were either plain sexist—girls and women being exclusively assigned traditional female roles—or 'cop-out' books, in which a heroine appears to be developing promisingly but in the end adjusts to the stereotype. Since then pressure groups in both America and Britain have examined a great many books and have made similar charges.

The assumption, explicit or implicit, of those who are concerned about racism or sexism in children's books is that the books children read affect their attitudes. This assumption is not, so far as I know, based on the results of any organised research. I have not been able to trace any study which has produced substantial evidence of a formative effect. It would in fact be extremely difficult to set up a valid research project. Effects of books on attitudes are hard to isolate and to measure, and at best there would have to be a good deal of reliance on subjective assessment.

It seems fair however to suppose that if stereotypes of racial characteristics or the roles of the sexes are constantly presented to children, they must to some extent be absorbed. (And in any case, ordinary decency suggests that people should not be demeaned for being of the 'wrong' sex or colour, even if no actual harm can be proved.) At the same time, common sense indicates that children's attitudes will be formed by the whole atmosphere of their society: books are only a rather small part of most children's environment, and children's books indeed tend to reflect the attitudes of society at large rather than to shape them.

Much good has probably been done by pressure groups in causing publishers to think hard about unconscious racism and sexism in school readers, textbooks, and information books. But when we come to creative literature for children I begin to feel serious doubts, especially where there appears to be determined fault-finding. Rather curiously, the greater part of the material I have seen on racism and sexism has concerned itself with children's 'quality' fiction and picture books: hardly any has tackled films or television, though some work has been done on comics and series-books. I say 'curiously' because one might have thought that television and films were much more popular, insistent, and influential media than books. Also, to be frank about it, 'quality' books are largely read in the kind of homes where parents and children are least likely to take their opinions at second hand from outside.

It's hard to avoid suspecting that books may well be scrutinised in preference to films or television because books are handy and stay still while you look at them. One also wonders whether good books may be investigated rather than poor ones because good books are more interesting for the investigator. Who wants to spend months researching the Famous Five or the Bobbsey Twins? In America, the books that win major awards have been particularly thoroughly worked over, sometimes with disconcerting results.

The introduction to the booklet on *Racist and Sexist Images* says, over the signatures of Children's Rights Workshop in London, that 'we can no longer base critical assessment solely on literary merit. Content and values, explicit or implicit, deserve similar critical attention'. And in a statement on Children's Books, CRW (to which, incidentally, I am indebted for the sight of a good deal of material) says: 'We maintain that, in any critical assessment of a children's book, its message and social values are all-important; at least, they concern us more than the criteria of style, beauty, or form.' I think there is a misconception here of the nature of literary criticism. It seems to be implied that the literary merit with which critics are concerned is a kind of ornamentation: the turrets and twiddles of a building rather than its structure. But in fact every self-respecting critic is concerned with the book as a whole: of course its content and values deserve and receive attention: it's merely that a good critic will refuse to take a narrow monocular view.

And when one finds articles, such as one in *Interracial Books for Children*, vol. 5, no. 3 (1974) on showing children how to detect racism and sexism in a book, one must surely feel uneasy.

Is this not itself a racist or sexist activity, creating the kind of division it purports to oppose?

To my mind, the literature on this subject includes too many wild generalizations made by people who obviously haven't read enough books or have managed only to see what they are determined to see. When they come down to actual cases, the humourlessness and stridency of campaigners often make it easy—perhaps too easy—to pour scorn. Pat Hutchinson's *Rosie's Walk*, a marvellously funny picture book featuring a hen who walks around the farmyard totally unaware that a fox is after her, while the fox is comically thwarted at every turn, has been attacked because a hen is seen as a symbol of stupid womanhood. With similar lack of humour it is suggested, seriously, in America that Cinderella should be rewritten in a less sexist vein:

Cinderella is pleasing in appearance, but as she spends much of her time at household labour, her body bears the signs: dishpan hands and flat feet. At the ball, she is interested in meeting as many new and interesting people as she can, and during the evening she dances with many men. Since she knows that the coach will turn into a pumpkin if she doesn't leave before the stroke of twelve, she plans her exit well in advance. . . .

Sometimes it seems that authors just can't win. Pippi Longstocking, the independent self-assertive supergirl in a series of books by Astrid Lindgren, might appear to be a feminist's dream: but no, a writer in *Interracial Books for Children* has seen through her:

It is soon apparent that Pippi isn't a girl at all, even a tomboy, but a boy in disguise. Astrid Lindgren has simply equipped Pippi with all the traits we have come to think of as male . . . Pippi acts like a 'real' man.

One of the dangers of the sillier and wilder attacks is that they are counter-productive, provoking ridicule and diverting attention from the genuinely difficult cases, of which there are several. A well known one is that of *Little Black Sambo*, first published in 1899. His author, Helen Bannerman, certainly meant no harm: her trouble was that she couldn't draw very well and was a bit confused about the races anyway. Sambo's crudely drawn features have given offence to large numbers of nonwhites, but he has also given great pleasure to many children, including nonwhites. Should he be removed from library shelves in this country, as in the United States? There are arguments both ways, and I do not seek to resolve them here.

Of the books mentioned in my opening paragraph, *The Story of Doctor Dolittle*, which dates from 1920, does undoubtedly contain offensive facetious references to blacks. Hugh Lofting obviously saw them as comic figures; his own drawings make that clear. Like Mrs Bannerman, he meant no harm; he was in fact a sincere internationalist, and his views on race were advanced for his day, but he lacked foresight and sensitivity. He leaves us with a problem.

The main objection to *Sounder*, as I understand it, is that it shows an oppressed black family as spiritless and submissive, rather than actively fighting injustice. But these were poor, ignorant, friendless people, and the setting is a good many years in the past; to me, as to many other commentators, the story has the ring of truth. The attack on Peter Rabbit is too silly to need refutation; but the criticism of *Watership Down* from which I quoted—and which incidentally does not seek to condemn the whole book—is sensible and cogent; it would be a pity if it were met with yawns or instant resentment.

Another danger is that—as is already happening to some extent—authors and editors run scared and go to absurd lengths to avoid giving offence. (An American editor rejected *Polar*, a picture book about a toy polar bear which is published in England by Andre Deutsch, on the ground that the text, written by Elaine Moss, states explicitly that the bear is white). A demand to avoid stereotypes can easily become in effect a demand for a different stereotype: for instance that girls should always be shown as strong, brave and resourceful, and that mothers should always have jobs and never, never wear an apron. And books written to an approved formula, or with deliberate didactic aim, do not often have the breath of life. Some members of women's groups in North America have published their own anti-sexist books, featuring such characters as fire-fighting girls or boys who learn to crochet. Good luck to them; but those I have seen are far below professional standard.

If seems to me that authors and publishers should avoid on the one hand jumping hastily on to the bandwagon, and on the other hand reacting over-sensitively and negatively to criticism. They should consider suggestions and complaints on their merits, act on them where action is justified and possible, but also be prepared to reject unfounded condemnation. They have, it is true, a responsibility to children and to society in general: they also have an obligation to practise their craft as best they can, to tell the truth as they see it, and to hold on to artistic freedom for themselves and their successors.

[1976]

Notes on the children's book trade: all is not well in tinsel town

JOHN GOLDTHWAITE

*When I was a little girl, I was satisfied with about six books. . . .
I think that children now have too many.* —BEATRIX POTTER

No children's book publisher would dream of suggesting that he
was in business for reasons other than to bring children what
Walter de la Mare, the librarians' darling, called 'only the rarest
kind of best'. With 80 per cent of the sales of the more than 2,000
titles published each year going to institutions staffed by the
secular legions of the muse, allowing any motive less noble would
be folly. A children's publisher, to succeed, must assume the
guise of doing good deeds, and to do that he must keep the muse,
old and toothless though she be, out front in a rocker, gumming
platitudes. Some publishers and editors are not insincere about
this. Excellent children's books do get published. On the other
hand, the department must profit the house; each editor must
earn his keep. That means marketing a whole heap of books that
are less than good, and warehouses of books that are downright
awful. Every trifle must be decked out as handsomely as possible,

every author and illustrator made out to be God's gift to children. This requires a certain suspension of disbelief on the part of publisher and editor, and inevitably some insensibility will set in, until the publisher and the editor, and soon the librarians as well, can themselves no longer tell the difference between a work of art and a commodity.

Sales now assume their spurious legitimacy; the search for excellence is lost to the art of the hype. Librarians, be it noted, do not buy books in hand but promises out of catalogues and trade reviews that read like a cross between a card-catalogue entry and a publicity release. The publishers' easy optimism and librarians' frequent lapses of literary discretion, riding high on public moneys and the lack of resistance from most quarters, enable endless crates of stuff to be bought sight unseen. It is a nice piece of work for the many writers and illustrators who have come to this lucrative field from the only incidentally literate worlds of the kitchen and the commercial arts. Really, it is a nice piece of work for everyone, for there is much at stake beyond literature—careers, prizes, income, fame; and often, as one Caldecott Medal winner pointed out, paying the bills may call for the production of two and preferably four titles a year, every year, forever.

So the proliferation of pretty little books must continue unabated, and not only unabated but celebrated. A multi-billion-dollar industry knows no law but the momentum of its own survival. The prizes must come thick and fast, the muse be rocked more and more quickly. Sooner or later some enthusiast will conjure up an aesthetic that makes it all ring good and true. College courses will spring up coast to coast. The people at the paper mills will be happy, the printers, the binders, and jobbers will be happy. The entrepreneur who manufactures the little chairs kids sit in during story hours can add another snowmobile to the family fleet.

People with a vested interest in children's books suffer from feelings of cultural inferiority. They are also hungry for the prestige of yesteryear, when children's books were the

Cinderella of literature. Accordingly, they are eager to promote the illusion that the present day is a second Golden Age, all aglitter with the glories of the picture book, and loud with the brave clatter of its mounted authors. To anyone not dazzled by the shine and show, the place may look suspiciously like tinsel town; but saying so can be a risky business. To point a finger is to get it lopped off. The replies awaiting those who would seek to rescue Cinderella from the ashes are prompt and humorless. If you don't like the books you see, snaps one voice, you haven't seen the right books. It is the illusion of people in the snug world of children's books that no one can read the 'right' books and not love them. They have been turning up in tinsel town since the mid-Twenties at the rate of a dozen or so to half a hundred each year. Only the laziest malcontent could fail to see it.

The child psychologist Bruno Bettelheim, an unlikely prince but one with his wits still intact, stuck up a finger recently in behalf of Cinderella, and, as was to be expected, they took a good whack at it. Dr Bettelheim's serious critical study of fairy tales, *The Uses of Enchantment,* is exactly the kind of book that you would expect children's authors, critics, and librarians to have written many times over. The truth is, what good essays we have on children's stories are the work of such gifted amateurs as J.R.R. Tolkien and C.S. Lewis, or of folklorists such as Iona and Peter Opie. They have come, in other words, from everywhere but inside the field of children's books itself, where the most popular form of disquisition seems to be the after-dinner speech. They ought to be a little embarrassed about this in tinsel town, but they are not. They are miffed. Not only has Dr Bettelheim bested them at their own game, he has had the temerity to suggest that in contrast to the fairy tales modern children's books are shallow and at cross-purposes with their didactic aims: 'Strictly realistic stories run counter to the child's inner experience . . . [and] inform without enriching.' Illustrated storybooks 'direct the child's imagination away from how he, on his own, would experience the story.' 'The trouble with some of what is considered "good children's literature" is that many of these stories peg the child's imagination to the level he has already reached on his own. Children like such a story, but benefit little from it beyond momentary pleasure.' And so on. A frightful man, this Freudian. *The Horn Book,* the most prestigious of all children's book journals, whose opinion of a book can make or break its library sales, gathers up her skirts and sniffs haughtily. Dr Bettelheim is a carper. Shame!

Dr Bettelheim might be dismayed to think that this is what his good work could come to, but he does not make his living writing for children and so can be excused for not caring less what *The Horn Book* thinks. A children's book author, on the other hand, has a much riskier time of it. Should he agree that modern children's books are shallow—and even dishonest—the people with the vested interests have his fortune and his personal honour squeezed tight in the notion that a children's author is by definition sweet and reasonable. Reasons for his lighting the fuse of disgust, reasons perhaps desperate and aesthetic and good enough for an incident or two of autocatharsis on the adult circuit, will at the great seminar on children's literature only soil his reputation as a good person, worthy to write for children. In the second Golden Age of Children's Books Hans Christian Andersen, to survive, must come whistling down the lane a certified Danny Kaye.

Children's authors generally write in one of two ways, either to please children or to please themselves. The more numerous of them, those who write to please children, have traditionally been the purveyors of ephemera and dreck; those who write to please themselves have given us most of the best children's books we have, though they, too, have produced many sad and silly books of the sort penned by the old lady down the lane. The quality of literature is not threatened by the latter, the child is not deprived by them, but by the book consciously directed at the child and written presumably to his or her liking. This book, the 'Chopsticks' of children's literature and virtually the only tune we hear being played today, has been deplored by nearly every writer on the subject who is not in thrall to the industry; yet it is what most people have been led to assume a good children's book to be, and so it is precisely the sort of book—short of another *Babar* or *Charlotte's Web*—that every editor is most eager to publish. Each new season brings an avalanche of such kiddie confetti, and the air right now is thick with it. In addition to the usual superfluity of ABCs, counting books, folk tales 'retold', holiday and Bicentennial specials, and other commercial artifacts, we have—many from notable authors out of the most reputable houses—such three-minute epics as *Oh, What a Busy Day! The Most Delicious Camping Trip Ever; A Special Birthday; A Wet Monday; Around Fred's Bed; Betsy and the Chicken Pox; Much Bigger Than Martin; Everett Anderson's Friend; My Teddy Bear; It's Not Fair! Two Is Company; A Little at a Time; I Love You, Mouse; I Like You; Like Me; I'll Tell on You; I'm Going to Run Away; I Wish I Was Sick, Too;* and *You Can't Catch Me.*

No less numerous than your local author's home movies are Casper the Friendly Ghost cartoons—*Monster Mary, Mischief Maker* and *Clyde Monster,* for example—and cat tales. Writers and illustrators with only a few cute tricks to turn on paper can always be counted on for funny monsters and cats; indeed, some respectable careers have been built on the low but universal appeal of funny monsters and cats and precious little else. Sifting through the latest batch of kitty litter, we find *Count the Cats, More Cats, Oh, No, Cat!, The Christmas Cat, The Convent Cat, The Post Office Cat, Kittens for Nothing, The Surprise Kitten, A Cat Called Amnesia,* and *Great Grandmother's Cat Tales.* Granny does rattle on these days. Who else but some venerable goodbody could be responsible for such geriatric titles as *Rupert Piper and the Dear, Dear Birds; Coo-My-Dove, My Dear;* or *Grandparents Around the World, Loving and Sharing?*

No more serious corruption of literature can be imagined than one which cheats children of their language even before they can read, and trivializes life before they have lived. Yet we are enjoying such an affluence of cultural frivolity that in the next few months librarians will, without blinking twice, spend tens of millions of tax dollars on these trifles. Call them educational toys, which many of them are, or pet rocks, which are more rewarding, or funny T-shirts with too much starch; but do not call them literature. *Pinocchio* is literature and so is *Babar*. *Peter Rabbit*, *The Wind in the Willows*, the *Jungle Books*, and the tales of the Brothers Grimm are literature. Take a good look at the next picture book your child brings home. Is it really any different in kind from the Saturday cartoons and Sunday funnies which children's-book people profess to despise? Or is it just an episode, when you come right down to it, from a TV family sit-com; a dramatization from a mother's field notes on the neighborhood kids; a case study from a child-training manual; a bit of toothless Aesop; or one more imitation of any children's book that ever showed a profit or won a prize? It is called 'children's literature', this bit of merchandise. It will probably win a prize. The author will move to Connecticut because 10,000 librarians said what the hell, and bought the thing. Children, because they cannot choose wisely for themselves, ought to be better served.

We have come to accept less and less and somehow the familiarity of it all comforts us. In a recently published fantasy the reward for saving the kingdom is not the kingdom but a roller skating party. Sad, paltry fare, but fully in accord with our lowered expectations. Like most of the rest of us, editors hope to reduce life to a series of small, manageable moments, and so they encourage authors to find their stories close to home, in the everyday, and publish whatever comes of it: timid little thoughts about snowflakes and shoes, lunch pails, snails, and sidewalks; inane fables about losing friends, making friends, being fat, hating war, holding hands. The clichés are old and tired and suspicious even to children: there's no place like home, a boy's best friend is his mother, one step at a time, arms are for hugging. These are not good thoughts for children to grow on; they are the sentiments of adults writing to pacify the next generation, not excite it; to make the world a safer place for people without curiosity, dreams, or bravery. Such books as *The Happy Day*, *The Snowy Day*, *So What If It's Raining!*, *I Love My Mother*, *I Like Old Clothes*, *A Tree Is Nice*, *Hold My Hand*, *That Makes Me Mad!*, *The Unfriendly Book*, *The Quarreling Book*, *Just Me*, and thousands of homey primers as like them as clothespins on the line do little but suggest to the child, if only subliminally, that he is so small, so afraid, and so blind that he cannot, as children have always done, discover the horrors and wonders of his backyard for himself, without some well-meaning, tedious grown-up playing tour guide. Apparently no one believes anymore that tales told by the fireside ought to be about the big, dangerous, rewarding world outside the door. Anatole France once wrote that children 'find the writer who binds them in the contemplation of their own childhood a terrible bore,' but senior editors throughout the industry have for some forty years been operating on a contrary assumption. They have made this the age of the domestic children's book—until now our best writers, housebroken, suffer from daring too little.

Our best writers have been in thrall to the domestic sensibility too long, and they have had to bow to the primacy of illustration too long. In so doing they have all but forgotten how to do what writers are supposed to do, which is use language to animate the world. Our worst writers, trying to please children by writing about childish things, think they have been able to do this in their stead. Whether or not they actually do please children is of little concern. You can please a child by slipping on a banana peel; it proves nothing. What is of concern is that even in pleasing children they will have failed them utterly. Their books are bad because the world has been left out of them. So has an intuition about life that once informed all our greatest children's books and most of the lesser ones as well, an intuition unknown to children's writers content to busy themselves with the details and worries of childhood itself. It is indefinable but there is no mistaking it, once heard. It is as detectable in the slightest picture book as in the longest epic—a naive longing in the author's voice, an acceptance that one cannot embrace the world without fearing its kick, and at the same time a celebration of curiosity and bravery. This is behind every great children's book from the tales of the Brothers Grimm to *Pinocchio,* from the verses of Mother Goose and Edward Lear to Wanda Gag's *Millions of Cats* and Carl Sandburg's *Rootabaga Stories.* G.K. Chesterton caught its spirit when in praising fairy tales he wrote, 'Life is not only a pleasure but a kind of eccentric privilege.' That is the voice of the comic spirit talking, and it is a voice both missing and sorely missed.

How has so much that is bad for literature and children been allowed to eat away at what ought to be—whether high, humble, or vulgar in origin—at the very least honest work honestly arrived at? Failures of nerve and the imperatives of profit aside, much of the hanky-panky (tinkering with classics, the attendance on special-interest groups) can be attributed to ordinary lapses in taste and good sense. Much more can be laid to the work of nepotism, cronyism, and the energies of not a few people without modesty or shame, despite their public resemblance to your favorite aunt. Here, for example, can be lumped the published efforts of those ethically suspect pains in every honest writer's billfold, the editors themselves. Gone are the days when a senior editor, feeling the need for a particular book, commissioned an author to write it. Now, assuming neither her daughter nor best pal needs a shot of glory at the moment, she will write it herself, appropriating a top illustrator and a goodly slice of the ad budget to do herself justice. One senior editor did recently do the honorable thing, submitting her manuscript elsewhere under a pseudonym; but here is an ethical standard a world apart from the realities of the children's-book industry.

Naturally, no one who lives in such a cozy niche of literature would for a moment entertain the following modest proposals:

1. *The pink slip for every other children's editor who is a woman.* There are too many women in children's books, and far too many holding down editorial positions. This imbalance of male and female sensibilities might have been accepted in 1919, when Macmillan put together the world's first juvenile department, and, under the delusion that children's books belonged to the ladies, gave it over to one; but there is no excuse for it today. There is no evidence that women understand more than men

what children need and want; and, even if there were, it would hardly affect the verdict on books given us by several generations of women editors who have proven that, whatever their good intentions, their standards are timid and commercial.

2. *The termination of the picture book.* Even with superior examples offered at prices that would allow for home use, one cannot avoid suspicions that what is told in a picture book is not worth a book for the telling, and that too many pictures, however good, may only divert the child away from any lasting encounter with his imagination. Worse, it is guilty of absolving parents of having to read—really *read*—to their children. The idea that children can learn to read words by first learning to read pictures is so bizarre one wonders if the educators responsible for it have got their heads screwed on straight. No one, children least of all, can get the feel of a language from nothing, nor from a few sentences. They must hear the sounds of whole books. Language is more than pretty captions; it is the rhythms of action and ideas, of expectation and consequence. It is the ultimate music. To abandon the verbal at an early age is to abandon the child.

3. *The promotion of the storybook.* Not to be confused with the picture book, the storybook is longer, livelier, and usually more complex. Books in the tradition of *The Tale of Peter Rabbit, Millions of Cats, The Story of Babar,* and Maurice Sendak's *Higglety Pigglety Pop!* are, together with the children's novel (see below), the best hope for reaffirming Chesterton's eccentric privilege of life and for redeeming children's books from commercialism and banality.

4. *The termination of teen-age fiction.* No one has ever satisfactorily explained why there is or ought to be such a thing as teen-age fiction at all. In the case of science fiction and fantasy, for example, there is little being written for adults that could not be understood by any literate twelve-year-old. Conversely, some prizewinning fantasies for teen-agers have a turgidity of style the worst SF hack would be hard put to achieve. As for all that novelized stuff about alienation, drugs, and pregnancy, the great bulk of it might be more enjoyable presented in comic books. There are any number of very good underground cartoonists on

the West Coast who need the money and might be willing to make something halfway real of such material.

5. *The rediscovery of the children's novel.* This is a form not much practiced by American writers, perhaps because of all books for children it is the hardest to do well, and perhaps too because by the time a writer has acquired the necessary skills he may be too corrupted or too dispirited either to make the attempt or to keep from botching the job. In this henpecked world, no one speaks the unspeakable: that, with the exception of Beatrix Potter, every great children's novel was written by a man, and nearly all of them by a man with little or no professional interest in children or their literature: Perrault, the Grimms, Andersen, Lear, Carroll, MacDonald, Stevenson, Twain, Collodi, Kipling, Grahame, Milne. (Carl Sandburg's *Rootabaga Stories* and more recent books by E.B. White, Tolkien, C.S. Lewis, and I.B. Singer seem to make it axiomatic that any remarkable children's book of this category will be the work of a gifted male 'amateur'.) It is instructive to note that while the Grimms, Andersen, Lear, and Carroll were doing their work, the ladies, self-appointed pros every one, were busy as bees edifying children with religious tracts and moral instructions. They have been at it ever since.

6. *The termination of the Newbery/Caldecott awards.* Each year for fifty-three and thirty-seven years respectively, the Newbery and Caldecott Medals have been awarded by the American Library Association to 'the most distinguished contribution to American literature for children' and to 'the most distinguished American picture book.' That's ninety distinguished books in all, and a taste of dust in the mouth. The average N/C book is just another average book—often decently done, always terribly earnest, always ordinary. The best Newbery books, such as *The Slave Dancer,* by Paula Fox, glide along on good ideas that never wake up even the sympathetic reader. Most are haunted by the genteel ghost of that winner who announced she had never done anything to make her mother ashamed. Even less can be said for the prints and posters which have dominated the Caldecott awards for the past thirty years.

Everyone has a right to his style and his prize, of course. Were it not for the pernicious effects of the N/C awards, they would hardly matter. But mediocrity tends to gather glory these days, and everywhere the N/C books are set up as little idols of sensibility and style by teachers and librarians dedicated to the cultural uplift of kids who just might be on their way to some larger literacy than is encouraged by such books.

7. *The removal of writers, poets, and illustrators from the schools and libraries.* They mean to spur the imagination of the child, but all they do, I suspect, is make the world a little more banal. Artists cannot enter the classroom without the emphasis shifting, however subtly, from art to celebrity. I do not care, as a reader, and I do not think most children, unaided, care how or why or by whom a book is made. That they are asked to know as much as they are can only debase the mystery of what is in a particular book, and the mystery of all books as magical things.

8. *The termination of undergraduate college courses in children's literature.* These courses are doing literature and generations of children more harm than good by following the texts now standard in the field—chronologies, most of them, and appreciations of librarians, editors, booksellers, and other good souls who were legends in their time—the sort of uncritical histories in which nosegays are thrown Howard Pyle's mother for raising such a nice boy, and Margaret Wise Brown, author of *The Runaway Bunny,* is elevated to the rank of genius. Children's-book scholars can't help but write these clubhouse surveys, of course, because there is not a lot you can say about most children's books (they resist explication in a way adult literature does not), and because the usual scholar does not often have the perception to cut through the wisdoms that pass for critical thought in the enchanted world of children's literature. Elaborating for more than two minutes on, say, *The Wind in the Willows,* she will likely tell you that what she reveres about the book—what sets it apart for her as a work of literature and raises it to the level of the sublime—is the chapter 'The Piper at the Gates of Dawn', that intrusive prelude to Kahlil Gibran in which Rat and Mole hear

the unearthly pipes of Pan and fall to their knees in teary reverence. C.S. Lewis was quite right that the child who has met the creatures of *The Wind in the Willows* 'has ever afterwards, in its bones, a knowledge of humanity . . . which it could not get in any other way'; but the child encouraged to swallow the pseudo-classical pantheism of Grahame's piper runs the risk of growing up soft at the core and of wearing fads for a soul. Such rambles with the muse are nice for American college students, however, who seem at last to have found, in children's literature, the universal gut course.

9. *The hiring of a few fast guns; or, a good critic is hard to find.* Despite the high regard in which our several trade journals are held, professional reviewing of children's books in America is depressingly second rate. Only a handful of outsiders—Jean Stafford in *The New Yorker* for example, or the collectively disgruntled voice of the *New York Times*—have anything worthwhile to say on the subject, and they, because they operate sporadically and from without the field, can be discounted as having much effect on sales, let alone on the way we think about our children's books.

How we do, and at the same time, do not, think about our children's books, is best reflected by that infuriating form of benign neglect, the roundup review. In varying degrees the roundup rules the shape of each of the journals on whose brief opinions the fortunes of every new book must ride: *School Library Journal*, the American Library Association's *Booklist*, *Publishers Weekly*, *Kirkus Reviews,* and, to a lesser extent, *The Horn Book*. With a nice feel for democracy in action, a list of books for review is gotten up, a paragraph of a certain length is allotted to each book, and pretty near equal space is shown to all. Week after week, year after year, mountains of these paragraphs heap up, and few are willing to sort them out. The industry which knows no law but the momentum of its own survival rolls on like a great conveyor belt, and the journals have their pages full just maintaining a spot check on the titles.

In this way children's journals and reviewers inadvertently

become what Eliot Fremont-Smith has called shills for the industry because, accepting not the performance but the *occasion* of each book as equal to that of all others, they allow themselves to be made into list-makers. No idea of quality is put forward; none is recalled and none demanded.

The visible results of such a leveling of literature will be evident to anyone who has ever come up against the fact of what retailers and librarians do and do not carry on their shelves as a consequence of the reviews they read. Among bookstores only a Scribner's or an Eeyore's in New York or a small-town gem like the Andover Bookstore in Massachusetts is likely to salt its stock with anything worthwhile. For the rest, relying heavily on *PW*'s roundups of winsome and commercial choices, it's the same old story: bad but noticeable books by name authors, didactic tracts, domestic candy, calendars, and the like. What is depressing is not that the stores carry such books, but that they carry them to the exclusion of too much else that is as good and better. A parent in an above-average store with a selection of perhaps 300 children's titles—say, one in a college town supplying a course in children's literature, to go to upstate New York for an example—ought reasonably to expect to find among the current crop of titles at least a few of the highest quality. What he will find, typically, is a fat sampling of the domestic dross mentioned earlier in this article. He will not find *Lizard Music* (Manus Pinkwater), *Moon Whales* (Ted Hughes/Leonard Baskin), *Nightmares* (Jack Prelutsky/Arnold Lobel), *The Red Swan* (John Bierhorst), or any number of other promising new books. He will find no books at all, from this or any other season, by Tove Jansson, William Steig, Natalie Babbitt, Nancy Elkholm Burkert, M.B. Goffstein, William Kurelek, Margot Zemach, Edward Gorey, or Uri Shulevitz. He will find one entire shelf devoted to the once-amusing and now repetitive books of James Marshall, and another to wordless picture books and miniature boxed sets. Wordless books—most of them idiot cartoons about sneezing, running, falling down—are a bastard genre, but they sell like bubble gum. Boxed sets derive from no compelling cause beyond the desire to be cute and make money. Having borrowed every one of Maurice Sendak's turns of style, the hacks must now rip off his *Nutshell Library* as well—in two instances without even doing him the courtesy of calling their junk by another name. But that's business.

Given half a chance, children will often choose to read, or be read, much humbler fare than the best we can offer them, and they will be moved in strange, unknowable ways by it. They will always want comic books, for example, which they love because comic books are theirs, not ours. Unless we can claim to know what we are doing—and I suspect when it comes to children none of us can—they may be better off with their own choices, insofar as their freedom to choose anything may kindle a love of reading. In my own childhood, before I took up with such pleasing stuff as Donald Duck and D.C. Comics, the humbler fare was *Old Mother West Wind* and *Uncle Wiggily*, good stories too easily despised today, appearing in none of our many so-called studies of children's books, save in passing—a misplaced snobbery and a shame. Thornton Burgess and Harrison Cady were hardly Joel Chandler Harris or Beatrix Potter; nonetheless, they created an inexhaustible landscape in their nature tales of the Green Meadows and Dear Old Briar Patch and deserve to be remembered for honest and often magical stories. Howard Garis and Lang Campbell gave us in the Uncle Wiggily stories the Skeezicks and his rowdy gang, among the looniest of all nursery villains. Where is there anything like these today? Where is the generosity of effort?

The following sixteen titles, representing less than one-tenth of 1 per cent of all those published in the past decade or so, seem to me to be among the best that have been done in that period, aside from the books of Maurice Sendak and the excellent work of Tomi Ungerer, whose talents are better viewed overall than in any one title:

1. *All the Way Home,* by Lore Segal. Illustrated by James Marshall. Farrar, Straus and Giroux. One of the funniest picture

books in years, told and illustrated with classical precision.

2. *The Animal Family*, by Randall Jarrell. Decorations by Maurice Sendak. Pantheon. A love story inspiring complete belief in a realm previously known only through the tales of George MacDonald.

3. *The Bear Who Had No Place to Go*, by James Stevenson. Harper & Row. This writer's favorite. Ralph, the bicycling bear, pedals through a series of comic adventures that are gently haunted by sorrow until he finds his rightful place in the sun.

4. *Everything About Easter Rabbits*, by Wiltrud Roser. Translated by Eva L. Mayer. Crowell. *Father Christmas*, by Raymond Briggs. Coward, McCann and Geoghegan. The two best holiday books for children in decades.

5. *Father Fox's Pennyrhymes*, by Clyde Watson. Illustrated by Wendy Watson. Crowell. *Frog and Toad Are Friends*, by Arnold Lobel. Harper & Row. *Sylvester and the Magic Pebble*, by William Steig. Windmill. Mother Goose in Vermont, two nifty amphibians, and a donkey on the spot, having in common a greatly deserved popularity.

6. *A Little Schubert*, by M.B. Goffstein. Record by Peter Schaaf. Harper & Row. A droll biography of anyone's humanity by the mistress of picture-book precision, and a nice corrective to today's image of the artist as celebrity.

7. *Lumberjack*, by William Kurelek. Houghton Mifflin. Hard to imagine a boy not getting up an absolute lust for the deep woods with this book. Then again, in the age of the Evel Knievel doll, maybe not.

8. *Snow White*. Translated by Randall Jarrell. Illustrated by Nancy Elkholm Burkert. Farrar, Straus and Giroux. Forget Bruno Bettelheim's proscription against the illustrated fairy tale for the sake of this book, whose pictures are too beautiful and too thoughtful to be missed.

9. *Tuck Everlasting*, by Natalie Babbitt. Farrar, Straus and Giroux. Probably the best work of our best children's novelist— a quiet fable about immortality, with a stunning and perfectly underplayed finish.

10. *The Wedding Procession of the Rag Doll and the Broom Handle, and Who Was in It,* by Carl Sandburg. Illustrated by Harriet Pincus. Harcourt Brace Jovanovich. Of all the tales in Sandburg's *Rootabaga Stories,* the perfect choice for a picture book, with illustrations that are homely as the dickens, and all the more fascinating for it.

11. *How Tom Beat Captain Najork and His Hired Sportsmen,* by Russell Hoban. Illustrated by Quentin Blake. Atheneum. *The Shrinking of Treehorn,* by Florence Parry Heide. Illustrated by Edward Gorey. Holiday House. *The Slightly Irregular Fire Engine,* by Donald Barthelme. Farrar, Straus and Giroux. Three books that may prove sophisticated or esoteric for some children, but which are well worth trying in spite of that—or because of it, depending on your point of view. In praise of sophistication, in fact, I would go so far as to recommend that you leave your own picture books lying about wherever your children can get at them—Brueghel, Goya, Edward Gorey's *Amphigorey,* the albums of Saul Steinberg, whatever. At the age of ten I had a run-in with the political drawings of Thomas Nast, and though I was filled with fear and loathing by the experience, I wouldn't trade it for all the Newbery books in Boston.

[1977]

Precepts, pleasures, and portents: changing emphases in children's literature

SHEILA EGOFF

When Caxton began printing in England in 1476, the child was still looked upon as a miniature adult and was merged into the adult world. With the gradual realization that the child's natural carefree ways were a barrier between adult and child, adults hastened to teach the child 'manners', and the first books for children were books of manners and 'courtesie'. What more palatable candy coating for the traditional morals of mankind than Aesop's *Fables*? Here was an ideal way to present acceptable actions to the child—by means of talking animals. Caxton printed the first English edition in 1484 and the work rapidly became part of the schoolroom tradition.

The Puritan concept of sin that took hold in the seventeenth century led to a change in the accepted view of children: they were still thought of as miniature adults but they now had to be specially trained. And so a separate stream of children's books began. 'Children are not too young to die,' said the Puritans, 'they are not too little to go to hell,' and a great spate of writing and publishing supported this view. What was described by later generations as the 'brand of hell' school of writing reached its peak in 1671 with James Janeway's *A Token For Children: Being an Exact Account of the Conversion, Holy and Exemplary Lives and Joyful Deaths of several Young Children*. The Puritans contended that books of this kind gave the highest pleasure to children, 'that of studying and enjoying the Will of God'. What emerges from an overall look at the children's books of this period is a picture of a society that was narrow and intolerant, that saw children as separate from adults even while it brought the full force of adult values to bear upon them. It also reveals a remarkably consistent viewpoint. This society knew exactly what it wanted for its children: happiness in the next world.

Although the tone of religious ferocity was to abate in children's books until they became only mildly moralistic, the spirit of fear engendered by the Puritan era lingered in them for about a hundred and fifty years. Few books were free of religious overtones. The title of a spelling book of 1705 reads: *A Help to True Spelling and Reading . . . Here are also the Chief Principles of Religion laid down in a plain and easie Metre*. In Dr Aikin's and Mrs Barbauld's *Evenings at Home* (1792), a kind of junior encyclopaedia, with suggestions for keeping children out of mischief, a section on geography reads:

Asia lies east of Europe; it is about 4,800 miles long, and 4,300 broad; bounded on the North by the Frozen Ocean, by the Pacific on the East, by the Red Sea on the West, and the Indian Sea on the South. This, though the second, is the principal quarter of the globe; for here our first parents were created, and placed in the garden of Eden . . .

A somewhat less grim view of pleasure in the Puritan sense was offered by a seventeenth-century philosopher. In *Some Thoughts Concerning Education* (1690) John Locke urged that children should be brought to pleasure in reading, but through animal stories accompanied by pictures. Although his choice of books was very narrow—Aesop's *Fables* and *Reynard the Fox* were his strongest recommendations—he enunciated the first great principle about children and reading. 'Children do not like to be constrained to read,' he warned, 'any more than adults.'

John Locke was not listened to in his day and it would appear that he had only one disciple, in the person of John Newbery who, in 1744, set up his bookshop for children in St Paul's churchyard. Newbery intended to please children, but his break with tradition came in the way he approached them rather than in the contents of the books he published for them: he provided stories with the obvious morals of the time but in a gayer, more childlike way than his contemporaries. He covered his books with 'flowery and gilt' Dutch paper; he added woodcuts that illustrated the text, though they were crude in execution; with his bookshop he provided a place children could call their own and he supplemented his stock of books with baubles to delight a child—tops, pincushions, and games. Newbery has been called the 'commercial dynamo' of his time in the field of publishing. As a publisher his activities included much of what is good and bad in publishing for children today. He commissioned writers (it is supposed that Oliver Goldsmith was the author of Newbery's *Goody Two Shoes*); he saw the market for children's books as well as the need; and he had other ventures associated with his publishing (in *Goody Two Shoes* it is noted that little Marjory's father died from a want of Dr James's fever powder—a patent medicine sold by Newbery).

The overall influence of John Newbery was slight and fleeting—although the marketing lesson remained. The deliberate motives of both writers and critics throughout the eighteenth century and well into the nineteenth were the constraint and edification of children through books written for them. The emphasis continued to be on children and what was thought to be their needs rather than on literature, and children's books became tools for the educational process. The chief influence on English children's books came from France with the publication of Rousseau's *Emile* (1762) and its translation into English in 1762.

Rousseau's idea of bringing up a child in a natural state, far from the corrupting influences of civilization but with an adult always at hand to teach and explain, was seized upon by writers for children. A flood of books was unleashed that portrayed children as constantly and of necessity under the surveillance of adults, who turned even a glance at a butterfly into a lesson on entomology or a sermon on the brevity of life. Hence Thomas Day in *Sandford and Merton* (1795-8) shows a minister, Mr Barlow, undertaking the complete education of two boys (obviously at the expense of his clerical duties) and turning the rich, bad child into a duplicate of the good farmer's son. Mrs Sherwood in *The History of the Fairchild Family* (1818-47) shows a father and mother devoting all their time to their children, who get into trouble whenever they are freed from parental supervision. Who in the 1960s would not expect such children to get into trouble the moment parental supervision was relaxed? For Rousseau's disciples the solution to this problem was not to encourage children to develop moral responsibility of their own from an early age; it was to make the external application of a moral code yet more stringent. The naughty Fairchild children are taken to visit a gibbet to see the body of a criminal who 'had hung there some years'.

Time brought modifications. The grip on children's books shifted from the French master (much misinterpreted by his English followers) to a group of English women and clergymen of Established, Unitarian, Evangelical, and Quaker persuasion. This included Dr Aikin, Mrs Barbauld, Mrs Trimmer, Mrs Sherwood, Maria Edgeworth, Mary Belson, Mary Elliott, Dorothy Kilner, and many others. Their motives were best expressed by Mrs Trimmer in her magazine *The Guardian of Education* (1802): 'to contribute to the preservation of the young and innocent from the dangers which threaten them in the form of infantine literature.' Their vehicles were the Moral Tale and the Matter-of-Fact Tale, which were devoted to telling children how to behave, extolling missionary work among the heathen, and cramming the children with elementary information that was little more than religious didacticism. A geography book of 1818 contains this passage:

Q. *What do the I-tal-i-ans wor-ship?*
A. *They wor-ship i-dols and a piece of bread.*
Q. *Would not God be ang-ry that I-tal-ians wor-ship i-dols and a piece of bread?*
A. *God is ang-ry.*

The literature of the 'moral' school mixed a liberal dose of menace in with its precepts. If children do not obey adults they will be punished and the punishment will be carried out. The heroine of Maria Edgeworth's *Rosamond* is told not to buy a purple jar. She does so and has to go shoeless and misses out on a treat. In much of the writing, death, the ultimate threat, is introduced. Moreover, God will see to it that death is the outcome of wrongdoing. In a little book of 1801 called *Pleasant Tales, to improve the mind and correct the morals of youth* (no irony is intended in the word 'pleasant'), we meet Patty's cousin who was haughty and arrogant and who, having the misjudgement to marry her father's valet, was thrust out into the snow in true *East Lynne* style. The book ends thus:

Patty put her poor Cousin to bed, where she lingered a few hours, and then expired, saying—'had I been GOOD, I should have been HAPPY; the GUILTY and the UNFEELING can never taste of PEACE.' Patty lived long and happily, a striking example to the world, that HONESTY, FILIAL DUTY, and RELIGION, are well-pleasing in the sight of the Almighty who is the punisher of VICE, and the liberal rewarder of VIRTUE.

Charles Lamb in a famous letter to Coleridge commented on the effects of this type of book rather than on its spirit: 'Mrs Barbauld's stuff has banished all the old classics of the nursery... Think what you would have been now, if instead of being fed with tales and old wives' fables in childhood, you had been fed with geography and natural history.' The old classics of the nursery were not specifically designed for children but were literature they had taken for themselves—myth, faerie and folklore, romances, nonsense rhymes, and such adult books as *Pilgrim's Progress* (1678), *Robinson Crusoe* (1719), and *Gulliver's Travels* (1726). These classics existed in a kind of underground movement, however—they were not dead.

Each era has produced what can be described as a public literature for its children; that is, a model of what society desired for them. Leonard de Vries's *Flowers of Delight* (1965), which gives a sampling of what was available for children from 1765-1830, shows how prominent this public literature was. Here is the round of *Easy Lessons*, *The Parental Instructor*, and stories containing 'caution and instruction for children'. Mr de Vries has included a few folktales and nonsense rhymes that tend only to heighten the dreariness of the writing considered 'good' for children. This literature came in horizontal waves from 1700 to 1900, but always cutting across it vertically was the literature of delight, the literature of mankind. As Paul Hazard has put it, children have simply refused to be oppressed and have taken what they wanted, be it Malory's *Le Morte d'Arthur* or Blake's *Songs of Innocence*. They had in addition the hundreds of little chapbooks that flooded England in the eighteenth century through the chapmen who sold them for a penny along with ribbons and needles and pins and thread. In these crude little books was stuff to make the sky turn round —*The Babes in the Wood*, *Valentine and Orson*, and *The Death and Burial of Cock Robin*.

Since 'Up with didacticism!' was the battle cry of the guardians of public morality, the fairies were in retreat. Denigrations of imagination, pleasure, and faerie were not new of course. Plato in *The Republic* condemned the Homeric epics for portraying the passions of men in the form of gods. In 1554 Hugh Rhodes, a gentleman of the king's chapel, urged parents in his *Book of Nurture to* keep their children from 'reading of feigned fables, vain fantasies, and wanton stories, and songs of love, which bring much mischief to youth.' About the same time, Roger Ascham, the otherwise enlightened tutor of Queen Elizabeth I, was exclaiming against *King Arthur* for the young. The Puritans almost succeeded in driving out imagination and pleasure by the sheer numbers of their own kind of book, but nothing exceeded the attempts of the writers of the moral tale in the late eighteenth and early nineteenth century for either ferocity or length of attack on imaginative literature. And when George Cruikshank in his *Fairy Library* rewrote the old tales such as 'Puss in Boots' and 'Cinderella' as temperance tracts, it seemed as if fear and didacticism in children's books were to last forever. Even Charles Dickens's now-famous article, 'Frauds on the Fairies'—a spirited attack on Cruikshank's emasculated moralizing versions of the old tales—was seemingly an insufficient counterthrust. Time, however, was on the side of the underground movement.

Yet the authors of the moral tale meant so well. Their concern for the good of children is obvious: they were the first to pay attention to the children of the poor through the Sunday School movement. As writers they often used the English language with power and precision; they wrote with a passionate conviction that most modern writers for children should envy; and their plots were skilfully contrived to give concrete support for abstract ideas. In *Simple Susan* (1796) Maria Edgeworth uses a disagreement between a farmer and a lawyer to make her point:

'Then why so stiff about it, Price? All I want of you is to say—'

'To say that black is white, which I won't do, Mr Case; the ground is a thing not worth talking of, but it's neither yours nor mine; in my memory, since the new lane was made, it has always been open to the parish, and no man shall enclose it with my good will.—Truth is truth, and must be spoken; justice is justice, and should be done, Mr Attorney.'

'*And law is law, Mr Farmer, and shall have its course, to your cost,*' cried the attorney, exasperated by the dauntless spirit of this village Hampden.

In retrospect it can be seen that until about 1850 the books deliberately intended for children were judged on their extra-literary qualities. They were used to preach, teach, exhort, and reprimand. However, their captive audience, children, resisted literature that was didactic and explicitly moral in favour of literature that was pleasurable—and *implicitly* moral. They were helped by the indestructible qualities of literature itself and by a few defenders such as Charles Lamb and Charles Dickens. As a result the underground movement held its own sufficiently to provide the inspiration for the flowering of children's literature that was to come.

Linked to this flowering was a change in attitude towards children. If the seventeenth century discovered the child, the Victorians may be credited with discovering childhood—that is, a state distinct from that of adulthood. While the writers of the past had said, in effect, 'Give me a child and through books we will see to it that his manners, religion, and outlook on life are exactly what we adults want', the writers of the late Victorian period idealized and sentimentalized the child. They saw child-hood as the time of innocence untrammelled, as epitomized in Wordsworth's famous lines, 'Heaven lies about us in our infancy!/Shades of the prison-house begin to close/Upon the growing boy.' Influenced also by Coleridge and William Morris, who had released fantasy and mythology for adults, they expressed this new spirit of childhood through the play of their original and inventive minds. Their audience was ready-made in the offspring of the wealthy middle class that emerged in the second half of the nineteenth century. These children were kept in the nursery, guarded and cherished by nannies who, while excellent disciplinarians, seemed to have had their heads stuffed with 'old wives' tales'. For these children, and sometimes for individual children or groups of children, there appeared works of original genius (some by writers who were strongly entrenched in the world of adult literature): Ruskin's *The King of the Golden River* (1851), Thackeray's *The Rose and the Ring* (1855), Kingsley's *The Water-Babies* (1863), Carroll's *Alice's Adventures in Wonderland* (1865), Mrs Ewing's *The Brownies* (1870), MacDonald's *At the Back of the North Wind* (1871) and *The Princess and the Goblin* (1872), Mrs Molesworth's *The Tapestry Room* (1879), and many, many more. There is no evidence to show that these books were attacked as being unsuitable fare for children. This may be because they in no way broke the moral tradition of children's literature. While telling fascinating tales, their authors simply raised morality to a higher degree, indeed to a universal order. Children's literature in the best moral and humanistic tradition had been born.

But no one type of literature ever has its way completely. Another brand of fantasy, helped by a revolution in the method of printing, was reaching out to another group of readers. Rotary presses disgorged masses of boys' sensational magazines, perhaps as a reaction to the moral constraints of previous ages or even as a revolt against the Victorian social conscience that was expressed in the works of Dickens and Thackeray. In literary lineage the serial stories in magazines such as *The Boys of England* (1866), *The Boy's Standard* (1875), and *Jack Harkaway's Journal* (1893) were related to gothic novels like Horace Walpole's *The Castle of Otranto* (1764) and Mrs Radcliffe's *The Mysteries of Udolpho* (1794) and were reinforced by the rise of the 'penny dreadfuls' and the 'penny parts' of the 1830s. In format, illustration, content, and popularity, these magazines were matched only by the rise and influence of the comic book in the mid-twentieth century. This was the beginning of mass-media publishing for the young and of the syndicated writer.

One of the chief publishers of these magazines was Edward Lloyd, who boasted that they were given to the office boy to read to test their suitability for the general public. At first they were not aimed at the juvenile market, but the scalp-tingling subject matter easily enticed boys who had little else to read in the adventure line after they had read *Robinson Crusoe* and *Quentin Durward*. One good book creates a desire for another and in those days there was virtually little else that was in the class of these two novels.

It is hard to believe that the 'bloods', as these stories came to be called, formed a part of the stream of children's literature, and it is harder to be objectively critical of them. Highly noticeable is the monotonous style, which was lavish in description and overloaded with detail. Pages are spent in building up an atmosphere of dread and mystery by utilizing mouldy dungeons, clanking chains, rusty daggers, and ethereal music. Then at the end comes a refusal to admit the existence of the supernatural: a laboured explanation of the mysterious events reduces the tale to nothing more than an illusion or a prank. Like the series books of today, anyone who understood the formula—even the office boy—could take over the writing. And the most cavalier approach was allowable. It is said that on one occasion the writer of a boy's serial became ill and left his hero bound and gagged on the edge of a cliff with the villain ready to do him in. The substitute writers could not think of a way to rescue the hero. The more practised writer, returning a few days later, picked up his pen and wrote: 'With one bound the hero broke his bonds.' (Syndicated writing is still with us today, both in its sensational magazine form and in the Bobbsey Twins and Nancy Drew series, in which the ten-year-old twins can out-detect the Japanese police force and Nancy can drive a golf ball two hundred and twenty-five yards straight down the fairway.) The boys' 'bloods', like their modern counterparts, were often regarded as quite legitimate escapism. In a seeming reinforcement of this attitude a noted critic of the time observed that 'the British boy cares as much about style as a pig about asparagus'. It is ironic that the remark was made about *Treasure Island*: Stevenson was considered to be wasting his talent on books for boys. However, when children had an opportunity to escape to genuine romance in *Treasure Island* they did so in great numbers, and succeeding generations of all nations have kept it very much alive. According to the pattern set by the boys' magazines, this novel was first serialized in the magazine *Young Folks* in 1881. It was called *The Sea Cook* and the author used a pseudonym, Captain George North.

Along with the literature of fantasy and sensationalism, in which *Treasure Island* showed that high adventure was not incompatible with good writing, didactic novels were still being produced—survivors from the earlier trend. The *Peter Parley* annuals (from the 1820s to the 1870s) were a long series chiefly composed of mini-essays of encyclopaedic variety compiled or written by numerous writers, both English and American. In the annual for 1871 appears a typical fictional effort entitled 'Found Wanting; or He Would Be a Traveller'. In this story a boy who has the sea in his blood agrees to stifle his own natural desires and enter his grandfather's counting-house. Eventually the grandfather sees the boy's unhappiness and allows him a trip on a luxury liner. On the voyage the boy falls down the stairs (the captain's, no less) and is crippled for life. Both he and the grandfather 'comprehend the hand of Providence in the matter'.

All this time English children's books travelled across the Atlantic and were published in the United States, many in pirated editions. Original American children's books paralleled the English ones, as can be seen from such titles as *Spiritual Milk for Boston Babes* (1684), *The School of Good Manners* (1796), *Little Nancy; or, The Punishment of Greediness* (1824). Richard Darling's excellent book, *The Rise of Children's Book Reviewing in the United States, 1865-1881* (1968), shows that it was in the United States rather than in England where some soul-searching was first done about the nature and mission of children's books and the nature of the child. The Reverend Samuel Osgood, a Unitarian clergyman, stated a philosophy close to that of the early twentieth century. Boys and girls are adults in 'nature', he said, but not in 'development'. Children have intelligence and wills that should be respected. 'Children not only want the true thing said to them, but want to have it said in a true and fitting way.' By thus emphasizing literary execution as early as 1865, Osgood helped to provide the climate of taste and talent in which the great American children's books of the nineteenth century were to flourish: Louisa May Alcott's *Little Women* (1868), Frank Stockton's *The Bee-man of Orn and Other Fanciful Tales* (1887), Mark Twain's *The Prince and the Pauper* (1881), Howard Pyle's *Otto of the Silver Hand* (1888) and *Men of Iron* (1891).

According to evidence supplied by Mr Darling, American reviews of children's books were of a higher order than those appearing in England at the time. Few books, however, were judged on their intrinsic merit as literature; the effect of the book on the child still took priority. Nevertheless the whole ferment of the time regarding children's books, the rise of children's libraries, the influx of talented writers and illustrators from Europe, and the development of criticism pointed to what in fact turned out to be the case: that in all the activities surrounding the production and use of picture books and the many categories of non-fiction for children, the twentieth century would belong to the United States.

The major writers of children's books from about 1900 to the late 1950s exhibited a tremendous unanimity of purpose in their view of childhood. For in spite of the changes in books for adults caused by two world wars, a depression, advances in medicine, transportation, and communication, and a freer expression about morality as well as changes in literary style, children's literature remained stable. It seemed as though twentieth-century writers for children had learned a lesson from the Golden Age of Victorian children's books: literature was for pleasure rather than for admonition. Fantasy, with its revelation of great truths and its strong appeal to the imagination, was still the highest form of writing engaging the talents of acknowledged serious writers. Kenneth Grahame, J. R. R. Tolkien, E. B. White, C. S. Lewis, and Rumer Godden did not shy away from difficult themes. *The Wind in the Willows* celebrates human relationships as well as the joys of the countryside; *The Hobbit* offers a quest that never ends as well as a search for gold; *Charlotte's Web* makes death acceptable by dealing with it in terms of the life-and-death cycle of an insect; the Narnia books speak gently of the beliefs and ethics of Christianity; and *The Dolls' House* exposes jealousy and hatred in the miniature world of dolls. Such themes were not used didactically or obtrusively, however. These writers stripped away the last vestiges of sentimentality and preaching from the classics of childhood. With consummate artistry they welded their own moral philosophy to a dramatic form, and it is probably this accomplishment as much as any other that makes a great book great.

Adult attitudes to children in the first half of the twentieth century can be directly seen in the realistic stories of child and family life. On the whole they are set in a world of delight and innocence, which is described lovingly and nostalgically, almost with Maurice Sendak's 'near-obsession' with childhood. The world of childhood is still separate from that of adults: the children are busy and happy about their own affairs while the adults hover on the periphery of their lives, ready to step in at times of danger or need. But the children are generally equal to most situations. There is little introspection and less ugliness or downright hardship than in real life. There were war stories, stories of poor children, stories of children with problems, but they were few in number, and such subjects were not empha-sized. Most books were primarily adventure stories that, in the hands of writers of talent, gave a clear, steady, conservative view of life for children. Childhood, it seems, was the best of all possible states. This is the literary world of Edith Nesbit, Arthur Ransome, Eleanor Estes, Lois Lenski, Noel Streatfeild, Lucy Boston, William Mayne, and many others.

The survival rate of books written between 1900 and 1960 has been remarkably high. Only a few books deliberately written for children before 1900 have survived to be read today. The most notable examples are: Edward Lear's *The Book of Nonsense* (1846), Lewis Carroll's *Alice's Adventures in Wonderland* (1865), Louisa May Alcott's *Little Women* (1868), George MacDonald's *The Princess and the Goblin* (1872), Robert Louis Stevenson's *Treasure Island* (1882). An extremely large group from the turn of the century on, however, now forms much of the basic reading of children of today: *Mary Poppins, The Borrowers, Island of the Blue Dolphins, Call It Courage, Johnny Tremain, Doctor Dolittle, The Eagle of the Ninth, The Children of Green Knowe, The Moffats,* and *The Wolves of Willoughby Chase* are only a few lasting books out of hundreds. This difference cannot be accounted for solely by an increase in the number of books published. In the nineteenth century the book business for children was also remarkably big, widespread, and affluent. The difference is in the writers. The major writers of the twentieth century have seen children as a challenging audience demanding their highest efforts and children have responded to their integrity.

'Only the more rugged mortals should attempt to keep up with current literature,' said George Ade many years ago. What would he have said if he had been faced with just one year's publications in the 1960s? With some 6,000 titles in the English language published annually for children (including some few hundred reissues and new editions), it would be futile to attempt a survey and misguided to try to offer genuine criticism. Generalizations are always tempting, however, and the subject invites some.

It appears that current children's books reflect the society they were written in to a degree not known since the seventeenth century and that they are overwhelmingly carrying on the traditional mission of children's books: to inform and instruct the young. There have been changes in style and theme in the books published in the last few years, and it is not surprising that the greatest changes appear in American fiction. Even a superficial study of North American society in the sixties reveals confusion, uneasiness, a shifting of values, a preoccupation with the psychology of individual and group problems, and a strong desire, particularly on the part of young people, to be told the truth, no matter how it distresses adults to tell it to them. Technical and electronic advances admit us to McLuhan's global village and force immediate decisions of conscience on us all, but we have very sketchy background information about the problems brought to our attention. Almost every hitherto accepted idea and principle about the conduct of life is being challenged. Pressure on the individual is intense and the feeling of being threatened is very real. The age of faith has passed and what is to fill the void? For many of the young the solution is to withdraw from bigness, from the multiversity and corporate business, from government and the mass media, and to become engaged in a rediscovery of humanity on a more personal level.

Where American books are concerned the condition of North American society is being translated into children's books quite clearly, but with one notable difference from the past. As society in general does not seem to know what to say to its children and cannot express itself with one voice, we have both a literature of 'personal decision', which suggests that each young person has to come to terms with life on an individual basis, and a literature of conformity. Many writers move uneasily between the two, exhibiting their own cloudy view of life and of contemporary problems. The form most writers use is realistic fiction or contemporary-scene fiction and they try to 'tell it like it is' in areas such as the 'personal' problems of young people, race relationships, alcoholism, drug addiction, violence, and war. These books are chiefly aimed at the senior elementary-school child or the junior high-school student.[1]

---

[1]For Professor Egoff's current (1980) views on the problem novel, see her essay on pp. 356-69.

Many books deal with family problems or problems of growing up, such as Lee Kingman's *The Year of the Raccoon* (1966), Christie Harris's *Confessions of a Toe-Hanger* (1967), and Maia Wojciechowska's *The Hollywood Kid* (1966). In most cases the young people are at odds with their parents and/or their siblings. Such books tend to be facile exploitations of tensions that are quickly and remarkably resolved by conformity.

In other books tensions are built up because of such social problems as divorce—Vera and Bill Cleaver's *Ellen Grae* (1967) and *Lady Ellen Grae* (1968); alcoholism—Regina Woody's *One Day At a Time* (1968); poverty—Frank Bonham's *The Nitty Gritty* (1967); and war—John R. Tunis's *His Enemy His Friend* (1968). All of these books have a brittle style that could be considered 'mod' by the younger generation, but unfortunately they have soft and flabby answers to the questions they deliberately raise. It is perhaps too simple to say that children's books are bringing children faster into the adult world than ever before. Television has a prior influence in this regard; and in many cases these books are merely a reflection of what the child has already encountered on TV. (Indeed they share their most notable characteristic with the mass media: superficiality.) Due to the mass media and the pressures of modern society, children have now rejoined the adult world from which they were separated in the previous century. However, we adults of the 1960s only half accept them and in our half acceptance we provide them with books that are only half honest. The alcoholic mother in Regina Woody's book makes a remarkable recovery when her young daughter solves the family's financial crisis and John Tunis would have us believe that his German officer made a decision when he did not.

The authors of all these books show quite clearly society's ambivalent attitude toward children: wanting them to be informed and yet to conform; wanting problems to be presented realistically while taking such a hesitant step towards realism that only half-truths result, which can be more dangerous than ignorance.

Most of the children's books on Negro life and problems lack, besides literary qualities, honesty, integrity, and genuine knowledge. The best books about Negroes will be written by black writers; hopefully these writers will have the power and insight of the many black writers who have distinguished themselves in the adult field.

The personal decision-making stream of writing can be represented by such books as Martha Stiles's *Darkness Over the Land* (1966), about the inner conflict of a boy growing up in Nazi Germany in the Second World War; Nat Hentoff's *I'm Really Dragged But Nothing Gets Me Down* (1968), on the problems of American boys facing the Vietnam draft; and Barbara Wersba's *The Dream Watcher* (1968), about a boy who worries because he is 'different':

I'm the only person in America who doesn't belong to a group. I'm not square and I'm not hip. I'm not a hood. I'm not an intellectual. I'm not an athlete. And what else is there?

Darkness Over the Land, with all its commonplace writing, has a clearly defined theme that makes the whole greater than the sum of its parts. In most other books of this type the major issues are either complicated or simplistic; in both cases they are undramatic. They also frequently imply that the young protagonist's decision—to engage in draft counselling, for example, or to become 'somebody'—is *the* big decision and that he need never make another one.

It is a fact that the desires of young people—to know what adults are all about, to understand themselves in the most complicated and diversified era man has yet experienced, to fulfil themselves in a world where the socially acceptable nine-to-five jobs and suburbia are holding less and less appeal, to see reflected in books written for them the view of the world that they really hold—do *not* preclude satisfying their requirements in genuine works of literature. That problems should provide themes for children's literature is not being questioned, for they should if literature is to reflect life, but it is clear that in most cases the demand for problem books is being filled by highly superficial and mediocre writing.

One view of the problem books, which says that if a problem exists it should be presented to the young reader in as realistic a way as possible, often implies that such literary values as style, characterization, plot, and the welding of a philosophy of life to a literary form must take second place. The opposite view is based on a literary standard and all that it demands. Generally speaking the modern American realistic school of writing is almost aggressively unliterary. Most authors appear to be amateur writers dragged into active existence by the great demand for the problem book, not because they have something to say to the young and can say it well. Their efforts are almost without plot and read like socio-psychological case-studies that are entirely devoid of interpretation and significance. Is bibliotherapy really an excuse for poor literature even though the problems—racial inequality, drug addiction, unmarried mothers, alcoholic fathers —are important ones? What answers do these books give to the problems they set up? Whatever they are, they tend to be one-dimensional answers to multi-dimensional problems. The vision in most current writing is very, very narrow—in the setting up of the problem, in the resolution of it, and in the intended reader-ship. In most instances several problems are settled for a lifetime in the last chapter. One can only wonder if the generation gap is so great that adults have to suspend their reasoned judgement in order to 'keep with it' so far as young people and their cares are concerned. It can be argued that in the hands of a real writer the problems of a fifteen-year-old with a famous movie-star mother could be made absorbing and significant. So they could, but only if the writer can make pain and sorrow and joy uni-versal, so that every reader can say of the protaganist 'That's me!' and of the theme 'I know it's true.'

We now know a great deal about children clinically and psychologically, but what do we know of their literary needs?

It would appear that in purporting to be realistic, present-day writers forget that realism is a distillation, not a simple ingredient or a fixed attitude. Realism as it is presented in most books for children is an encumbrance rather than a release. As Sir Laurence Olivier once pointed out, 'If you cut out the nose of a portrait by Rembrandt and pushed your own nose through, the nose would be real enough, but as a painting it would be disastrous.' Much of modern realistic writing for children is just this: adults ludicrously playing at deception. The artificial quality of these books is never more evident than in their endings. All too often they conclude on a note of moralizing or of sweetened uplift. At the end of Barbara Wersba's *The Dream Watcher* (1968) the young hero 'finds' himself, as do most other young American heroes and heroines.

Of course not all current writers contribute to the slice-of-life genre; there are a few who do not slavishly pursue verisimilitude but prefer to write on a more symbolic level. Significantly it is such authors—notably Louise Fitzhugh in *Harriet the Spy* (1964) and *The Long Secret* (1965) and Julia Cunningham in *Dorp Dead* (1965)—who are the most controversial. The objectives and successes of these two writers can be seen in contrast to a more obviously realistic book, such as Marilyn Sachs's *Veronica Ganz* (1968).

In *Harriet the Spy* we gather first of all that Harriet's parents have not found the time to take a large part in her upbringing and have entrusted most of it to her nurse, Ole Golly. We are given a fairly detailed portrait of Ole Golly, though not of the other adults in the book. She comes from an impoverished and uninspiring background (the book begins with a visit to her grotesque, simple-minded mother), but she compensates for the dreariness of her youth with enormous intellectual pretensions. She has a fondness for inserting into a conversation dimly understood quotations from famous writers, no matter how irrelevant they may be. Undoubtedly it is Ole Golly who influenced Harriet to keep a diary as a prelude to her future writing career. Harriet's character is really quite consistent with the description we are given of Ole Golly's part in her upbringing. In a permissive atmosphere in which her ideas are taken seriously by her nurse, she has come to believe that all experience must be explored; at the same time she has been taught that she can and indeed must be objective in her observation of this experience:

Miss Whitehead's feet look larger this year. Miss Whitehead has buck teeth, thin hair, feet like skis, and a very long hanging stomach. Ole Golly says description is good for the soul, and clears the brain like a laxative.

Harriet gets carried away and deliberately spies upon people to get the material she so accurately records in her diary. She comes to realize that 'some people are one way and some people are another and that's that.' In the book's denouement, which has horrified many adults, Harriet learns about human relations that 'Ole Golly was right. Sometimes you have to lie.'

The people she spies upon are her neighbours, her teachers, her parents, and her friends. None of them is 'real' in the sense that we could imagine such people existing in our own world. They are all exaggerations, even caricatures, yet they are real as symbols of the follies of contemporary society. Harriet's parents are presented far more realistically than most parents in modern children's books. At the beginning they ignore their parental responsibilities, but they do come to Harriet's aid when she is in trouble and so do her teachers. This runs counter to the current American trend of making adults ineffectual, which implies that children are in opposition to adults. (American children seem to be hurried into adulthood; yet in books, adulthood is not presented as an entirely felicitous state. But this is a topic for another paper.)

Opinions of *Harriet the Spy* have been sharply divided. It has been lauded for its 'realism' and condemned as being 'warped and unpleasant'. Both views misinterpret Miss Fitzhugh's approach to life, which, if it is to be pigeon-holed, should be described as 'naturalistic' rather than 'realistic'. She introduces into children's literature a mode of fictional writing that adults have learned how to deal with adequately in their own literature but that they do not quite know what to make of in a children's book. For example, an adult would not read Evelyn Waugh's *The Loved One* and think it was an accurate representation of American funerary practices, yet through its distortions the book tells us a great deal about life in southern California and indeed about contemporary life in general. But when Louise Fitzhugh in somewhat the same way brings a child to terms with adult life and in the process reveals its unpleasantness and dishonesty, she is criticized for her lack of fidelity. What is hampering judgement here is simply an old tradition of children's literature that life is fundamentally good and beautiful and that all the virtues will have their own reward.

Marilyn Sachs's *Veronica Ganz* might be described as a more realistic and generally 'acceptable' book than *Harriet the Spy*. But it is precisely Mrs Sachs's faithfulness to a limited reality that ultimately makes this book a lesser accomplishment than either of Miss Fitzhugh's novels. The turning-point comes when Veronica, realizing the power and privileges of being a female, loses all the aggressive instincts that have dominated her mind and actions up to that moment. Certainly Veronica has suffered from the break-up of her parent's marriage, from having lived in grinding poverty, and from having to fight all her fellow pupils into submission in order to gain a sense of position among them. Is it consistent with the realistic background that Mrs Sachs has so faithfully described that Veronica could undergo such an instantaneous and presumably permanent transformation? Because Mrs Sachs is not faithful to the inner reality of her book, it is marred by a certain dishonesty. Her message of the power of womanhood goes against the laws of both her created universe and the universe of the reader. In *Harriet the Spy* the reader only has to look at its inner reality to see the relevance of that reality to the one he knows. In *Dorp Dead* Julia Cunningham also portrays life as she sees it, believing that, in the total experience, the unhealthy lip-licking kind of brutality that she has been accused of exploiting is actually inseparable from the realization of love and personal fulfilment of the young protagonist, Gilly: had he not been the victim of a sadistic adult, he would have become entrapped in a cage of self-alienation.

The disapproving critical reception of these unusual novels by Louise Fitzhugh and Julia Cunningham suggests that while mediocrity is acceptable or at least tolerated, distortion for artistic reasons and anything pathological are not, even when they are used to widen the reader's vision of life and society. It is sadly apparent that the majority of adult critics of children's books prefer a message imposed from without rather than one that grows out of the novel itself.[2]

Realistic novels in the established tradition of children's literature, while not neglected by American writers, are being produced in greater numbers in England and Australia. Echoes of Louisa May Alcott, Arthur Ransome, and Eleanor Estes continue to reverberate in stories that have real plots, self-reliant children, and timeless themes and settings. These books have fewer instant problems and solutions. In John Rowe Townsend's *Gumble's Yard* (1961) a group of poor children, deserted by an uncle and his common-law wife, solve a mystery and help capture some criminals. At the end of the story Kevin quite naturally feels that after all the exciting events some dramatic change should come into his life, but circumstances do not allow a change. The children have a choice between an unsatisfactory life and public welfare. Yet the book ends on a note of practical cheer:

We walked three abreast, with Sandra in the middle. And as we turned the corner into our own street I felt happy and burst out singing.

---

[2]See Anthony Metie, 'Notes on Some Recent Fiction for Children,' Canadian Association of Children's Librarians *Bulletin* (Fall 1968), pp. 37-43.

'Hark at him!' said Sandra. 'Not a care in the world.'
'Where does it hurt, Kevin?' asked Dick with mock sympathy.
'I'll hurt you in a minute!' I said.
And we started a friendly scuffle, the kind that happens a
dozen times a day.

On the whole, British children's fiction tends to carry on the tradition of children's literature that was set in the late-Victorian age and was carried on into the 1950s; a large proportion of these novels reflect literary discipline and a flair for language, and (more frequently than in American novels) the resolution of theme usually stems from characterization and from the inevitability of events. Not all British books are praiseworthy, of course, nor do they all avoid current issues: British publishers are not above offering books like Gertrude Kamm's *Young Mother* (almost a 'how-to-do-it' book on illegitimacy). But the mainstream of writing tends toward the realistic adventure story rather than the problem book. Gerald Durrell's *The Donkey Rustlers* (1968) is a zany 'cops-and-robbers' story and the fact that two wealthy children help a poor friend is an integral part of the plot rather than a lesson in generosity. Helen Cresswell's *The Piemakers* (1968) is a charming and original 'tall tale'. Patricia Wrightson's *I Own the Racecourse* (Australian, 1968), in which a group of boys disagree over how to help a mentally retarded friend who takes their game of owning things seriously, manages to convey a world of concerned childhood rather than the American concept of 'growing up' or 'coming to terms with life'. None of these writers, and indeed fewer British writers than American, inhibit their style because they are writing for children.

While current American writing is notable for a group of new writers who are busy with immediate social and personal problems, a goodly number of established and new British writers prefer to write about the past, an area in which American writing has been weak. The British historical novel for children has had a long tradition and its modern practitioners are among the best:

Rosemary Sutcliff, Geoffrey Trease, Hilda Lewis, Naomi Mitchison, Ronald Welch, and Hester Burton. The rising star in this field is Leon Garfield, who has called forth comparisons with Fielding, Hogarth, and Dickens. Not merely concerned with creating a strict historical setting, he conveys the very atmosphere of time past. Using the ingredients of melodrama—pickpockets, highwaymen, smiling villains, cut-throat sailors, stolen documents and diamonds, escapes and hurried journeys—he welds them into tales of high adventure that have their own inner purpose. The only direct problem Mr Garfield poses to readers is how to put a book of his down.

[1969]

In North America the sixties and seventies were chiefly the decades of the problem novel. This genre of fiction for children, which began in the early sixties by focusing on unexceptional family conflicts, pushed ever outward for subjects into the domains of the psychologist and the social worker. It tackled sex, alcoholism, mental retardation, drugs, divorce and death, confronting deep anxieties about sexuality and alienation and what was seen as the corruption of the adult world and its indifference to the young. Gratifying the need of children and young adolescents to 'find' themselves in a society that provides them with a confusing array of choices and influences, these books gained a large and avid readership, particularly among young girls. Though tending to be simplistic and narrow of aim, they explored their hitherto taboo subjects with an openness, an explicitness, and a seriousness that influenced the writing of more creative and imaginative novels in every genre. Their influence even reached across the Atlantic. While it was not as strong in the United Kingdom as in the United States, on both sides of the Atlantic it combined with the period's changes in social attitudes and the felt need for new modes of expression to alter children's books irrevocably.

Although today each genre—realistic fiction, historical fiction, science fiction, or fantasy—is marked by a distinct identity, they all share qualities that reflect a new approach to writing for children: stylistic and thematic maturity, seriousness, psychological probing, and highly individualized characters (gone are the interchangeable children of Arthur Ransome and his school). The finest writers—such as Jill Paton Walsh, William Corlett, and Virginia Hamilton in realistic fiction, Hester Burton and Katherine Paterson in historical fiction, Rosemary Harris and Peter Dickinson in science fiction, and Ursula Le Guin and Susan Cooper in fantasy—have introduced young people to some terrifying and enlightening realities of the adult world. In Robert Cormier's *The Chocolate War* (1973) Jerry Renault may never recover from his inhuman experience at the hands of both boys and masters in the closed world of a boys' school. Like the kidnapped David in William Corlett's *The Dark Side of the Moon* (1976), he faces the void of despair. In the fantasies of Susan Cooper (the 'Dark is Rising' quintet[3]) and in Natalie Babbitt's *Tuck Everlasting* (1975), the responsibilities and ethical trials forced upon the young characters are far removed from the joyous play of earlier fantasies by such writers as Pamela Travers. Children are made to bear physical and moral burdens even in the new science fiction, such as Elizabeth Mace's *Ransome Revisited* (1975), which depicts a future of enforced child-labour camps. This is a far cry from David Craigie's *The Voyage of the Luna I* (1949), in which an accidental trip to the moon by two children is treated as a lighthearted adventure.

Appearing to write from their adult rather than their child selves, many authors today engage their characters in intense struggles for emotional and psychological survival: stripped of every traditional stereotype of childhood, the protagonists stand forlorn, in an environment controlled by adults, amid crisis situ-

---

[3]*Over Sea, Under Stone* (Harcourt, Brace 1966); *The Dark Is Rising* (1973), *Greenwitch* (1974), *The Grey King* (1975), *Silver on the Tree* (1977), all published by Atheneum.

ations that require a decisive choice that will change their lives. The best of such writing is often almost Dostoyevskian in purpose, treating despair ruthlessly in order to exorcise it. But while much of it is bleak, expressing a misanthropic view of society, it is also deeply humanistic in the importance it places on human relationships, which are a more dominant feature of recent fiction than even traumatic incidents. In portraying the intricacies of familial, romantic, peer, and generational relationships, virtually all writers of note give recognition to the fact that love and other forms of emotional sustenance are central to human existence.

The theme that is most common in all the best recent fiction is personal struggle—marking the passage from childhood to adolescence or from adolescence to adulthood—played out in the context of death, war, responsibility, human relationships, social attitudes, or psychological crises. The presence in much recent fiction of the two most disturbing and disruptive events in life, death and war, is remarkable. Death is of overriding importance in such realistic fiction as Alan Garner's *Tom Fobble's Day* (1977), Mollie Hunter's *A Sound of Chariots* (1972), and Katherine Paterson's *Bridge to Terabithia* (1977). Death mated to war appears in historical fiction such as Rosemary Sutcliff's *Sun Horse, Moon Horse* (1977), Leon Garfield's *The Prisoners of September* (1975), and James and Christopher Collier's *My Brother Sam Is Dead* (1974). While death occurred in earlier historical novels, it was always presented at one remove from the main protagonists; frequently, as in Dickens's *A Tale of Two Cities*, it was used as a symbol of courage and self-sacrifice. In the new historical novels, death—coming with appalling swiftness—is close, personal, and leaves an indelible mark on the young. Although death occurs in some of the books that have war as a theme—such as Robert Westall's *The Machine Gunners* (1975) and Bette Green's *Summer of My German Soldier* (1973) —it is the disruption of children's lives and the *effects* of war that concern Nina Bawden in *Carrie's War* (1973), Penelope

Lively in *Going Back* (1975), and T. Degens in *Transport 7-41-R* (1974). Even the American Civil War, in Betty Sue Cummings's *Hew Against the Grain* (1977), provides little more than background for Matilda's emotional upheavals. Fantasy, in its epic form, also deals with war. But while it is elevated to a contest between Good and Evil in such books as Susan Cooper's the 'Dark is Rising' quintet (1966 to 1977), Joy Chant's *Red Moon and Black Mountain*, and Alan Garner's *The Weirdstone of Brisingamen* (1960), the action and the symbolism are of the battlefield.

With such themes it is not surprising that the tone of most fine modern children's books is one of extreme seriousness, deteriorating in lesser works to solemnity. However, some writers infuse their otherwise sober themes with a kind of joy—indeed, a celebration of life—in spite of heavy odds. Such serious and thought-provoking books as Ivan Southall's *What About Tomorrow* (1977), Jill Paton Walsh's *Unleaving* (1976), and Mollie Hunter's *A Sound of Chariots* (1972) leave one with a sense that, in spite of everything, life is worthwhile simply because it is such a miracle in itself. And in rare novels, such as Jane Gardam's *Bilgewater* (1976), life is viewed with a truly humorous rather than an ironic eye. As the decade closed, there were some indications that the tone of children's literature might be lightening. Picturebooks showed less concern with socializing the young child and a happier turn toward simple good fun. And the success of Helen Cresswell's surprising trilogy about the zany 'Bagthorpe Family'[4], who move from one hilarious crisis to another without a psychological or social purpose in sight, perhaps gives hope of the return of humour to children's books.

The seriousness of themes and tone of the new literature permits of no condescension in style. The young reader is treated as an equal, capable of appreciating maturity of presentation—

---

[4]The Bagthorpe Saga consists of four volumes: *Ordinary Jack* (1977), *Absolute Zero* (1978), *Bagthorpes V. the World* (1978), and *Bagthorpes Unlimited* (1978).

of language as well as content. Most of the new literature is episodic rather than strongly plotted in the old adventure-story sense. Each incident builds on another, but chiefly for the purpose of psychological resolution. Drawing on the adult in themselves, writers pursue stylistic expression without concern for reading levels. Alan Garner's 'Stone Book' quartet (historical fiction), with its use of poetic country dialect, Virginia Hamilton's effective use of Black English in *The Planet of Junior Brown* (1971), and Robert Cormier's introduction of the taped interview in *I Am the Cheese* (1977) are only a few examples of a new linguistic and structural freedom that reflects authenticity and imagination rather than mere aesthetic experimentation. The writers of fantasy in particular have broken the bonds of tradition by adopting highly cinematic techniques to explore states of consciousness and transformations, as in the books of Susan Cooper and in *A Castle of Bone* (1972) by Penelope Farmer, *The House in Norham Gardens* (1974) by Penelope Lively, and *A Game of Dark* (1971) by William Mayne. Such books, and many others, cry out to be filmed.

Despite the major changes enumerated here, contemporary children's literature is not as cut off from the past as it may appear: there is an underlying link with earlier periods. In a broad sense it still fulfils the major ground rule: that of reflecting the manners and mores of society and the child's place in it. While the psychological approach of the seventies is very much in tune with the times, it also calls to mind the precept literature of the first 250 years of writing for children. Contemporary authors are telling children how to live emotionally, as their predecessors told them how to behave. The saving graces of this new didacticism are its literary sophistication, its compassion, and its concern for the individual.

The most significant features of the literature of the seventies, then, are its maturity and its seriousness. Most of the best books are calculated to appeal to the adult within the adolescent. One looks in vain for fine writers for the middle-aged child (ages nine to eleven), those who were served in the recent past by such writers as Pamela Travers, Eleanor Estes, E. B. White, Mary Norton, and Lucy Boston, among others. It would seem that when contemporary children's literature gained, with a vast expansion of subject matter, the world of adult freedom, it lost some of its soul—its identity as a separate and distinctive branch of writing. In society itself we have taken down the walls of convention that once surrounded children. Whether or not one believes that they are 'growing up too fast' as a result, the recent literature that reflects liberated attitudes suggests that we run the risk of losing permanently those characteristics of warmth, wonder, gaiety, sentiment, and simplicity that pervade the finest books of the past. The 'classics' are still read and enjoyed, however, so these 'childlike' qualities cannot be considered *passé*. Is it unrealistic to hope that the predominantly bleak vision of today's gifted writers will brighten and warm sufficiently to bring about their restoration? The books of the seventies have unquestionably reached a high peak of literary achievement. But the decade just over is perhaps more suitably described as an iron age than a golden one.

[1980]

Contributors

EDWARD ARDIZZONE   One of the best-loved illustrators of children's books, Ardizzone died in 1979. He illustrated over a hundred books, both for adults and children, and his name is particularly associated with the *Tim* books, the first and perhaps most popular of which, *Little Tim and the Brave Sea Captain*, was published in 1936. He won the Kate Greenaway Medal for *Tim All Alone* in 1956.

JORDAN BROTMAN   A Canadian by birth, Brotman lived in Calgary and Vancouver before moving to the United States. He got his doctorate at the Berkeley campus of the University of California and now teaches English at Sacramento State College. He is a journalist and novelist. His best-known novel is *Doctor Vago*.

ROGER DUVOISIN   After spending his childhood in Switzerland, Duvoisin studied design as a young man in Lyons and Paris and later settled in the United States, where he has become well known as an author and illustrator of children's books. *Petunia* and *Lovely Veronica* brought him recognition as an artist capable of combining imagination and humour. In 1948 he was awarded the Caldecott Medal for *White Snow, Bright Snow*.

SHEILA EGOFF   Born in Maine, Sheila Egoff was educated in Ontario. She graduated from the University of Toronto and went to the University of London for graduate studies. Returning to Canada, she became actively engaged in library work, first in the east and, since 1962, in Vancouver where she is a Professor in the School of Librarianship at the University of British Columbia. Her special interest for many years has been literature for children. She is the author of *The Republic of Childhood: A Critical Guide to Canadian Children's Literature in English* (Second Edition, 1975), and was the co-ordinator of the first Pacific Rim Conference on Children's Literature, held in Vancouver in 1976, and edited the collection of its papers: *One Ocean Touching*.

T. S. ELIOT   American-born, but resident in England from 1914 until his death in 1965, Eliot is recognized as one of the most influential writers of the twentieth century. His poetry, though generally serious and complex, includes a few diversions such as 'The Hippopotamus' and *Old Possum's Book of Practical Cats*. His best-known essays deal with poetic theory, doctrines of criticism, the classics, and the place of religion in society.

SYLVIA ENGDAHL   After a brief period of teaching and ten years as a computer-systems specialist, Engdahl became a full-time writer in 1967. Her novel *Enchantress From the Stars* was a 1971 Newbery Honour Book and Junior Literary Guild selection. Besides several works of fiction, she has written books about the scientific aspects of space exploration and recent developments in high-energy physics.

JASON EPSTEIN   Vice-president and editorial director of Random House, he is also a director of the New York Review of Books Inc., and has served as a consultant to the Children's Television Workshop.

CLIFTON FADIMAN   Known to the general public through his appearances on radio and television programs, Clifton Fadiman has also been a frequent contributor of articles, essays, and reviews to periodicals in the United States. Some of these writings were collected in *Party of One* (1955), *Any Number Can Play* (1957) and *Enter, Conversing* (1962). He has been a Senior Editor of the children's magazine *Cricket* since 1972.

MARTIN GARDNER   American journalist and freelance writer. Many of his articles have been published in philosophical journals, and his column on recreational mathematics appears regularly in *Scientific American*. He is the author of *Relativity for the Million, Codes, Ciphers and Secret Writing*, and *The Ambidextrous Universe*.

JOHN GOLDTHWAITE   In addition to periodical articles, Goldthwaite has written a number of popular books for children, including *Dracula Spectacula, Eggs Amen*, and *The Kidnapping of the Coffee Pot*.

ROGER LANCELYN GREEN   Author of *Kipling: The Creative Heritage, C. S. Lewis, Andrew Lang*, and other biographical works, Green has made a particular study of children's books and authors. His publications include retellings of the great myths and legends.

GRAHAM GREENE   Noted writer of fiction. Some of his novels (*The Power and the Glory, The Heart of the Matter, A Burnt-Out Case*) reveal the author's concern with moral and theological dilemmas; in others (*The Third Man, Our Man in Havana*) the element of entertainment predominates. Graham Greene has also written short stories, travel books, and critical essays and articles on many different subjects. His *Collected Essays* was published in 1969.

MICHAEL HORNYANSKY   His popular children's book, *The Golden Phoenix and Other Folk Tales from Quebec*, is a retelling of French-Canadian stories collected by Marius Barbeau. He is Professor of English at Brock University, St Catharines, Ont.

ELIZABETH JANEWAY   Born in Brooklyn, New York, she attended Barnard College. She is a frequent book reviewer and the author of several novels, including *The Walsh Girls* and *Daisy Kenyon*. Mrs Janeway's two sons supplied ideas for some of her children's books. In recent years she has turned her attention to the social context of change that produced the women's movement. *Man's World — Women's Place: A Study in Social Mythology* was published in 1971.

EDMUND LEACH   Professor of Social Anthropology and until 1979 Provost of King's College, Cambridge, Leach has conducted research in anthropology in Formosa, Borneo, Ceylon, and many other places. He has reported on his work in professional journals and in such studies as *A Village in Ceylon*. In 1967 Dr Leach gave the Reith Lectures for the BBC, taking as his subject, 'A Runaway World?'.

C. S. LEWIS   After holding other academic appointments, Lewis was Professor of Medieval and Renaissance English at Cambridge University from 1954 until his death in 1963. He was a man of varied literary gifts: a novelist, literary critic, and the author of essays on Christian theological and moral problems. Three of his novels, including the well-known *Out of the Silent Planet*, are philosophical fantasies of life on other planets. His *Narnia* stories for children, written between 1950 and 1956, are allegorical in character.

MARION LOCHHEAD   Born in Lanarkshire, Scotland, Marion Lochhead was educated at Wishaw High School and Glasgow University. She is the author of numerous biographical and historical works. Of the latter, *Their First Ten Years* examines the place of children in Victorian society. *St. Mungo's Bairns* and *On Tintock Tap* are children's stories.

WALTER LORRAINE Director of Children's Trade Books for the Houghton Mifflin Company. A graduate of the Rhode Island School of Design, he served as president of the Children's Book Council, 1978-9.

HELEN LOURIE Psychiatrist and author, wife of Lord Balogh, the economist. Since 1962 she has devoted her full time to writing. *Stories for Jane* (1952) was the first of several books for children. Her other writings have included *Freud for Jung* (1963), written under the pseudonym Irene Adler, and frequent contributions to *Nova* and *Cosmopolitan*.

DONNARAE MAC CANN After studying music at Santa Monica City College and international relations at the University of California, she was librarian at the University Elementary School on the Los Angeles campus of the University of California from 1957 to 1965. Since then she has held various university appointments and written a study of book illustration, *The Child's First Books: A Critical Study of Pictures and Texts* (1973).

WILLIAM H. MAGEE For four years Dean of the College of Arts and Letters at the University of Alaska, Dr Magee is at present Professor of English at the University of Calgary. He has contributed papers to the *University of Toronto Quarterly*, *Culture*, the *Dalhousie Review*, and other Canadian periodicals. The subjects in which he has a special interest are Canadian literature and the eighteenth-century British novel.

PENELOPE MORTIMER Film critic for the *Observer* from 1967 to 1970, Penelope Mortimer is best known as a writer of fiction. Many of her short stories have been published in the *New Yorker*. Her novel *The Pumpkin Eater* was made into a film by Harold Pinter. In 1975-6 she lectured at the New School for Social Research at Boston University.

WILLIAM NOBLETT He studied history at Christ's College, Cambridge, and librarianship at the University of Sheffield. Currently employed at the Cambridge University Library, he has written several articles on the social and economic aspects of the eighteenth-century book trade in Great Britain.

JOHN PUDNEY Since his first book, *Spring Encounter*, was published in 1933, John Pudney has been active as a writer of stories for children, biographical works, and books on flight and flying. He has also written poetry. From 1953 to 1963 he was a director of Putnam.

EDWARD W. ROSENHEIM, JR   Professor of English at the University of Chicago. His books include *What Happens in Literature* (1960) and *Swift and the Satirist's Art* (1963).

MAURICE SENDAK   The distinguished American illustrator of children's books, can number among his many productions some of the most popular picture-storybooks of today, which are entirely his own creation. They include *The Nutshell Library, Where the Wild Things Are, Hector Protector, Higglety, Pigglety Pop; or, There Must Be More in Life,* and *In the Night Kitchen.* He won the Caldecott Medal for *Where the Wild Things Are* in 1964 and the Hans Christian Andersen Award in 1970 for his works to date. He illustrated *The Juniper Tree and Other Tales from Grimm,* selected by Lore Segal and Maurice Sendak and translated by Lore Segal—an illustration from volume 1 of which is reproduced on page 333.

LILLIAN H. SMITH   A Canadian librarian, now retired, Miss Smith is remembered for her long and distinguished service at the Toronto Public Library. Starting with limited resources, she built up in over forty years a children's collection that has become recognized as one of the best in North America. Her approach to the evaluation of children's books has had enormous influence. In 1962 the American Library Association presented her with the Clarence Day Award for her work in Toronto and for her book on children's literature, *The Unreluctant Years: A Critical Approach to Children's Literature.*

PETER A. SODERBERGH   Dean of the College of Education at Louisiana State University, Baton Rouge, since 1976. Before this, Dr Soderbergh held appointments at the University of Virginia and the University of Pittsburgh. He is the author of many articles on historical subjects, juvenile literature, and the mass media.

ANTHONY STORR   Educated at Winchester College and Cambridge University, Anthony Storr qualified as a physician in 1944 and has since specialized in psychiatric work. In addition to his practice as an analyst, he finds time for appearances on British television and radio and writes articles and book reviews. He has also written six books, including *The Dynamics of Creation* (1972).

ROSEMARY SUTCLIFF   Born in Sussex, the daughter of an English naval officer, Rosemary Sutcliff first embarked on a career as an artist and was elected a member of the Royal Society of Miniature Painters. After the Second World War she gave up painting for writing historical fiction for children and adults. Her many outstanding children's novels include *The Eagle of the Ninth, The Shield Ring, Song for a Dark Queen,* and *Sun Horse, Moon Horse.* In 1959 she was awarded the Carnegie Medal for *The Lantern Bearers.*

J. R. R. TOLKIEN First reaching a wide public as author of the threefold saga *The Lord of the Rings,* Tolkien was also an authority on medieval English literature and philology and was Merton professor of English language and literature at Oxford University from 1945 to 1959. The mythical creatures who inhabit *The Lord of the Rings* originally made their appearance in a children's book, *The Hobbit,* written in 1937 when Tolkien was professor of Anglo-Saxon at Oxford. He died in 1973.

JOHN ROWE TOWNSEND Born and brought up in Leeds, Towsend attended Cambridge University where he edited the university newspaper. Subsequently he embarked on a career in journalism, gaining much of his experience on the staff of the *Guardian,* first as sub-editor then later as editor of the international edition. An active interest in the social conditions of poor children prompted him to write his first novel, *Gumble's Yard.* Its success led to other books for children, including *The Visitors, Noah's Castle,* and *Top of the World.* In the last few years he has conducted courses in children's literature at English and American universities, and gave the Whittall Lecture at the Library of Congress in 1976.

PAMELA TRAVERS A native of Australia, Pamela Travers has spent most of her life in England. Her literary career began with the writing of poetry; then for a number of years she contributed articles to the *Irish Statesman* and to English magazines. For her own entertainment while recovering from an illness she began to write the *Mary Poppins stories,* which have brought her international fame.

ALAN MORAY WILLIAMS A graduate of King's College, Cambridge, Williams entered the field of journalism and was appointed special correspondent of the *Sunday Times* in Norway in 1950. His newspaper work has taken him to all parts of Scandinavia, and since 1956 he has been managing editor of Scandinavian Features Service, with offices in Copenhagen. Apart from contributions to newspapers and periodicals, he has written *Children of the Century, The Road to the West,* and *Russian Made Easy.*

Selected bibliography

ANDERSON, W. AND P. GROFF. *A New Look at Children's Literature.* Belmont, California, Wadsworth, 1972.

Anderson and Groff are concerned to show that, as a part of the mainstream of literature, children's books are worthy of the same standards of evaluation as those of adults. *A New Look* is especially useful for its survey of various doctrines of literary criticism and for a rationale for curriculum design. It also contains an extensive annotated bibliography.

AVERY, GILLIAN. *Childhood's Pattern: A Study of the Heroes and Heroines of Children's Fiction, 1770-1950.* London, Hodder and Stoughton, 1975.

Avery explains how, during two centuries, children's books have mirrored a constantly shifting moral pattern. The book addresses itself to questions such as: 'What in any given age do adults want of children?' What are their values?' 'What are the virtues they are trying to inculcate, the vices they are trying to root out?'

BADER, BARBARA. *American Picture books: From Noah's Ark to the Beast Within.* New York, Macmillan, 1976.

This large book with its profuse illustrations goes a long way to meet the author's objectives: to attempt to identify all the picturebooks published; to examine as many as possible; and to investigate publication backgrounds. Almost anyone interested in children's books (and not merely the illustrations) will find this an invaluable browsing and reference work. It contains a wealth of material not readily found elsewhere.

CIANCIOLO, PATRICIA. *Illustrations in Children's Books,* 2nd edition. Dubuque, Iowa, Brown, 1976.

With the increasing attention being given to art-work, this is a most useful reference and there has been considerable updating of the original edition. As one of a series intended for the elementary classroom teacher who wants to design and implement an effective program, the book offers fine coverage of such matters as evaluation of illustration, artistic styles, media, and techniques.

DARLING, RICHARD. *The Rise of Children's Book Reviewing in America, 1865-1881.* New York & London, R. R. Bowker, 1968.
A valuable piece of research that will have to be taken into account in any future histories of children's literature and in the development of criticism about it. The activity that surrounded children and their books during this period, particularly as it was reflected in the major literary periodicals, is well described and documented. The author occasionally mistakenly considers book reviewing—excellent though many of the examples are—to represent a genuine, objective body of critical writing on children's literature.

DARTON, F. J. HARVEY. *Children's Books in England: Five Centuries of Social Life.* 2nd edition. Cambridge University Press, 1958.
The first major work to relate children's books to evolving social and moral attitudes towards young people, *Children's Books in England* is a work no serious student should be unacquainted with. It gives a scholarly review of the historical conflict between instruction and entertainment in children's literature.

EGOFF, SHEILA. *The Republic of Childhood: A Critical Guide to Canadian Children's Literature in English.* 2nd edition. Toronto, Oxford University Press, 1975.
Sheila Egoff's provocative survey of Canadian children's books since 1950 frankly compares the relative weaknesses and strengths of a burgeoning literature with significant British and American publications. The annotated booklists provide honest and objective judgements.

FENWICK, SARA I., ed. *A Critical Approach to Children's Literature.* University of Chicago Press, 1976. (Midway Reprint Series)
Twelve papers originally presented at the 31st Annual Conference of the University of Chicago Graduate Library School. They deal with important current issues and stress the need for informed criticism.

GLAZER, J. I. AND G. WILLIAMS. *Introduction to Children's Literature.* New York, McGraw-Hill, 1979.
This book is oriented to the requirements of students of children's literature and, as such, incorporates a good deal of very useful and thought-

ful material. It includes a survey of genres, with appropriate criteria for evaluation; strategies for teaching; and ideas for discussion of selected topics.

HAZARD, PAUL. *Books, Children and Men.* Translated by Marguerite Mitchell. Boston, Horn Book, 1960.
A wide-ranging philosophical discourse about children and their books. Some think the 'Give us wings' approach limits its usefulness, but for its richness of allusion and its profound interpretation of childhood it continues to occupy an important place in the literature on children's books.

HÜRLIMANN, BETTINA. *Three Centuries of Children's Books in Europe.* Translated and edited by B. W. Alderson. London, Oxford University Press, 1967.
Bettina Hürlimann gives a highly informative and warm appraisal of children's literature. She discusses European authors and books against a background of British and American developments. Her lively style is admirably complemented by the translator's comments and booklists.

MEIGS, CORNELIA AND OTHERS. *A Critical History of Children's Literature.* Revised edition. New York, Macmillan, 1969.
This survey is one of the most comprehensive works of its kind and is widely used as a text. Most of the book is concerned with American writing, though there is some discussion of parallel developments in Great Britain.

OPIE, IONA AND PETER. *The Classic Fairy Tale.* London, Oxford University Press, 1974.
A lucid and well-researched treatment of a fascinating subject. As usual with the Opies' work, the material is at the same time authoritative and eminently readable.

QUAYLE, ERIC. *The Collector's Book of Children's Books.* London, Studio Vista, 1971.
Although published as the 'first survey of children's books for the collector', Quayle's book will provide information and insight for anyone interested in the development of literature for children. Subjects dealt with include fairy tales, folk tales, and fantasia; poetry and nursery rhymes; stories before and after 1850; and adventure, toy, and moveable books. The whole production is an attractive blend of text and pictures.

RUGOFF, MILTON. *A Harvest of World Folk Tales.* New York, Viking, 1968.
A very worthwhile anthology of materials from many diverse cultures, with introductory comments. The selection is perceptive, reflecting each culture's particular 'atmosphere' within the universality of themes.

SMITH, LILLIAN H. *The Unreluctant Years: A Critical Approach to Children's Literature.* Chicago, American Library Association, 1953.
Miss Smith brings sound literary taste, a wide background of reading in both adult and children's literature, and a fine writing style to her discussion of traditional and modern children's books, which is also given distinction by her high standards and a sound knowledge of children's reading interests. Her analyses of outstanding children's books offer criteria for evaluation that cannot fail to benefit anyone working in the field. The book was reissued as a Penguin paperback in 1977.

THWAITE, MARY F. *From Primer to Pleasure in Reading: An Introduction to the History of Children's Books in England from the Invention of Printing to 1914, with an Outline of Some Developments in Other Countries.* Boston, Horn Book, 1972.
Intended as an introduction to more detailed studies, *From Primer to Pleasure* possesses considerable merit in its own right. Of particular interest to teachers and librarians is the coverage of nineteenth-century literature. This Horn Book edition contains many additions to the original text of 1963, and considerably expanded appendices.

TOWNSEND, JOHN ROWE. *Written for Children: an Outline of English Children's Literature.* New edition. Harmondsworth, Middlesex, Penguin, 1976.
A survey of quality, this very informed study offers the kind of enlightened views to be expected from a distinguished critic and author.

WAGGONER, DIANA. *The Hills of Faraway: A Guide to Fantasy.* New York, Atheneum, 1978.
Students of literature and devotees of fantasy will welcome Waggoner's panoramic survey of a wide-ranging field of writing. The various subgenres of fantasy are delineated with careful reference to specific examples. The book features a 'time-line of fantasy, 1858-1975'. It contains a useful bibliography and an excellent index.

Index

offers fine coverage of such matters as evaluation of illustration, artistic styles, media, and techniques.

DARLING, RICHARD. *The Rise of Children's Book Reviewing in America, 1865-1881.* New York & London, R. R. Bowker, 1968.

A valuable piece of research that will have to be taken into account in any future histories of children's literature and in the development of criticism about it. The activity that surrounded children and their books during this period, particularly as it was reflected in the major literary periodicals, is well described and documented. The author occasionally mistakenly considers book reviewing—excellent though many of the examples are—to represent a genuine, objective body of critical writing on children's literature.

DARTON, F. J. HARVEY. *Children's Books in England: Five Centuries of Social Life.* 2nd edition. Cambridge University Press, 1958.

The first major work to relate children's books to evolving social and moral attitudes towards young people, *Children's Books in England* is a work no serious student should be unacquainted with. It gives a scholarly review of the historical conflict between instruction and entertainment in children's literature.

EGOFF, SHEILA. *The Republic of Childhood: A Critical Guide to Canadian Children's Literature in English.* 2nd edition. Toronto, Oxford University Press, 1975.

Sheila Egoff's provocative survey of Canadian children's books since 1950 frankly compares the relative weaknesses and strengths of a burgeoning literature with significant British and American publications. The annotated booklists provide honest and objective judgements.

FENWICK, SARA I., ed. *A Critical Approach to Children's Literature.* University of Chicago Press, 1976. (Midway Reprint Series)

Twelve papers originally presented at the 31st Annual Conference of the University of Chicago Graduate Library School. They deal with important current issues and stress the need for informed criticism.

GLAZER, J. I. AND G. WILLIAMS. *Introduction to Children's Literature.* New York, McGraw-Hill, 1979.

This book is oriented to the requirements of students of children's literature and, as such, incorporates a good deal of very useful and thoughtful material. It includes a survey of genres, with appropriate criteria for evaluation; strategies for teaching; and ideas for discussion of selected topics.

HAZARD, PAUL. *Books, Children and Men*. Translated by Marguerite Mitchell. Boston, Horn Book, 1960.

A wide-ranging philosophical discourse about children and their books. Some think the 'Give us wings' approach limits its usefulness, but for its richness of allusion and its profound interpretation of childhood it continues to occupy an important place in the literature on children's books.

HÜRLIMANN, BETTINA. *Three Centuries of Children's Books in Europe*. Translated and edited by B. W. Alderson. London, Oxford University Press, 1967.

Bettina Hürlimann gives a highly informative and warm appraisal of children's literature. She discusses European authors and books against a background of British and American developments. Her lively style is admirably complemented by the translator's comments and booklists.

MEIGS, CORNELIA AND OTHERS. *A Critical History of Children's Literature*. Revised edition. New York, Macmillan, 1969.

This survey is one of the most comprehensive works of its kind and is widely used as a text. Most of the book is concerned with American writing, though there is some discussion of parallel developments in Great Britain.

OPIE, IONA AND PETER. *The Classic Fairy Tale*. London, Oxford University Press, 1974.

A lucid and well-researched treatment of a fascinating subject. As usual with the Opies' work, the material is at the same time authoritative and eminently readable.

QUAYLE, ERIC. *The Collector's Book of Children's Books*. London, Studio Vista, 1971.

Although published as the 'first survey of children's books for the collector', Quayle's book will provide information and insight for anyone interested in the development of literature for children. Subjects dealt with include fairy tales, folk tales, and fantasia; poetry and nursery rhymes; stories before and after 1850; and adventure, toy, and moveable books. The whole production is an attractive blend of text and pictures.